Governing California in the Twenty-First Century

THE POLITICAL DYNAMICS OF THE GOLDEN STATE

FOURTH EDITION

J. Theodore Anagnoson
CALIFORNIA STATE UNIVERSITY, LOS ANGELES

Gerald Bonetto
CALIFORNIA STATE UNIVERSITY, LOS ANGELES

J. Vincent Buck
CALIFORNIA STATE UNIVERSITY, FULLERTON

Richard E. DeLeon
SAN FRANCISCO STATE UNIVERSITY

Jolly Emrey
UNIVERSITY OF WISCONSIN–WHITEWATER

James J. Kelleher
CALIFORNIA STATE UNIVERSITY, DOMINGUEZ HILLS

Nadine Koch
CALIFORNIA STATE UNIVERSITY, LOS ANGELES

 W. W. NORTON AND COMPANY
NEW YORK ★ LONDON

W. W. Norton & Company has been independent since its founding in 1923, when William Warder Norton and Mary D. Herter Norton first published lectures delivered at the People's Institute, the adult education division of New York City's Cooper Union. The firm soon expanded its program beyond the Institute, publishing books by celebrated academics from America and abroad. By midcentury, the two major pillars of Norton's publishing program—trade books and college texts—were firmly established. In the 1950s, the Norton family transferred control of the company to its employees, and today—with a staff of four hundred and a comparable number of trade, college, and professional titles published each year—W. W. Norton & Company stands as the largest publishing house owned wholly by its employees.

The text of this book is composed in Berlin
with the display set in Interstate.
Book design: Sandra Watanabe
Composition: Jouve International—Brattleboro, VT
Manufacturing: Courier—Kendallville, IN
Associate Editor: Jake Schindel
Copyeditor: Candace Levy
Project editor: Christine D'Antonio
Associate Director of Production, College: Ben Reynolds

Library of Congress Cataloging-in-Publication Data has been applied for.
  ISBN 978-0-393-91915-8 (pbk.)

W. W. Norton & Company, Inc., 500 Fifth Avenue, New York, N.Y. 10110
www.wwnorton.com

W. W. Norton & Company Ltd., Castle House, 75/76 Wells Street, London W1T 3QT

1 2 3 4 5 6 7 8 9 0

Contents

10 ★ Public Policy in California *217*

Preface

We began this project over a decade ago with a working title asking whether California's political system and its politics were simply "broken." That is, politicians were caught within a system that was so contradictory in its rules, norms, and mores that budgets simply couldn't be passed on time or balanced, programs and departments couldn't be managed under the existing set of rules, and citizen expectations were so out of line with the ability of the political system to satisfy them that the level of negativism and cynicism was about as bad as could be found anywhere in the nation.

We think after a decade of false and halting starts that the picture needs some modification. California has begun to repair its infrastructure. The state has new incentives for politicians to be less ideologically extreme on the right or the left, in particular the "top two" primary system and the commission that is now drawing new districts for the Assembly, the state Senate, and congressional districts every 10 years after the Census. Decision rules in Sacramento still leave much to be desired, but at least a budget can be passed with majority rule instead of having to have two-thirds, a rule that necessitated some votes from the minority party and, unfortunately, some pork projects or other incentives to gain those votes. And the nation's strictest term-limit rules have been modified to allow members of the Assembly or state Senate to serve 12 years in a single house before being "termed out" and forced to seek another office outside the state legislature. Hopefully this will increase the level of expertise available among legislators.

At the same time, if the distance to be traveled to reach a political system that would actually "function" and make decisions is one mile, we have gone perhaps 1,000 feet. There still is no way to adjust the tax system without a two-thirds vote, and California's tax system badly needs modernization from its last overhaul more than 50 years ago. While the economy has moved toward a services base, California's tax system remains based on the manufacturing that was more common a half century ago. The income tax relies much too heavily on the capital gains tax, and that in turn creates revenue peaks and valleys that tempt Sacramento politicians to build the periodic surges of revenue into the base and in turn to run deficits when times are tough.

Proposition 13, passed in 1978, caused over the next decade a massive centralization of authority in Sacramento at the expense of cities, counties, and school districts. As a result, local governments have little authority over their own revenue. State government proved to be unable to provide local governments the revenue and authority they needed to deal with the recent recession, financial collapse, and defaulted mortgages that plague certain parts of the state, resulting in a number of local government bankruptcies, and in governments that are not bankrupt, the inability to help people in a genuine time of need. In some dire cases, state government cutbacks combined with the revenue-depleting impacts of home mortgage foreclosures, high unemployment, business failures, and grossly overburdened public sector pension and benefit obligations created local "perfect storms" of economic and political conditions that bankrupted Stockton and other cities and still threaten others. The state has been unable to help.

In these circumstances, the fourth edition of *Governing California in the Twenty-First Century* offers a ray of hope but the reality of a long distance to go. We hope you enjoy our analysis of California's politics, not quite "broken"—but not as yet "fixed" either—at this point.

We divided the writing of this book as follows:

1. California Government in Crisis—Anagnoson (tanagno@calstatela.edu)
2. The Constitution and the Progressive Legacy—Bonetto (Gerry@piasc.org)
3. Interest Groups and the Media in California—Bonetto
4. Parties and Elections in California—Koch (nkoch@calstatela.edu)
5. The California Legislature—Buck (vbuck@fullerton.edu)
6. The Governor and the Executive Branch—Buck
7. The California Judiciary—Emrey (emreyj@uww.edu)
8. The State Budget and Budgetary Limitations—Anagnoson
9. Local Government—DeLeon (rdeleon@sfsu.edu)
10. Public Policy in California—Anagnoson

There are websites for the second, third, and fourth editions of this book. For the fourth edition, go to http://www.silcom.com/~anag999/g4.html. For the second or third edition sites, substitute "g2" or "g3" (without the quotes) for "g4." The sites contain:

- A link to the publisher's own site for this book.

- A list of *errata*. If you find any error in the book, please email the lead author, J. Theodore Anagnoson, at anag999@silcom.com or tanagno@calstatela.edu.

- The answers to the short answer questions at the end of each chapter

- PowerPoint slides used by Anagnoson in Spring 2009 to teach an upper division course in California politics. These are up to date only to the end of Spring 2009.

We have constructed, in addition, a test bank for instructors. To gain access to the test bank, visit wwnorton.com/instructors.

We would like to acknowledge the helpful recommendations from a series of reviewers, whose comments have assisted us in updating events and materials. We would also like to thank the many students who have communicated their comments. I would also like to acknowledge the assistance of Alexandra Jimenez in gathering data used in Chapter 1. Any errors that remain are strictly our own, much as we would like to attribute them to others.

We would be glad to hear from you about the book. Use the e-mail addresses above to communicate with us.

J. Theodore Anagnoson
Professor of Political Science
California State University, Los Angeles

1 California Government in Crisis

WHAT CALIFORNIA GOVERNMENT DOES AND WHY IT MATTERS

Which of the following actions does not involve the use of an object or action regulated by the federal, state, or local government?

★ Driving on the freeway

★ Driving on a tollway

★ Driving across a bridge

★ Walking to the grocery store

★ Buying fruit at the grocery store

★ Going to school at any level, public or private

★ Working for the California Highway Patrol

★ Working for a private security guard service

★ Working for a grocery store

★ Eating dinner in a restaurant

[Answers at the end of the chapter.]

The California Dream?

For almost 200 years, the dream of California has attracted immigrants from the United States and abroad. Governor Arnold Schwarzenegger, in one of his state of the state speeches (2004), said that California represents "an empire of hope and aspiration," a place where "Californians do great things." To some, the California dream is sun and surf; to others, the warm winter season; to still others, a house on the coast in the redwoods and acres of untrammeled wilderness, or three or four cars per family. Many of these dreams can be summed up in the phrase *freedom from restraints* or *freedom from traditions*. These are typical themes in statewide elections and gubernatorial state of the state speeches—bringing back our image of an older, less crowded California.

The reality is that some of the dream is attainable for many—we live in a place with winter weather that is the envy of most of the rest of the nation—but much of it is not. One of the themes of this book is the conflict between the dream and the reality, between the ideals that we set for ourselves and the reality of our every-day lives. One conflict particularly vivid to politicians is the conflict between the expectations we have for them and the reality of the constraints and incentives we saddle them with, so that they cannot possibly meet our expectations.

The Crisis of California Politics

The question before us is whether California government is capable of making the decisions needed for California to thrive and preserve its standard of living through the twenty-first century. The general sentiment among informed observers is that California is hamstrung by voter-approved rules and regulations, all admirable individually but a nightmare collectively. However, during the Schwarzenegger administration from 2003 to 2011, some progress was made:

- Proposition 11, approved in November 2008, took the power to apportion the districts of the Assembly and State Senate away from those bodies and gave it to a citizens' commission. Later, the voters added congressional districts to the duties of the new citizens' commission. In 2012, the first year the new districts were used, they seemed to be fair (that is, not gerrymandered). Future years will establish whether unbiased districts will produce more moderate legislators willing to compromise for the good of the state as a whole, which was the goal of changing the reapportionment method. So far, we have had significantly more competition.

- In 2010, the voters decided to change the state's party primary elections from a party primary to a new top-two system, used for the first time in June 2012. Under the new system, there is no party primary. Instead the election system is like a swimming or track meet, in which there are preliminary heats and finals. Following the preliminary election, the top two candidates advance to the finals in November, even if they are from the same party or they are not in a major party.

- In 2010, the voters also approved changing the majority needed to approve the state budget in the legislature from a two-thirds vote of the total number of legislators in each chamber, the Assembly and the State Senate, to a simple majority (50 percent plus one). The budgets approved in June 2011 and June 2012 were the first to be approved using the new system. However, the state constitution still requires a two-thirds majority of both houses of the legislature, plus the governor's signature, to raise or lower taxes.

Schwarzenegger also made progress through the approval of reforms to the workers' compensation system in 2004 and several initiatives to rebuild California's infrastructure (levees in the Central Valley, highways) in 2006.

Yet under Governor Jerry Brown, elected in November 2010, the frustrating budget stalemate has continued in spite of the majority rule for passing the budget. As of June 2012, the budget gap was $16 billion, more than the total revenues received for the general fund in 40 of the 50 states. However, the Legislative Analyst's Office reported in January 2012 that although the deficit still persists, the long-term trend is moving in the right direction, toward smaller deficits. While the majority budget rule might not be the only factor, clearly it has helped in cutting the long-term deficits projected in Figure 1.1.

The downward trend is the result of difficult and tough decisions. Every college student in California knows some of them, having seen cut after cut after cut to the budgets of the community colleges, the California State University system, and the University of California system. These cuts have been partially replaced by tuition and fee increases. Other reductions have included Medi-Cal (California's medical program for the poor) rate and service reductions, many cost-containment measures in the state developmentally disabled programs, and the elimination of the state's local government redevelopment agencies and their state funding (see Chapter 9). Prisoners are being sent from the state prisons to local jails, and many state responsibilities are being devolved to the local level of government. Figure 1.1 reflects the results of those decisions and the continuing, if slow, improvement to the state's economy.

California state government thus faces a series of paradoxes. On the one hand, we see progress in cutting the deficit and in making the hard decisions necessary

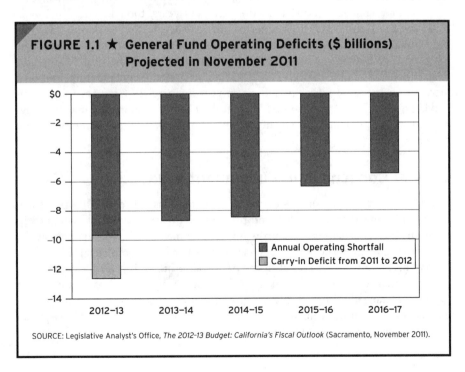

FIGURE 1.1 ★ General Fund Operating Deficits ($ billions) Projected in November 2011

SOURCE: Legislative Analyst's Office, *The 2012-13 Budget: California's Fiscal Outlook* (Sacramento, November 2011).

to weather the national economic storm. But on the other hand, the difficulty of those decisions and the fact that taxes can still be only raised by a two-thirds majority has meant that there has been a budget crisis for months every single year. And every decision in the state government is a budget decision—a decision made solely, or almost solely, on the basis of whether there is enough money and a budget source for the particular activity.

Let us take a closer look at some reasons we seem to have a continual crisis in California state government.

The Two-Thirds Requirement for Raising Taxes

As noted earlier, until November 2010, when the voters passed Proposition 25, California's constitution required a two-thirds vote of the total membership—not just those present and voting—in each house of the legislature to pass the budget. Proposition 25 lowered the vote required to pass the budget to 50 percent plus one. It will take several years to see if this change makes a substantial difference. So far, the first two budgets passed under the new rules—which penalize legislators' salaries if the budget is not passed on time—have been passed around June 15, the constitutional deadline, but have not been any more balanced than previous budgets. Obtaining a balanced budget clearly requires improving the quality of the state's economy and tax system as well as changing procedural deadlines.

Herein lies the problem. A two-thirds vote of the absolute number of legislators in both houses of the state legislature is still necessary to raise or lower any tax level. With a Republican Party that refuses to countenance any tax increases of any kind (plus the taxpayer groups that promise to sue the instant any tax increase is passed), the burden of balancing the state budget has fallen on low- and moderate-income state residents, who benefit disproportionately from state programs (which are now being cut). For higher-income state residents, state services are at least partially irrelevant, as the major "service" is a low tax rate, and this has not been raised in at least three years.

This may change somewhat in the next few years, though. The 2012 elections saw the Democrats win a supermajority of seats in the legislature, meaning they would have enough votes without any Republican support to raise taxes (see Chapter 4). Whether this supermajority will hold remains to be seen. Meanwhile, Proposition 30 on the November 2012 ballot passed, implementing four-year increases in the state sales tax and seven-year increases in tax rates for citizens making over $250,000 in income (Chapter 4). These developments may have significant impact, but they do not negate the two-thirds rule for raising taxes that currently exists.

Lack of Consensus in Fundamental Questions

Another reason for California's perpetual state of crisis is the inability of legislators to unify in matters of policy and principle. How can a political system overcome the inertia generated by narrow interests to make decisions that benefit the broader general interest of the public as a whole? In a large complex state like California, this issue will persist, but in the past, California politicians have been able to overcome the lack of consensus to make progress on significant questions. Has California changed? Why do interest groups cause impasse now, after the 2000s, when they did not back in the 1970s and 1980s? After all, we have always had interest groups, and we had the two-thirds decision rule for adopting the budget or raising taxes in the legislature from 1935 until 2010. Dan Walters suggests that the blame heaped on the legislature is inappropriate.

> In fact, California's governance maladies stem from the complex, often contradictory nature of the state itself. With its immense geographic, economic, and cultural diversity, California has myriad policy issues, but those same factors also have become an impediment to governance. The state lost its vital consensus on public policy issues, and without that civic compass, its politicians tend to ignore major issues and pursue trivial ones. . . . The real issue is whether the public's anger at Gray Davis will morph into a new sense of civic purpose or whether California is destined to be . . . ungovernable.[1]

So far, the experience since the recall of Governor Gray Davis in 2003 indicates very slow progress, with no "new sense of civic purpose." The same old problems seem to vex California's political class, over and over.

The Ease of Passing Initiatives

One factor is certainly the ease with which special interests propose and collect signatures, campaign for, and sometimes pass initiatives to help their own cause. The initiative was added to the California constitution by the Progressive movement just after the beginning of the twentieth century as a way to promote the involvement of the public in public policy and affairs. Two recent examples include Proposition 15 on the June 2010 ballot, ostensibly allowing taxpayers to have more control over their government but in fact designed to keep local public utilities from competing with PG&E, and Proposition 33 on the November 2012 ballot, ostensibly allowing insurance companies to give longevity discounts to drivers who had continuous insurance coverage from another insurance company but in fact designed to give one insurance company the ability to raise rates on drivers who had lapses in insurance coverage. In general, the initiative has ceased to be a measure promoting direct democracy for at least the last two decades. It is instead just one more method by which special interests convince voters who are paying little attention to government and politics that they should enact some rule, law, or constitutional amendment that will benefit the particular interest and hurt the public as a whole.

Term Limits

The term limit movement found fertile ground in California in the 1980s and 1990s. Proposition 140 in 1990 imposed the severest term limits in the nation on the legislature and the elected officials of the executive branch, and the voters in many cities in California enacted term limits as well. Part of the statewide anger was directed against Willie Brown, then Speaker of the California Assembly, whose flamboyant lifestyle and prolific fund-raising raised the ire of voters.

The theory of the term limits movement is that if term limits are imposed, members of the Assembly and state Senate will pay more attention to their jobs and raise less money for future campaigns, and the system will be opened up to more minority and female candidates. Since term limits have been imposed, the proportion of Latino legislators in particular has indeed risen, but paradoxically, members have much less expertise on the matters they vote on and many—perhaps most—members of the legislature spend a good deal of their time worrying about their next position and raising funds for those campaigns.

The result is that most observers think that term limits have worsened the legislature, not bettered it. By the time legislators acquire the expertise to make good decisions, they are term-limited out. One of the reasons our limits are the strictest in the nation is that there is a lifetime ban on running for the same position again. While voters strongly support term limits, they have recently taken steps to address some of the institutional problems they present. In June 2012, the voters approved Proposition 28, which allows legislators to serve as many as 12 years in the legislature, providing the 12 years is served in one house. (The previous total service time had actually been higher—14 years—but with caps of 6 years in the Assembly and 8 in the Senate.) Currently the term limits are 12 years (six terms) for the Assembly, 12 years (three terms) for the state Senate, and 8 years (two terms) for all statewide officials (governor, lieutenant governor, attorney general, controller, secretary of state, treasurer, superintendent of public instruction, insurance commissioner, and the four members of the Board of Equalization).

The Safe-Seat Reapportionment

Every 10 years, after the census, state legislatures realign their seats in accordance with the census numbers. In California, until recently, this process was usually partisan. In some reapportionments, the legislature came together across party lines to form a coalition in which most incumbent seats became safe seats—that is, seats for which the incumbent generally wins by more than a 10 to 15 percent margin (a 55 to 45 percent win is a 10 percent margin). Short of a surge in voter anger, most incumbents are safe, meaning that their votes in the Assembly or state Senate are not restricted by considerations of what their opponent will say about the vote in the next election campaign.

In November 2008, however, voters passed Proposition 11, which substituted a citizens' commission for the legislature itself in drawing up the Assembly and state Senate districts. It was expected to reduce the proportion of extremely safe seats in the 2012 and subsequent elections.

Here are the results from the 2010 and 2012 legislative elections, combining congressional, state Senate, and Assembly seats:

	WON BY	<10%	10–19.9%	20–29.9%	30–44.9%	45–99%	100%
2010	Total of 153 districts	10	21	38	49	28	7
	percent	7%	14%	25%	32%	18%	5%
2012		29	38	38	22	25	2
		19%	25%	25%	14%	16%	1%

SOURCE: Compiled by the author from the Secretary of State's website. Data from 2012 include one additional district, from a special state Senate election.

In 2010, 7 percent of the districts were competitive, won by less than 10 percent of the vote. That percentage was 19 percent for 2012, meaning roughly 80 percent of all districts were still safe. The category of districts that were won by 10–19.9 percent of the vote moved from 14 percent to 25 percent, and the districts won by 30 percent of the vote or more dropped from 55 percent in 2010 to 31 percent in 2012. The combination of the top two primary and the newly reapportioned seats has indeed produced more competitive races for the Assembly, state Senate, and House of Representatives in California.

Reform Ideas

In addition to the steps already taken (as discussed earlier), numerous additional reforms have been suggested over the years to address the institutional hindrances to effective California governance. Some of the standard ones are listed here. See how many you agree with as you begin this book.

On the liberal side:

- Instituting public financing of election campaigns.

- Loosening further the term limits for members of the Assembly and Senate.

- Lowering the required super-majority to raise taxes from two-thirds to some lower, more achievable percentage, such as 55 or 60 percent.

- Restricting the initiative process to allow more citizen participation and decreasing the necessity to hire professional firms to collect signatures and run initiative campaigns. This would require lengthening the time allowed to collect signatures.

- Making it more difficult to amend the state constitution, which now requires 807,615 valid signatures for an initiative and a 50 percent vote of those who turn out at the next election.

From California Forward, a politically moderate reform organization:

- Instituting performance-based budgeting, with clear goals and performance measures for all programs.

- Engaging in multi-year budget planning.

- Mandating that all new programs, including those in initiatives, should have budget sources identified.

- Using spikes in revenue for the state's "rainy-day fund" and for paying down debt.

- Realigning the tax structure to match the state's shift from a manufacturing economy to a service-based one (see Chapter 8).

- Decentralizing and devolving more power to local governments.

- Investing more in K–12 education.

- Encouraging state and local leaders to reform public pensions.

On the conservative side:

- Changing the legislature from full time to part time.

- Imposing caps on public sector pensions.

- Making all new programs pay-as-you-go.

- Lowering California's tax rates, making the system less progressive in the process.

- Improving California's business climate with lower taxes and fewer regulations.

- Making it easier to terminate incompetent public sector workers, including teachers.

Most of these ideas involve so much controversy that they have little chance of being enacted, at least in the short run. In general, enacting major reforms such as those just listed is much easier through the ballot box (that is, via an initiative) than it is through the legislature, where constitutional changes require a two-thirds vote of the Assembly and the Senate before being placed on the ballot for ratification.

Why Study California Politics?

We know the obvious answer to the question, Why study California politics?—the course meets some requirement for graduation or your major. The State of California decided that every college student should know something about the California Constitution and California government and politics. But more important—why?

- You are *the citizens and voters of the present and future*. The policies and political trends occurring today do and will continue to impact your lives, from university tuition fees to the strength of the job market.

- California politics is plagued by *low levels of participation and turnout,* so much so that the electorate is distinctly older and more conservative than would be the case if every eligible adult voted. Your vote and participation can make a difference.

- California politics also suffers from *too much interest-group participation and not enough citizen participation*. The general interests of large groups of citizens need to be represented at the Table.

That's the narrow answer. A broader answer as to why we study California politics is that California's government and politics are distinctive and worthy of study. How are we different?

- We have much *more cultural diversity* than other states, including a much higher proportion of Latino and Asian residents. By some measures, we are the multicultural trendsetter among states.

- We are *one of the 10 largest economies in the world*. We are much larger than other states and larger than most entire countries. The 38 million citizens of the state of California produce as much in goods and services as France or Great Britain. However, we need to be cautious about statements about the economy—not only are there different ways to measure the size of the economy but governors and state government have much less control over that economy than do nations. Nations can run deficits and print money; governors and states can't, at least not in the long run. Nations can influence the money supply through their reserve banks; governors and states cannot.

- We *are the most populous state, and we have grown more quickly than other states*. In 1960 New York had 41 members in the U.S. House of Representatives; California had 38. The 2010 Census resulted in California having 53 seats, followed by Texas with 36 and Florida and New York both with 27.

- We are *more majoritarian than other states*, meaning that we rely more on the measures for direct democracy—the initiative, the referendum, and the recall—that were added to the state constitution by the Progressive movement in 1912. Every state uses majority rule for most decisions, but when we use the term *majoritarian*, we mean that the public makes policy decisions, rather than our elected representatives.

Consider the following continuum:

Majoritarian   Republican

A *majoritarian* government is one that is highly influenced by the public at large, through public-opinion polls that politicians take and through such measures as the initiative, referendum, and recall that enable the public to decide government policies directly.

A *republican* government is one in which we elect representatives to make our decisions for us, very much based on the Madisonian model for the federal government.

California government has moved much more toward the majoritarian model than other states. Not only are initiatives to amend the constitution routine but interest groups often begin collecting signatures for an initiative just to pressure the legislature into voting on their legislation. Californians like being majoritarian: surveys show that most don't want to restrict use of the initiative, in spite of its extensive use by interest groups.[2]

A report from the nonpartisan Initiative and Referendum Institute at the University of Southern California shows that Oregon has had more initiatives in the period from 1904 to 2009 than any other state, with 351. California is close behind at 329, followed by Colorado (209), North Dakota (178), and Arizona (171). Twenty-seven states do not have the initiative at all, and the top five states account for more than half of all initiatives considered from 1904 to 2009.[3]

What Determines the Content and Character of California's Politics?

Three factors shape the content and character of California's politics:

- The underlying demographic and sociopolitical trends that affect California and the other states;

- The rules of the game, as set out in the federal and state constitutions and in state laws; and

- The decisions of voters and politicians.

In Chapters 1 and 2 we will discuss the underlying demographic and sociopolitical trends and the rules of the game. What voters and politicians do in different areas is the subject of the rest of the book.

Underlying Socioeconomic Trends

Socioeconomic trends have driven many of the problems that have faced California voters and politicians. Some of these are discussed in the following sections.

POPULATION GROWTH Except for the four years from 1993 to 1996, California's population has grown by about 450,000 people per year for more than two decades. The 2010 Census results show California's 2010 population as 37,691,912. Current growth is 350,000 people per year. This strong and consistent growth means that the political controversies that have plagued the state in the past cannot be expected to abate in the future. Some of those controversies include:

- *Housing and Transportation*—Even with the decline brought on by the recession of 2008–09, housing prices in many middle-class areas have skyrocketed since the early 1990s. Many lower- and middle-class people must live in the Central Valley and commute to work in the San Francisco Bay Area or live in Riverside and San Bernardino counties and commute to the Los Angeles area. In both of these places, commutes of one to two hours—and even more—each way are not uncommon. Our transportation systems have not kept pace and were built for a much smaller population.

- *Schools*—Population growth means more schoolchildren, and there is a high demand for teachers across the state, along with a lack of fully qualified or credentialed teachers in many urban areas. Projections of the educational requirements of the future job market show that approximately 35 percent of jobs will require a college degree. Budget cuts to the University of California, California State University, and community college systems are already resulting in fewer students receiving their degrees and will make it impossible to meet this employment goal. The proportion of students who receive a college degree should be rising to meet future job requirements, but instead the proportion is falling.

- *Immigration*—California has had high levels of immigration since the 1950s, so high in some areas that candidates for the presidency of Mexico have campaigned here. Between 1970 and 2010 the number of immigrants in the California population increased from 1.8 to about 10.2 million; 27 percent of the state's current population was born somewhere else, a much higher proportion than in any other state. Most immigrants in California are from Latin America or Asia, with 4.3 million from Mexico, some 43 percent of the total immigrant population in California. Immigrants live in all parts of California, with those from Latin America more likely to live in Southern California and those from Asia in Northern California. Immigrants are younger than nonimmigrant Californians and more likely to be poor, and although some have relatively high levels of education, most immigrants are less educated than the native population.[4] Table 1.1 shows the 11 largest countries of origin for immigrants in California in 2006.

As of 2009, there were approximately 2.6 million illegal immigrants in California's population of 38 million, estimated the Urban Institute, using the census figures on the foreign-born population and subtracting the numbers we know are naturalized or here on legal visas and work permits.[5] Illegal immigrants are a continuing political issue. In 1994, Proposition 187 would have refused public services to anyone who could not show documentation, but it was found to be unconstitutional. A driver-license bill allowing undocumented immigrants to receive licenses was so controversial in the 2003 that it contributed to the recall of Governor Gray Davis

TABLE 1.1 ★ Leading Countries of Origin of Immigrants in California, 2009

COUNTRY	NUMBER OF IMMIGRANTS IN CALIFORNIA	PERCENT NATURALIZED
Mexico	4,308,000	28
Philippines	783,000	68
China (including Taiwan)	681,000	68
Vietnam	457,000	82
El Salvador	413,000	37
India	319,000	46
Korea	307,000	55
Guatemala	261,000	28
Iran	214,000	76
Canada	132,000	49
United Kingdom	125,000	40

SOURCE: Public Policy Institute of California, "Just the Facts: Immigrants in California" (April 2011), www.ppic.org (accessed 7/17/12). PPIC cites the U.S. Census and the 2009 American Community Survey.

TABLE 1.2 ★ Undocumented Immigrants by State, 2009

STATE	NUMBER OF UNDOCUMENTED IMMIGRANTS	SHARE OF STATE'S TOTAL POPULATION (%)
California	2,600,000	7.0
Texas	1,680,000	6.8
Florida	720,000	3.9
Illinois	554,000	4.3
New York	550,000	2.8
Georgia	480,000	4.9
Arizona	460,000	7.0
New Jersey	360,000	4.1
North Carolina	370,000	3.9
Other states	2,976,000	1.9
All states	10,750,000	3.5

SOURCE: Public Policy Institute of California, "Just the Facts: Illegal Immigrants" (December 2010), www.ppic.org (accessed 7/17/12). Estimates shown are from the U.S. Department of Homeland Security.

and was repealed before it took effect. Times have changed sufficiently that Governor Brown signed a bill in October 2012 that would allow illegal immigrants to drive legally in California if they qualified for the new federal work permit program announced by the Obama administration earlier that year. However, during the presidential elections of both 2008 and 2012, several of the more conservative candidates took strong stands against immigration. Table 1.2 shows the number of undocumented immigrants by state, along with the share of that state's total population that they make up. Arizona and California have the highest proportion of undocumented immigrants at 7.0 percent.

Reflecting the controversies over immigration, both legal and undocumented, in recent years, California has seen a number of demonstrations on the immigration issue. They have taken both sides: against more immigration, in favor of closing the borders, in favor of a "path to citizenship," both for and against the Arizona immigration law of 2010, and so forth. At least one of the demonstrations was the largest ever seen in Southern California to that date—over 1 million people. Little policy action has taken place at the state level, however.

RACE AND ETHNICITY In many respects, California's population is notably diverse compared with the U.S. population (see Table 1.3). Latino or Hispanic is not a racial category in the official census, but a separate question asks about Hispanic or Latino origin. About 17 percent of the United States is Latino, but about 38 percent of California is. Almost 60 percent of California's Latino population is of Mexican heritage.

AGE California's population is relatively young, mostly because of immigration. Immigrants tend to be younger and to have larger families than those who have been residents for longer periods.

EDUCATION Californians are highly educated. A greater proportion of Californians have gone to college or completed a bachelor's or higher degree than in the United States in general.

MOBILITY AND FOREIGN-BORN About 60 percent of all Americans live in the state in which they were born, but only 50 percent of all Californians were born in California. One-quarter, in fact, were foreign born, a much higher percentage than in the United States as a whole (12 percent). Most foreign-born residents are not U.S. citizens; only 40 percent of the foreign-born in both the United States and California are citizens. As one might expect with such a large foreign-born population, only

---

TABLE 1.3 ★ Ethnic Composition of California and the United States, 2011

	CALIFORNIA	UNITED STATES
White persons	74%	78%
Black/African American persons	7%	13%
Asian persons	14%	5%
American Indian/Alaskan Native persons	2%	1%
Native Hawaiian/other Pacific Islander persons	1%	0%
Two or more races	4%	2%
Persons of Hispanic or Latino origin	38%	17%
White persons not Hispanic	40%	63%

SOURCE: U.S. Census Bureau, "California Quick Facts from the U.S. Census Bureau," http://quickfacts.census.gov/qfd/states/06000.html (accessed 11/12/12).

61 percent of those over age five speak English at home in California. In the United States as a whole, 82 percent of those over age five speak English at home. That is a substantial difference by the standards of social science. There have been many political issues over this, ranging from debates over whether local store signs should be in foreign languages to the "English as the official state language" movement.

INCOME The U.S. Census Bureau has estimated California's median household income at $60,883 for 2006–10, about $9,000 higher than the national figure of $51,914. The state poverty rate is almost the same as the national figure, 13.7 percent for 2008 (California) compared with 13.8 percent (United States).

Conclusion

In this book we are going to consider the real world of California politics and the possibilities, both fascinating and frustrating, of the present, as well as changes that might make the future more positive for both politicians and the public. We will investigate what makes California different from other states and examine its unique political problems, including

- the inability to balance the budget, year after year.
- the malapportioned districts for the California legislature that, in combination with the primary system, produce legislators who are more liberal than the public on the Democratic side and more conservative than the public on the Republican side. We shall see whether the new top-two primary system and the non-gerrymandered legislative districts make any difference in this area.
- the public's attachment to the strictest term limits in the nation.
- the public's attachment to extreme majoritarianism, which produces the longest ballots in the nation as well as some of the lowest turnout rates.

Our coverage includes subjects that the newspapers and bloggers discuss in great detail as well as some subjects, such as the California tax system and the impact of Proposition 13, that are taken for granted but that have kept the state from updating its structure and services. Welcome to the journey.

A Guide to This Book

Chapter 2, "The Constitution and the Progressive Legacy," deals with California's state constitutions and the Progressives, the two crucial factors that defined the shape and direction of today's California government.

Chapters 3 and 4 deal with the bodies outside government that influence what government can accomplish. Chapter 3, "Interest Groups and the Media in California," deals with the groups that are as prevalent and influential in California as they are in our nation's capital. Chapter 4, "Parties and Elections in California," deals with parties and voters, and how both influence government through elections and campaigns.

Chapters 5, 6, and 7 deal with the institutions of government. Chapter 5, "The California Legislature," deals with the legislature, the body we love to hate. We try in this book to understand the legislature and why it functions as it does rather than simply condemn it. Chapter 6, "The Governor and the Executive Branch," asks whether California has become ungovernable. Chapter 7, "The California Judiciary," deals with judges and the criminal justice system.

Chapters 8, 9, and 10 deal with some policy problems and governmental structures that are particularly relevant today. Chapter 8, "The State Budget and Budgetary Limitations," addresses taxes, spending, and the California budget, asking whether the budget can be controlled in today's political and policy environment with the tools we have available to us. Chapter 9, "Local Government," deals with local government and its dependency on the state, a dependency that localities are taking action to remove in part through the initiative process. Chapter 10, "Public Policy in California," deals with several contemporary public policy problems, illustrating how the institutions and voters have acted in these areas.

FOR FURTHER READING

"California in Crisis." *California Journal*, August 2003, pp. 18–27.

Davis, Mike. *City of Quartz: Excavating the Future in Los Angeles*. New York: Vintage, 1990.

Goldmacher, Shane. "New Rules, New Tactics, in U.S. Races: Lessons Learned in the Free-Spending State Campaigns Now Apply to Candidates Seeking Office at the Federal Level." *Los Angeles Times*, February 24, 2010, p. AA3.

Gramlich, John. "California's Worst Enemy: Its Own Political System." *Stateline*, May 17, 2011. http://stateline.org. Accessed 7/17/12.

Hofstadter, Richard. *The Age of Reform*. New York: Washington Square Press, 1988.

Horwitz, Sasha. *Termed Out: Reforming California's Term Limits*. Los Angeles: Center for Governmental Studies, October 2007. www.cgs.org. Accessed 7/17/12.

Legislation by Initiative vs. through Elected Representatives. San Francisco: Field Institute, November, 1999. www.field .com/fieldpollonline/subscribers/COI-99-Nov-Legislation .pdf. Accessed 7/17/12.

Lewis, Michael. "California *and* Bust." *Vanity Fair*, November 2011.

Matthews, Joe, and Mark Paul. *California Crack Up, How Reform Broke the Golden State and How We Can Fix It*. Berkeley: University of California Press, 2010.

McGhee, Eric, and Daniel Krimm. *California's Political Geography*. San Francisco: Public Policy Institute of California, February 2012.

Olin, Spencer C. *California's Prodigal Sons: Hiram Johnson and the Progressives, 1911–1917*. Berkeley: University of California Press, 1968.

Public Policy Institute of California. "Just the Facts: Illegal Immigrants." San Francisco: Public Policy Institute of California, December 2010. www.ppic.org. Accessed 7/17/12.

———. "Just the Facts: Immigrants in California." San Francisco: Public Policy Institute of California, April 2011. www.ppic .org. Accessed 7/17/12.

———. "Research Brief: How Have Term Limits Affected the California Legislature?" No. 94. San Francisco: Public Policy Institute of California, November 2004. www.ppic.org. Accessed 7/17/12.

Reyes, Belinda I., ed. *A Portrait of Race and Ethnicity in California, An Assessment of Social and Economic Well-Being*. San Francisco: Public Policy Institute of California, 2001.

Skelton, George. "California's Capitol—The Long View. A Columnist Looks Back on 50 Years Covering the Ups and Downs of Sacramento." *Los Angeles Times*, December 1, 2011.

Slater, Dashka, and Gary Rivlin. "Economy, California on the Brink." *Newsweek*, September 5, 2011, pp. 26–27.

Walters, Dan. "California Makes It Easier to Cut Taxes Than to Raise Them." *Sacramento Bee*, May 16, 2010.

Wilson, James Q. "A Guide to Schwarzenegger Country." *Commentary*, December 2003, 45–49.

ON THE WEB

California Choices: www.californiachoices.org (accessed 7/17/12).

California Forward: "The California Forward 2010 Reform Principles." www.cafwd-action.org (accessed 7/17/12).

Center for Governmental Studies: www.cgs.org (accessed 7/17/12). A think tank that specifically focuses on promoting citizen participation in government.

The Field (California) Poll: Field Institute. www.field.com (accessed 7/17/12).

Los Angeles Times: www.latimes.com (accessed 7/17/12).

Public Policy Institute of California: www.ppic.org (accessed 7/17/12). A think tank devoted to nonpartisan research on how to improve California policy.

Sacramento Bee: www.sacbee.com (accessed 7/17/12).

San Francisco Chronicle: www.sfgate.com (accessed 7/17/12).

SUMMARY

I. Many observers question whether California is governable, at least as far as budgets and taxes are concerned.
   A. The Democratic majority won't consider cutting programs substantially but does not constitute the two-thirds necessary to raise taxes.
   B. The Republican minority will not consider any tax increases and has more than one-third of the votes in both chambers, thus preventing any agreement that might be a compromise for both sides.

II. The crisis has many roots.
   A. The requirement that two-thirds of the total membership of each house of the legislature is needed to raise taxes.
   B. Interest-group impasse reflected in the legislature on many issues.
   C. The ease with which the voters can pass initiatives designed to help an interest group with its cause, set aside funds from the general fund for a single cause, etc.
   D. Severe term limits—the strictest in the nation—leading to a loss of knowledge and interest in staying in the legislature and learning the issues involved there.
   E. Gerrymandered districts that are safe for most legislatures. The districts for the 2012 election are the first in many decades that have not been gerrymandered by the legislature; the new citizens' commission proposed them in 2011.

III. Reform ideas are abundant. Several from both sides of the political spectrum are listed in the text.

IV. California's politics are important for several reasons.
   A. California is the biggest state, has an economy in the top 10 among nations of the world, and has a population more multicultural and diverse than the rest of the nation.
   B. California is strongly majoritarian, and its citizens like it that way.
   C. California has experienced some of the strongest population growth of any state, resulting in a number of political conflicts over the years.
   D. California has more immigrants—and more undocumented immigrants—than any other state, although Arizona has the same proportion of undocumented immigrants.
   E. California is younger than many states, has a greater percentage of its population that is college-educated, and is richer than most states.

PRACTICE QUIZ

1. The budget must be passed by a majority of those present and voting in both chambers of the legislature.
   a) true.
   b) false.

2. Most states require a two-thirds majority to pass their budgets each year.
   a) true.
   b) false.

3. What proportion of California legislative seats in 2012—those in the Assembly, state Senate, and Congress—were safe (that is, the won by a margin of 10 percent or more)?
   a) about 50 percent.
   b) about 65 percent.
   c) about 80 percent.
   d) 90+ percent.

4. California's population, the foreign-born population, and the approximate number of undocumented immigrants, according to the text are:
   a) 50 million, 5 million, 2 million.

   b) 34 million, 8.8 million, 2.4 million.
   c) 25 million, 20 million, 18 million.
   d) 38 million, 10.2 million, 2.6 million.

5. Latino or Hispanic has been a racial category in the U.S. Census that is taken every 10 years.
   a) true.
   b) false.

6. The proportion of immigrants in California who speak English at home as compared to the United States as a whole is
   a) greater.
   b) lesser.
   c) the same.

7. According to this book, the inability of the California legislature to make decisions that benefit the state as a whole is due to
   a) the number of interest groups.
   b) the two-thirds requirement to raise taxes.
   c) California's size.
   d) all of the above.

8. California's term limits are
   a) 8 years for the governor, 4 years for the Assembly, and 6 years for the state Senate.
   b) 6 years for the governor, 6 years for the Assembly, and 8 years for the state Senate.
   c) 8 years for the governor, 12 years for the Assembly, and 12 years for the state Senate.
   d) 8 years for the governor, 8 years for the Assembly, and 12 years for the state Senate.

9. Some undocumented immigrants can obtain a driver license in California.
   a) true.
   b) false.

CRITICAL-THINKING QUESTIONS

1. How distinctive is California compared with other states? Are we really that different?

2. California's population differs from that of other states on several levels: what are the two or three most significant, and why are they significant?

KEY TERMS

At this point you should have a general understanding of the following concepts and terms:

California dream (p. 2)
cultural diversity (p. 8)
foreign-born (p. 10)
Latino/Hispanic (p. 12)

majoritarian (p. 9)
racial and ethnic diversity (p. 12)
reapportionment (p. 6)
recall (p. 8)

safe seat (p. 6)
term limits (p. 5)
undocumented immigration (p. 10)

ANSWERS TO QUESTIONS IN "WHAT CALIFORNIA GOVERNMENT DOES AND WHY IT MATTERS"

Every action named involves government at some level and in some way:

- Driving on the freeway: Freeways are built by state government with federal and state funds; traffic is monitored by the California Highway Patrol.

- Driving on a tollway: California has several privately owned tollways; these are freeways built with private funds typically raised by selling bonds, itself a market regulated by government. State government approves the rights of way for these tollways and otherwise regulates their operations.

- Driving across a bridge: Standards for bridges come from both the federal government and the California Department of Transportation; most bridges were constructed with public funds.

- Walking to the grocery store: Sidewalks were constructed with public funds and to local government construction standards.

- Buying fruit at the grocery store: Scales are certified by county government; both imported and domestic fruit must meet U.S. Department of Agriculture and State Department of Agriculture standards.

- Going to school at any level, public or private: States have standards for what must be taught at each grade level, as well as tests to determine whether schools are meeting the standard.

- Working for the California Highway Patrol: The CHP is a state government agency.

- Working for a private security guard service: Security guards must meet local police department standards.

- Working for a grocery store: Wages, hours, and working conditions are governed by the state Department of Employment Security or by union contract.

- Eating dinner in a restaurant: County Departments of Health oversee restaurant food quality and cleanliness.

2 The Constitution and the Progressive Legacy

WHAT CALIFORNIA GOVERNMENT DOES AND WHY IT MATTERS

The current problems in California are hard to miss. Look anywhere and you'll find a crisis. For many, the root cause is an age-old, deeply flawed constitution and particularly the ballot box initiative. The initiative was the result of the attempt to gain control of the state's political process over special interests. Ironically, nearly 100 years later, the initiative has become a means through which individuals, interest groups, and elected officials pursue outcomes they cannot achieve in the legislature.

Any individual or group can propose a statute or an amendment to the California constitution. Of course, having sufficient funds to wage an effective campaign and having an issue appealing enough to the voters to have one's measure approved are other matters. Only about a third of initiatives are approved by the voters, and the amount of money spent correlates only very loosely with the probability of approval.

In 2006, for example, California voters cast their ballots on Proposition 87, a high-profile initiative that was also the most costly in history, with over $156 million being spent. Supporters contributed $61.9 million (with $49.6 million alone coming from film producer Steve Bing), and opponents contributed $94.4 million (with Chevron Corporation, Aera Energy, and Occidental Oil and Gas contributing $38 million, $32.8 million, and $9.6 million, respectively).[1]

The initiative brought out celebrities on both sides, including prominent individuals, companies, and organizations. These included former President Bill Clinton, Brad Pitt, and the Coalition for Clean Air in support of the measure, and Governor Arnold Schwarzenegger, Chevron Corporation, and California Chamber of Commerce in opposition.

The measure established a $4 billion program, the primary goal of which was to reduce petroleum consumption by 25 percent, with research and production incentives for alternative energy, alternative-energy vehicles, and energy-efficient technologies, as well as funding for education and training. The program would be funded by a tax of 1.5 to 6.0 percent (depending on oil price per barrel) on California oil producers.

The stakes were high because California was the fourth largest oil-producing state in the nation: roughly 37 percent of California's oil was pumped in the state, and another 21 percent came from Alaska. The rest was imported.

The campaign was bitter and acrimonious. Accusations of dirty tactics thrived, and lawsuits were filed by both sides. Supporters alleged that the opposition's print and television advertisements created the false impression that it was financed by a broad coalition, including educators and public-safety officials, when in fact it was subsidized by the oil industry. On the other side, opponents to the measure accused their adversaries of illegally registering several "no" sites that, when accessed, redirected viewers to the "Yes-on-87" website. In the end, little came of either lawsuit; however, each helped sharpen and intensify feelings on both sides.

In the end, Proposition 87 failed to pass, getting 45.3 percent of the vote, as voters feared that passage of the initiative would cause higher gas prices, resulting in a greater demand for foreign oil. It is a prime example, however, of an issue that, rather than being debated by experts and elected officials in the legislature, was seized by wealthy individuals and interest groups in the name of direct democracy. Such examples abound in California politics.

In Chapter 1, we discussed some of the demographic differences between California and other states. We also mentioned that California's government is institutionally designed to foster (or at least not be able to solve) critical state issues. Here are some of the unique features in the political process:

- The **sheer size of the state** increases the cost of political campaigns and media cost.

- The **competing network of interest groups** causes groups to jockey for position and influence.

- The **increasing use of the initiative** significantly impacts state and local governance and policy.

- The **divided executive branch**, composed of nine separately elected officials, each with his or her own area of authority and responsibility, leads to overlapping responsibilities and fragmentation in the execution of state policy.

- The **widespread, almost universal use of nonpartisan elections at the local level of government** eliminates a valuable clue for voters to identify the policy positions of the candidates on the ballot.

Aside from the size of the state and the interest-group network, these other characteristics are a result of the Progressive movement, which flourished from 1900 to 1917. The leaders of this movement focused on one goal: making government more responsive to the political, social, and economic concerns of the people. Their reforms continue to shape California government and politics in ways that sharply differentiate it from other states. To some, these features hamper the political process and should be changed. To others, they are the essence of California, and if they were changed, California would be just another state.

The Rules of the Game: California's Constitution

The California constitution is long and very detailed, with numerous amendments added over the years, dealing with both the fundamental principles and power of government as well as commonplace issues such as the right to fish on government property, English as the state's official language, and grants for stem cell research. Today California has the second highest number of constitutional amendments, behind Alabama, and has the second longest state constitution, behind Louisiana. The California constitution is over 100 pages long.

The constitution defines the rules under which political actors and the citizens interact with each other to fulfill their goals as individuals, members of a group, or a population as a whole. Its long and storied history can be divided into four stages:

- **The 1849 constitution.** Written by residents of the territory in anticipation of statehood, this constitution contains many of the basic ideas underlying California government today.

- **The 1879 constitution.** Written by a constitutional convention in 1878, this is the basic document, with amendments, that is in force today.

- **From 1900 to 1917.** During this period, the Progressives amended the constitution and passed laws to return government to the people, temper the power of special interests, and make government responsive to the people's desires and needs. The most prominent reforms of this period were the initiative, referendum, and recall.

- **From 1918 to the present.** Amendment after amendment lengthened the state's constitution, resulting in a document that at one point was almost 100,000 words long. Several commissions proposed substantive changes, but the only changes adopted came from two constitutional revision commissions, one in the 1960s and the other in the 1990s, that shortened and clarified language in the constitution but made no substantial changes to its provisions.

The 1849 Constitution

By 1849, 80,000 unruly gold miners had moved to California, giving the area enough people to apply for territorial status, and the settlers of the territory drafted a constitution. Admitting California as a free state, however, would have upset the balance between free and slave states that had existed in the Union since 1820; therefore, admission as a territory was delayed. In 1849, the newly elected president of the United States Zachary Taylor proposed that California draft a constitution and apply for admission as a state directly to Congress, instead of applying as a territory first and moving to state status later. California citizens elected delegates to a constitutional convention; the delegates in turn met and drew up the proposed constitution in 43 days.

The constitutional convention, 48 elected men who met in Monterey in September of 1849, used a book of constitutions that contained the constitutions of the federal government and some 30 states. Several of the provisions were taken directly from the constitutions of New York and Iowa. The basic provisions of the 1849 constitution are still in force:

- The framework of the government rested on a separation of powers—executive, legislative, and judicial—and checks and balances, like the federal government.

- Executive power was divided, as it is today, with the separate election and jurisdiction of the governor, lieutenant governor, comptroller, treasurer, attorney general, surveyor general, and superintendent of public instruction. This division weakens the governor, who cannot appoint—or remove—senior members of his or her own administration. Moreover, each of these statewide officials is a potential competitor for the governor's office, and each can put out statements that contradict what the governor is saying.

- An extensive bill of rights begins the constitution.

- The legislature was elected and consisted of two houses, one called the Senate, the other the Assembly.

Features that were different from what we have today include

- The right to vote at that time was limited to white males 21 years of age or older who had lived in California for at least six months.

- The legislature by a two-thirds vote could grant Native Americans the right to vote "in such special cases as such proportion of the legislative body may deem just and proper."

- The judiciary was elected, as judges are today, but they were organized into four levels as was Mexico's judiciary at the time.

- All laws and other provisions were to be published in both English and Spanish, since California was a bilingual state.

The first California constitution read very much like any other state constitution—it had about 9,000 words, compared with the present U.S. Constitution's 4,500 words, plus another 3,100 words of amendments. Over time, as we shall see, the constitution evolved into a much longer document.

In 1850, the federal government passed a series of bills that made up the Compromise of 1850. These bills admitted California to the union as a free state, established territorial governments in Utah and New Mexico, allowed residents of those states to decide whether to be free or slave states, settled a dispute over the border between Texas and New Mexico, compensated Texas with $10 million to repay debts to Mexico, abolished the slave trade in the District of Columbia, and put the Fugitive Slave Act into effect.

The 1879 Constitution

Voters approved the convening of a constitutional convention in 1877, but the actual convention was held in 1879. A new political party, the Workingmen's Party, which supported many Populist ideas (see p. 24), and which held 51 of the 152 seats at the convention, played a significant role in the discussion.[2] The new party supported restrictions on corporations and railroads and was also strongly opposed to the presence of Chinese workers in California. One of its rallying cries was "The Chinese must go!"[3] The party also opposed centralized governmental power and a powerful legislature, proposing unsuccessfully to the convention that California collapse the two houses of the legislature into one, a unicameral legislature, and abolish the lieutenant governor's office.

All kinds of provisions were adopted. For example, stockholders were to be responsible for the debts of a corporation. The railroads could not give free passes to those holding political office; they could not raise rates on one line to compensate for reductions made to compete on alternative lines; and they would be regulated by a Railroad Commission. Other provisions restricted Chinese workers, prohibiting them from being employed on public works projects or by corporations chartered in California.

These additions added words—almost doubling the constitution's size—and policies that read very much like a series of laws rather than a fundamental framework within which laws would operate. By 1948, the California constitution, with amendments, reached 95,000 words.

The new constitution was approved by a 54 to 46 percent vote in May 1879, with 90 percent of those eligible to vote participating. In the end, however, most of the reform measures were not put into practice right away, as corporations and other special interests sued to block their implementation, continuing the domination of the state by corporate and railroad power. These setbacks were temporary, however. In a matter of three decades the broad reforms of the Progressive movement gained passage, weakening the grip of these special interests in the legislature and reshaping the landscape of California politics.

You can get a sense of California's constitution and how different it is from the federal constitution by examining California's bill of rights, called "Declaration of Rights." The federal bill of rights consists of the first 10 amendments to the U.S. Constitution, and while other amendments may be passed, the first 10 will remain the Bill of Rights as they were written. California's bill of rights, meanwhile, can be expanded or rewritten as times change. Because of this factor, California's bill of rights reflects the political changes and conflicts that have occurred over time, which means that some of the rights can be much more specific than the corresponding federal right. You can see the result of that specificity in the provisions for freedom of speech as they apply to a newspaper. The federal constitution has the familiar First Amendment:

> Amendment 1: Congress shall make no law respecting an establishment of religion, or prohibiting the free exercise thereof, or abridging the freedom of speech, or of the press; or the right of the people peaceably to assembly, and to petition the Government for a redress of grievances.

California's corresponding section has both more detail and more specificity, since it has been amended over time.

> SEC. 2. (a) Every person may freely speak, write and publish his or her sentiments on all subjects, being responsible for the abuse of this right. A law may not restrain or abridge liberty of speech or press.

(b) A publisher, editor, reporter, or other person connected with or employed upon a newspaper, magazine, or other periodical publication, or by a press association or wire service, or any person who has been so connected or employed, shall not be adjudged in contempt by a judicial, legislative, or administrative body, or any other body having the power to issue subpoenas, for refusing to disclose the source of any information procured while so connected or employed for publication in a newspaper, magazine, or other periodical publication, or for refusing to disclose any unpublished information obtained or prepared in gathering, receiving, or processing of information for communication to the public. Nor shall a radio or television news reporter or other person connected with or employed by a radio or television station, or any person who has been so connected or employed, be so adjudged in contempt for refusing to disclose the source of any information procured while so connected or employed for news or news commentary purposes on radio or television, or for refusing to disclose any unpublished information obtained or prepared in gathering, receiving, or processing of information for communication to the public.

Note the use of modern language, such as *wire service* and *television*.

California's Declaration of Rights can also be amended through the initiative process, which allows individuals or groups to put proposed changes before the voting public at any election.

From 1900 to 1917: The Progressive Movement

Pressure for political reform continued. Beginning with the turn of the twentieth century, the Progressives pursued three goals: to attack corporate political influence, eliminate the political corruption that went with such influence, and democratize the political process.[4]

They understood that these goals had to be accomplished before they could address equally pressing but more mundane concerns of the time. They accomplished all of this—and much more. Beginning with the 1911 legislative session, these reformers passed dozens of constitutional amendments and statutes that changed the face of California government and politics.[5] The most prominent of the political reforms were the following:

- **Nonpartisanship.** This is the norm in local elections, by which no party label is affixed to the candidates' names on the ballot. Of the more than 19,000 elected public officials in California, less than 300 are elected in partisan races.

- **Primary elections.** Before the institution of primary elections, political parties chose their candidates in party conventions (with their stereotypes of the smoky back rooms) or caucuses—meetings of party members at the local level. In a primary election, each prospective party nominee has to obtain more votes than any other prospective nominee to run as the party's candidate in the general election in November.

- **The office block ballot.** This is the ballot that we vote on today, with a "block" for each office and the candidates listed for that office. Before this reform, in some elections, voters cast ballots for their preferred party, not for individual candidates.

- **Direct democracy.** These grassroots processes—the initiative, referendum, and recall—give citizens the ability to rein in the abuse of power by elected officials or to ignite those same public officials if they are paralyzed by inaction and partisan bickering.

During this period, the California constitution grew substantially as the legislature enacted dozens of constitutional amendments and statutes. In the first three months of 1911 alone, the legislature passed more than 800 statutes and 23 constitutional amendments.

From 1960 to the Present: Late Revisions

In 1963, the legislature created a constitution revision commission as a result of an initiative passed in 1962. The commission, composed of 50 citizens, three state senators, and three Assembly members, submitted two major reports with recommended revisions to the state constitution. The legislature incorporated these into 14 constitutional amendments that were submitted to the voters for their approval between 1966 and 1976, and the voters approved 10 of these. These simplified, shortened, and reorganized the constitution but made few substantive changes in it.

In 1993, the legislature again established a constitution revision commission, which proposed a number of substantial changes to the constitution, provisions reformers had discussed in some cases for generations. For a variety of reasons, many having to do with the two-thirds vote in the Assembly and Senate to place them on the ballot, they were never submitted to the voters.

How well do the constitution of 1879 and the Progressive-era amendments fit a California that is 10 to 20 times larger than in the early twentieth century? Not terribly well, it must be admitted. The legislature is the same size, 40 state Senators and 80 Assembly members, but the districts have grown from just over 60,000 for the state Senate to almost 1,000,000 people, with much less personal service

---

BOX 2.1 **Amending the California Constitution**

The constitution can be amended in one of three ways. In each case, the proposed amendment must be ratified by majority vote in the next statewide election.

1. **A constitutional convention can propose an amendment.** The convention can be called either by the legislature with a two-thirds vote or by a majority vote of the electorate through an initiative. Voters must ratify the amendment by majority vote in the next statewide election.

2. **Citizens can propose an amendment directly through the initiative.** The process requires the proponents to submit a petition with the signatures of 8 percent of the voters in the last gubernatorial election. The proposed amendment then is placed on the ballot for approval in the next statewide election.

3. **The legislature may propose an amendment to the constitution.** The process requires a two-thirds vote of both houses of the legislature. The proposed amendment is then placed on the ballot for approval in the next statewide election.

than what occurred in an earlier era. The initiative could be mounted by small amateur groups in the early twentieth century, but now it is strictly a tool for use by well-funded interest groups. Serious efforts to modernize state government, unfortunately, have been few and far between, and when they have occurred, as with the constitutional revision commission of the 1990s, the results were subject to partisan voting and insufficient majorities to send them to the people for a final decision.

The Progressive Movement and Its Impact on California Politics

The Progressive movement had its roots in the economic and political changes that swept the United States after the Civil War. It was foreshadowed by the Populist movement, which dominated American politics from 1870 to 1896.

Some of the political concerns and much of the moral indignation expressed by the Populists about the changes taking place in America are reflected in the Progressive movement. One major difference between the two movements is geographic. The Populist movement began in the rural areas of the country; the Progressive movement was urban, born in the major cities.[6] While the Progressive movement was identified mostly with the Republican Party, there were notable Progressive leaders in the Democratic Party as well, such as Woodrow Wilson.

The Progressives perceived many of the same problems as the Populists. From the Civil War on, the United States had rapidly industrialized, and wealth became concentrated in the hands of a new breed of corporate entrepreneurs. *Monopoly* was the word of the day. These corporate giants dictated economic policy, which in turn had significant social and political consequences. In California, one giant corporation, the Southern Pacific Railroad, stood above all others. It represented a concentration of wealth and power that gave it undue influence not only economically but also politically. To a degree perhaps unparalleled in the nation, the Southern Pacific Railroad and a web of associated interests ruled the state. The Southern Pacific Railroad had the money and resources to influence political decisions. Bribing public officials was not unusual, nor was handpicking candidates for the two major political parties.[7]

The Progressives countered the powerful corporations, specifically the Southern Pacific Railroad, by prosecuting the corrupt politicians who served them. Eventually, this tactic unraveled the railroad's domination of state and local politics and led to a series of regulatory reforms that loosened the choke hold that they—and specifically the Southern Pacific Railroad—had on state and local politics.

Local Politics

Progressive reforms began at the local level, in the cities of San Francisco and Los Angeles. The battle against the Southern Pacific Railroad and corporate influence in general started in San Francisco in 1906, with the reform movement fighting to rid city government of graft and bribery. President Theodore Roosevelt stepped in to help. Working hand in hand with James D. Phelan, the former mayor of San Francisco, Roosevelt sent in federal agents led by William J. Bums to investigate bribery and corruption charges.[8] Public officials were put on trial for the bribery, bringing to the public's attention the extent of graft and political corruption in municipal government.

Seventeen supervisors and a number of corporate leaders were indicted.[9] The mayor was forced to resign, and his henchman, Abraham Reuf, who implicated officials of the Southern Pacific Railroad and several utility companies, was convicted and sentenced to 14 years in jail. While Reuf was the exception, and the graft trials largely failed to convict those indicted, they were nonetheless an important step in breaking the power of the Southern Pacific Railroad and its political allies.

In 1906, the Southern Pacific Railroad also dominated Los Angeles.[10] During this time, a group dedicated to good government, the Non-Partisan Committee of One Hundred, was formed. They selected a reform candidate for mayor who was opposed by the two major parties, labor, and the *Los Angeles Times*. While the reform candidate lost his bid for the mayoralty, 17 of 23 reform candidates for other city positions were elected.[11] The nonpartisan reformers were on the way to ridding the city of the Southern Pacific machine.

State Politics

The 1907 legislative session was one of the most corrupt on record, with no action taken without the blessing of the political operatives of the Southern Pacific Railroad. At the end of the session, the editor of the Fresno *Republican*, Chester Rowell, wrote: "If we are fit to govern ourselves, this is the last time we will submit to be governed by the hired bosses of the Southern Pacific Railroad Company."[12]

At the same time, Rowell and Edward Dickson of the Los Angeles *Express* began to organize a statewide movement to attack the Southern Pacific's power. At Dickson's invitation, a group of lawyers, newspaper publishers, and other political reformers met in Los Angeles. They founded the Lincoln Republicans, later to become the League of Lincoln-Roosevelt Republican Clubs, dedicated to ending the control of California politics by the Southern Pacific Railroad and linking themselves to the national Progressive movement.

The Lincoln-Roosevelt League participated in the statewide legislative elections of 1908 and managed to elect a small group of reformers to the legislature. Two years later it fielded a full-party slate, from governor down to local candidates.

STATEHOUSE VICTORY In 1910, Hiram Johnson became the candidate for governor of the Lincoln-Roosevelt League. He campaigned up and down the state, focusing on one main issue: the Southern Pacific Railroad. He claimed the Southern Pacific Railroad, acting in concert with criminal elements, had corrupted the political process in California. He defined the battle as one between decent, law-abiding citizens and a few corrupt, powerful individuals who were determined to run the state in their own best interests.

Johnson won the election and met with leading national Progressives—Theodore Roosevelt, Robert La Follette, and Lincoln Steffens—to discuss a reform program for California. The new administration in Sacramento set out to eliminate every special interest from the government and to make government solely responsive to the people and Johnson. Through a series of legislative acts and constitutional amendments, they went a long way in that direction. In 1911, the voters passed the initiative, the referendum, and the recall. These three reforms, widely known as *direct democracy*, placed enormous power and control over government in the hands of the voters. Now citizens could write their laws or amend the constitution through the initiative, approve or disapprove constitutional amendments through the referendum, and remove corrupt politicians from office through the recall.

In addition to these reforms, a new law set up a railroad commission with power to fix rates beginning in 1911. Other reforms included the *direct primary*, which gave the power to ordinary citizens to select the candidates of the political parties for national and state offices. Women obtained the right to vote in California in 1911. Legislation was also enacted that limited women to an eight-hour workday, set up a workmen's compensation system, put into practice a weekly pay law, and required employers to inform strikebreakers that they were being hired to replace employees on strike (and thus might face verbal abuse and physical violence).

The Progressives in California more than kept their campaign promises to limit the influence of the corporations and the political parties in politics. In the first two years in office, the Johnson administration succeeded in breaking the power of the Southern Pacific Railroad.[13]

LAST HURRAH The national Progressive Party lost its bid to capture the White House in 1912, with a ticket of Theodore Roosevelt for president and Hiram Johnson for vice president. The failure to win an important national office weakened the party by lessening the enthusiasm of its supporters. It also meant that the party had no patronage with which to reward its followers between elections. Electoral failure was just one of several major problems that plagued the Progressives. Several other factors also contributed to the decline of the party: the public grew tired of reform, there was a major falling out among the leadership in California, the Progressives generally opposed World War I, and the party failed to support reforms that labor so badly wanted.

While the Progressives were hoping that Roosevelt would run again in 1916, he was working to prevent another third-party fiasco. When the Progressives learned that the Republican Party would not nominate Roosevelt, they offered him the nomination, but he turned them down. At a dinner in San Francisco in July 1916, the California Progressive Party disbanded. Hiram Johnson urged his followers to go back to either the Republican or the Democratic Party. Later that year Johnson, now a Republican, was elected to the U.S. Senate, where he served for 28 years.

If there was one major flaw in Progressive thinking, it was the belief in the active, informed citizen willing to participate in politics. Progressives believed that given the opportunity, citizens would be happy to support the democratic process and spend whatever time and effort was needed to participate in elections. Since the late 1940s, a host of studies has shown that large numbers of people don't vote or pay attention to politics. But the Progressives cannot be faulted for today's diminished interest in politics and government. In the end, they gave the people of California tremendous political power, if or when they choose to use it.

This political power was appropriate for 1910, when California had 2.4 million people. Since then, California has grown so much and so quickly that its constitution has been unable to catch up, and the reforms that allowed "the people" to propose initiatives and recall public officials in particular cannot be exercised on a *statewide*[14] level in a state of now 38 million people without money, organization, and professional help. We haven't had an initiative that did *not* use paid, professional signature gatherers since 1990, and that one needed a paid coordinator for the campaign. A totally volunteer initiative organization hasn't been successful since 1984.

Direct Democracy

The Progressives established civil service reforms, nonpartisan commissions to control key state regulatory functions, nonpartisan elections to cripple local machines, office block voting (a ballot listing all candidates for a given office under the name of that office), and primary elections. If these innovations failed to check the power of special interests, they gave voters the power of direct action through the initiative, referendum, and recall. These three mechanisms work in the same way. Citizens circulate petitions to gather a required number of signatures to bring the measure to statewide vote. The number of signatures, as we shall see, varies depending on the mechanism.

Initiative

THE PROCESS Of the three direct voices in government, the initiative is the most well known and most frequently used. The process, also known as direct legislation, requires the proponent to obtain a title (e.g., "Public Schools: English as Required Language of Instruction") and summary of the proposed initiative from the state attorney general. Upon obtaining the title and summary, the proponents have 150 days to circulate a petition to gather the required number of signatures to qualify for the ballot—5 percent of voters in the last gubernatorial election for statutes, and 8 percent for constitutional amendments. The secretary of state submits the measure at the next general election held at least 131 days after it qualifies or at any special election held before the next general election. The governor may call a special election for the measure.

Before 1960, initiatives appeared only on the general election ballot, thus limiting their use to the two-year election cycle. Since 1960, they have appeared on the primary, general, and special-election ballots, which allows for more frequent opportunities to qualify and vote on them. The freedom to qualify them in all elections keeps the public aware of them and excited about using them.

FREQUENCY OF USE Initiatives have become a staple of California's political fabric. From 1912 to 2012, over 1,600 initiatives were titled and summarized for circulation. Of this number, 360 qualified for the ballot, 3 were removed by court order, and 121 were approved by the voters—for an overall passage rate of 34 percent. Of the 121 initiatives approved, 40 were constitutional amendments and 10 were constitutional/stationary changes.[15]

Figure 2.1 presents the use of initiative by decade. Note these two points: the increasing frequency of initiatives since 1970, and the varying, but generally low, level of success for the measures that made it to the ballot.

For discussion purposes, we can compress the 100-year history of initiatives into four time periods: 1912–39, 1940–69, 1970–1999, and 2000–12.

1912–39 From the beginning, various individuals and special interests understood that the initiative could be used to forward their special causes. Social and cultural issues, such as outlawing gambling on horse races, professional fighting, prostitution, and land ownership by Asians, drew the highest voter turnout during this period. Labor issues (closed versus open shops) and tax propositions were also volatile issues.

No one issue, however, dominated the initiative process during this period more than the so-called liquor question.[16] These initiatives were among the most controversial, and they drew high voter turnouts. Twelve measures related

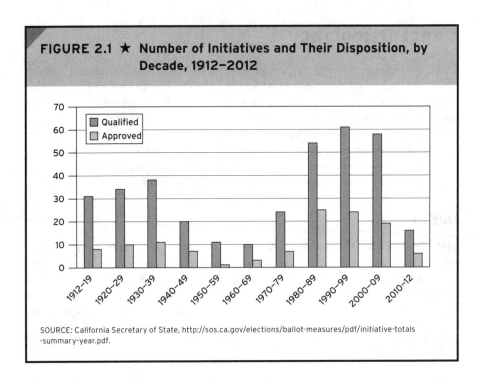

FIGURE 2.1 ★ Number of Initiatives and Their Disposition, by Decade, 1912–2012

SOURCE: California Secretary of State, http://sos.ca.gov/elections/ballot-measures/pdf/initiative-totals-summary-year.pdf.

to liquor control appeared on the ballot between 1914 and 1936, for and against full prohibition and antisoloon measures, and state regulation versus local control. Voting was consistent throughout this period, with the anti-Prohibition forces generally prevailing on every measure. The issue, however, wouldn't go away; in 1948, after many failures to qualify an initiative, the antiliquor forces qualified another local option measure, which was rejected by 70 percent of the voters. After this vote, the issue lost its appeal, never to appear on the ballot again.

1940–69 In this time period, use of the initiative declined markedly. Compared to the previous 27 years, a higher percentage of proposed measures failed to gather enough signatures to qualify for the ballot. The subject matter of the initiatives also varied from those of 1912–39. Newer issues came to the forefront: race and civil rights, property taxes, and labor and welfare issues.

Proposition 14 (1964) was the most prominent of a number of initiatives that dealt with fair housing. The initiative was drafted to nullify the Rumford Fair Housing Act, which prohibited discrimination in the rental, lease, or purchase of housing on the basis of race and national origin. The Rumford Act, supporters of Proposition 14 claimed, interfered with their private property rights. Real estate and homeowners' associations led the forces in support of the proposition and a coalition of Democratic Party leadership, organized labor, churches, and a variety of other groups led the forces against it. The broader issue of race, specifically African Americans, lingered in the background of the campaign; by all accounts, race was the deciding factor in how people voted. Proposition 14 passed by a 2–1 margin in November 1964. Its victory was a major factor in the Watts riots in the summer of 1965.[17] Over the next two years, Proposition 14 was overturned, first by the California Supreme Court and then by the U.S. Supreme Court, because it violated the Fourteenth Amendment.

1970–99 In this period initiatives abounded, with over 1,000 being titled, 141 qualifying, and 56 being approved. The subjects addressed social, cultural, and economic issues, including the death penalty, gun control, busing, property tax, nuclear power, water resources, air quality, coastal preservation, English as the official language, affirmative action, illegal immigrants, and gay marriage.

The most controversial initiative of this period was Proposition 13, titled the "People's Initiative to Limit Property Taxation" (1978). Sponsored by longtime antitax activists Howard Jarvis and Paul Gann, Proposition 13 was a reaction to the spiraling appreciation of property throughout the 1970s. In just one year, some properties were reassessed at a value 50 to 100 percent higher, and their owners' tax bills jumped correspondingly.

Proposition 13 was a grassroots effort. Nearly every state employee and labor union, and most Democratic leaders, opposed it. The pro side raised $2.2 million, and the con side raised $2 million. On June 6, 1978, nearly two-thirds of California's voters passed Proposition 13, reducing property tax rates by about 57 percent.

Now, 30 years later, Proposition 13 is still hotly debated. Critics argue that it creates tax inequities because it treats residential and commercial property the same and assesses similar properties differently based solely on when a homeowner bought a house. Supporters argue that pegging property taxes to the yearly assessed value of the property exposes homeowners to accelerated yearly property taxes, which leaves them vulnerable to losing their homes.

2000–12 During this period, California voters decided on 75 initiatives in 16 separate elections, 3 of which were special elections, including the special election to recall Governor Gray Davis. Twenty-five passed, including measures on farm animal confinement practices, redistricting the state legislative boundaries, victims' rights, and parole procedures.

The most controversial and long-lasting ballot issue deals with same-sex marriage. The issue goes back some 35 years. In 1977, the state legislature passed a law that said that marriage is a "personal relation arising out of a civil contract between a man and a woman." This was reaffirmed in 2000 when the voters passed Proposition 22, a statutory—not constitutional—amendment that revised the California Family Code to formally define marriage to be between a man and a woman.

In 2004, San Francisco Mayor Gavin Newsom began performing same-sex marriages, which were judicially annulled. However, in May 2008, the California Supreme Court ruled Proposition 22 invalid. At about the same time, fearing such a decision, the proponents of Proposition 8 ("Eliminates Right of Same-Sex Couples to Marry") had already begun to qualify the initiative for the ballot, anticipating this time that a constitutional amendment, not a statute, would put the issue to rest.

The campaign over Proposition 8 was fiercely contested. In the end, the initiative passed by a margin of 52.3 to 47.7 percent. Both sides attracted significant amounts of money: those supporting Proposition 8 contributed $40.3 million, and those opposing Proposition 8 contributed $64.4 million, making it the second most expensive initiative campaign—to Proposition 87 in 2006—in state history and the highest same-sex marriage initiative campaign expenditure ever nationally.

After the election six lawsuits were filed by gay couples and government bodies, with the California Supreme Court challenging the constitutionality of Proposition 8. Three of the six were accepted together to be heard by the court, but the court denied the request to stay the enforcement of Proposition 8. On May 26,

2009 (*Strauss v. Horton*), the court ruled that Proposition 8 was valid but allowed existing same-sex marriages to stand.

On August 4, 2010, a federal court declared the ban unconstitutional in *Perry v. Schwarzenegger* (now *Perry v. Brown*), and this decision was upheld by the Ninth Circuit in February 2012. The supporters of Proposition 8 had the choice of appealing the decision to the full 11-judge Ninth Circuit Court or appealing directly to the U.S. Supreme Court. They chose the former route, and this is where the issue stands today.

How can we account for the increase in initiatives over the past four decades? The simplest explanation is that it is a consequence of several factors—the complexity of modern society, the increased willingness to regulate and specify legally things that had been left to individual citizens in the first half of the twentieth century, and the move from a part-time to full-time legislature in 1968. As a result of the latter change, politics became a career, more legislation was passed, the budget grew, and decision making and power shifted to Sacramento.

These shifts, coupled with the other reforms started by the Progressives to rid the capital of political corruption and an unresponsive legislature—direct primaries, term limits, regulation of campaign contributions, and the various devices used to weaken political parties—undermined the influence voters have on elected officials. Accordingly, voters, frustrated by the action or inaction of the legislature, have turned to the initiative to get what they want.

During this time period, special interests also frequently turned to initiatives to promote policies they couldn't get through the legislature. More and more, all a group needs is the money to fund an initiative campaign. As a result, an industry of professional campaign managers and signature gatherers is flourishing. In fact, these so-called policy managers now identify hot issues and then go out and search for clients who will pay for the privilege of sponsoring the initiative.

Referendum

THE PROCESS A referendum allows voters to approve or reject statutes or amendments passed by the state legislature. The process is as follows: the measure may be proposed by presenting to the secretary of state a petition with signatures equal to 5 percent of the voters in the last gubernatorial election. The filing of the signatures must take place within a 90-day period after the enactment of the statute. If it qualifies to be on the ballot, the measure prevents the law from taking effect until the electorate decides whether it should become a law.

FREQUENCY OF USE The referendum is used infrequently. In fact, it has almost faded from use. Between 1912 and 2012, 48 referenda have appeared on the ballot. Using the same periods that we used for the initiative, there were 33 referenda from 1912 to 1939, 2 from 1940 to 1969, and 13 from 1970 to 2012.

Voters rejected a law 27 times; they approved a law 21 times. Moreover, only 14 referenda have appeared on the ballot since 1942: 1 in 1942, 1 in 1952, 4 in 1982, 3 in 2000, 1 in 2004, 4 in 2008, 2 in 2010 and 1 in 2012. Three of the 4 referenda of 1982 had to do with the redistricting of congressional, state Senate and state Assembly district boundaries. The Democratic state legislature had drawn district boundaries for all three bodies that the Republican believed were unfair. The voters concurred and rejected all three Democratic laws, forcing new boundaries to be drawn, which, from the Republican point of view, were more reflective of political reality.[18]

Recall

THE PROCESS The recall allows voters to determine whether to recall an elected official before his or her term expires. Proponents first submit a petition alleging the reason for recall. They have 150 days to present to the secretary of state a petition with the required number of signatures to qualify for the ballot. At the same time, if required, a successor is elected if the sitting official is recalled.

For statewide offices, the number of signatures must be equal to 12 percent of the last vote for the office, with signatures from at least five counties equal to 1 percent of the last vote for the office in the county. For the Senate, Assembly, members of the Board of Equalization, and judges, the number of signatures must be equal to 20 percent of the last vote for the office. Upon receiving the petitions, an election must be held between 60 and 80 days from the date of certification of sufficient signatures.

FREQUENCY OF USE Recalls of statewide offices or the state legislature are rare. There have been eight recalls out of 118 filings against state office holders. Seven of the eight were state legislators; Governor Davis was the other. Four of the state legislators were tossed out of office. The recall was put into use almost immediately after its passage against three state legislators—twice in 1913, against Senator Marshall Black for involvement in a banking scandal, which succeeded, and against Senator James Owen for corruption, which failed. The next year Senator Edwin Grant, who represented the red-light district in San Francisco, was recalled for opposing prostitution, which succeeded.

Four other state legislators faced a recall vote in 1994 and 1995. The National Rifle Association failed in its attempt to recall Senator David Roberti for his position on gun control legislation. Two Republican members of the Assembly, Doris Allen and Paul Horcher, were voted out of office for supporting Willie Brown for speaker in a battle between the parties for control of the Assembly. And an attempt to recall Democratic Assemblyman Mike Machado for backing Republicans failed.[19]

The most notorious recall, however, was that of Governor Gray Davis. He is the only California governor to have been recalled, although there had been over two dozen previous attempts to gather enough signatures to recall a governor, including three against Ronald Reagan in the 1960s and one against Pete Wilson in the 1990s. During the 2002 campaign for governor, Davis had claimed that the budget deficit was $18 billion, but a week after his election he revealed it was actually $35 billion. Proponents of the recall immediately accused Davis of misleading voters about the severity of the state's budget crisis during his reelection campaign.

Each of the direct democracy processes—initiative, referendum, and recall—is available as well in local politics, where they first appeared and where they still thrive today.

Debating the Merit of Direct Democracy

The debate about the merits of direct democracy—initiative, referendum, and recall—has been ongoing since its adoption in the early twentieth century. As we have seen, one device, the initiative, has been employed more than the other two and is generally the focus of the debate on the value of direct democracy.

Many scholars believe the initiative blurs the complexity of many issues and reduces them to clichés or sound bites upon which the voter is asked to make a yes/no choice. Furthermore, they are concerned about the influence of money in the initiative process. Some writers, like journalists David Broder and Peter Schrag, believe that special interests with deep pockets dominate the initiative process, undermining the efficacy of representative government, with its built-in checks and balances. Other writers, such as academics Elisabeth R. Gerber and Shaun Bowler, take a broader view, arguing that money plays a vital role in defeating initiatives but not in the passage of initiatives. They argue that successful initiatives are the product of grassroots movements that have more to do with visceral social and economic issues than with well-financed campaigns. Supporters of the initiative also claim that the initiative is a more effective means of serving the majority in California than the legislative process in any event. Therein lies the catch-22 that largely defines California politics: the legislature is argued to be hamstrung by the zealous use of direct democracy, while direct democracy is argued to be necessary to overcome an unproductive legislature.

A recent Field Poll[20] reveals that Californians still support the institution of direct democracy but not as strongly as in the past. In 1979, just after the passage of Proposition 13, 83 percent of voters viewed statewide ballot proposition elections as a good thing. While the favorable rating has dropped considerably since then, a majority of Californians (53 percent) still favor statewide ballot proposition elections.

Californians also think that the voting public trust fellow citizens, by use of initiatives, more than they do their elected representatives "to do what is right on important government issues" (63 percent), and especially when it comes to deciding on large-scale government programs and projects.

It's not surprising, then, that a majority of voters oppose two proposed changes to the initiative process. By a 59 to 33 percent margin, voters oppose giving the legislature the right to amend or repeal an initiative four years after its passage, and they also oppose the idea that the legislature should be able to amend an initiative after it qualifies for placement on the ballot.

In final analysis, according to the Field Poll, voters don't fully trust their elective representatives. They believe elected officials, by a 56 to 29 percent margin, "are more easily influenced by interest groups." Until that trust is gained or regained, Californians will continue to hold strong in their support of direct democracy.

California's Constitution: Where Are We Now?

California's constitution has been through three stages—establishment in the mid-1800s, rewriting in 1879, and extensive amendment during the Progressive era. Since then, a fourth, ongoing stage has been defined by political scientists and others—most notably the 1996 California Constitutional Revision Commission—making numerous suggestions to update the constitutional framework. The 1996 commission made many suggestions to strengthen the governor and make state government less susceptible to interest-group influence. These suggestions included:

- Having the governor and lieutenant governor run as a team.
- Having the other elected members of the executive branch be appointed by the governor.

- Merging the several tax administration agencies.

- Lengthening term limits for legislators.

- Requiring a simple majority instead of a two-thirds majority for the enactment of the budget each year.

Most of these proposals have never come before the voters. In 2010, however, with the state's decade-long budget crisis looming in the background, California voters passed Proposition 25, which changed the legislative requirement to pass the budget from two-thirds to a simple majority. Proposition 25 also requires state legislators to forfeit their pay in years in which they fail to pass a budget in a timely fashion. So Democrats—currently the majority party—can pass a budget without any Republican votes; however, they still can't raise taxes without a two-thirds vote. This makes the Democrats fully responsible for the budget, which, under current economic conditions, can be balanced only by cutting spending.

In the meantime, voters continue their love–hate relationship with the political parties. In 2008, the passage of Proposition 11 removed the legislature from the process of drawing its own district boundaries; a citizen commission will draw the boundaries beginning with the 2012 elections, based on the 2010 Census. And in 2010, the voters approved a top-two primary initiative, with candidates from all the parties listed on one ballot and the top two candidates, regardless of party, moving to a runoff in the November election.

FOR FURTHER READING

Allswang, John M., *The Initiative and Referendum in California, 1898–1998*. Stanford, CA: Stanford University Press, 2000.

Broder, David. *Democracy Derailed: Initiative Campaigns and the Power of Money*. New York: Harcourt, 2000.

California Secretary of State. "Initiative Totals by Summary Year 1912–March 2012." http://www.sos.ca.gov/elections/ballot-measures/pdf/initiative-totals-summary-year.pdf. Accessed 8/3/12.

Donovan, Todd, S. Bowler, D. McCuan and K. Fernandez. "Contending Players and Strategies: Opposition Advantages in Initiative Elections." In *Citizens as Legislators: Direct Democracy in the United States*. Ed. S. Bowler, T. Donovan, and C. Tolbert, pp. 133–52. Columbus: Ohio State University Press, 1998.

Gerber, Elisabeth. *The Populist Paradox: Interest Group Influence on the Promise of Direct Legislation*. Princeton, NJ: Princeton University Press, 1999.

Hofstadter, Richard. *The Age of Reform*. New York: Washington Square Press, 1988.

Johnson, Hiram. "First Inaugural Address." January 3, 1913. http://governors.library.ca.gov/addresses/23-hjohnson01.htm. Accessed 8/3/12.

Mowry, George. *The California Progressives*. Chicago: Quadrangle Paperbacks, 1963.

Olin, Spencer C., Jr. *California's Prodigal Sons: Hiram Johnson and the Progressives, 1911–1917*. Berkeley: University of California Press, 1968.

"Policy Forum: Do Ballot Initiatives Undermine Democracy?" *Cato Policy Report* (July–August 2000): 6–9. www.cato.org/pubs/policy_report/v22n4/initiatives.pdf. Accessed 6/20/12.

Schrag, Peter. *Paradise Lost: California's Experience, America's Future*. Berkeley: University of California Press, 1998.

Starr, Kevin. *Inventing the Dream: California through the Progressive Era*. New York: Oxford University Press, 1985.

Swisher, Carl Brent. Motivation and Political Technique in the California Constitutional Convention 1878–79. New York: Da Capo Press, 1969.

ON THE WEB

Ballot measure updates: www.sos.ca.gov/elections_j-htm (accessed 6/20/12).

California State Constitution: www.leginfo.ca.gov/const.html (accessed 6/20/12). This site makes the California State Constitution searchable by keyword.

Initiative & Referendum Institute: www.iandrinstitute.org (accessed 6/20/12).

LearnCalifornia.org: www.learncalifornia.org/doc.asp?id=1606 (accessed 6/20/12). LearnCalifornia.org offers a guide to the history of progressivism in California.

Southern Pacific Historical & Technical Society: www.sphts.org (accessed 6/20/12).

SUMMARY

I. The California constitution originated with the version of 1849.
  A. The basic structure of government is still the same.
  B. The most significant changes were the inclusion of the provisions for direct democracy, the initiative, referendum, and recall, in 1911.

II. The history of the constitution has four stages.
  A. 1849: basic structure of government established. Includes separation of powers, bicameralism, federalism, and popular election of most state offices.
  B. 1879: a constitutional convention added nine new articles and 8,000 words to respond to the reform needs of the time.
  C. 1910–17: the Progressive era added the initiative, referendum, and recall and hundreds of reform laws.
  D. 1960–present time: California voters have authorized a few significant reforms.

III. Proposing an amendment to the California constitution is easy.
  A. Amendments can be proposed in three ways:
    1. Through a constitutional convention. The legislature can convene the convention by a two-thirds vote or it can be convened by a majority vote of the electorate from an initiative. A Bay Area business group tried to collect sufficient signatures for a new constitutional convention in 2009–10 but gave up because professional signature-gathering firms refused to work with the group, feeling that the effort would imperil their future existence.
    2. Amendments may be proposed by collecting signatures through the initiative process.
      a) Signatures totaling 8 percent of the vote in the last gubernatorial election are required, collected over a five-month period.
      b) Most amendments are proposed this way. The cost is approximately $1 million to $2 million, mostly for signature gathering.
      c) The legislature may propose an amendment by a two-thirds vote.
  B. In each case, the electorate must then ratify the amendment before it goes into the constitution. A majority vote is required.

IV. The Progressive reformers had several key goals.
  A. Ending the dominance of big business over the state, especially the Southern Pacific Railroad.
  B. Reforming the corrupt political process.
  C. Removing from office corrupt political officials at the state and local levels of government.
  D. Returning political power to the people.

V. Progressive laws and constitutional amendments wrought many significant changes.
  A. Ended child labor.
  B. Established a state park system.
  C. Enacted protections for working people.
  D. Established nonpartisan elections.
  E. Instituted primary elections.
  F. Created office block voting.
  G. Set in motion the process of direct democracy—the initiative, referendum, and recall.
  H. Resulted in the vast bulk of the Progressive reforms that are still in operation today.

VI. Direct democracy is a vital aspect of California politics.
  A. The initiative is the most popular of the three direct democracy mechanisms.
    1. Proponents need to gather signatures equal to 5 percent of voters in the last gubernatorial election for statutes and 8 percent of the voters for constitutional amendments.
    2. Since 1912, roughly 33 percent of initiatives that are voted on pass.
    3. The initiative has increasingly become a mechanism by which special interests or wealthy individuals can pass legislation by circumventing the legislature.
  B. The referendum allows voters to approve or reject statutes or constitutional amendments passed by the legislature.
    1. Proponents need to gather signatures equal to 5 percent of voters in the last gubernatorial election.
    2. The referendum is infrequently used and has appeared on the ballot less than 50 times since 1912.
    3. In 2008, four referenda appeared on the ballot, all dealing with Indian gaming. All four passed.
  C. Recall allows voters to remove a public official from elected office before his or her term is up.
    1. The number of signatures that needs to be gathered depends on the office: 12 percent of the last vote for statewide office from at least five counties equal to 1 percent of the last vote in the

county; 20 percent of the last vote in for office for Senate, Assembly, and Board of Equalization.

2. Since 1912, there have been only eight recalls of statewide officials and legislative members.

3. Governor Gray Davis is the only statewide official to have been recalled.

PRACTICE QUIZ

1. The popular democracy process by which citizens can place a constitutional amendment or statute on the ballot is called a(n)
   a) referendum.
   b) initiative.
   c) recall.
   d) nonpartisan election.

2. The individual who served as governor during much of the Progressive period was
   a) Chester Rowell.
   b) Edward Dickson.
   c) Hiram Johnson.
   d) Samuel P. Huntington.

3. The process by which a certain percentage of those who vote in the last gubernatorial election can sign petitions to vote on a law enacted by the legislature is a(n)
   a) referendum.
   b) initiative.
   c) recall.
   d) nonpartisan election.

4. The process by which an elected official is removed from office before his or her term expires is called a(n)
   a) referendum.
   b) initiative.
   c) recall.
   d) nonpartisan election.

5. Progressive reformers pointed to this company whenever they spoke about machine politics and corporate privilege in Sacramento:
   a) Standard Oil Company.
   b) Bank of America.
   c) Southern Pacific Railroad.
   d) Northern Securities Company.

6. The only sitting California governor to be recalled from office was
   a) Ronald Reagan.
   b) Jerry Brown.
   c) Gray Davis.
   d) Pete Wilson.

7. Which of the following direct democracy devices allows voters to approve or reject statutes or amendments passed by the legislature?
   a) referendum
   b) direct primary
   c) initiative
   d) recall

8. In which historical block was the greatest number of initiatives titled?
   a) 1912–39
   b) 1940–69
   c) 1970–99
   d) 2000–12

9. Which of the following is not a Progressive Era reform?
   a) nonpartisan elections
   b) primary elections
   c) the office block vote
   d) party caucuses

10. Which of the following is not a legal way to amend the California constitution?
    a) The legislature can convene a constitutional convention by a two-thirds vote.
    b) The governor can sign into law a proposed amendment passed by the legislature.
    c) The legislature may propose a constitutional amendment by a two-thirds vote.
    d) The electorate can propose a constitutional amendment through the initiative process.

CRITICAL-THINKING QUESTIONS

1. The California constitution has gone through a series of revisions. Identify the periods of those revisions and discuss the contribution that each made to the state's political structure.

2. Suppose you worked for a coalition of interest groups supporting legislation to increase the state sales tax to fund a state-run health care system. The coalition is frustrated by the lack of action in the legislature. They come to you

for advice about the initiative process and the possibility of success. What would you tell them from what you've read in this chapter?

3. Some people argue that direct democracy provides citizens with another way to correct the behavior and decision making of public officials. Others argue that it is merely the instrument of those special interest groups that have enough money to manipulate the political process. Present an argument for each position. Where do you stand in this debate?

4. California is the model Progressive state. The key components, however, greatly weakened the role of political parties in the state. Identify and discuss how some of the reforms of this period have weakened the state's party system. Is this a good or a bad thing? Do you think there are any correlations between weak parties and the increasing use of the initiative process?

KEY TERMS

California Constitutional Revision
    Commission (p. 32)
direct democracy (p. 23)

initiative (p. 17)
Progressive movement (p. 18)
recall (p. 25)

referendum (p. 30)

3 Interest Groups and the Media in California

WHAT INTEREST GROUPS DO AND WHY THEY MATTER IN CALIFORNIA POLITICS

Consider the diversity of organizations that try to influence governmental policy or legislation:

★ A **student organization** opposes legislation to raise tuition at state universities

★ A **business trade association** supports legislation that would reform the state's workers' compensation insurance system

★ A **telecommunications company** opposes legislation mandating the use of hands-free telephones in cars and trucks

★ A **citizens' group** supports legislation that would impose stricter penalties on people convicted of drunk driving

★ An **association of county governments** opposes legislation that prohibits the placing of certain juvenile offenders into group homes that are located in residential neighborhoods

★ A **public employees' union** supports legislation that prohibits state agencies from contracting with businesses unless the businesses pay their employees the equivalent of a living wage

Each of these organizations is an interest group. Interest groups have always been part of California's (and America's) political landscape. They are a product of freedom of association that is a First Amendment right under our democratic system of government.

Interest groups are associations of individuals who seek to influence policy decisions primarily in the legislature, with the executive branch, at administrative agencies, and through direct legislation (the initiative). They are a way, in addition to voting, for individuals to voice their opinion on issues that concern them.

Interest groups are also called pressure groups, political advocacy groups, special-interest groups, and lobbying groups. Because they focus primarily on influencing policy decisions in the legislature, interest groups are often referred to as the third house, a term that describes their standing and influence in the legislative process.[1]

In California, interest groups are especially influential because of the state's unique political landscape. As we shall see, open primaries, top-two primary elections, term limits, and non-partisan elections at the local level have freed candidates from party dependence and turned candidates to interest groups for financial backing and mobilizing voters. At the same time, interest groups have realized that they could successfully use the initiative process to achieve political goals, and there has been no shortage of initiatives—and money spent—to do so, even if the propositions are in conflict with broad-based citizen interests.

Interest-Group Dynamics in Politics

All Californians are represented by interest groups, whether wittingly or not, such as county and city governments, trade associations, labor unions, professional and religious organizations, educational institutions, and environmental groups. When a government recognizes the right of association, citizens will exercise that right, and groups of all types will form. There is much debate about the influence of interest groups in the political arena, especially about whether the theories of pluralism or elitism best explain their status and power in the political process.

In pluralist theory, the political system is considered a marketplace in which a multitude of interests compete, with no one interest or combination of interests powerful enough to dominate, and in which government sits outside as an umpire or referee. Pluralist theory argues that power is dispersed. To achieve success, interests often have to join together to bargain and negotiate with opposition interests, and through bargaining and negotiating, policy decisions are made. Pluralist theory acknowledges that some groups are stronger and even more successful than others; however, it also contends that these groups do not necessarily succeed all or a majority of the time. They point out that weaker but well-organized groups do succeed in achieving their goals or checking stronger groups.

Elitist theory acknowledges that there are many interest groups active in the political process, but most of them have minimal power. Power rests in the hands of a few groups, such as large national and multinational corporations, universities, foundations, and public policy institutes, where leaders (elites) set the agenda and determine the policy outcomes of government. Accordingly, when it comes to important policy matters—the economy and noteworthy social policies—elites representing a narrow range of groups determine the basic direction of public policy. Still, elite theory recognizes that less powerful groups, most commonly in coalition with other less powerful groups, are occasionally able to check the proposals of elites. This is especially true when elites can't agree among themselves on policy choices.

Which theory best describes interest groups in California? Neither elitism nor pluralism fully explains California politics. In practice, California politics is a blend of pluralism and elitism. In each legislative session, there is widespread interest group activity, with literally thousands of interests competing for influence on more than 2,000 bills. Most of these groups, from child care facilities and auto repair shops to environmental organizations, trade unions, and businesses, focus on measures that directly affect their interest. Often these issues are of limited concern to the public at large. In these circumstances, the groups involved in the issue, whether for or against, work to create policy through competition and compromise. Here the pluralism theory fits well. Yet on some broad-based issues, a small number of (elite) groups, such as public employee unions and multinational corporations, influence decision making to favor their own special interests. They exert power downward, on the legislature, other groups, and the public. They are able to do this because of their economic clout and ability to contribute great sums of money to candidates, independent committees, ballot initiatives, and public relations campaigns. In the end, California politics is a mixture of pluralism and elitism, depending on the issue in question and the stakes presented.

Lobbying the Legislature

The people who do the work for interest groups are called lobbyists, and the work they do is called lobbying. Lobbyists have played a visible and sometimes controversial role in California politics. The most notorious figure was Arthur Samish, whose influence in the state legislature during the 1930s and 1940s drew national attention. Samish represented the most powerful industries in the state: oil, liquor stores, transportation, breweries, and racing. Samish was not shy about his influence. He once told a grand jury looking into his lobbying activities, "To hell with the governor of California. I'm the governor of the legislature."[2]

Samish's downfall came as a result of two articles in *Collier's* magazine in 1949 about "the man who secretly controls the state."[3] In the article, when asked who had more influence, himself or Samish, Governor Earl Warren responded, "On matters that affect his clients, Artie unquestionably has more power than the governor."[4]

Soon after the articles appeared Governor Warren asked for legislation to regulate lobbyists and require the disclosure of lobbyists' financial activities. The legislature obliged first with the Collier Act and later with the Erwin Act. The legislature also voted to ban Arthur Samish from the capitol building. Somewhat thereafter, Samish was convicted of income tax evasion and sentenced to three years in federal prison, thus ending his career as a Sacramento power broker.

Diversity of Interest Groups

The term *interest groups* is all inclusive, covering a wide range of businesses and organizations. The California secretary of state classifies interest groups into 19 categories and shows the amount spent by each category for lobbying for a two-year legislative session. Table 3.1 shows the figures for the 2009–10 session.

Many organizations openly state in their literature and on their websites that lobbying or advocacy is a major part of their activity and a principal reason why many individuals and businesses join the group. For example, the California Applicants' Attorneys Association claims to be "the most powerful and most knowledgeable legal voice for the injured workers of California"; the California Labor Federation, AFL-CIO, professes to promote "the interests of working people and

TABLE 3.1 ★ Lobbying Categories and Spending, 2009–10

CATEGORY	AMOUNT (MILLIONS)
1. Government	$89.3
2. Miscellaneous*	79.4
3. Health	61.5
4. Manufacturing, industrial	50.0
5. Education	37.6
6. Finance, insurance	33.3
7. Labor unions	32.8
8. Utilities	32.0
9. Professional, trade	31.4
10. Oil and gas	22.3
11. Transportation	13.6
12. Real estate	11.6
13. Entertainment, recreation	10.8
14. Agriculture	8.7
15. Merchandise, retail	8.5
16. Legal	6.5
17. Public employees	5.9
18. Lodging, restaurants	2.1
19. Political organizations	0.4

*Includes hundreds of interest groups, such as professional and trade associations, environmental organizations, and religious groups.

SOURCE: Data from California Secretary of State, http://cal-access.ss.ca.gov/Lobbying/Employers/list.aspx?view=category.

their families for the betterment of California communities"; and the California Alliance of Child and Family Services lobbies "on behalf of its member agencies and the children and families they serve."

Individual businesses and academic institutions, however, rarely identify lobbying as one of their activities. This is understandable and perfectly legitimate. Lobbying is not a primary reason for the existence of these organizations; profits are. They participate in politics to protect or expand their markets. They are careful not to call attention to their involvement in politics out of fear that they may alienate customers or tarnish their image. Accordingly, information about their lobbying activity must be obtained from newspaper accounts and public disclosure documents.

Many businesses do join professional or trade associations to give them a voice on issues that affect their industry. "We're the champion of California businesses, large and small," the California Chamber of Commerce proudly asserts on its website. "For more than 120 years, CalChamber has worked to make California a better place to do business by giving private-sector employers a voice in state politics." The more than 13,000 member businesses give the chamber tremendous clout and stature. In turn, individual members enjoy several advantages—sharing of cost, strength in numbers, and, perhaps most important, anonymity.

Government also lobbies government. Taxpayer protection groups have come to call these interests—education, health, special districts, local government, state agencies—"the spending lobby" because they are motivated by the desire to maintain or increase their revenue. In 2008, for instance, government was the highest spender among the 19 categories of lobbyist employers registered with the secretary of state.

According to governmental lobbyists, the passage in 1978 of Proposition 13, which limited the property tax revenues to local government, spurred the growth in governmental lobbying and the competition for funds. John P. Quimby Sr., a former Assemblyman who lobbies for San Bernardino County, told the *Riverside Press Enterprise* in 1997: "I wish government wasn't for sale like this, but the fact is you have to hustle to get your share. Local governments without lobbyists see the ones with representation doing better so they say, 'We need to get our butts on board and get one or they're going to steal everything from us.'"[5] Or, to put it another way, government agencies spend taxpayers' money to lobby government for more money to spend on taxpayers.

The Increase in Interest Groups

In California over the last two decades, the number of interest groups and lobbying expenditures has grown steadily. In 1990, lobbyists represented approximately 1,300 interest groups; in 2000, the number had nearly doubled to 2,552; and in 2010, it had increased to 3,094.[6] During the same period, lobbying expenditures also grew substantially, with just a slight dip in 2009–10, as seen in Table 3.2. However, during the first three-quarters of the 2011–12 legislative session, groups spent nearly $216 million on lobbying activity, a 5 percent increase over the first three-quarters of the 2009–10 session, which suggests that lobby spending for 2011–12 will again set a record amount.[7]

TABLE 3.2 ★ Growth in Lobbying Expenditures

LEGISLATIVE SESSION	LOBBYING EXPENDITURES	PERCENT INCREASE
1989–90	$193,575,480	
1991–92	233,872,097	20.8
1993–94	250,119,667	7.0
1995–96	266,939,559	6.7
1997–98	292,615,513	9.6
1999–2000	344,318,650	17.7
2001–02	386,829,719	12.4
2003–04	413,376,146	6.9
2005–06	500,326,710	21.0
2007–08	558,419,109	11.0
2009–10	538,638,251	–3.5

SOURCE: Data from California Secretary of State, http://cal-access.ss.ca.gov/Lobbying/Employers.

California continually ranks first nationally in number of interest groups and amount spent on lobbying activity. California accounts for one-third of all lobbyist activity in the country. Texas and New York rank second and third behind California, and together they spend around 60 percent of what is spent in California on lobbying activities.[8] What Carey McWilliams said about California politics during the 1930s and 1940s still holds true today: "Interests, not people, are represented in Sacramento. Sacramento is the marketplace of California where grape growers and sardine fishermen, morticians and osteopaths bid for allotments of state power."[9]

Several factors encouraged the proliferation of interest groups:

Weak Political Parties

California has weak parties for a variety of reasons, but largely because of the Progressive reforms of the 1910s. The reforms were directed at the spoils system in government, the control parties had over which candidates would represent the party in general elections, and the influence of interest groups in the legislature. To balance these influences, they gave voters the direct democracy practices of initiative, referendum, and recall. These measures and subsequent reforms—many of which were considered citizen initiatives, such as the direct primary, term limits, redistricting by an independent commission, and top-two open primary—greatly free officials from party structure and discipline and tie them to interest groups that can ensure their reelection. In this way, Progressive attempts to curb interest group influence actually strengthened it.

Growth of Government

California government has grown substantially over the past half century. Californians, like other Americans, initially were suspicious of government. They perceived government as a force whose powers had to be kept in check to protect individual rights. As time passed, however, citizens began to perceive government differently, as a force that could be used to solve myriad social and economic problems. The legislature has eagerly taken up the challenge.

Term Limits

In 1990, California voters approved term limits for all state and legislative offices. Term limits, it was argued, would break the cozy relationship between elected officials and lobbyists. Yet this is not what has happened. As legislators with years of institutional memory left office, the legislature became more chaotic and less efficient. "Experts say it is this institutional memory that has swung the legislature toward the 'third house' of special interests. In short, the lobbyists have it. Legislators don't." Legislators rely on lobbyists to write intricate legislation and counsel them on the flood of complex issues that come across their desks.[10]

Public Interest Groups

The growth of public interest groups, what some call the New Politics movement, began in the 1970s and continues through today. Examples of such groups are AARP, Sierra Club, and the Foundation for Taxpayers and Consumer Rights. As the textbook *We the People* explains, these "groups sought to distinguish themselves from other groups—business groups, in particular—by styling themselves as 'public interest groups,' terminology that suggests they served the general good rather than their own selfish interests." Although these so-called public interest groups claim to represent *only* the public interest, they should be judged critically, for they are sometimes facades behind which narrow private interests hide.

Interest-Group Politics

Today, in California, politics *is* interest groups. Not all interest groups, however, are equal. Some have considerably more clout than others. The success of an interest group depends on several factors: a clear message, group cohesiveness, the alignment of the group's interests with those of other groups and elected officials, an understanding of the political process, technical expertise, and money. As we shall see, money is especially important.

Table 3.3 shows the top employers of lobbyists. This list has remained relatively stable over the past several years, with four or five groups moving in and out of the ranks from one year to the next, depending on their agenda in the legislative session. By most standards, the lobbyists for these groups are some of the most successful in Sacramento.

It is not surprising that with the growth of the "lobbying industrial complex" in California, allegations of influence peddling follow and sometimes turn out to

---

TABLE 3.3 ★ Top 10 Lobbyist Employers, January 1, 2009–December 31, 2010

ORGANIZATION	CUMULATIVE EXPENDITURES
Western States Petroleum Association	$9,345,305
California Teachers Association	9,164,421
California State Council of Service Employees	8,665,881
California Chamber of Commerce	6,715,018
California Labor Federation, AFL-CIO	5,967,560
California Hospital Association	4,483,216
California School Employees Association	4,475,376
Kaiser Foundation Health Plan	4,255,622
California Manufacturers & Technology Association	3,950,754
Chevron Corporation	3,846,857

SOURCE: Data from California Secretary of State, http://cal-access.ss.ca.gov/Lobbying/Employers.

be true. For example, Clay Jackson, one of the most influential lobbyists in Sacramento, was accused of offering large campaign contributions to Senator Alan Robbins in return for the lawmaker's support on legislation benefiting Jackson's clients. The FBI uncovered Robbins's part in the plan, and he agreed to wear a wire to expose Jackson in exchange for a reduced sentence. In the end, Jackson, Robbins, and former State Senator Paul Carpenter (who funneled campaign money through a public relations firm for Robbins's personal use) were convicted of engaging in a money-laundering scheme.

The incident raised questions about the connections among interest groups, money, and power in Sacramento. It revealed how a legal fund-raising system can be used to benefit legislators, especially in an environment in which there is a fine line between campaign contributions and influence over the way in which legislators vote on issues—even when these processes are conducted legally.

Lobbyists

Lobbyists are at the forefront of interest-group activity. They coordinate the efforts to secure passage, amendment, or defeat of bills in the legislature and the approval or veto of bills by the governor. Having a good lobbyist is paramount to the success of any group.

There are citizen lobbyists and professional lobbyists. A citizen lobbyist is not paid to advocate for a particular issue or set of issues. Citizen lobbyists interact with their representatives to express their personal views on an issue and to attempt to influence legislation on that issue. Professional lobbyists are paid for their services and must register with the secretary of state. They also must submit quarterly disclosure reports detailing for whom they are working, the amount of money earned, and payment such as gifts and honoraria made to public officials they lobby.

There are two categories of professional lobbyists: contract and in-house. Contract lobbyists make up 50 percent of all lobbyists in Sacramento; in-house lobbyists account for the other half.[11] Contract lobbyists offer their services to the general public; they are advocates for hire and often represent multiple clients on a variety of issues at the same time. In-house lobbyists are employees of a trade, professional, or labor association and represent that group's interest only. Many of these interest groups also use contract lobbyists because the group is involved in too many issues for its in-house staff to handle, or it may want to use a lobbyist who specializes in a specific subject area such as health insurance or who has a close relation with a particular legislator or members of a specific committee whose support is vital for the group's success.

Lobbying

Few issues are just lobbied—that is, discussed with a public official or staff during the legislative process. Most issues are managed using a combination of techniques: public relations (marketing), grassroots mobilization, and coalition building.

The first job of the lobbyist is to know the group's objective. Is the goal new legislation? Is it to amend existing law? Or is it to stop another business or interest group from passing new legislation or amending an existing law that may affect the group's interest? The goal may not even be legislation. The group may want to amend current regulatory policy or shape the content of new regulations that will affect its members.

The lobbyist must also identify other groups that may have an interest in the issue, and assess whether these groups, legislators, the executive branch, regulators, or the general public will support or oppose the group's activity. Moreover, lobbyists who can rely on the group's members, especially if they reside in the legislator's district, can more easily influence policy making. The most successful efforts are built around networks of activists who have made it a point to know their elected officials. These relationships can be built in many ways: working on election campaigns, commending a representative in writing for an action he or she has taken, contributing to political campaigns, and connecting in other ways so as to have a positive relationship with these officials.

With this preparation in hand, the lobbyist has a greater chance of success. Of course, several other factors are also important: knowledge of the legislation process, strong communication skills, established relationships, credibility, adaptability to change, and the ability to negotiate.

Campaign Contributions to Candidates

Besides expenditures on lobbying to influence legislative action, interest groups also make campaign contributions, which enable them to become familiar with and gain access to legislators. They do so through political action committees (PACs).

There is a connection between lobbying success and campaign contributions. Those who invest heavily in lobbying generally invest heavily in PAC contributions, and vice versa.[12] Table 3.4 shows the top 10 contributors for the 2009–10 legislative year. The table shows only the amount directly contributed to candidates for the

TABLE 3.4 ★ Top 10 Contributors to Legislative Candidates, 2009–10	
California Association of Realtors	$781,354
AT&T	775,900
California Teachers Association	702,541
California Dental Association	671,049
California State Council of Laborers	604,035
Pechanga Band of Luiseño Mission Indians	562,699
California Medical Association	509,385
PG&E	488,816
California Professional Firefighters	477,018
California State Pipe Trades Council	474,737

SOURCE: National Institute on Money in State Politics, www.followthemoney.org/database/state_overview .phtml?s=CA&y=2010.

state legislature—the total of which was $105,822,734. This figure does not include what these organizations may have contributed to the Democratic or Republican Party committees ($67,574,985), candidates for statewide office, ($307,677,930), or ballot initiatives ($235,674,934), which, when totaled, comes to an additional $610,927,849.[13] Campaign contributions enable a lobbyist to gain access to legislators. The lobbyist can then make his or her argument—at which time he or she can provide the legislator with important, often technical information.

In 2010, the U.S. Supreme Court in *Citizens United v. Federal Election Commission* held that political action committees could raise unlimited funds from individuals, corporations, and unions to support or oppose candidates for office. Though a landmark case nationally, *Citizens United* had little impact on political spending in California because California had allowed such practice before the Supreme Court's ruling.

California's disclosure laws require independent committees to file the same financial reports as candidate committees and ballot measure committees. In a study of independent committees in California from 2005 to 2010, Linda Casey of the National Institute on Money in State Politics showed that independent spending amounted to 9 percent ($228.8 million) of the total amount spent directly for candidates and initiatives ($2.5 billion).

Jesse Unruh, former speaker of the Assembly, once said, "Money is the mother's milk of politics." This adage still holds true today. Most interest groups have PACs and carefully target their campaign contributions. They support individuals in positions of power (e.g., incumbent state officers, party leaders in the legislature, committee chairs, and rising stars). Contributions have little to do with the legislator's

TABLE 3.5 ★ Top 10 Independent Spenders on Initiatives, 2005–10	
California Teachers Association	$101,738,213
Pharmaceutical Research & Manufacturers of America	70,819,206
PG&E	61,856,250
Pechanga Band of Lucerño Mission Indians	47,618,135
Morongo Band of Mission Indians	46,525,977
Chevron Corporation	43,607,500
California State Council of Service Employees	42,121,506
Philip Morris	38,079,500
Agua Caliente Band of Cahuilla Indians	34,840,025
AERA Energy	33,235,243

SOURCE: National Institute on Money in State Politics, www.followthemoney.org/database/state_overview.phtml?s=CA&y=2010.

or a party's political ideology. The only question is, Can this legislator help me achieve my goals?

An example of the dynamics of campaign contributions and lobbying can be seen in the California Correctional Peace Officers Association (CCPOA), one of the most powerful interest groups in Sacramento. It has achieved this status through a combination of aggressive lobbying, large campaign contributions, and skillful public relations.

The union is one of the biggest contributors to candidates running for statewide and legislative office. Over the past decade, the union has spent nearly $40 million in lobbying and campaign activities,[14] contributing aggressively to the campaigns of its supporters and just as aggressively to defeat those who oppose its agenda. The union is one of the few public employee groups to give generously to both Republicans and Democrats. For example, when Pete Wilson ran for governor in 1990, prison guards gave $1 million to his campaign. Wilson reciprocated with substantial pay increases and stronger sentencing policies. The union, however, really stepped forward with Gray Davis. Besides early endorsement in the primary, which guaranteed his selection as the Democrat candidate for governor, they contributed more than $3 million between 1998 and 2002 to his campaign war chest. During the same period, the union contributed millions of dollars to members of the legislature, with especially large sums going to the leadership of both parties. Governor Davis responded in kind. Correctional officers' wages were tied to those of highway patrol officers. Retirement benefits, sick leave and overtime provisions, and uniform allowances were greatly increased.

CCPOA also spent heavily—$1.8 million—in support of Jerry Brown's 2010 gubernatorial victory. In March 2012, the legislature and Governor Brown agreed on a new contract, which the union overwhelmingly approved. The contract increases pension contributions of officers, reduces pay in one year by requiring one day of unpaid leave each month, and eliminates a state-funded, $42 million-a-year 401(k)-type plan that correctional officers received in addition to their pensions. However, as the *San Francisco Chronicle* pointed out, the contract eliminates limitations on accrual of vacation time, currently estimated at more than 33 million hours and estimated to cost the state another $1 billion.[15]

Governor Brown argued that collective bargaining is about "give and take" and claimed the deal with the correctional officers was comparable to what other public employee unions received under Governor Schwarzenneger. Moreover, according to some, the union contract is a bargaining chip to gain union support for the governor's prison reform agenda, including closing youth prisons and transferring up to 30,000 low-level offenders from state prisons to local jails, which is intended to save the state millions of dollars. Still, the returns from CCPOA's campaign spending and lobbying suggest that the strategy has paid off handsomely. Today, "California's prison guards are the nation's highest paid, a big reason that spending on the state's prison system has rocketed from less than 4.3 percent of the budget in 1986 to more than 11 percent today."[16]

Regulating Interest Groups

With the passage of the Political Reform Act (PRA) of 1974, California lobbyist and interest groups are required to report campaign and lobbying expenditures. At the same time, the PRA shifted the filing of lobbying statements from the state legislature to the independent Fair Political Practice Commission.

Since its passage, the PRA has undergone numerous amendments, the most significant being in 2000 with the passage of Proposition 34. The following rules now govern interest groups and lobbyists:

- A lobbyist or lobbying firm cannot present a gift to a state-elected official or legislative official in aggregate of more than $10 a month. Anyone who is not a registered lobbyist can give up to $250 in gifts in any calendar year.

- A lobbyist cannot contribute to state candidates or officeholders if he or she are registered to lobby that candidate or officeholder's agency. However, the various interest groups that employ lobbyists have no such restrictions.

- Interest groups, individuals, and businesses have specific limits on election contributions to candidates or officeholders. The limits for legislative candidates are $3,200; for all state offices except the governor, $5,300; and for governor, $21,300.

Some public interest groups, such as Common Cause, Clean Money Campaign, and the League of Women Voters, have called for further restrictions on lobbying expenditures and campaign contributions by both individual and interest groups. Such measures, they argue, would constrain the power of special interests and allow public policy decision to reflect the overall interest of society.

Recommendations to restrict the power of interest groups fall into three categories: clean-money elections, contribution restrictions, and conflict-of-interest laws. The first category, clean-money elections, would provide public funding to candidates who demonstrate a base of public support by getting a qualifying number of voter signatures and a certain number of small contributions and who agree to forgo any other private donations. Such measures would cover all state legislative and statewide offices and have recently been adopted by Maine and Arizona. In California, it would be difficult to get the political parties and most legislators, who are tied to the current funding system, to support the idea. It would also be difficult to convince the public that they should subsidize campaigns for elective office. Over the years, only 35 to 40 percent of California voters have supported public financing of election campaigns.

The second category, contribution limits, has been a focal point of campaign reform for some time. Most of the effort has come from citizen groups disgruntled with the current system. Together they have established stricter reporting requirements and limits on campaign contributions and loans to state candidates and political parties. The changes have been accomplished almost wholly through initiatives sponsored by these groups over the past decade—Propositions 63 and 78 in 1993, Proposition 208 in 1996, and Proposition 34 in 2000. These efforts will continue in the future as various groups attempt to rein in the free flow of money into political campaigns.

One of the biggest issues involving campaign finance has been the rise of super PACs. Technically known as independent expenditure-only committees, super PAC committees may raise unlimited sums of money from corporations, unions, associations, and individuals and then spend unlimited sums to overtly advocate for or against political candidates. Super PACs must, however, report their donors to the Federal Election Commission on a monthly or quarterly basis—the super PAC's choice—as a traditional PAC would. Unlike traditional PACs, super PACs are prohibited from donating money directly to political candidates, though this has not prevented them from exhibiting enormous influence in elections.

The last category, conflict-of-interest laws, covers a multitude of situations. Sometimes simultaneous activity falls into this category. For example, the California Senate offers lobbyists who contribute to its charity the opportunity to travel with the lawmakers to various foreign countries.[17]

The Senate's California International Relations Foundation, a charity, helps fund the entertainment of foreign delegations that visit the state capital and a high school students' exchange between California and Japan. The idea is new in lobbyist-legislator relations.

Each donor contributes $2,000 to $3,000, which gives the donor a seat on the foundation's board of directors and the invitation to travel with legislators on trade and cultural trips to foreign countries. Since 2004, there have been 18 trips to places such as Tokyo, Jerusalem, and Rio de Janeiro.

The foundation operates out in the open, and it does not underwrite the expenses of either the traveling legislators or the supporters. Critics, however, contend that it provides a unique opportunity for supporters. They gain the goodwill of and access to legislators. This is especially convenient when the supporter's interest group has a bill pending in the legislature.

Outside the Legislature

Up until now, we have focused on the influence of interest groups on the state legislature. Interest groups, however, flex their muscles in other ways in the electoral process: through get-out-the-vote and initiative (direct legislation) campaigns.

GET OUT THE VOTE Many interest groups engage in get-out-the-vote (GOTV) operations among their members to help a candidate (and political party) or an issue win at the ballot box. This is especially true in what is perceived to be a hotly contested election. In such instances, GOTV can be the most important activity undertaken because there are many examples of an election being won or lost by a handful of votes.

GOTV operations are often considered "outsider strategies"—that is, they take place outside the traditional arena of interest-group activity, the legislature, and they are supported by groups that feel they have a vital stake in the outcome of the election, as Hispanics did in 1994 with Proposition 187, making illegal aliens ineligible for public services, and as the Protect Marriage Coalition did in 2008 with Proposition 8, eliminating same-sex couples' right to marry.

Some interest groups, like organized labor, religious denominations, and minorities, have a long history in mobilizing their members to vote—and to vote for or against a candidate or critical issue. Other interest groups, like gays, environmentalists, and gender-based groups, have more recently begun to participate in GOTV activities. They mobilize their supporters at the grassroots level, employing a variety of techniques, including direct mail, door-to-door canvassing, telemarketing, poll watching, pickup, phoning, and assistance. Months of work go into planning the campaign. While the goal is simple—delivering members' votes—the outcome is unpredictable until the final tally of ballots.

INITIATIVES Chapter 2 explored the history of the initiative and the impact of some of those that passed. What was initially considered a tool for citizens to check the actions of elected officials and indirectly the influence of interest groups in the legislature is still considered so today. The majority of voters support the initiative because they believe that the public, and not elected representatives, are better suited to decide "important government issues," although many also believe that a few narrow economic interests also shape public policy through the initiative process.[18]

Yet, as Elisabeth Gerber shows, this may not be as big of an issue as voters think. Although there are now more initiatives and considerably more money spent on them, groups with different goals use the initiative process differently. On the one hand, narrow (economic) interest groups, whose members join because of their occupation or professional status, rely primarily on the mobilization of money for initiative campaigns. They use these monetary resources and, to a lesser extent, personnel in two ways: "to protect the status quo or to pressure the legislature." When they sponsor initiatives, the measures generally fail. On the other hand, citizen groups, whose members join as free individuals committed to some personal belief or social issue, rely primarily on the mobilization of personnel who "volunteer their personal time and energy . . . to pass new laws by initiative."[19] In the end, the measures citizen groups back succeed at a higher rate than those sponsored by narrow economic interests.

For most Californians, the media—news stories, paid political commercials, public debate, direct mail—are the most influential sources of information on the activity of interest groups, the amount of money spent on lobbying and political campaigns, and the increasing frequency and amount of money spent on initiatives. The media keep citizens actively involved in politics.

The Media

The term *media* refers to the dispensers of information, including broadcast media (radio and television), print media (newspapers and magazines), and electronic media (the Internet). When we speak of these sources individually we refer to it as a *medium* (the Latin singular of *media*). Sometimes we speak about mass media but most often the limiting adjective (*mass*) is assumed.

Television

Today, television is the medium of choice for political information for the vast majority of Americans, and Californians are no exception. This medium can spread messages quickly, covering a wide variety of topics, including car chases, earthquakes, and the latest political scandal. Television is particularly important for conducting political campaigns in a large state with a diverse population, such as California. Yet for all its speed and ability to reach large numbers of viewers, television is a medium that provides little information on government.

Two facts account for this lack of information: (1) California is so big and diverse that it is difficult to cover statewide political and governmental news, and (2) Californians in general are not that interested in state government and policy. These dynamics, along with a fragmented political structure, produce a stark reality—the largest state in the nation, with some of the largest media resources and markets in the nation, provides relatively little political and governmental news, particularly on television news programs.[20] There are few media correspondents in Sacramento. More important, because there is no newspaper distributed statewide, there is no incentive to cover news on a statewide basis.

The nightly news stations compete with one another for viewers. But in reality, the news formats provide little in the way of important political information. The half-hour news format is crammed with commercials, weather reports, entertainment news, sports coverage, and a host of other topics that do little to inform the viewer about the political problems that affect the state and nation. Those topics that are reported with any depth are calculated to achieve ratings and are structured to last over several newscasts.

Each local station has its own version of some type of "action" news team or consumer protection group bringing audiences the latest artificially hyped crisis. From the nature of the issues covered, it is clear that local television, for the most part, has made a concerted effort to treat political news as a secondary issue. Issues related to political parties, government, or interest groups in California don't have the power to reach and energize large populations on a day-to-day basis.

Local television stations focus our attention on issues like crime in a way that government representatives cannot. Sensational undercover stories are frequently broadcast, such as the financial deceptions practiced by automobile dealers, the unsanitary conditions in local restaurants, and the health risks of cosmetic surgeries. These exposés help identify dishonest practices in our communities, but they are also examples of how the ability to identify important political issues has passed from the political parties to the media. The media place an issue on the agenda, often based more on its sensational appeal than its practical importance, and the next day government representatives are telling the public what must be done to fix the problem. They are reacting to the media's promotion of the issue.

In California, where voters have the ability to put statute and constitutional initiatives on the ballot, local television plays a major role by getting information to the voters about these issues through extensive advertising campaigns. These messages are drafted and paid for by the interest groups that support the initiatives, and the political parties may or may not play a role in the process. The broadcast media have the power to reach a vast audience, something the parties cannot do on their own.

Newspapers

The number of newspapers across the United States has fallen during the last 25 years, and newspaper circulations have declined in every recent year as well. Newspapers still remain active in identifying political corruption, reporting the workings of state and local government, covering political campaigns, and helping keep the public focused on important political issues. But newspapers in the final analysis are businesses and must be able to generate revenues and profits. To adequately cover state government, reporters and news staff have to be located in Sacramento. At the same time, on-the-spot coverage of county and local government requires a second set of reporters and news staff. The expense is prohibitive, and, over time, newspaper coverage at the state and local levels has noticeably declined. The public is not as fully informed about the activities of its various levels of government as it needs to be. The *Los Angeles Times* and the *Sacramento Bee* cover developments in Sacramento more extensively than other newspapers, but both have become victim to cost pressures and the need to reduce news reporting staffs in the 1990s and 2000s.

The drive for profits has reduced the news reporting capabilities of broadcast and print media, which cover only the big stories at the state government level. Ultimately, this means the public receives little information about the political activities of state and local government. This leads to a public that constantly finds itself surprised by political crises that seem to develop suddenly, such as rising state deficits, electricity shortages, declining state bond ratings, school facilities that are falling apart, and an overwhelmed freeway system. But for all their failings, broadcast and print media still play an important role in the election process and in formulating the political agenda. The media continue to identify the major political issues, report on the political progress of candidates at all levels, question the candidates and officeholders, and edit the replies the public gets to hear and read. These powers continue to undermine the role of political parties in California.

With Arnold Schwarzenegger's election as governor in October 2003, the public had a renewed interest in state politics. People were curious. A few stations that had closed their Sacramento news bureaus announced their reopening. This wasn't surprising. Nationally known figures have generally drawn more media attention than regional or local personalities. There was more coverage of Governors Edmund G. Brown, Ronald Reagan, and Jerry Brown, each of whom was a presidential contender, than of Governors Deukmejian, Wilson, and Davis, who were not.[21]

As time passed, however, the increase in coverage wasn't due to Schwarzenegger's celebrity but the state's economic woes: record budget deficits, sinking bond ratings, high unemployment, and staggering foreclosure filings. These concerns still persist today under Governor Jerry Brown. Local government, interest groups (especially public employee unions whose members are impacted by the budget deficits), and the general public have turned to Sacramento for solutions. Economic issues are the big concern, not the political personalities who have been thrust in the position of resolving these problems.

The Internet

Today the Internet offers instant access to political information and the opportunity to communicate one's views quickly to political leaders, news outlets, interest groups, and other individuals through blogs, Twitter, Tumblr, Facebook, and other social media channels. Many experts see the Internet as a catalyst for enhancing the democratic process. It offers candidates the opportunity to communicate rapidly with supporters and to recruit campaign workers. During the presidential election season, it has proven to be an excellent tool for raising campaign funds. The Internet offers political parties the opportunity to disseminate their issue positions to millions of potential voters in a quick and inexpensive fashion. Whether it will restore some of the power political parties have lost remains to be seen. The Internet is open to all users, and in that environment, political parties will still have lots of competition to control the political agenda.

With the growth of the Internet, access to California political and news sources has expanded exponentially. The major newspapers provide daily e-mails that focus on topics of the reader's interest, and research organizations, libraries, and blogs provide political information, background, and research beyond what any individual can absorb. A list of some of the major sources covering California politics is provided in Table 3.6.

Media and Political Campaigns

Running for office is a very expensive endeavor and it requires highly focused political messages. Because of these requirements, electronic media are the media of choice to reach large numbers of citizens. The media are also very useful in mobiliz-

TABLE 3.6 ★ Internet Sources Covering California Politics

MAJOR NEWSPAPERS

Los Angeles Times (www.latimes.com)
Sacramento Bee (www.sacbee.com)
San Francisco Chronicle (www.sfgate.com)
Capitol Weekly (capitolweekly.net)

ORGANIZATIONS

Rough & Tumble (www.rtumble.com)
California Progress Report (www.californiaprogressreport.com)
Flashreport (www.flashreport.org)
Fox & Hounds (www.foxandhoundsdaily.com)
Calitics (www.calitics.com)
Around the Capitol (www.aroundthecapitol.com)

PUBLIC POLICY SITES

Public Policy Institute of California (www.ppic.org)
California Health Care Foundation (www.chcf.org)
California Policy Inbox (http://inbox.berkeley.edu)

UNIVERSITIES

University of California at Berkeley (http://igs.berkeley.edu/)
California State University Bakersfield (www.csub.edu/library/)

MAJOR COLUMNISTS

Dan Walters, Daniel Weintraub, and Peter Schrag of the *Sacramento Bee* (www.sacbee.com)
George Skelton of the *Los Angeles Times* (www.latimes.com)

ing supporters on Election Day. Mobilizing a candidate's base of support is essential to winning elections. Without the media, no effective message is conveyed to the electorate, and consequently no money can be raised to fuel the modern type of media campaign that candidates must use to get elected. The media have the dual role of getting out the message to one's supporters and energizing them so they will contribute the money needed to win public office. Candidates cannot depend on local campaign appearances to reach enough people. They must depend on the power of electronic media to reach the mass audience needed to win elections.

In some cases, the media themselves and their coverage can become a central issue in the campaign, with a candidate running against the media and positioning himself or herself as outside the political establishment. During the recall election of 2003, the *Los Angeles Times* ran a story just before the election about inappropriate sexual behavior on the part of Schwarzenegger during his acting days. The reaction of many citizens was that the newspaper was taking incumbent Governor Gray Davis's side, not that it was uncovering important information that citizens might want to consider in their voting decisions.[22]

Interest-Group Politics in California: Where Are We Now?

Interest groups play an important and often dominant role in California politics. The continued growth in the number of groups and their lobbying expenditures attest to this fact. Moreover, if the past decade is any indication, the number of interest groups doing business in Sacramento will continue to grow, and lobbying expenditures will continue to increase. The size and structural deficit of the state budget, weak political parties, mandated term limits, increase in public interest groups, and continued dependence of local governments on Sacramento for financial assistance are all factors that will continue to promote interest group politics.

Much of the time, these groups are self-regulating, checking one another and forging broad-based coalitions of interests to achieve important policy decisions. Of course, interest groups will always be able to achieve advantages for narrow issues affecting their members, and the most powerful will generally be the most successful, as long as they can get a group of legislators to fall in behind them. That's why interest-group disclosure rules, campaign expenditure limits, and other reporting requirements are necessary. They enable us to keep these groups in check. That's the theory, at least.

Today, however, there is a disjunction between theory and practice. Interest groups have undue influence on politics in the state. Without some limit on the amount of money an interest group can spend on lobbying and campaign contributions, the only check on their power may be divided government, whereby one party controls the executive and one controls both or one house of the legislature, so that no one interest or coalition of interests can ride roughshod over government.

That's the state of affairs in California today. Although California's politics are not broken, unless these concerns are addressed, California will continue to hobble along, and interest groups will continue to flourish and prosper at the expense of the general public.

FOR FURTHER READING

Baldassare, Mark. "The California Initiative Process—How Democratic Is It?" Public Policy Institute of California, February 2002.

Gerber, Elisabeth R. "Interest Group Influence in the California Initiative Process." Public Policy Institute of California, 1998. www.ppic.org/main/publication.asp?i=49. Accessed 8/4/12.

McWilliams, Carey. *California: The Great Exception.* Berkeley: University of California Press, 1999.

Michael, Jay, Dan Walters, and Dan Weintraub. *The Third House: Lobbyists, Power, and Money in Sacramento.* Berkeley, CA: Berkeley Public Policy Press, 2000.

Rasky, Susan F. "Covering California: The Press Wrestles with Diversity, Complexity, and Change." In *Governing California: Politics, Government, and Public Policy in the Golden State.* Ed. Gerald C. Lubenow and Bruce E. Cain. Berkeley: Institute of Government Studies Press, University of California, 1997, pp. 157–88.

Samish, Arthur H., and Bob Thomas. *The Secret Boss of California.* New York: Crown Publishers, 1971.

ON THE WEB

Around the Capitol: www.aroundthecapitol.com (accessed 8/4/12). A portal to California legislative information.

California Alert: http://blogs.sacbee.com/capitolalertlatest/ California and national political news and commentary.

Capitol & California: www.sacbee.com/capitolandcalifornia (accessed 6/22/12).

Capital Weekly: www.capitolweekly.net (accessed 6/22/12).

Lobbying activity: http://cal-access.ss.ca.gov/lobbying (accessed 6/22/12); the secretary of state's office reports on lobbying in California politics.

SUMMARY

I. Interest groups are at the center of California's campaign and lobbying activities.
   A. Some believe they play a necessary role in our democratic society.
   B. Others see them as detrimental to our political system.

II. Interest groups exhibit the following characteristics:
   A. They are associations of individuals who join together for the purpose of influencing governmental or legislative policy.
   B. They can be individual businesses, trade and professional associations, or labor unions.
   C. They have proliferated over the past three decades for four reasons: growth in government, weak political parties, public interest groups, and term limits.

III. Lobbyists do the work of interest groups.
   A. The activity referred to as lobbying.
   B. There are three different categories of lobbyists.
      1. citizen lobbyists
      2. contract lobbyists
      3. in-house lobbyists
         a) Citizen lobbyists are individuals who have an interest in an issue and want to make their view known to their public official.
         b) Contract lobbyists and in-house lobbyists are professionals who must register with the secretary of state and submit a variety of disclosure statements yearly regarding their activities.

IV. The number of interest groups (and registered lobbyists) has grown substantially in each legislative session since 1990.
   A. In the 2007–08 legislature, interest groups employed over 3,200 lobbyists.
   B. In the same legislature, they spent over $500 million on lobbying activities.
   C. The public ranks lobbying at the bottom of professions for honesty and integrity.

V. Lobbyists perform a variety of activities to accomplish their goals.
   A. Preparation for the legislative or regulatory campaign:
      1. set campaign goals
      2. learn as much about the interest group as possible
      3. establish a grassroots network
      4. identify other organizations that could support or oppose the goals

   B. The campaign (lobbying basics):
      1. draft language, amendments, etc.
      2. prepare a fact sheet, position papers, etc.
      3. contact committee members before the committee hearing
      4. initiate a grassroots campaign to contact key legislators
   C. Legislative activity:
      1. testify in person
      2. bring expert witness from legislator's district

VI. There is a strong correlation between lobbying expenditure and campaign contributions.
   A. Interest groups that invest heavily in lobbying also invest heavily in political campaigns.
   B. The California Correctional Peace Officers Association is a prime example.

VII. Interest groups contribute to candidates' and officeholders' campaigns to leverage their influence.
   A. The Political Reform Act of 1974 was passed to regulate lobbying practices and requires the disclosure of lobbying financial activity.
   B. Proposition 34, the most recent initiative amendment to the act, includes new restrictions:
      1. Lobbyists cannot contribute to the campaigns of anyone they are lobbying for.
      2. Lobbyists are limited in the amount of money they can contribute during any election cycle.

VIII. The media are important vehicles in mobilizing and informing voters and candidates' supporters.
   A. Television and newspapers have traditionally had the greatest influence, with the Internet (through political websites and blogs) gaining in influence.
   B. Little of this mobilization, however, comes from news programs, which generally provide scant political information.
      1. It comes indirectly through the ability of television news programs to cover scandals and dishonest practices of politicians and focus viewers' attention on the latest special investigation.
      2. This demonstrates how the power to set the political agenda has passed from the political parties to the media.

PRACTICE QUIZ

1. The term *third house* refers to which of the following entities?
   a) judicial branch
   b) executive branch
   c) interest groups
   d) media

2. Over the past two decades, interest-group expenditures in California have
   a) declined.
   b) increased.
   c) remained relatively the same.
   d) fluctuated from year to year.

3. An individual who offers his or her lobbying services to multiple clients at the same time is called a(n)
   a) contract lobbyist.
   b) "hired gun."
   c) citizen lobbyist.
   d) in-house lobbyist.

4. The principal function of an interest group is to
   a) provide its members with educational and social opportunities.
   b) contribute money to candidates for public office who favor its programs.
   c) attain favorable decisions from government on issues that it supports.
   d) seek to inform the public on the role of interest in the economy.

5. Political action committees (PACs)
   a) have declined in popularity in recent years.
   b) must disclose campaign contributions and expenditures in connection with state and local elections.
   c) may make unlimited contributions to political candidates.
   d) provide candidates with public funding for their campaign.

6. According to the text, all of the following factors are involved in the media's decision not to cover more political and governmental news except
   a) Californians are not that interested in political and governmental news.

   b) the ratings for political and governmental news are lower than other kinds of news, such as the weather, consumer news, and sports coverage.
   c) so many news programs cover California political and governmental news that there is little for each station to report.
   d) political and governmental news, except during election campaigns, does not lend itself to sensational coverage.

7. What former speaker of the California Assembly said, "Money is the mother's milk of politics?"
   a) Jesse Unruh
   b) Willie Brown
   c) Antonio Villaraigosa
   d) Fabian Nuñez

8. Over the past two decades, the number of newspapers across the United States has _____, and newspaper circulations have _____ in every recent year as well.
   a) risen, increased
   b) remained the same, increased
   c) risen, declined
   d) fallen, declined

9. Which of the following is *not* a reason for the increase in interest groups in California?
   a) divided government
   b) weakness of political parties
   c) term limits
   d) growth of public interest groups

10. Many experts see the Internet as a catalyst for _____ the democratic process.
    a) threatening
    b) enhancing
    c) having little effect on
    d) undermining

CRITICAL-THINKING QUESTIONS

1. Over the past several decades, interest groups have grown and expanded their influence over public policy decisions in the legislature and at administrative agencies. Identify the reasons for this phenomenon.

2. Interest groups use a variety of techniques to accomplish their goal. Suppose you worked for an interest group that opposed stricter requirements for the recycling of plastic bottles. Outline a campaign to achieve your goal. Justify why you would take the action you propose.

3. Some people argue that interest groups provide citizens with another way in which to become involved in the political process. Others argue that interest groups undermine the political process. Discuss the arguments for both positions. Give your opinion on the controversy.
4. Interest groups play a significant role in the funding of political campaigns. Should more restriction be put on their activity? You decide that interest groups should be limited or altogether prohibited from contributing to political campaigns. How would this policy affect political campaigns? What would be the outcome of this reform?
5. What are the factors that have led to relatively low levels of coverage of politics and government in California?

KEY TERMS

California Political Reform Act (p. 47)
citizen lobbyist (p. 44)
contract lobbyist (p. 44)
in-house lobbyist (p. 44)

interest group (p. 37)
lobbying (p. 39)
media (p. 50)
political action committee (PAC) (p. 45)

public interest group (p. 42)
third house (p. 38)
trade association (p. 40)

4 Parties and Elections in California

WHAT CALIFORNIA GOVERNMENT DOES AND WHY IT MATTERS

As described in previous chapters, the Progressive movement brought to California three important tools of direct democracy: the initiative, the referendum, and the recall. All three of these have had a fundamental impact on electoral politics in our state. More recently, there has been a spate of initiatives and referenda that have dramatically changed how and when we conduct elections. In the abstract, many of these changes and reforms appear to strengthen the democratic process in California. However, some would argue that legislating by the ballot box (using initiatives or referenda to change policy) has produced some unanticipated consequences.

As this chapter will describe, California's primary election system has been changed numerous times as a result of various propositions. First, Proposition 198 in 1996 changed our long-held primary system to a new "open" primary. This new primary system was in place for the following two primary elections. Then, the new system was overturned by the U.S. Supreme Court and we reverted to a variation of the old primary election method. In 2010, voters, unhappy with the status quo, passed Proposition 14, which once again changed our primary system, this time in a very dramatic way (described in detail in this chapter). It is believed that this new primary system might very well be challenged in the courts, as was the previous one. June 2012 was the first time voters used this new primary system.

Initiatives brought additional changes to the 2012 primary election. It was the first election that manifested the results of the implementation of Propositions 11 and 20. Proposition 11, passed in 2008, mandated the creation of an independent, bipartisan Citizens Redistricting Commission that would be responsible for redrawing the boundaries of the state Senate and state Assembly districts after each U.S. Census. Proposition 20 added to the responsibility of the commission by granting it the authority to redraw U.S. House of Representative district boundaries in the state. Predictably, groups unhappy with the law—which was adopted through direct democracy—wanted voters to overturn it. So a new referendum appeared on the November 2012 ballot statewide that aimed to undo parts of Proposition 11. This ballot measure required that voters approve the revised state Senate boundaries set by the commission. If voters fail to approve the new districts, for which we've already held elections, court-appointed officials would set interim boundaries for use in the next statewide election until permanent boundaries can be set. Voters approved the measure by a wide margin.

One has to wonder how voters feel about all of these changes brought about through the ballot box. Our primary system has been changed four times over the past nine primaries; the ballot voters now receive looks very different as a result of Proposition 14, and votes now are tallied in a very unusual way; the ballot independent voters receive could potentially change with every primary election, depending on decisions made by the qualified political parties about ballot access, and newly redrawn state and federal legislative districts have included new neighborhoods and excluded others that had been historically part of the district.

Many observers believe voters are confused with all of these changes, and the result has been a decline in voter turnout rates. Case in point: the June 2012 primary, with its proposition-mandated changes, had one of the lowest voter turnout rates in state history, with only about 31 percent of registered voters casting ballots. Typically, primaries in which none of the candidates is a viable presidential nominee do not garner a lot of voter interest, and that was the case for the June 2012 primary. However, this turnout rate of less than one-third of registered voters broke the record low of 42 percent in 1996 by a wide margin. One has to wonder if all of these changes, brought to us by the initiative and referenda, are partly responsible for this dismal rate of voter participation. We have voters passing initiatives and referenda that change, in fundamental ways, our elections. Those who disagree with the outcome produced by direct democracy bring legal challenges or again use the initiative or referendum to change or undo what the voters had passed. The march of new initiatives and referenda, and lawsuits challenging them, just seems to continue. You have to ask, Is this any way to run a democracy?

Political Parties

A political party is an organization of people with roughly similar political or ideological positions who work to win elections to take control of the government and change public policy. Political parties perform many valuable functions in a democratic society. One of their most important roles is to mobilize voters at election time, helping to get out the vote. They also function as opposition points to the policies pursued by government at all levels, thereby promoting discussion of important political issues. Parties help recruit candidates for office and play a major role in the selection process. They are directly involved in political campaigns, providing workers, raising money, and identifying important political issues. Parties help bring about consensus on important political issues and serve as two-way communication channels between government and the people. Consequently, most political scientists consider them vital to the health of a democratic state.

California has a *winner-take-all* system of voting in which the candidate receiving the highest vote wins the election. Political scientists have long known that such a system promotes two dominant political parties. As a result, two major political parties dominate the political process in California: the Republicans and the

Democrats. *Third parties*, which are defined as any party other than the Republicans and Democrats, play only a limited role in California politics, although several third parties are considered qualified and are entitled to appear on the California ballot. They are the American Independent Party, the Americans Elect Party, the Peace and Freedom Party, the Green Party, and the Libertarian Party.

Party Organizations

All political parties in California have *state central committees*, which are made up of partisan officeholders and other party officials. The average political party member or supporter is not represented by this organization. The state central committee helps build support for the party's campaign efforts. Members of *county central committees* are elected by the voters in each assembly district. They generally help in campaigns. Because of the Progressive reforms, state and county committees are weak and play a diminished role in the party's affairs.

The Progressive Impact on Political Parties

The Progressive movement viewed political parties as corrupt organizations operating in concert with big corporations with the intent of controlling and manipulating the political system for their own benefit. Spencer Olin describes the attitude that Progressives had toward political parties:

> Accompanying their democratic faith in the wisdom of the individual voter was a distrust of formal party organizations, which were viewed as the media of special-interest power.... Furthermore, it was argued by progressives that science and efficient management would solve the problems of government; parties were irrelevant and unnecessary.[1]

The Progressives attacked the power of the political parties with reforms such as party primaries. Primaries were designed to take the power to select candidates for office away from the parties and put it into the hands of voters. The primary system also opened up the opportunity to run for office to anyone capable of meeting the basic qualifications, such as age and residency requirements. Instead of the party leadership and their corporate allies having the power to select candidates and subsequently manipulate them while they held office, the people now participated in a whole new class of elections, forcing candidates to direct their political messages and loyalty to the average voter.

Nonpartisan elections further weakened parties by preventing party designations from appearing on the ballot. Voters were no longer able to use their party loyalties to make voting decisions on Election Day at the county and city level. The Progressives wanted the electorate to do its homework and find out about the candidates. Instead of a party label on the ballot, voters were to be given only the current occupational status of the candidate. This meant that voters had to inform themselves by reading up on the candidates or even attending a candidate's forum.

The Progressives also installed a new ballot, the *office block ballot*. This type of ballot made it difficult to vote the straight party ticket, which was easy in many other states. Ballots that favored voting for one party, or voting the *straight ticket*, listed all the candidates running for each office by party. The use of the office block ballot in California discourages such behavior by listing each office separately and requiring the voter to make his or her choice.

The weakening of political parties in the form of nonpartisan elections at the county and city levels are believed to have an impact on voters. Contrary to the beliefs of the Progressives, voters are not known to devote a lot of time conducting research on each candidate in an attempt to determine how to cast their vote. However, we do know that voters who identify with a political party view the party affiliation of candidates as important and this information helps them in their vote decision. Typically, county and city races are not exciting, high-profile contests, and not allowing candidates to have their party label on the ballot means voters don't have that additional information to assist them in their vote choice. Researchers have found that a voter's attachment to a political party also may motivate them to vote. As Schaffner, Streb, and Wright describe it, "party identification is a, or even the, central component of voter decision making. As an effective attachment, it motivates individuals to participate as a display of party support."[2] Therefore, nonpartisan elections may have lower turnout rates than partisan ones.

Third Parties in California

Voters in California have long had the opportunity to vote for third-party candidates. In the 2012 presidential race, voters could vote for the Republican or Democratic candidates or for the candidates of four other parties: the American Independent Party, Green Party, Libertarian Party, and the Peace and Freedom Party.

Traditionally, third-party candidates do not win in a *winner-take-all* system like that in the United States. Both major parties make much of the fact that third parties do not win and warn voters against throwing their votes away. However, a significant percentage of voters reject their advice and continue to vote for third-party candidates anyway.

The American political system, which is a *federal system*, delegates power to three levels of government: national, state, and local. One of the powers that states retain is to determine how political parties may organize and gain access to the ballot. Because the legislature in California is dominated by the Republicans and Democrats, they have not made it easy for third parties to qualify to get on the ballot. As a consequence, California politics is almost totally dominated by the Republicans and Democrats.

There are two ways that political parties can qualify to get on the ballot in California. The first method is by *registration*; the second is by *petition*. Both methods are based on a percentage of those persons who voted in the last preceding gubernatorial election. In the election held in November 2010, some 10,300,392 persons turned out to vote. To qualify a new party by the registration method, the law requires that 103,004 persons or 1 percent of those who voted in the 2010 gubernatorial election officially register with the new party. The law also requires that the registrations be completed and mailed in by the 154th day preceding the upcoming primary. The second option, the petition method, is even more difficult and tedious. It requires a new political party to collect signatures equal to 10 percent of those who voted in the last gubernatorial election on petitions asking that the party be included in the upcoming primary. Currently, that number stands at over 1 million signatures. Obviously, qualifying as a new political party is not an easy task and requires time, manpower, expertise, and resources.

So what is the role of third parties in politics, particularly in California? One theory is that third parties act as spoilers. They may draw enough votes from one or the other of the two major parties to alter the election outcome. Third parties also help focus public attention on important political issues. Once an issue attracts

AMERICAN INDEPENDENT PARTY	www.aipca.org
AMERICANS ELECT PARTY	www.americanselect.org
DEMOCRATIC PARTY	www.cadem.org
GREEN PARTY	www.cagreens.org
LIBERTARIAN PARTY	www.ca.lp.org
PEACE AND FREEDOM PARTY	www.peaceandfreedom.org
REPUBLICAN PARTY	www.cagop.org

enough public attention, it will be taken over by one or both of the two major political parties. Altering election outcomes and raising political issues relegates third parties to a lesser role in politics. Whether that will change over time remains to be seen. Box 4.1 provides the URLs of those parties currently qualified in California.

Party Affiliation of California Voters

A plurality of California voters identify with the Democratic Party. As of October 2012, about 44 percent of voters are registered with the Democratic Party compared to 29 percent affiliated with the Republican Party. A substantial 21 percent of voters have no party preference, and 6 percent identify with one of the minor parties. Party affiliation is fairly easy to determine in the state, because when you register to vote, you are asked to declare your political party. Of the seven political parties that have qualified for the ballot in California, two are major parties and five are minor or third parties. The Democratic and Republican parties receive the lion's share of votes and members.

As Figure 4.1 illustrates, since 1996, registration in the two major political parties has declined. Identification with the Democratic Party declined by only 3 percent compared to an 8 percent decline in those registering with the Republican Party. The most dramatic change has been among those who have no political party preference (also referred to as independent voters). This group has nearly doubled its size over the past 16 years; now more than one in five voters claim no party preference when they register to vote.

Now let us look at political-party affiliation and some demographic factors. Figure 4.2 presents the results of a California statewide survey conducted in July 2012 that asked respondents about their party affiliation, age, gender, race, educational level, and place of birth. The results suggest that nearly 45 percent of all young, middle-aged, and older Californians prefer the Democratic Party. Younger

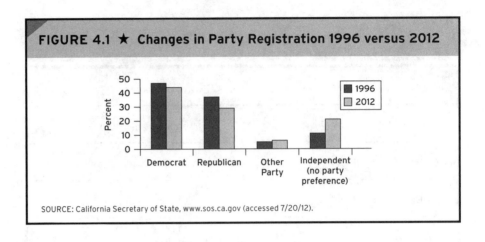

FIGURE 4.1 ★ Changes in Party Registration 1996 versus 2012

SOURCE: California Secretary of State, www.sos.ca.gov (accessed 7/20/12).

people are less inclined than are middle-aged and older people to affiliate with the Republican Party (19 percent compared to 36 percent and 34 percent), and younger people appear to be more likely than the other age groups not to affiliate with one of the major political parties, with 30 percent registering as independents. Conversely, a recent California Field Poll (2011) found that the Republican Party is becoming the party of senior citizens. Currently, those 50 years of age or older make up 54 percent of the party, and this number is growing annually as the population ages. Many are questioning what the Republican Party of the future will look like in California with the passing of these older Republicans. Will the party be able to survive this demographic trend?

We also observe gender differences in party affiliation, with a majority of women affiliating with the Democratic Party (compared to 37 percent of men) and more men than women registering as independents (27 percent and 16 percent, respectively). Educational level seems to have an impact on party preference. Regardless of educational level, the Democratic Party has more support than the Republican Party. However, a majority of those with a high school degree or less prefer the Democratic Party, and only 26 percent in this category identify with the Republican Party. Latinos, by over a 40 percent margin, prefer the Democratic Party over the Republican Party (57 percent Democratic versus 15 percent Republican), while whites are evenly split between the Democratic Party and the Republican Party (40 percent Democratic versus 39 percent Republican). In comparing the U.S.-born to immigrants, more U.S.-born Californians prefer the Republican Party (32 percent to 25 percent) and nearly equal numbers of U.S.-born and immigrants support the Democratic Party. It is interesting that more of the foreign-born identify themselves as independents, 27 percent, compared to 20 percent of U.S.-born.

Some of these demographic trends suggest that politics in our state will change in the future. Older white males' proportionate decline in the population will continue to have an impact on the Republican Party, a party that will continue to lose a large segment of its support. It is important to note another impact of changing demographics: the Latino population is increasing, and this portends well for the future of the Democratic Party. Recently released Census data showed that from 2000 to 2010 the Latino population grew by nearly 28 percent to 14 million, whereas the white population declined more than 5 percent to just under 15 million. Currently, Latinos favor the Democratic Party over the Republican Party by sizable percentages, and there is no reason to expect this to change in the future. Many are predicting an even stronger Democratic Party presence in the state.

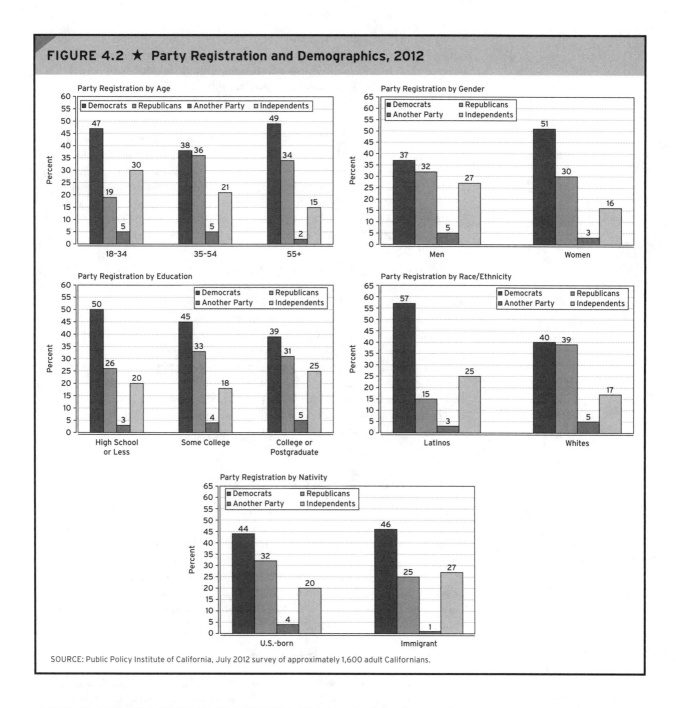

FIGURE 4.2 ★ Party Registration and Demographics, 2012

Party Registration by Age

Party Registration by Gender

Party Registration by Education

Party Registration by Race/Ethnicity

Party Registration by Nativity

SOURCE: Public Policy Institute of California, July 2012 survey of approximately 1,600 adult Californians.

THE RED AND THE BLUE IN CALIFORNIA Thinking back to the presidential election of 2012, you may recall that most television programs focusing on the election outcome had maps of the United States color-coded to represent the states that voted Republican (red) and those states that voted Democratic (blue). The map was very interesting—the West Coast and most of the Northeast as well as major urban areas of the United States were blue (Democratic) and the South, agricultural regions, and the Great Plains states were red (Republican). The map nicely illustrated the national split between urban areas, predominantly Democratic, and rural, agricultural, and suburban areas, mostly Republican.

As the map in Figure 4.3 shows, the same geographic split appears within the state of California—a split between the coastal counties and the inland counties. Most of the Democratic counties are coastal and encompass major urban areas, whereas most of the Republican counties are inland and rural.

As reported by the *Los Angeles Times:*

> Over the last decade, Republican influence has grown more concentrated in conservative inland California—largely the Central Valley and Inland Empire but also the Antelope Valley, the Sierra and rural north. . . . At the same time Democrats have strengthened their domination of counties along California's coastline, building overwhelming advantages in the San Francisco and Los Angeles areas as Latino voters have expanded the party's base. And from San Diego's beachfront suburbs to the Central Coast, Democrats have eroded Republican support among moderates, especially women.[3]

Overall, the Democratic Party has an electoral advantage in California, largely due to the fact that nearly 70 percent of the state's population resides in Democratic-leaning coastal regions. Republicans have an uphill battle winning statewide elections and are more likely to succeed if they nominate ideologically moderate candidates who are able to win the support of Democratic voters. What this suggests for California's political future is that California will remain a distinctly blue state. The fact that the urban and coastal population centers are largely Democratic and moderate to liberal, coupled with the fact that a majority of independent voters lean toward the Democratic Party, puts California solidly in the "blue" column. This is not to suggest that all populated coastal regions are the same politically and ideologically. As the next section illustrates, there are some interesting variations.

California's Local Political Cultures from Left to Right

Political culture is difficult to define and quantify. However, we can offer at least a few statistics to show how three of the state's most populous counties differ in terms of political partisanship, political ideology, political activism, political tolerance, and voting tendencies on important issues. Table 4.1 compares and contrasts San Francisco City/County, Los Angeles County, and San Diego County on those selected indicators of local political culture.

Political Party Registration

As of October 2012, registered Democrats outnumbered Republicans in San Francisco by more than six to one and by more than two to one in Los Angeles County. In San Diego County, however, Republicans and Democrats were nearly equal at 34 and 35 percent, respectively.

Political Ideology

Based on community surveys conducted in late 2000, about one in five San Franciscans identify themselves politically as "very liberal" and only 4 percent as "very conservative." In both Los Angeles County and San Diego County, conservatives outnumber liberals by about two to one.[4]

FIGURE 4.3 ★ Percent Difference between Democratic and Republican Registration by County (2012 Presidential Election)

SOURCE: California Secretary of State, October 22, 2012, www.sos.ca.gov.

Del Norte 3%
Siskiyou 9%
Modoc 24%
Humboldt 16%
Trinity <1%
Shasta 20%
Lassen 24%
Tehama 14%
Plumas 11%
Mendocino 25%
Glenn 15%
Butte 3%
Sierra 14%
Nevada
Colusa 11%
Sutter 12%
Yuba 8%
Placer 19%
Lake 13%
5%
Yolo 23%
El Dorado 15%
Alpine 7%
Sonoma 30%
Napa 20%
Sacramento 12%
Amador 13%
Marin 36%
Solano 23%
Calaveras 12%
Tuolumne 10%
Mono 4%
Contra Costa 25%
San Joaquin 7%
San Francisco 47%
Alameda 42%
Stanislaus 1%
Mariposa 15%
San Mateo 32%
Santa Clara 24%
Merced 9%
Madera 11%
Santa Cruz 38%
San Benito 18%
Fresno 2%
Inyo 13%
Tulare 10%
Monterey 27%
Kings 10%
San Luis Obispo 6%
Kern 6%
San Bernardino 3%
Santa Barbara 11%
Los Angeles 29%
Ventura 2%
Orange 10%
Riverside 4%
San Diego 1%
Imperial 26%

Dominant political party affiliation
☐ Democratic advantage
■ Republican advantage

TABLE 4.1 ★ Regional Political Cultures: Three California Counties Compared from Left to Right

INDICATOR	SAN FRANCISCO	LOS ANGELES	SAN DIEGO
1. Percent Democrats (2012)	56	51	35
2. Percent Republicans (2012)	9	22	34
3. Percent very liberal (2000)	21	8	6
4. Percent very conservative (2000)	4	15	14
5. Percent high protest activity (2000)	47	30	30
6. Percent voter turnout (Nov. 4, 2008)	79	77	84
7. Percent voter turnout (Nov. 2, 2010)	62	53	64
8. Percent voter turnout (Nov. 6, 2012)	57	52	56
9. Percent yes on Proposition 13 (1978)	47	67	60
10. Percent yes on Proposition 187 (1994)	29	56	68
11. Percent yes on Proposition 209 (1996)	29	45	63
12. Percent yes on Proposition 215 (1996)	78	56	52
13. Percent yes on Proposition 22 (2000)	32	59	63
14. Percent yes on Proposition 8 (2008)	25	50	54
15. Percent yes on Proposition 30 (2012)	77	60	46
16. Percent yes on Proposition 34 (2012)	70	54	45
17. Percent vote Brown for governor (2010)	79	63	44
18. Percent vote Whitman for governor (2010)	18	32	50
19. Percent vote Obama for president (2012)	83	69	51

SOURCES: Indicators 1-2, 6-18: California Secretary of State, various official statements of vote. Indicators 3-5: Analysis of sample survey data obtained from the Social Capital Benchmark Survey 2000.

Political Protest and Voter Turnout

Those same surveys show that San Franciscans are much more inclined to engage in political protest than are their counterparts in the southland. Specifically, 47 percent of San Francisco citizens scored "high" on a nationally normed political protest activity index, as compared with only 30 percent in both Los Angeles and San

Diego Counties. In terms of more conventional forms of political participation, however, San Diego County's citizens are on top, with higher voter turnout rates than San Franciscans and Angelenos in both the November 4, 2008, general election and the November 2, 2010, general election. The November 6, 2012, general election saw both San Diego and San Francisco with near equal turnout rates, with Los Angeles lagging behind.

Support for Proposition 13

Proposition 13, the 1978 initiative that rolled back property tax rates and limited the government's ability to raise local property taxes in the future, regarded by some observers "as one of the most significant political events in California's history,"[5] won by a landslide vote nearly everywhere throughout the state, including a 67 percent yes vote in Los Angeles County and a 60 percent vote in San Diego County. In San Francisco, however, it mustered only 47 percent, not even a majority.

Political Tolerance and Support for Racial and Cultural Diversity

Table 4.1 reports county voting results on seven different statewide ballot propositions over the period 1994–2012. All seven can be viewed as indicators of political tolerance and support for racial and cultural diversity.

- Proposition 187 was a 1994 initiative constitutional amendment that made undocumented immigrants ineligible for various public social services. The state's voters approved it by a wide margin, with 56 percent voting yes in Los Angeles County and 68 percent in San Diego County. Only 29 percent voted for it in San Francisco.

- Proposition 209 was a 1996 initiative constitutional amendment that prohibited state and local government agencies from giving preferential treatment to any individual or group on the basis of race, sex, color, ethnicity, or national origin. Widely viewed by friends and foes alike as an attack on affirmative action, this measure also passed in the statewide vote, with 63 percent support in San Diego County. It received only 45 percent in Los Angeles County, however, and a mere 29 percent in San Francisco.

- Proposition 215 was a 1996 initiative statute that permitted the medicinal use of marijuana. This measure passed in the statewide vote, but only barely in San Diego County with 52 percent, more comfortably in Los Angeles County with 56 percent, and by a landslide 78 percent vote in San Francisco.

- Proposition 22 was a 2000 initiative statute declaring that only marriage between a man and a woman is valid or recognized in California. This measure was approved by a landslide statewide vote, with 59 percent support in Los Angeles County and 63 percent in San Diego County. In San Francisco, however, a resounding 68 percent voted no.

- Proposition 8 was a 2008 initiative constitutional amendment that eliminated the right of same-sex couples to marry. Backers of the proposition placed it on the ballot as a direct challenge to the California Supreme Court's ruling in May 2008 affirming the constitutionality of same-sex marriage. The measure was approved 52 to 48 percent in the statewide vote. Only 25 percent of San Francisco County's voters voted yes, however, compared with 50 percent in Los Angeles County and 54 percent in San Diego County.

- Proposition 30 was a 2012 initiative constitutional amendment that would temporarily raise taxes to fund education. Personal income taxes would increase on those earnings over $250,000 for seven years and the sales tax would increase by .25 cent for four years. This increased state revenue would be used to fund education at the K-12, community college, and university levels. Teacher unions and Governor Brown campaigned aggressively for the passage of this initiative. Failure of the proposition would result in extensive budget cuts to the already struggling public school and university systems. Proposition 30 was approved statewide by a 54-to-46 percent vote. Over three-quarters of San Francisco voters approved of the measure, as did 60 percent of Los Angeles county voters. In San Diego, however, only 46 percent voted yes.

- Proposition 34 was an initiative statute asking voters to approve the repeal of the death penalty and replace it with life imprisonment without the possibility of parole. This measure would apply retroactively to those inmates currently on death row. The measure failed to pass with a statewide vote of only 47 percent. Contrary to the statewide vote, 70 percent of voters in San Francisco and 54 percent of voters in Los Angeles voted in favor of this measure. In San Diego county, only 45 percent voted yes.

The Presidential Election of 2008

In the November 4, 2008, presidential election, California voters supported Barack Obama in a landslide over John McCain by 61 to 37 percent. Majorities in all three counties voted for Obama, with San Francisco County leading the pack with 84 percent for Obama, followed by Los Angeles County at 61 percent and San Diego County at 54 percent.

The Gubernatorial and U.S. Senate Elections of 2010

In the 2010 race for governor, the winner, Democrat Jerry Brown, easily beat Republican Meg Whitman, 79 percent to 18 percent in San Francisco and 63 percent 32 percent in Los Angeles County. In San Diego County, however, Whitman beat Brown 50 percent to 44 percent. In the race for U.S. Senate that year, the winner incumbent Democrat Barbara Boxer handily defeated Republican Carly Fiorina, 80 percent to 16 percent in San Francisco and 62 percent to 33 percent in Los Angeles County. But in San Diego County, Fiorina came out on top, 51 percent to 44 percent.

The Presidential Election of 2012

In the November 6, 2012, presidential election, voters preferred President Barack Obama over former Massachusetts Governor Mitt Romney by 59 to 38 percent. San Francisco county overwhelmingly voted for President Obama with a resounding 83 percent, voters in Los Angeles county supported him at 69 percent, and San Diego county at 51 percent.

To Sum Up

The statistics in Table 4.1 show that political life varies dramatically in California from region to region. If you happen to reside in San Francisco, you live in one of the nation's most liberal, tolerant, and activist political cultures.[6] The political environment in San Diego County, on the other hand, is more conservative, less tolerant, and more passive. Los Angeles County falls somewhere between these two extremes. These three counties reflect the range of political cultural differences that exist across the state. You can easily see why local representatives in the state legislature fight so much and so fiercely and have a very hard time agreeing on anything.

Elections in California

The Battle over the Primary

The past decade has seen much controversy, upheaval, and court challenges regarding the type of primary system used in California. In primary elections, voters cast votes to select who will run as their party's nominees in the general election. In the United States, there are three general types of primary-election systems, and states have the authority to determine which system they will operate under.

- *Closed primary system*—Only voters who declare a party affiliation when they register to vote are permitted to vote in their party's primary election. Each party has its own ballot, listing the names of the candidates from their party competing to be the party's candidate in the general election. Registered Democrats receive the Democratic ballot, registered Republicans receive the Republican ballot, and voters registered with minor parties receive their party's ballot. Voters who decline to state a party affiliation when they register are not eligible to receive a party ballot because it is only party members who have the privilege of electing the party's nominees.

- *Open primary system*—Registered voters, regardless of their party affiliation, can vote in the party primary of their choice on primary election day. As an example, a registered Democrat can decide he or she would like to vote in the Republican Party primary and request that ballot. The choice of party ballot on primary election day does not affect the voter's permanent party affiliation. Approximately 20 states operate under this system.

- *Blanket primary system*—One ballot lists all candidates from all of the parties. All registered voters, including those not affiliated with any party, are permitted to vote, and all voters receive the same ballot. For instance, a voter who is not affiliated with a party may vote for a Democrat to run as the nominee for governor and a Republican to run as the nominee for the U.S. Senate. Under this system, voters who are not affiliated with a party help choose that party's nominees. Alaska, Louisiana, and Washington State all use this primary system.

California operated under the closed primary system until the passage of Proposition 198 in 1996 (incorrectly named the "Open Primary" proposition). Proposition 198 instituted a blanket primary system in which all voters received a single ballot containing the names of all candidates from all parties. California held two blanket primaries—in June 1998 and March 2000—before the U.S. Supreme Court (in the case of *California Democratic Party v. Jones*) invalidated Proposition 198. The Court ruled that, based on the First Amendment's guarantee of freedom of association, California's political parties did have a right to exclude nonparty members from voting in party primaries. In an effort to include the growing number of nonaffiliated voters, California adopted a *modified closed primary system*. Beginning with the March 2002 primary election, political parties still had their own party ballots but now had the option of adopting a party rule that would allow unaffiliated voters to vote in their party primary. If an unaffiliated voter is not allowed to request a party's ballot, he or she is given a ballot containing only the names of candidates for nonpartisan races and ballot measures.

Proponents of the blanket primary were not satisfied with the modified closed primary system, arguing that the blanket primary system is the most inclusive one and would result in more-moderate candidates running in primary elections, thus producing more competitive races. The logic is that if independent, ideologically moderate voters participate in the primary election, they will bring a counter-balance to the more extreme and ideological views of traditional primary party voters, the party loyalists. Primary candidates would, therefore, need to moderate their positions to attract the votes of moderate, independent voters. So, in June 2010, voters once more passed a proposition that changes California's primary-election system.

Proposition 14 mandates a form of a blanket primary system known as the "top-two vote getters" system. This primary system would be used for state legislative and congressional seats as well as for statewide offices, such as governor and attorney general. All registered voters, even those stating no party preference, receive a ballot listing all candidates from all qualified political parties. The top two vote getters for each office are then in a runoff in November's general election. An interesting feature of this new primary election system is the possibility that the top two vote getters could be of the same political party, resulting in two Democrats or two Republicans competing against each other in the general election. California's new primary system does not apply to candidates running for the U.S. president, county central committee, or local offices. The June 5, 2012, primary election was the first statewide election held under this new system, and the results were quite interesting. Of the 53 primary elections for U.S. House seats, 8 of these races resulted in candidates from the same party being the top-two vote getters: November 2012 had 6 contests with Democrats pitted against each other and 2 contests featuring Republican candidates competing against each other. Of the 20 primary contests for the California state Senate, 5 resulted in November match-ups between two of the same party members (Democrats), and for the state Assembly, we had 15 contests with Democrats going head to head and 6 contests with two Republicans battling for the Assembly seat.

This new primary system also allows candidates to designate whether they have a political party preference and how it should be stated on the ballot. According to California law, "a candidate for nomination to a voter-nominated office shall have his or her party preference, or lack of party preference, stated on the ballot, but the party preference designation is selected solely by the candidate." What this means is that candidates can state the party they identify with or they can state they don't have a party preference. In this age of voter frustration, directed at party politics and legislative gridlock, having the ballot state "Party Preference: None" appears to be a strategy adopted by some candidates. This is what happened in a race for a hotly contested congressional seat in Ventura County. The redrawing of the state's congressional district boundaries created a new swing district in this area. A *swing district* is one in which there are near equal numbers of Republican and Democratic voters and a significant number of independent voters. This new district consisted of 41 percent Democrats, 35 percent Republicans, and 19 percent with no party preference (independent voters). In this type of a district it is usually the independent voters who often decide the winner. There is no electoral edge given to either party candidate—the district is competitive. There were four Democrats, one Republican, and one independent (no party preference) running in this primary. The "independent" candidate was actually a Republican who switched her party registration to no party preference just before filing her papers to run, hoping to win the support of enough independent and moderate voters to be one of the top two winners. A number of candidates have used this strategy, hoping voters wouldn't remember or even know that they had been party loyalists before the campaign. Unfortunately for this candidate, the only Republican on the ballot and the better-known Democrat captured the top two positions and competed against each other in the November general election.

Will this new primary system have the intended impact of encouraging more moderate candidates running in primaries and being elected to office? Louisiana and Washington operate under similar primary systems, and analyses of their election outcomes found that these states have not experienced the election of more moderate candidates. However, some argue that blanket primaries can boost voter turnout by 3 to 6 percent by attracting voters with no party preference. It is too soon to tell the impact of this new primary system on California electoral politics.

Presidential Primaries: Maximizing California's Clout?

Until 2000, California held its presidential primaries in June of election years, one of the last states to cast its votes for the parties' nominees. It was often the case that states holding earlier primaries and caucuses determined who the presidential nominees were before Californians had a chance to go to the polls. To have more influence in the nomination process, California changed its presidential primary election date to early March. Many believed it was only fitting that the most populous state should have an early primary date. Sadly, this earlier primary date did not result in California voters' having more clout in the presidential nomination process, as other states moved their primaries to even earlier dates. So California changed its primary date back to June, effective 2006. However, for the 2008 presidential primaries, California changed the date once again, from June 3 to February 5, the earliest permissible date under national party rules.

Many political analysts and journalists heralded the early-February presidential primary date. But did this move really have the intended impact, as hopefully reflected in a 2007 *Los Angeles Times* article titled, "Earlier Primary Gives California a Major Voice"? Many who had argued for the early-February 2008 presidential primary believed that candidates would have to campaign early and hard in the Golden State and would have to win support from a very racially and ethnically diverse population, especially the growing number of Latino voters. To win voters' support, issues important to Californians would need to be addressed, and all this would result in California's greater prominence in presidential campaign politics. Or so the theory went.

One of the unanticipated consequences of California's adoption of an early primary date was that a number of states with long-standing early primaries set their election dates even earlier, not wanting to be overshadowed by the most populous state in the nation. And 23 other states also moved their primaries to February 5, resulting in something akin to a national primary. California's dream of being in the electoral limelight quickly faded.

Another consequence of the early-February primary was that the June 2008 primary election for statewide offices cost the state and counties $100 million and resulted in a historically low voting turnout rate of less than 25 percent of the registered voters. Including the November 2008 general election, California voters were asked to vote in three elections in less than 10 months. Now California's presidential primary is once again back to the June date. Some believe this frequent changing of primary election dates contributes to California's less than spectacular voting turnout rates because voters might be confused as to when elections will be held.

Initiative Campaigns: Direct Democracy or Tool of Special Interests?

One legacy of California's early-twentieth-century reform movement is the initiative process. Californians can completely bypass the state legislature, their elected representatives, and place proposed policies on the ballot for direct vote by the people. As the name suggests, the electorate *initiates* initiatives. Most people think of the initiative process as direct democracy in action—concerned citizens circulate petitions to qualify their issue for the ballot and then hold an election allowing the public to state its preference for or against the proposed policy. In reality, only a small number of ballot initiatives emerge as a result of grassroots efforts. Initiatives are largely a political tool used by special-interest groups to achieve their policy goals. Depending on the issue, interest groups sometimes find it politically expedient to bypass the legislature altogether, believing they have a better chance of achieving their policy goals if they take the issue directly to the voters.

For example, many members of the California legislature would find it politically unwise to introduce legislation that would legalize marijuana or abolish the death penalty or raise taxes. Positions on these issues are sure to outrage some voters, making reelection more difficult. That is why these types of issues find their way onto our ballots as initiatives or referendums. Likewise, legislation that would curb the power of special interests, interests that make sizable campaign contributions to legislators, also are unlikely to be dealt with by our elected representatives. Recently, some local ballot measures have passed that reduce retirement benefits of public employees. If an elected official introduced this type of proposal, he or she would be targeted by unions representing public employees for reelection defeat. So, for many of these types of issues, interest groups realize the most productive route is to go directly to the voters via the initiative process. In addition, citizen groups have found the initiative process to be the only avenue for policy change in the areas of legislative term limits, nonpartisan redistricting, and the blanket primary system. These changes would never have been proposed or approved by legislators because these reforms would curb their own and their political party's powers.

Since 1912, the first year initiatives were permitted, over 350 statewide initiatives have appeared on the California ballot. These ballot initiatives have dealt with a wide range of issues, such as legalization of marijuana, campaign finance reform, same-sex marriage, taxation policy, legalization of gambling casinos, the establishment of a state lottery, environmental regulations, affirmative action policy, the criminal justice system, and labor issues. Of these hundreds of initiatives, only about one-third have been approved by the voters. In the past three decades, there has been a dramatic surge in the number of initiatives that have been proposed and that have qualified for the ballot. Many surmise that the reason for this increase is that special interests have become more sophisticated in their use of the initiative process to achieve their policy goals.

To qualify for the ballot, the state requires over 500,000 signatures of registered voters for initiatives creating new laws (statutes) and over 800,000 signatures for propositions that aim to amend the state constitution. Signatures are gathered on petitions, which are then submitted to the secretary of state's office for verification. Collecting hundreds of thousands of signatures of registered voters is a daunting task. Rarely is this a grassroots movement in which ordinary citizens fan out across the state, knock on doors, and stand in front of supermarkets, asking strangers to support their initiative by signing a petition. More common is the hiring of professional signature gatherers. There are political consulting firms who specialize in this very activity. They hire individuals to go to college campuses, supermarkets, malls, and other places where voters congregate, and they are paid an average of $1.50 per signature for every signature they acquire. This means that it costs over $750,000 just to collect the signatures to qualify a proposition for the ballot.

For the more controversial initiatives, in order to wage a successful campaign either in support of or in opposition to an initiative, one needs to have ample political resources. Money is probably the most important of these resources. Not only must a statewide initiative campaign hire political consultants, but it must also plan and implement a sustainable media campaign. Such campaigns are very costly because of California's size and expensive media markets. Therefore, it is not surprising to find the more high-profile and controversial initiative campaigns costing tens of millions of dollars. In 2008 slightly over $60 million was spent on the highly controversial initiative Proposition 8, a constitutional amendment that would eliminate same-sex marriage in California. Proposition 8 was put on the ballot in response to the State Supreme Court's May 2008 ruling (4–3) declaring that the state constitution protects a fundamental "right to marry" that extends equally to same-sex couples. Both sides of the issue collected near equal sums of contributions totaling $74 million, with the majority of the contributions in support of Proposition 8 coming from members of the Mormon Church throughout the United States.[7] As expensive as Proposition 8 was, it did not break the record for the most expensive initiative campaign. In 2006 both sides spent more than $150 million on Proposition 87, the alternative energy initiative, which was soundly defeated by a 55 percent vote. This was, by far, the most expensive proposition campaign not only in California history but in U.S. history.

It should be noted, however, that spending more money than the opposing side does not always guarantee victory. Case in point: Proposition 19, the legalization of marijuana initiative on the November 2010 ballot. Proponents had raised and spent nearly $4 million on the yes campaign, whereas the opposition spent only a paltry $300,000 in defeating this measure.

Political savvy is another important resource. The chances of winning an initiative campaign increase if one understands how the game is played. For example, the naming of the proposition can increase its chance of passage. In the November 1996 election, Proposition 209, officially titled "Prohibition against Discrimination or Preferential Treatment by State and Other Public Entities," appeared on the ballot. Its supporters referred to the proposition as the "California Civil Rights Initiative." Considering these titles alone, it would be difficult to imagine this proposition failing; in these progressive times, it is fair to say that most voters are opposed to discrimination and are supportive of civil rights. However, in reality, Proposition 209 was not what most would consider to be a civil rights statute. The proposition proposed to eliminate affirmative action programs in California for women and minorities in public employment, education (college admissions, tutoring, and outreach programs), and contracting. Proposition 209 passed and is now state law.

Critics of the initiative process believe that too many complicated issues are presented to the voters as ballot propositions. In some recent elections, voters have had to vote for candidates for federal, state, county, and city elective offices as well as cast their votes for over a dozen important state propositions and numerous county and city measures.

Some argue that many of the issues that appear as ballot initiatives are best suited for debate and deliberation by our elected representatives and should not be decided by misleading television ads aimed at the public. Sometimes the propositions are very confusing in name and in substance, and some question whether we are asking too much of the electorate to wade through all this information. Another problem with the initiative process is that the constitutionality of many propositions approved by the voters is later challenged. It takes years for the courts to render a decision, and it is not uncommon for the courts to declare the law based on the passage of the proposition to be unconstitutional, null, and void. Not only does this complicate the process; it also frustrates the public who voted for a new policy only to see the courts invalidate the public's will.

The legislature understands some of the problems associated with the initiative process and has created state commissions to investigate and reform the process. Some suggested reforms have been to prohibit the use of paid signature gatherers whom only the well-funded interest groups are able to afford; to increase the number of signatures required in an effort to reduce the number of initiatives; to restrict the types of issues that can appear as ballot initiatives; and to review the constitutionality of initiatives prior to placing them on the ballot. Although there have been a couple of commissions to examine these ideas, none of these reforms has been adopted.

The 2003 Gubernatorial Recall Election: A Perfect Political Storm

On October 7, 2003, Governor Gray Davis made history. Only 11 months after he successfully won his reelection bid, he was recalled from office. He was the first and only governor in the state of California and the second governor in the nation's history to be recalled. The recall movement and election of Arnold Schwarzenegger was in every sense dramatic, historic, and stunning.

Davis was reelected in November 2002, thanks to a very weak challenger, even though just before the election a majority of voters disapproved of his overall performance as governor.[8] Voters held Governor Davis responsible for the 2000–01 energy crisis during which Californians had to reduce their energy consumption while experiencing or being threatened by blackouts and, to add insult to injury, had to pay more for their electricity. News reports focused on this issue for many months and this issue had a negative impact on Davis's popularity. Compounding the problem was a dramatic decrease in state revenues. The governor had to announce that the state was short $23.6 billion and the 2003–04 budget shortfall would rise to nearly $35 billion. The state legislature could not produce a budget on time and voters were very uneasy about the economic future of the state. Davis entered his second term as a wounded, unpopular governor, viewed as distant, too beholden to special interests, and ineffectual.

Darrell Issa, a multimillionaire Republican member of Congress from the San Diego area, was a dominant force in the movement to recall Davis. He injected nearly $2 million into the recall effort and had hopes of running for governor if the recall succeeded. Nearly 1.5 million voter signatures were collected on recall petitions, meeting the state requirement for an October 2003 recall election. Unfortunately for Representative Issa's hopes of capturing the governorship, appearing on the scene was a well-known, highly likable, charismatic, moderate Republican antipolitician, antiestablishment actor/businessman: Arnold Schwarzenegger. In the summer of 2003, Schwarzenegger announced his candidacy and immediately became the front-runner among Republican candidates, making national and international headlines with his decision to run.[9] Politically, it was the making of a perfect storm: a weak and unpopular governor, an unhappy electorate, and an internationally known celebrity. Schwarzenegger was elected governor and was reelected again in November 2006. An unpopular war, a series of corruption and sex scandals implicating prominent Republican officeholders, and an unpopular president all contributed to the defeat of Republican candidates in the 2006 national elections. In contrast, Schwarzenegger won his reelection bid by a whopping 17 percent margin. His adoption of moderate positions—pro-choice on abortion, moderate on the environment, and cooperating with the Democratically controlled state legislature—placed him in sync with voters, resulting in his reelection victory.

The 2008 Election: Demographic and Ideological Shifts

The 2008 election was somewhat unusual, even by California standards. A very popular, young, charismatic candidate, Barack Obama, topped the ticket as the Democratic candidate for the presidency, winning 61 percent of the popular vote, the biggest margin in the state of California since 1964.

The *Los Angeles Times*, in an article aptly titled "State's Shifting Political Landscape," described the election results:

> Those unpredictable decisions by voters, however, were accompaniments to the election's main theme: the demographic and ideological shifts that have delivered the state into Democratic hands and demonstrated anew the tough road ahead for the Republican minority.[10]

The Democratic Party was hopeful that it could continue to win the support and allegiance of the overwhelming number of voters who cast their votes for Obama, especially 83 percent of first-time voters. Seventy-six percent of those 18–29 years of age voted for Obama compared to only 48 percent of those 65 and older. However, some analysts were not confident that future elections would see high percentages of young voters turning out to vote or see substantial increases in support for the Democratic Party.

By November 2, 2010, the evidence was in. The lead headline from Scott Fahey's *Elections 2010* blog from Southern California Public Radio read, "Low youth voter turnout hurts Democrats." As he described it, "In California, one of every five voters in 2008 was between the ages of 18 and 29, compared with about 1 in 10 on Tuesday." California reflected the overall national trend with fewer young, liberal, and black voters casting votes in the November 2010 general election.

The 2010 General Election

While the nation witnessed a historic "shellacking" of the Democratic Party, as President Obama called it, with an unprecedented loss of Democratically held seats in Congress, Californians voted to the beat of a different drummer. All of the Democratic candidates running for statewide elective office won and nearly all won by respectable margins. The *Los Angeles Times*, in an analysis of the vote based on exit poll data, concluded that the strength of the Latino vote was a key factor in the success of Democratic candidates. Latino voters made up 22 percent of the California voter pool, a record tally that mortally wounded many Republicans.

THE GOVERNOR'S RACE The costliest statewide race in the nation's history pitted novice politician and billionaire Meg Whitman against political insider Jerry Brown. Whitman spent a record-breaking $160 million on her general election campaign (see Table 4.2, p. 85), with over $140 million from her own personal wealth. Of this total, she poured nearly $110 million into TV and radio advertising, and Californians quickly became aware of her candidacy and voters easily recognized her name. In contrast, Jerry Brown, who had served two terms as governor (1975–83), had been mayor of Oakland (1999–2007), and more recently served as state attorney general, spent only $25 million on his campaign. In the end, Brown won by a very comfortable margin, 54 percent to 41 percent. Furthermore, Brown's cost per vote was only $1.24, whereas Whitman spent a whopping $51.82 per vote! What accounted for Brown's victory and Whitman's defeat?

- *Voters wanted an experienced leader*—Whitman, a politically inexperienced mega-wealthy businesswoman, believed her money and outsider status would win her the governorship. Exit polls, however, revealed that 54 percent of voters wanted "an insider who knows how to get things done" compared to only 36 percent who wanted "an outsider who wants to shake things up."[11] Voters were very concerned about the economy, and Brown campaigned as the candidate with the experience to deal with the state's fiscal crisis and legislative gridlock.

- *Immigration issue*—Just weeks before the election, Whitman, who ran on an anti-illegal immigration platform, was forced to admit that she had employed a housekeeper for nine years who did not have legal residency status. Whitman had fired her housekeeper and stated during her campaign that she would support deportation of her former employee. Any progress the Whitman campaign had made on reaching out to Latino voters dissipated with the news of this scandal. Exit polls found that Latinos, more than any other voting group, said it was the governor's race that impelled them to vote, with 60 percent voting for Brown and only 34 percent voting for Whitman. Likewise, independent voters, who tend to be anti-illegal immigration, were concerned that Whitman knew of her housekeeper's illegal status (evidence was presented to support this allegation) and yet took no action until it became a campaign issue. In order to win the election, Whitman needed the support of independent voters. Polling data suggest that this scandal, so close to election day, was the turning point in the governor's race.

- *Demographic divide*—Brown won the election with the support of women and Latino voters. Although male voters were evenly split between Brown and Whitman, a majority of female voters favored Brown (54 percent) over Whitman (42 percent). Anglo voters favored Whitman over Brown (53 to 45 percent) but Latino voters, who are largely credited with the electoral success of Democratic candidates in this election, overwhelmingly favored Brown. Analysts believe that Brown's experience and moderate positions on the issues attracted the support of women and Latino voters.

- *Political landscape*—It is not surprising that inland voters preferred Whitman and coastal and urban voters largely preferred Brown. Because most of California's population resides in the coastal regions and urban centers, Democratic candidates have a distinct edge over Republican candidates in statewide contests.

THE U.S. SENATE RACE Barbara Boxer, a liberal Democrat, running for her fourth term in the U.S. Senate, had a tough reelection challenge, the toughest of her political career. Boxer, a career politician, ran against outsider and novice campaigner Carly Fiorina, a Republican and former CEO of Hewlett-Packard (HP). Typically, incumbents such as Boxer, running for reelection in a state where her political party dominates, would have had a relatively easy time keeping their seat. The situation was different this time around. California's economy was in shambles; Boxer's popularity had been declining; and Fiorina was a formidable opponent. In the end, Boxer prevailed, winning reelection with 52 percent of the vote compared to Fiorina's 43 percent. Many pundits believe that Fiorina's failure to moderate her position on social issues (she was ardently anti-abortion and anti-illegal immigration) along with Boxer's stinging ads highlighting the layoff of 30,000 HP workers under Fiorina's stewardship were responsible for Fiorina's loss.

PROPOSITION 20: REDISTRICTING CONGRESSIONAL DISTRICTS VS. PROPOSITION 27: ELIMINATING THE STATE REDISTRICTING COMMISSION
Propositions 20 and 27 were actually competing initiatives. Proposition 20 is an extension of Proposition 11, which passed in November 2008. Proposition 11 created the 14-member Citizens Redistricting Commission that would be in charge of drawing the boundaries of state Assembly and state Senate districts after each U.S. Census. November 2010's Proposition 20 asked voters to remove the authority for congressional redistricting from the legislature and give this power to the newly created Citizens Redistricting Commission. The commission would then be responsible for drawing congressional district lines as well as the already approved power of drawing state Assembly and state Senate district boundaries. The competing initiative, Proposition 27, on the other hand, would have eliminated the Citizens Redistricting Commission and returned to the legislature the power to draw state district boundaries (essentially repealing Proposition 11). California voters soundly endorsed the Citizens Redistricting Commission (defeating Proposition 27 with a 59 percent no vote) and gave the Commission the power to determine congressional districts as well (Proposition 25 passed with a 61 percent yes vote).

The Citizens Redistricting Commission completed its work in August 2011, and the impact of its work has been profound on a number of levels. As soon as the new district maps were finalized, lawsuits were filed against the commission's drawing of state Assembly and Senate district boundaries. A referendum was qualified for the November 2012 ballot that asked voters to prevent the revised state Senate boundaries from taking effect. Some of the most dramatic changes resulted from the redrawing of congressional district lines. Before the redrawing of district lines by this independent, bipartisan commission, very few house incumbents were ever defeated. They resided in safe districts with little or no reelection competition from challengers. The newly drawn political map has changed that. Some long-serving members of Congress have had their districts redrawn to where they are not guaranteed reelection. Some of the new districts are now electorally competitive, whereas others have been redrawn to where the voter demographics now favor the opposing political party. Take, for example, Representative David Drier, a Republican who chairs one of the most powerful committees in the House of Representatives. His congressional district was redrawn, and he would have faced a difficult reelection bid in this new district, which has more Democrats than Republicans. Rather than wage an expensive and likely losing reelection bid, he announced his retirement after serving 30 years in the House. One of the most watched congressional races in 2012 was between two well-known Democratic House members who found themselves in the same newly drawn congressional district in the San Fernando Valley. Representatives Howard Berman and Brad Sherman were forced to compete against each other in the primary election, which was nicknamed the "clash of the titans" or the "Erman Wars." They were the top two vote-getters and ran against each other again in November's general election, with Sherman winning over 60 percent of the vote. Overall, the new congressional district boundaries created by the commission resulted in 36 safe or leaning Democratic districts, 13 safe or leaning Republican districts, and 4 toss-up districts. In the November 2012 congressional elections, Democrats gained 4 more seats than they had before the redistricting, for a total of 38 seats compared to 15 Republican seats.

PROPOSITION 25: SIMPLE MAJORITY VOTE TO PASS BUDGET Proposition 25 changed the legislative vote requirement from two-thirds to pass the budget to a simple majority. In addition, all members of the legislature must permanently forfeit reimbursement for salary and expenses for every day the budget is late. California had not passed a state budget by the mandatory June 15 deadline in 23 years. Budget negotiations in 2010 extended 100 days past the deadline, just close enough to Election Day for it to be fresh in voters' minds. Californians passed Proposition 25, with a 55 percent affirmative vote. Supporters of this initiative were labor unions (especially teachers who received layoff notices when the budget was not passed on time), the League of Women Voters, groups representing retirees, and others who were able to devote resources to the "Yes on Prop. 25" campaign.

Since the passage of this proposition, the state budget has been passed on time and lawmakers were not forced to forfeit their pay or reimbursement for expenses. However, it is interesting to note that although lawmakers are technically in compliance with the law by meeting the June 15 deadline, they have fallen short of the intent of Proposition 25. As described by the *Sacramento Bee*, "While lawmakers sent Brown the main budget bill, Assembly Bill 1464, they did not send him the bulk of more than two dozen 'trailer' bills that actually explain how to cut programs and raise revenue"[12] to carry out the expenditures. Senate President Pro Tem

Darrell Steinberg (D-Sacramento) said that is because legislative Democrats and Brown still must resolve "small but important differences."

The 2012 Primary Election

The June 2012 primary was an interesting one. Usually, the major contest in the primary during a presidential election year is between the candidates competing for their party's nomination for the presidential race. But, as typically happens when states hold their primary late in the political season, Mitt Romney already had won enough delegates to secure his party's nomination, and President Obama had no Democratic challenger and was, by default, his party's nominee. Perhaps this explains why only 31 percent of California voters participated in this election with Los Angeles County having one of the lowest turnout rates, at less than 22 percent. There were two initiatives on the ballot, Propositions 28 and 29 and, as mandated by the passage of Proposition 14, this was the first statewide blanket primary using the new top-two vote-getter system. It was also the first election since the adoption of the newly drawn congressional and state legislative districts. The ballot looked different; all voters regardless of party affiliation were given the same ballot; the results were calculated differently; and some candidates found themselves running in new or very different districts. A very interesting election, indeed.

PROPOSITION 28: LIMITS ON LEGISLATORS' TERMS IN OFFICE; CONSTITUTIONAL AMENDMENT In 1990, voters passed Proposition 140, which implemented term limits for those elected to the California legislature. Legislators were limited to three 2-year terms in the Assembly and two 4-year terms in the Senate. This placed a 14-year limit of service in the California legislature. Proposition 28 is a constitutional amendment changing the term limit laws. This measure does two things: it reduces the total number of years an individual can serve in the legislature from 14 to 12 years, and it increases the number of years that can be served in either chamber. Six 2-year terms in the Assembly or three 4-year terms in the Senate are allowable. Individuals can still serve in both chambers but are not permitted to exceed the 12-year limit on service. Voters passed Proposition 28 by a rather wide margin of 61 to 39 percent. A major argument in support of this proposition was that allowing legislators to serve longer in the Assembly or Senate will reduce the habit of "flipping offices," by which individuals jump from one chamber to the other. Now, individuals can run for reelection for the same office and serve the maximum 12 years. Proponents also argued that serving 12 years in one chamber will allow members to pay more attention to the needs of their constituents and this focused attention might reduce the power of special-interest groups.

PROPOSITION 29: TAX ON CIGARETTES FOR CANCER RESEARCH Proposition 29 would raise the tax on a pack of cigarettes by $1. The revenue generated by the cigarette tax would be used for research on cancer and tobacco-related diseases. Antismoking advocates were frustrated that the legislature, in the past 30 years, had failed to pass more than 30 attempts to raise taxes on cigarettes. So, they decided to bypass an uncooperative legislature and go directly to the voters. Nearly $59 million was spent on ads supporting or opposing this proposition. The "no" campaign was very well funded thanks to the tobacco companies who contributed $44 million in hopes of defeating the measure. Groups supporting the measure, such as the American Cancer Society and the American Heart and Lung Associations, were able to raise only $12 million. The mayor of New York City, Michael Bloomberg, contributed $0.5 million to the yes campaign, and Lance Armstrong, well-known bicycling champion and cancer survivor, was its high-profile spokesperson. It was estimated that the cigarette tax would raise about $735 million annually. The *Los Angeles Times* did not endorse Proposition 29, and in its editorial stated a reason that seemed to resonate with voters: "It just doesn't make sense for the state to get into the medical research business to the tune of half a billion dollars a year when it has so many other important unmet needs."[13] Opponents argued that some of the revenue should be used to help California address its fiscal crisis. The budget crisis has resulted in the shortening of the school year, the closing of state parks, layoffs of teachers, and other difficult budgetary cuts in order to address the state's $16 billion deficit. Polls taken in March, before the onslaught of TV ads, showed 67 percent in support of the proposition. By election day, support had declined, and Proposition 29 failed to pass, with 50.8 percent voting no.[14]

The 2012 General Election: More Demographic and Ideological Shifts

THE PRESIDENTIAL RACE The outcome of the November 2012 presidential election looked similar to the 2008 presidential election, with young and minority voters favoring President Obama and older and white voters supporting Romney. Statewide, President Obama won 59 percent of the vote, slightly less than the 61 percent he won in 2008. He received 71 percent of the votes cast by 18–29-year-old Californians, which is close to the 76 percent he received in 2008. Of those 65 years of age and older, 48 percent voted for Obama, the same percentage as did in 2008. Other notable demographic results were based on race, marital status, and place of residence. Whereas only 45 percent of whites supported Obama, 79 percent of Asian Americans and 72 percent of Latinos voted for him. Marital status also made a difference in vote choice, with Obama receiving 67 percent of the votes of unmarried Californians and 51 percent of married voters. Voters living in urban areas voted to reelect the president by 65 percent compared to rural voters at 50 percent.

The 2012 election was interesting in terms of voter turnout rates. Although 5 percent fewer people voted in 2012 than in 2008, more young voters turned out to vote in 2012. The youth vote accounted for 20 percent of all votes cast in 2008 and 28 percent of all votes in 2012. That is a 40 percent increase in turnout among 18–29-year-old voters. Nationwide, there was a very slight increase in the youth vote, which grew from 17 percent in 2008 to 19 percent in 2012. What accounted for this dramatic increase in the turnout of young California voters?

According to Peter Levine, California's new online voter registration system (a description of which comes later in this chapter), made available shortly before the 2012 election, registered nearly 700,000 new voters, many of whom were young people.[15] Also, Proposition 30 (the initiative to fund higher education) was a salient issue for young voters. If the measure did not pass, college students were facing another round of tuition increases, crowded classes, and cuts in enrollment to the CSU and UC systems. This combination of an accessible online voter registration system and an important initiative impacting higher education motivated young voters.

CONGRESSIONAL RACES As mandated by the U.S. Constitution, all House members serve two-year terms in office. California has 53 House members, and in the November 2012 election, 11 new members were elected, the most new members in 20 years. Democrats won 38 of the 53 seats, and the number of seats held by Latinos also increased. These changes were a result of the recent remapping of House districts and changing demographics. A number of incumbent House members retired when their districts were redrawn after the 2010 Census, and they found themselves in competitive districts where their reelection was not assured. Prior to the 2012 election, only 1 House seat had changed between the parties during the last five Congressional elections. In 2012, Democratic candidates won 4 more House seats than they had in 2012. A second factor related to the strong showing by Democratic candidates is the growing number and clout of Latino voters, especially in southern California. As reported in the *Los Angeles Times*, "Voters in Riverside and San Bernardino counties elected three Democrats to Congress—two Latinos and a gay Asian American—after having sent only two Democrats to Washington in the last four decades."[16]

The Democratic Party had hopes of winning back control of the U.S. House of Representatives and needed to win 25 additional House seats around the country to reach this goal. California and its newly remapped competitive districts were seen as an opportunity for the Democratic Party to win some new seats. To that end, a whopping $53 million was spent on California House races by the political parties, interest groups, and individuals.[17]

CALIFORNIA LEGISLATIVE RACES The headline in the *Los Angeles Times* on November 8, 2012, read "Blue reign in Sacramento: Democrats' historic gains position them for unchecked power." Prior to the November 6 election Democrats had controlled both the state Assembly and the state Senate. They were expected to win enough seats to maintain their majority. Amazingly, the election not only allowed the Democratic Party to maintain their majority status but their electoral successes gave them *supermajority* status. Having a supermajority means that there are enough Democratic votes in each chamber to raise taxes without needing any votes from Republicans. Proposition 13, passed in 1978, mandates that legislation raising revenue must be passed by a two-thirds vote. As a result of this election, Democrats now control 70 percent of the seats in the state Senate and nearly 68 percent of the Assembly seats: a supermajority in both chambers. The last time a party had supermajority power was in 1933 when the Republicans were in charge. The Democrats last had this power in 1883.

PROPOSITIONS There were 11 measures on the November 2012 ballot. Voters were asked to weigh in on a number of issues ranging from increased taxes to fund educational programs to the repeal of the death penalty. A recordbreaking amount of money was spent on these campaigns. George Skelton, a *Los Angeles Times* columnist, wrote "It's almost unfathomable that $372 million was spent to promote or attack the 11 measures. To put it in perspective, that amount of money could pay for the annual tuitions of 31,000 undergrads at the University of California. The top 20 donors provided 69 percent of all initiative funding."[18] What follows is a description of some of the more high profile measures.

- *Proposition 30: Taxes to Fund Education versus Proposition 38: Tax to Fund Education and Early Childhood Programs*—These two competing propositions dealt with ways to raise revenue to fund education. Proposition 30, backed by the Governor, would temporarily raise the state sales tax for 4 years and increase taxes on the wealthy for 7 years. Proposition 38 would raise taxes on earnings for all Californians for 12 years. Since these were competing measures, if both passed, the one receiving the most votes would prevail. Proposition 30 passed with 55 percent of the vote. Proposition 38 received only 28 percent of the vote even though its sponsor spent $44 million of her own money on the measure. In addition, an outside political group from Arizona spent over $11 million to defeat both Propositions 30 and 38.

- *Proposition 32: Political Contributions by Payroll Deduction: Contributions to Candidates*—This measure would prohibit unions from using payroll deductions for political purposes. As expected, unions were opposed to this measure and poured over $50 million into campaigns to defeat this measure. They were ultimately victorious, as the initiative failed.

- *Proposition 34: Death Penalty*—This initiative statute would repeal the death penalty and replace it with life in prison without possibility of parole. Those currently on death row would have their sentences commuted to life imprisonment. Proponents of this measure spent over $8 million on this measure. Opponents spent a small fraction of that amount. The measure was defeated with a 52 percent "no" vote.

- *Proposition 36: Three Strikes Law: Repeat Felony Offenders*—This measure would revise the existing Three Strikes law to impose life sentences only when the offender is convicted of a new violent felony. Those previously convicted under this law for nonviolent felonies may have their sentences reviewed. The measure easily passed with 69 percent of the vote.

- *Proposition 37: Genetically Engineered Foods Labeling*—This proposition would require the labeling of food which is made from plants or animals containing genetically altered material. Agroscience opponents such as DuPont, Dow Agro, and Monsanto spent over $15 million to defeat this measure. The proposition failed, receiving only 48 percent of the vote.

Campaigning in California

California politics presents many challenges to those seeking elective office or the passage of a ballot measure. First, the immense size of the state means that state-wide propositions, candidates running for statewide office, and those running for federal offices, such as the U.S. Congress and the presidency, must plan campaigns that reach voters throughout the entire state. In fact, California has 13 distinct media markets, making it very expensive to communicate to its 38 million residents about politics. Second, California's population is very diverse, with many ethnicities, races, cultures, professions, occupations, and interests represented. Successful campaigns must find ways to effectively communicate their platform and messages to all of the 18 million registered voters in the state. And third, California has passed a number of political campaign reform acts in an attempt to regulate campaign spending and to provide public information on contributions and expenditures. These laws have proved beneficial to some and not as helpful to others.

Whatever the challenges of campaigning in California, one thing is certain: California's campaign politics are watched by the nation. California is a campaign trendsetter.

Money and Politics: California Style

As the record-breaking spending in the campaigns of 2010 showed, campaigning in California requires money, and lots of it. In fact, California is one of the most expensive states in which to conduct a political campaign. Table 4.2 compares the fund-raising of the 10 gubernatorial candidates who raised the most money in 2009–10. As you can see, amounts over $25 million landed a candidate on this list, and Whitman's $176 million is quite the anomaly. It is interesting to note that candidates running for governor in other large states, such as Texas and Florida, spent less than one-quarter of what Whitman spent on her campaign.

TABLE 4.2 ★ Fund-Raising by Top 10 Gubernatorial Candidates, 2009–10

CANDIDATE	STATE	PARTY	STATUS	TOTAL RAISED
Meg Whitman	California	Republican	Lost	176,684,951
Richard Scott	Florida	Republican	Won	67,421,942
Jerry Brown	California	Democrat	Won	40,556,608
Rick Perry	Texas	Republican	Won	39,328,540
Jon S. Corzine	New Jersey	Democrat	Lost	30,583,881
Tom Corbett	Pennsylvania	Republican	Won	28,561,987
Steve Poizner	California	Republican	Lost primary	26,660,173
Bill White	Texas	Democrat	Lost	26,291,532
Andrew Cuomo	New York	Democrat	Won	26,047,733
Dan Onorato	Pennsylvania	Democrat	Lost	25,116,397
			Total	487,253,745

SOURCE: *Follow the Money*, www.followthemoney.org/press/ReportView.phtml?r=487&ext=1#tableid3 (accessed 7/25/12).

Running for governor is not the only campaign that is costly. Running for the California legislature is also very expensive. Citing a Pew Center on the States study, Osorio notes that California is the costliest state in which to win a state Senate seat ($938,522). The least expensive state is North Dakota at $5,713. In Arizona it costs $36,696; in Wisconsin, $140,287; and in North Carolina, $234,031.[19] The prohibitive cost of campaigning in California restricts who can realistically run for office, another contributing factor to the state's governance challenges. Incumbents far outspend challengers, and incumbents' spending has increased over time while spending by challengers has not. On average, challengers spend only a fraction of what incumbents spend. This discrepancy helps to explain the high reelection rates of those elected to the California legislature. Some competitive races for the California legislature cost in excess of $1 million.

The following are some reasons that California campaigns are so expensive:

MEDIA-DOMINATED CAMPAIGNS Because of the size of the state and its 13 different media markets, candidates must spend enormous amounts of money producing political ads and buying the broadcast time to air them. During the 2003 gubernatorial recall election, it cost approximately $2 million a week to run political ads statewide.[20] In the 2006 governor's race, Schwarzenegger's campaign alone spent $9 million on TV ads in the short time span between July 1 and September 30. As is shown in Table 4.3, an astounding $138 million was spent in the November 2010 governor's race just on TV, cable, and radio airtime and production. This cost is in addition to the $57 million spent on the media during the primary campaign. As one media consultant described it, "There's a lot to be said for traditional politicking, kissing babies and shaking hands, but you have to get on TV to reach voters."[21]

POLITICAL CONSULTANTS Professional campaign managers and various consultants—media consultants, pollsters, fund-raisers, direct-mail experts, and voter mobilization professionals—cost money. Because of California's love of direct democracy, especially the initiative process, many well-known political consultants have established offices in California. There is money to be made in California politics, and candidates and supporters of ballot initiatives know that to win elections you must hire the costly services of top-notch political consultants.

WEAK POLITICAL PARTIES California has a comparatively weak political party system. The reform movement of Governor Hiram Johnson implemented many rules that reduced the organizational strength and clout of political parties within the state. Because of the weak party system in California, the party organizations are minimally involved in organizing and conducting the campaigns of candidates running for office. In addition, California has a relatively large number of registered voters who decline to affiliate with any political party and consider themselves politically independent. These unaffiliated, independent voters compose about 20 percent of all registered voters. The combination of weak party structure and less party attachment means that candidates themselves have to work harder—raise and spend more money—to reach these voters.

Campaign Finance Reform in California

To create more transparency in the electoral process and make public the flow of money in political campaigns, several campaign finance laws have been enacted in California over the past 100 years. Brief descriptions of the most recent laws follow.

TABLE 4.3 ★ Spending in California's Gubernatorial Election: How the Money Was Spent (spending through 10/16/10)

EXPENDITURE	WHITMAN ($)	BROWN ($)
Television and radio advertising	106,930,505.28	21,259,408.00
Campaign consultants	11,693,547.95	167,200.00
Campaign literature and mailings	10,582,303.93	2,532,801.36
Campaign workers' salaries	5,918,110.80	157,870.01
Radio airtime and production costs	5,472,228.17	0
TV or cable airtime and production costs	4,139,919.07	182,103.12
Information technology costs (Internet, e-mail)	3,177,977.76	23,345.51
Office expenses	2,321,340.46	132,023.40
Meetings and appearances	1,772,342.56	
Polling and survey research	1,410,893.36	93,728.30
Staff/spouse travel, lodging, and meals	1,260,616.12	2,618.30
Fundraising events	1,241,158.66	70,626.38
Candidate travel, lodging, and meals	950,890.17	12,071.76
Professional services (legal, accounting)	880,044.13	39,310.00
Postage, delivery, and messenger services	668,059.56	2,117.00
Campaign paraphernalia/miscellaneous	633,946.72	65,129.65
Phone banks	549,904.75	0
Contribution	252,500.00	0
Print ads	153,440.00	0
Voter registration	66,710.00	0
Civic donations	16,383.00	0
Returned contributions	0	99,364.14
Candidate filing/ballot fees	0	3,579.74
TOTAL	**160,092,822.45**	**24,843,296.67**

SOURCE: Campaign Watch, http://californiawatch.org/dailyreport/how-whitman-spent-160-million-6292.

1974: POLITICAL REFORM ACT In 1974 a group of reform-minded Californians crafted a statewide proposition that would require the most detailed campaign finance reporting in the nation. Proposition 9 appeared on the ballot during the Watergate scandal, and voters were ready for these reforms. Proposition 9 passed with an overwhelming majority of votes. This act created the Political Reform Division within the office of the secretary of state to administer and oversee key provisions of the law. A new independent state agency, the Fair Political Practices Commission, also was created for the purposes of interpreting and enforcing the act.

1988: PROPOSITION 73 In 1988 California voters overwhelmingly passed Proposition 73, which limited contributions to legislative and statewide candidates to $1,000 per donor, including individuals, labor unions, and corporations. A federal judge struck it down in 1990.

1996: PROPOSITION 208 Voters approved Proposition 208 by a 61 percent vote in 1996. Contributions to candidates from individuals, political parties, committees, corporations, unions, and political action committees (PACs) were limited. Spending limits also were imposed on candidates, although these were voluntary. Candidates who abide by the spending limits are allowed to collect larger contributions, whereas candidates who decide not to comply with the spending limits have lower contribution limits. Proposition 208 was being challenged in the courts when Proposition 34 was proposed and passed.

2000: PROPOSITION 34 Proposition 34 was placed on the ballot by the legislature. Spending limits were substantially increased, as were contribution limits. For example, under Proposition 208, individuals were permitted to contribute $1,000 to gubernatorial candidates—$500 if the candidate decided not to abide by the voluntary spending limits. Proposition 34 increased individual contributions to $21,200. Many reform-minded organizations that had supported Proposition 208, such as the League of Women Voters and Common Cause, were opposed to Proposition 34. They saw Proposition 34 as an attempt by the legislature to replace the more stringent Proposition 208 that was under review in the courts. Nevertheless, in November 2000, Proposition 34 passed with close to 60 percent of the popular vote and has replaced the provisions of Proposition 208.

Although it could be argued that Proposition 34 has resulted in less control of campaign financing, California does receive high marks when it comes to laws requiring public disclosure of campaign contributions and expenditures. The Campaign Disclosure Project conducted by UCLA in 2008 studied the campaign disclosure laws in all 50 states and ranked the states according to their campaign finance disclosure laws. California received a grade of A for its disclosure laws and ranked second in the nation; Washington State ranked first.

Campaign Contributions to Federal Candidates

As Table 4.4 illustrates, Californians are generous in their contributions to federal candidates and parties. In the 2012 election year, California ranked number one in the nation for its total amount of contributions. As the most populous state, California contributed nearly $300 million to federal candidates, with almost half of the contributions going to Democrats. Californians contributing to federal candidates and parties must abide by all federal campaign contribution laws, which limit the amount of money individuals and PACs may contribute to federal campaigns and parties.

TABLE 4.4 ★ Contributions by States to Federal Candidates in the 2012 Elections: The Top 10

RANK	STATE	TOTAL CONTRIBUTIONS ($)	TO DEMOCRATS (%)	TO REPUBLICANS (%)
1	California	297,098,839	49	37
2	Texas	242,325,942	18	51
3	District of Columbia	235,191,281	47	36
4	New York	222,137,461	48	34
5	Florida	150,831,110	29	57
6	Virginia	123,206,735	36	60
7	Illinois	104,654,233	42	45
8	Massachusetts	86,006,854	49	40
9	Pennsylvania	69,605,260	39	52
10	Nevada	62,123,429	11	22

Based on data released by the FEC on Oct 1, 2012 Totals include PAC and individual contributions to federal candidates and parties.

SOURCE: The Center for Responsive Politics, www.opensecrets.org.

Voting in California

Of California's nearly 39 million residents, approximately 17 million (72 percent) are registered to vote. To register to vote in the state of California you must meet the following criteria:

- You will be 18 years of age on or before Election Day.
- You are a citizen of the United States.
- You are a resident of California.
- You are not in prison or on parole for a felony conviction.
- You have not been judged by a court to be mentally incompetent to register and vote.

How You Can Register to Vote

Registering to vote is a simple process. Here are the options:

- Obtain a Voter Registration form from any U.S. post office or library. Forms are usually set out on counters. Fill out the preaddressed, stamped form and mail it in.

- Visit a California Department of Motor Vehicles office. The National Voter Registration Act of 1993 (also known as "Motor Voter") permits persons conducting business at a DMV office to register to vote or to update their voter registration information. In fact, since 1995 over 12.5 million people have registered or reregistered in conformance with this law.

- Register online. Go to the secretary of state's website, and use the new online voter registration system (registertovote.ca.gov). The process is very simple and completed entirely online if you have a California driver license or identification card. Since voter registration applications must be signed by the individual, the online system retrieves your signature from your driver license or ID card and electronically transfers it to your online registration application. This new system has proven to be so popular that of the record 1.4 million newly registered voters, over half of them registered online. California is one of only 15 states that offer electronic voter registration.

You will need to reregister to vote when

- you move;
- you change your name;
- you change your political party affiliation.

You must register at least 15 days before an election.

Who Votes in California?

Different groups vote at different rates. Figure 4.5 clearly illustrates this. Eight-five percent of white adults are registered to vote. The figure of African Americans is similar: a high registration rate of 82 percent. The number of Asian Americans voters has increased over the years with this group now having a 65 percent registration rate. Although Latino voter registration is increasing each year, only 38 percent of Latino adults are registered to vote. Over the decades the composition of the voting population has changed to where we have more minority voters. But overall the same pattern has held: whites vote at a higher rate than do Asian Americans and Latinos. Three factors help explain this discrepancy:

- *Eligibility*—A significant proportion of the Latino and Asian populations are not eligible to vote because they are not citizens.

- *Youth*—The Latino and Asian populations are both younger, and younger people are much less likely to vote than are older people.

- *Education*—The probability of voting increases significantly with a receipt of a college or advanced degree.

Research shows that if you control for these three factors, Latinos vote at rates comparable to whites.[22] The 2012 presidential election saw a decline in voter turnout. In 2008, 59 percent of eligible Californians turned out to vote. In 2012, nearly 2 million fewer adults voted, for a turnout rate of only 56 percent. As Figure 4.5 illustrates, the 2008 presidential election had the highest turnout rate since 1972. In analyzing voting statistics over the decades, political scientists have found that an exciting political

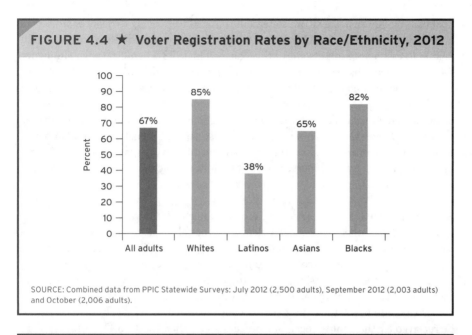

FIGURE 4.4 ★ Voter Registration Rates by Race/Ethnicity, 2012

SOURCE: Combined data from PPIC Statewide Surveys: July 2012 (2,500 adults), September 2012 (2,003 adults) and October (2,006 adults).

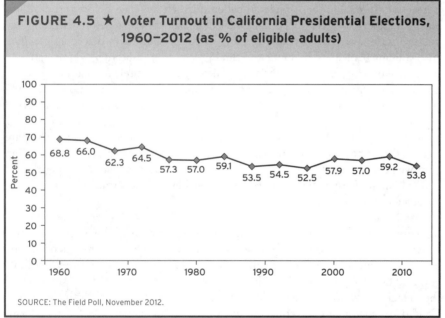

FIGURE 4.5 ★ Voter Turnout in California Presidential Elections, 1960–2012 (as % of eligible adults)

SOURCE: The Field Poll, November 2012.

race with charismatic candidates has the potential of encouraging more citizens to vote. Apparently, the 2008 presidential election was an example of this. Although more young adults and Latinos voted in 2012 than in 2008, the overall turnout rate declined, leading one to conclude that white voters did not come out to vote at the same rate as they had in 2008.

THE EVER-EXPANDING GROUP OF VOTERS: VOTING BY MAIL California now has very liberal vote-by-mail laws. Before 1978, a voter had to have a valid excuse for not voting at his or her designated polling place. You were eligible to receive a mail ballot if you signed a sworn statement that you were going to be away from your home precinct on Election Day or that you were infirm or bedridden and physically unable to cast a vote in person. All this changed in 1978 when California eliminated the requirement that voters present a valid excuse in order to vote absentee. Now, mail ballots are available to any voter who wants one. You are permitted to request a mail ballot for a particular election or you may request permanent vote-by-mail status, meaning that a mail ballot automatically will be sent to your home for each election.

From 1962 to 1978, the percentage of those voting by mail in primary and general elections averaged slightly under 4 percent of all votes cast. After the change in the law, voting by mail increased substantially. Of the over 10 million votes cast in November 2012, 51 percent were cast by mail ballots.

EARLY VOTING There is a special type of voter in California: the early voter. In fact, in the November 2012 general election, over half of all voters were early voters. There are several ways Californians can vote early (casting their votes before official Election Day). Most early voters voluntarily request vote-by-mail ballots. Virtually all of these voters are classified as "permanent vote-by-mail" voters, which means they have requested to automatically receive a vote-by-mail ballot for every election. Otherwise, one needs to request such a ballot for each election. These ballots must be received by the county registrar's office no later than Election Day, often making it necessary to mail in the completed ballot at least a few days before this deadline. And a number of voters fill out and mail their ballots weeks before Election Day because state law permits voting as early as twenty-nine days before an election. Also, a number of sparsely populated rural precincts in California, where staffing a traditional polling place makes little sense, have moved entirely to mail-in ballots for all voters. And in an attempt to lighten the volume of voters on Election Day, some counties have permitted "early voting," in which voters can go to various publicized locations (such as shopping malls, registrars' offices, civic centers) to cast their votes, again as early as twenty-nine days before an election. How does California compare to the other states? Well, twenty-nine states allow voting by mail without having an approved excuse, and California is one of only four states that allow for permanent voting by mail. Early voting, requiring no special excuse, is permitted by thirty-one other states and prohibited in fifteen states.

Many view these developments as positive changes, believing that by making voting more convenient, it will increase participation in this important civic activity. However, as with many reforms, there are unintended consequences. One major consequence is that early voting has had a direct impact on campaign strategy. Traditionally, political campaigns plan their strategy so that the weekend before the election is viewed as their last opportunity to communicate with the voters. Candidates spend an enormous amount of money in the last days of their campaigns trying to convince voters to vote for them or their initiative, or at least not to vote for their opponent or opposing side. During this time, they usually bombard viewers with TV ads and messages. Yet, in California, nearly half the voters have most likely already voted by mail or at an early-voting location. So candidates must now spend money earlier in the campaign cycle to reach these early voters before they cast their votes. As an example, State Senator Tom McClintock lost a race for state controller by less than one-half of a percentage point because he did not have enough money to buy TV ads until the final days of the campaign. Many absentee voters had already mailed in their ballots and did not see his campaign ads until after they had cast their vote. Earlier campaigning means more expensive campaigning in a state that is already prohibitively expensive.

HOW YOU CAN VOTE BY MAIL To apply for a mail ballot you may use the application form contained in the sample ballot mailed to your home before the election or you may apply in writing to your county elections official. Ballots can be returned by mail or in person to a polling place or elections office within your county on Election Day.

Modernizing Voting Machines

In the March 2002 election, voters approved Proposition 41, the Voting Modernization Bond Act. This act allocates $200 million to upgrade and modernize voting systems throughout the state. In the October 2003 recall election, three types of voting systems were used in California. Of California's 58 counties, 34 used some type of optical-scan ballot, 20 counties used some form of punch-card ballot, and only 4 counties used touch-screen ballots. After the controversial 2000 presidential election and the problem of punch-card voting in the state of Florida, the state legislature was concerned that if California did not replace its outmoded voting systems, the same calamity might strike here. Presumably, the remaining punch-card ballots and other outdated equipment will be replaced with more accurate voting machines.

What Reforms Are Needed?

It is fascinating to observe electoral politics in California. We live in a state where ballot initiatives are frequently used to make law, bypassing our duly elected representatives and the deliberative process of the legislature. In recent elections voters have been asked to weigh in on important policy matters such as same-sex marriage, abortion and parental notification, renewable energy, legalization of marijuana, the state budget process, tax issues, and the process by which state and congressional districts boundaries are determined. Many people question whether the initiative process is the best way to make public policy.

Although the legacy of the Progressives included the recall, referendum, and initiative, during the past few decades these tools of direct democracy have been taken over by special-interest groups. Some believe that reforms are needed to make it more difficult to recall an elected official or to bypass the legislative branch through the initiative process. Suggested reforms have included the prohibition of paid signature gatherers, judicial review of the proposed initiative before placement on the ballot and increasing the number of required signatures to qualify a recall or initiative for the ballot; for a recall to qualify for the ballot, California law requires the number of signatures to equal 12 percent of the votes cast in the last gubernatorial election, while other states require 25 to 40 percent.

Candidates and initiative campaigns spend enormous amounts of money in hopes of electoral victory. Proposition 34, the campaign finance initiative passed in 2000, substantially increased spending and contribution limits. California's limits on contributions to gubernatorial candidates are far more liberal than federal limits on contributions to presidential candidates. In fact, Californians can contribute more than 10 times the amount to gubernatorial candidates than they are permitted to contribute to presidential candidates ($25,900 versus $2,500). Many fear that these high limits will lead to spiraling campaign costs in a state where it is already expensive to campaign.

FOR FURTHER READING

Cain, B. "The California Recall." Interview, Brookings Institution, October 8, 2003.

Cain, Bruce E., and Elisabeth R. Gerber. *Voting at the Political Fault Line: California's Experiment with the Blanket Primary*. Berkeley: University of California Press, 2002.

California Fair Political Practices Commission. "Proposition 34." www.fppc.ca.gov. Accessed 7/25/12.

California Secretary of State's History of Political Reform Division, www.ss.ca.gov/elections. Accessed 7/25/12.

Douzet, Frédérick, Thad Kousser, and Kenneth P. Miller, eds. *The New Political Geography of California*. Berkeley, CA: Berkeley Public Policy Press, 2008.

Lubenow, Gerald C., ed. *California Votes: The 2002 Governor's Race and the Recall That Made History*. Berkeley, CA: Berkeley Public Policy Press, 2003.

Rarick, E. *California Votes: The 2010 Governor's Race*. Berkeley, CA: Institute of Governmental Studies, 2012.

Rasky, Susan. Introduction to "An Antipolitician, Anti-establishment Groundswell Elected the Candidate of Change." In *California Votes: The 2002 Governor's Race and the Recall That Made History*, ed. G. Lubenow.

UCLA School of Law, Center for Governmental Studies, and the California Voter Foundation. "Grading State Disclosure 2008: A Comprehensive, Comparative Study of Candidate Campaign Finance Disclosure Laws and Practices in the 50 States." 2008.

ON THE WEB

California Elections and Voter Information: www.sos.ca.gov/elections (accessed 7/25/12). The California Secretary of State offers a comprehensive guide to California elections, including information on how to register to vote.

California General Election Results: http://vote.sos.ca.gov (accessed 7/25/12). Detailed breakdowns of California election results.

The California Voter Foundation: http://calvoter.org (accessed 7/25/12).

Fair Political Practices Commission: www.fppc.ca.gov (accessed 7/25/12).

Join California: www.joincalifornia.com (accessed 7/25/12).

SUMMARY

I. Introduction
   A. There are several ways of voting in California.
      1. Voting by mail.
      2. Mail-in-ballot-only precincts.
      3. Early voting opportunities.
   B. Early voting has had an impact on candidates and campaign strategies.
      1. Traditional late spending on the weekend before Election Day is not as effective.
      2. Candidates must spend money earlier to communicate messages to early voters.

II. Political parties.
   A. Functions of parties.
   B. Two dominant parties: Democratic and Republican.
   C. Progressives' impact on parties was sizable.
      1. They disliked corrupt parties.
      2. They weakened the power of parties.
   D. Third parties struggle to compete.
      1. There are four certified minor parties.
      2. Third parties can impact the political agenda.

III. Party affiliation of California voters varies by region and demographics.
   A. The Democratic Party represents a plurality of voters.
   B. There has been an increase in the number of independents ("decline to state").
   C. Demographics and party affiliation.
      1. Whites tend to vote Republican; Latinos tend to vote Democratic.
      2. Younger voters comprise the highest percentage of Independents, compared to other age groups.
      3. Women tend to prefer the Democratic Party, as do non–U.S.-born citizens.
   D. Blue and red in California.
      1. Coastal and urban areas tend to be Democratic.
      2. Inland and rural areas tend to be Republican.

IV. Elections in California.
   A. There have been many changes in the primary system used.
      1. Closed primary until Proposition 198 in 1996.
      2. Blanket primary 1998–2000. *California Democratic Party v. Jones*: in 2002, California Supreme Court ruled blanket primary unconstitutional.
      3. Modified closed primary system, 2002–10: "decline to state" voters permitted to vote in party primaries if party grants permission.
      4. Proposition 14, passed in 2010, replaced modified closed primary system with another version of blanket primary.
   B. Presidential primaries.
      1. Changes in date of primaries.
      2. 2008 presidential primary: more clout for state unrealized.
   C. Initiative campaigns.
      1. Tool of special interests or grass-roots movements.
      2. 1912–2010: over 350 ballot initiatives.

3. How to qualify an initiative for ballot.
   a) Over 500,000 signatures of registered voters needed for initiative, and over 800,000 for constitutional amendment.
   b) Costs and other political resources needed to be successful.
D. 2003 gubernatorial recall election.
   1. Major players.
   2. Issues.
      a) Challenge by wealthy congressman Issa.
      b) Budget deficit.
      c) Enron and energy crisis; rolling blackouts.
E. 2006 election: Schwarzenegger's reelection. Unpopular governor beats weak challenger.
F. 2008 election: ideological and demographic shift to Democrat. Long-term or situational?
G. 2010 election: most expensive governor's race in history. Brown, former governor, beats wealthy billionaire. Initiatives pass that will have an important impact on state budget process and political representation and party politics.
H. 2012 election: results similar to 2008 but more of a Democratic shift. Democratic Party gains supermajority status in state legislature. Young voters' turnout increased but overall turnout declined. New online voter registration system. An important measure, Proposition 30, passed, increasing the state sales tax and taxes on the wealthy to fund education.

V. Campaigning in California is expensive.
   A. Money and politics.
      1. Record-breaking spending.
         a) Wealthy candidates.
         b) Personal fortunes.
      2. Media-dominated campaigns.
         3. Political consultants.
         4. Weak political parties.
   B. Campaign finance reform.
      1. 1974: Proposition 9, Political Reform Act.
         a) Created Political Reform Division.
         b) Established Fair Political Practices Commission.
      2. 1998: Proposition 73 limiting contributions passed; 1990 declared unconstitutional.
      3. 1996: Proposition 208 limiting contributions passed: Proposition 34 in 2000 invalidated Proposition 208.
      4. 2000: Proposition 34 passed increased spending and contribution limits.
      5. 2008: study of fifty states; California gets grade of A for campaign-finance disclosure laws.

VI. How to Register to vote in California.
   A. 39 million population, 17 million registered voters.
   B. How to register to vote: National Voter Registration Act (Motor Voter).
   C. Who votes?
      1. Whites overrepresented in voting population; Latinos and Asians underrepresented; African Americans vote in equal proportion to their percentage of population. Reasons: youth, eligibility, education.
      2. Voter turnout rates 1960–2012. November 2008 highest turnout since 1972.
      3. Absentee voter: over 50 percent of all registered voters.
      4. Modernizing voting machines: Proposition 41(2002) allocated $200 million to upgrade voting systems.

VII. Reforms may be necessary.
   A. Is initiative process best way to make policy?
   B. Need for campaign-finance reform to limit contributions and candidate spending.

PRACTICE QUIZ

1. In the 2012 general election, 18–29-year-olds voted at a higher rate than they did in 2008.
   a) true
   b) false
2. In running for the state legislature, winners and losers spend nearly the same amount of money on their political campaigns.
   a) true
   b) false
3. Political campaigns are so expensive in California because
   a) campaigns need to hire political consultants.
   b) campaigns need to spend a substantial amount of money on media advertising.
   c) political parties are not very involved in the planning and running of campaigns.
   d) all of the above

4. Special-interest groups often use the initiative process to achieve their policy objectives.
   a) true
   b) false
5. Which of the following is *not* true about Proposition 34, which deals with campaign finance:
   a) The League of Women Voters and Common Cause supported Proposition 34.
   b) Proposition 34 increased individual contributions to candidates to $21,200.
   c) Proposition 34 has resulted in less control on campaign financing.
   d) Proposition 34 replaced the stricter campaign finance law enacted through Proposition 208.
6. Of California's 38 million people, approximately how many are registered to vote?
   a) 30 million
   b) 25 million

c) 5 million

d) 18 million

7. Democrats are the plurality party in California.
   a) true
   b) false

8. The number of voters who decline to state a party affiliation at the time they register is declining.
   a) true
   b) false

9. Most of the Democratic counties encompass major urban areas, whereas most of the Republican counties are more rural in nature.
   a) true
   b) false

10. California presently operates under which of the following primary election systems:
    a) open primary
    b) blanket primary
    c) modified closed primary
    d) fully closed primary

CRITICAL-THINKING QUESTIONS

1. How might the cost of campaigning be reduced in California? Because incumbents spend much more money than challengers, what reforms might level the playing field of campaign politics?

2. What do you think have been the successes and failures of campaign finance laws in California? Do you think that additional reforms are needed? Why or why not?

3. How do you think the increase in unaffiliated voters and the increase in mail voters will affect campaigns and elections in the future?

4. Why do you think so many states follow California's lead in the areas of ballot propositions and recall efforts? Do you think this is a good or bad development? Explain why.

KEY TERMS

At this point you should have a general understanding of the following concepts and terms:

vote-by-mail ballot (p. 91)
ballot initiative (p. 74)
blanket primary (p. 71)
campaign finance reform (p. 86)
closed primary (p. 71)
decline to state (p. 71)
media-dominated campaign (p. 86)

media market (p. 75)
modified closed primary (p. 72)
Motor Voter (p. 90)
office block ballot (p. 61)
open primary (p. 71)
political consultant (p. 86)
political culture (p. 66)

political party affiliation (p. 60)
State Central Committees (p. 61)
Voting Modernization Bond Act (p. 93)
weak political parties (p. 86)
winner-take-all (p. 60)

The California Legislature

WHAT CALIFORNIA GOVERNMENT DOES AND WHY IT MATTERS

Consider the following activities of the legislature in 2011-12:

★ Passed legislation banning the sale of beer to which caffeine had been added. There had been incidents of severe intoxication from drinking this beverage.

★ Passed 1,884 bills. The governor vetoed 248 of them. No veto was overridden.

★ The Senate refused to confirm the reappointment of a member of the California State University Board of Trustees because he had supported a 12 percent increase in student fees while also supporting salaries in excess of $300,000 for campus presidents.

★ Passed legislation giving children age 12 and older the authority to get medical care for prevention of sexually transmitted diseases without parental consent.

★ Passed legislation making it illegal to sell live animals on any public right of way.

★ Passed a budget for the first time since the two-thirds vote requirement for budgets had been eliminated. Governor Brown vetoed the first attempt, saying it was not an honest budget.

Californians give little if any thought to their legislature. We have a general sense that it is made up of a group of elected individuals who write laws. Beyond that, our knowledge fades, although we believe strongly that the legislature does not work well. In fact, when the Field Poll has asked whether Californians approve of the job that the state legislature is doing overall in 20 different surveys since 2002, 40 percent or more of Californians have responded positively only once. In May 2010, only 16 percent approved, while 72 percent did not approve. At the same time, almost twice that number approved of the job that the U.S. Congress was doing.

Our lack of knowledge is related to the minimal coverage that legislatures receive in the media. The media find it difficult to cover institutions with multiple members who are doing many different things and have no single voice. They find it much easier to focus on a chief executive who has a press office to provide news-ready stories. In addition, media coverage of state politics is minimal. Although most people get their news from television, before the election of Governor Schwarzenegger no Los Angeles television station had a Sacramento bureau. But even the interest in a movie-star governor did not carry over to the legislature, and since his departure media interest in Sacramento in general has sharply declined.

Our dissatisfaction with the legislative process is related to the dysfunctional condition of our state. While the legislature is not the principal cause of this state of affairs, it is the most public arena in which the consequences are observed. Term limits and voting rules make it difficult for the legislature to function well, leading to gridlock and highly partisan disputes. Americans dislike politics in general and tend to believe that we should all be able to work together to achieve our common goals. Bipartisanship has a lot of appeal, but at the same time citizens want their individual interests forcefully represented against competing interests. We have conflicting expectations of legislatures, and the legislatures' attempts to balance these expectations often contribute to our dissatisfaction. The nineteenth-century German statesman Otto von Bismarck may well have been correct in suggesting that the making of laws, like the making of sausages, should not be observed.

In reality, legislatures, although poorly understood, play a critical role in our government. The framers of the national constitution, fearing a powerful executive, viewed Congress as the first branch of government and gave it the most significant and most explicit powers, including control of money and the writing of all laws. The fact that the president gets the most attention in the media today and that some congressional powers have gravitated to the president does not negate the fact that Congress is a very powerful body.

Most state legislatures have been modeled on the U.S. Congress in structure, process, and functions, and this is true in California, although there are some significant differences, explained later. Ours is a bicameral legislature (a two-house legislature) consisting of the 40-member Senate (sometimes called the upper house) and 80-member Assembly. Like Congress, members of both bodies represent geographically based districts and are elected by winner-take-all elections. As in Congress, bills become law by being approved by both houses and signed by the chief executive. The bulk of the work of each house is done in committees. Each house is organized by party and party leaders determine committee membership. Compared to Congress in Washington, in the state legislature seniority is much less important in determining committee memberships and chairs.

The recent history of the California legislature has been remarkable in its extremes. In the 1960s the legislature was changed from an often corrupt, amateur body to a well-paid, well-staffed professional legislature that was the envy of other states. It was regarded by many as the best state legislature in the country. This was accomplished under the leadership of the Assembly Speaker Jesse Unruh. Yet in 1990 the voters of California passed Proposition 140, imposing term limits on the legislature. Although this did not change the basic structure of the legislature, it did change the effectiveness and power of the legislature by reducing the time that legislators are permitted to serve and by reducing the size of the staff that makes legislative work possible.

Functions

Legislatures have two principal functions: representation and policy making. The tensions between these make it difficult for a legislature to perform as citizens might wish.

Representation

The legislature is the principal representative institution in our society, although the executive branch and interest groups also lay claim to this function. It is the duty of legislators (also called members, representatives, or assemblypersons or senators) to represent the voters and other residents (collectively known as constituents) within their districts, as well as the dominant interests within these districts. This is easier said than done. In the first place, the term *representation* has many meanings. Here we will simplify it to mean that our representative is our counterpart in Sacramento and that he or she will do what we would do were we there, especially when it comes to influencing legislation or voting. Of course, there are many of us, and we all do not see things the same way. Some of us are wealthy and educated; others, destitute. Some see government as the means to solve society's problems; others see government as the main problem.

Furthermore, representatives face many different and difficult issues—same-sex marriages, lower taxes versus improved services, new highways versus preservation of neighborhoods, more spending on prisons versus lower college tuition. We do not communicate with our representatives very well, and our wishes may have to be intuited rather than known. Under the best of circumstances, knowing what you should do for 450,000 or 900,000 constituents is difficult. Beyond that is the question of whether you should give your constituents what they want—maybe lower taxes and less regulation—or what they need—perhaps higher taxes and improved infrastructure. Political scientists talk about two polar forms of representation: the delegate who tries to find out what constituents want and does only that and the trustee who believes he or she is elected to use his or her own best judgment to do what is right. Delegates would most often try to provide what constituents want, whereas trustees would be more inclined to provide for their districts' needs as they perceive them. Both orientations involve difficulties because it is often impossible to know what constituents want, and determining district needs is often influenced by ideology or other subjective factors.

Some legislators identify closely with a particular group and view themselves as representatives of that group: women, ethnic minorities, sexual preference groups. There are others who want to get the representatives' ears: party leaders, the governor, campaign contributors, organized special interests. And those groups are better organized and have better access than average constituents. Large campaign contributors do not give their donations without expecting something in return, so the legislator is unable to ignore them. Ultimately it is the constituents who have the vote, but even this principle has been weakened in recent years because of big money, partisan gerrymandered districts, and term limits. Rarely do voters have a realistic chance to keep the good representatives and "throw the rascals out."

In addition to representing our policy views, representatives try to look out for us when we have specific problems with government—not getting an entitlement check, being treated unfairly by an inspector, worrying that a new highway will be built through our property, being opposed to liquor being sold near our

BOX 5.1 | Keep on Top, Keep in Touch

It is easy to stay on top of what is happening in the legislature by using the Internet. Both houses have Web pages. The Senate page is www.sen.ca.gov; the Assembly page is www.assembly.ca.gov. From these sites you can find out about the legislative process and about the status of individual bills. You can also find out how to stay in touch with your legislators. If you type in your address, the site will tell you who your legislators are and how you can contact them. Another useful site is that of the Legislative Counsel: www.leginfo.ca.gov.

State legislators are surprisingly accessible, especially in the district. If you have an issue for which you want to contact your legislator, be informed, call for an appointment, and be brief and forthright. Do not threaten. Information is helpful, and a good anecdote is always useful! Thoughtful letters are also helpful. E-mail is used too much, and staff can recognize form mail as soon as it is opened.

Of course, working through a lobby is also effective, and you may belong to an organization that lobbies; environmental groups, unions, and student organizations are just a few of many that write, track, and try to influence legislation in their area of concern.

kids' school. This ombudsman function is called "constituency service" or "casework," and it involves intervening with the bureaucracy to solve specific problems. Representatives also try to get favorable treatment for economic interests in their districts—a restaurant owner wants a liquor license that he or she believes is being unfairly denied, or a construction company wants to build more buildings at the local state university. Representatives will also take stands on issues that are largely symbolic but still important to their constituents, such as flag burning or prayer in schools.

Another important part of representation is being available to constituents. Representatives spend much of their time in their districts, attending many functions; speaking to many groups to educate them about the activities of government; and listening to many constituents in their offices. Constituents and representatives of organized groups also visit with them in Sacramento.

Policy Making

The representatives described earlier come together to make policy, most obviously through the complex process of making laws, which involves writing bills, holding committee hearings, conducting legislative debates, and adding amendments.

Policy making also involves seeing that legislation is carried out by the bureaucracy as the legislature intended and looking out for potential problems in the implementation of policy. This function, called oversight, is carried out through a variety of means, including legislative hearings, staff follow-up on constituents' concerns, budgetary hearings, and confirmation hearings. Congressional hearings on the role of federal regulation in the Gulf of Mexico oil spill is an excellent example of this.

The job of the legislator involves both representing the district and making policy. It also involves fund-raising. Legislators live in two worlds, Sacramento and their districts, and they have offices in both places. Mail and phone messages are answered from both places. In the districts they listen to the concerns of their constituents on the one hand, and on the other they tell these constituents about government activities, policy, and politics. In Sacramento they also interact with those constituents who travel to the capital as well as representatives of interest groups. In addition, they work on policy, mostly in committee. Fund-raising takes place largely in the state capital, often involving important interest groups. Most often legislators are in Sacramento Monday through midday Thursday and return to the district for the remainder of the week; however, this varies with the time of the year. Special events often bring them back to their districts. It is necessary to keep a high profile in the district to discourage potential election opponents. The worst charge that can be brought against legislators is that they are ignoring their districts.

Members and Districts

Unlike Congress, in which each state has two seats in the Senate regardless of population, both houses of the California legislature are apportioned by population. The state is divided into 80 Assembly districts and 40 state Senate districts. In each of these districts a single representative is elected. This means that representatives will be paying attention to local interests because local voters determine who gets to go and stay in Sacramento. As a former speaker of the U.S. House of Representatives once said, "All politics is local." Local interests often take precedence over statewide interests. Our legislative system is designed to favor local interests (and interests with money).

Legislative elections are winner-take-all elections, which means that minor or third parties are generally excluded from the legislature, even though they may have substantial support statewide. If they cannot muster the most votes in any one district, they will not have a representative in Sacramento.

Most members, if they have any previous elective experience, have served on school boards, city councils, or county boards of supervisors. Many are self-selected. Others are tapped by party leaders or interests who see them as viable.

Campaigns can easily cost half a million dollars and campaign expenditures are likely to be much higher in the future given the Supreme Court ruling in *Citizens United* (see Chapter 3), which rejected corporate spending limits, and given that the California Citizens Redistricting Commission has created more competitive legislative districts. Fund-raising is one of the big obstacles to winning an election. The nature of California and the size of the districts make winning elections by old-fashioned precinct work unlikely. Use of electronic media is also impractical in the larger media markets because of cost. Most candidates have campaign consultants and engage in polling and targeted distribution of literature.

Because of the relatively small size of the legislature, the districts are among the largest in the country. Senate districts have over 900,000 constituents, Assembly districts over 450,000. Historically, district lines were drawn by the legislature, often leading to charges of gerrymandering, a term dating to the early 1800s, when Massachusetts Governor Elbridge Gerry oversaw a redistricting that benefited his party and resulted in district lines that resembled, in a famous cartoon of the day, a salamander. *To gerrymander* means to draw district lines in a manner that favors one party over another, generally by packing most of the opponent's voters into a few districts and spreading the remainder thinly over the remaining districts. The courts have generally accepted this practice, saying only that districts must be equal in population and must not be drawn to diminish the voting strength of any minority.

Redistricting is done following each census and until 2012 had to pass both houses and be signed by the governor, like any other piece of legislation. The Democrats controlled both houses and the governor's office after the 2000 census but chose to preserve the status quo, which maintained a majority with which they were comfortable. Because the incumbent Republicans were not in danger of losing their seats, they did not challenge the scheme in court. The result was that the vast majority of seats in the legislature were safe seats for one party or the other, and an incumbent was unlikely to be defeated in the general election.

Most action, therefore, took place in the primaries, but since the advent of term limits, incumbents rarely faced a serious challenge. Knowing that an incumbent assemblyperson would be out of office in no more than six years, the astute challenger waited for that vacancy to occur rather than engaging in an expensive, divisive challenge. If one believes that the real power of voters is to throw the rascals out, then term limits had an unintended consequence of insuring that that was unlikely to happen. The legislature was more immune from direct electoral challenge than ever before.

However, as of 2012, two steps have been taken that entirely change the situation described in the previous paragraphs, which created safe districts with highly partisan incumbents. Whether they will change the ultimate outcome remains to be seen. As a result of their continued frustration with the legislature—and not recognizing their own contributions to the problem by establishing term limits—the voters approved two measures, Proposition 11 in November 2008 and Proposition 14 in June 2010, that should impact who gets elected to the legislature. Proposition 11 takes the task of drawing legislative districts away from the legislature and places it with a 15-person commission (see Chapter 1). This committee created new districts that have a closer partisan balance and have at times pitted incumbents of the same party against one another. The expectation is that this will result in fewer seats that are safe for one party and that would previously have been filled by highly ideological partisans, but the true effect of Proposition 11 will not be known until the voting patterns of the newly elected legislature become clearer over the course of several years.

Proposition 14 carried this theme forward by eliminating partisan primaries and, perhaps, general elections. It provided for an open primary in which all candidates run and all voters take part. Voters vote in the primary or preliminary election for the candidate of their choice for each office from a single list of all candidates from every party, and the top two candidates go on to the November election, which is like a runoff. The expectation here is that, even if both of these candidates are in the same party, the more moderate candidate will win by appealing to voters in the minority party (see Chapter 4). If there are only two candidates in the first election they will have to run against each other for a second time. While this may seem absurd, the electorate in November is almost always larger (and therefore less Republican) than in June, which could affect the outcome. In 2012, the 65th Assembly District in Orange County was an excellent example of an incumbent—Republican in this case—challenged by a single opponent, a Democrat. They ran against each other in June and the Republican incumbent won with over 58 percent of the vote. In the run-off in November the Democratic challenger won with about 52 percent of the vote, and this was a key seat in the Democrats gaining a two-thirds majority in the Assembly. Many factors were at work in the district, not the least of which was that about 50,000 people voted in June while over 120,000 voted in November.

The hope was that the combination of Propositions 11 and 14 would result in legislators being elected who are more moderate and more willing to engage in bipartisan compromise, but it is too early for us to feel confident that this will occur. However, these measures did result in at least one huge change in 2012: the Democrats gained a two-thirds majority in both houses, meaning they can act on tax measures without any Republican votes. Still, many of these new legislators are from marginal seats (such as the 65th in Orange County and 32nd in Bakersfield) and may be reluctant to take bold action which might endanger their chances for reelection in two years when—because it is not a presidential election and therefore turnout will be lower—most likely fewer Democrats will vote. And the theory is that new legislators will in general be more moderate. A new chapter in California politics has been started, and no one knows what will be written in it.

Organization

Leadership

The leader of the Assembly is the speaker, and he or she has a remarkable array of powers, although these are now diminished because no member of the Assembly occupies his or her position for a long period of time. In an attempt to increase the power of the speaker by increasing his or her time in the position, in 2003 and again in 2009 the Democrats elected a first-term legislator to the speakership. The Assembly speaker's powers are considerably more extensive than the Speaker of the U.S. House of Representatives. Most notable of these powers—which begin with control over parking spaces and offices—is the almost complete control over establishing committees, assigning members to serve on committees, and removing them if the speaker chooses. Because the bulk of legislative work is done in committee, members are dependent on the speaker if they are to have any meaningful role in the legislature. The speaker is also the presiding officer when the full Assembly meets and in this role controls debate. If the speaker does not personally preside he or she designates the person who does. The speaker also appoints the majority floor leader, who assists in running legislative sessions.

It is difficult to overestimate the power of the speaker. This power is used to move bills and can be used to help supporters and hurt opponents. It is also used to raise money, which in turn is used to solidify support. Members find it advantageous to cooperate with the speaker. The speaker is elected by the entire membership of the Assembly, but in most cases the outcome is determined in advance by the majority party caucus, which consists of all of the members of the majority party meeting together. Only when the majority is split does the full Assembly vote become significant.

The minority caucus elects the Assembly minority leader, who is the public voice of the minority party and who works with the speaker to determine minority party assignments on committees. The speaker, however, has the final say.

The other important element of the leadership is the Assembly Rules Committee, which is made up of nine members, four elected by each caucus plus a chair appointed by the speaker. Its responsibilities include hiring staff and assigning bills to committees and reviewing legislative rules. Rarely does this committee operate independently of the speaker's wishes.

The organization of the Senate is similar, but the leader, the president pro tempore, does not have the absolute power that the Assembly speaker does. Many of the speaker's powers in the Assembly rest with the Rules Committee in the Senate. Yet in recent years the president pro tempore—most notably John Burton—has become the most influential legislator, largely because of the impact of term limits, which have created an Assembly that is far less experienced than the Senate. Assembly members have a maximum of 6 years' experience, and their leaders may have only 1 or 2 years' experience. Senators have often been in the Assembly first and then have an additional 8 years to serve. By the time a senator becomes a Senate leader, he or she may have had 10 or 12 years' experience in Sacramento. John Burton, who may be the last of his breed, had far more experience than that, including experience in the U.S. Congress.

Committees

The bulk of legislative work is done in committees. Committees allow for greater specialization, greater expertise of those involved, and greater attention to detail. In 2009–10 there were 30 standing or permanent committees in the Assembly and 22 in the Senate (see Table 5.1). Each member sits on several standing committees. In addition to standing committees, there are many select committees that exist to study specific issues, and joint committees to look at issues that concern both houses. Members may serve on a dozen or more of these less important committees.

Committees are at the heart of groups of players often referred to as issue networks. These networks consist of committee members and staff, senior members of the respective executive branch agency, and interest groups concerned with issues in a committee's jurisdiction. The bulk of policy details are worked out in these networks. Lobbyists and bureaucrats tend to be specialists. They generally spend their careers in a single subject area and are experts in this area. It would be unusual for someone who has spent a career in transportation to move to education. Previously, legislators would spend their careers in specific issue areas as well. Term limits have changed that, or rather have shortened the length of careers. While policy is still worked out in these networks, power has shifted to those with greater permanency, experience, and expertise—namely, lobbyists and bureaucrats. The less experienced and less knowledgeable legislator is now more dependent than before on these individuals for policy details. Experienced staff can help, but often staff members are no more experienced than legislators.

Staff

Before Proposition 140, the staff of the California legislature was the best in the nation. The proposition required a staff cut of 40 percent and resulted in layoffs and the departure of many of the best staffers, especially the experts on which the committees relied. Staff is still a significant factor in the legislature, and over the years, it has inched back toward its previous size.

Without staff, the legislature cannot effectively do its job. Staff is crucial in both the policy-making and representative functions of the legislature. All legislators have staff in both their Sacramento and district offices to help with constituency contacts, including casework, scheduling appearances, and answering mail and phone calls from constituents. In addition, committees have staff, called consultants,

TABLE 5.1 ★ Standing Committees of the California Legislature, 2009–10

STATE SENATE

Agriculture	Judiciary
Appropriations	Labor and Industrial Relations
Banking, Finance, and Insurance	Legislative Ethics
Budget and Fiscal Review	Natural Resources and Water
Business, Professions and Economic Development	Public Employment and Retirement
Education	Public Safety
Elections, Reapportionment, and Constitutional Amendments	Rules
Energy, Utilities, and Communications	Transportation and Housing
Environmental Quality	Veterans Affairs
Governance and Finance	
Governmental Organization	
Health	
Human Services	
Insurance	

ASSEMBLY

Committee on Accountability and Administrative Review	Committee on Insurance
Committee on Aging and Long-Term Care	Committee on Jobs, Economic Development, and the Economy
Committee on Agriculture	Committee on Judiciary
Committee on Appropriations	Committee on Labor and Employment
Committee on Arts, Entertainment, Sports, Tourism, and Internet Media	Committee on Local Government
Committee on Banking and Finance	Committee on Natural Resources
Committee on Budget	Committee on Public Employees, Retirement and Social Security
Committee on Business and Professions	Committee on Public Safety
Committee on Education	Committee on Revenue and Taxation
Committee on Elections and Redistricting	Committee on Rules
Committee on Environmental Safety and Toxic Materials	Committee on Transportation
Committee on Governmental Organization	Committee on Utilities and Commerce
Committee on Health	Committee on Veterans Affairs
Committee on Higher Education	Committee on Water, Parks, and Wildlife
Committee on Housing and Community Development	
Committee on Human Services	

to help with the policy work of that committee, and consultants are critical components of the issue networks. Each legislator is allotted an office budget for staffing. Additional staff depends on having a committee leadership role or on the generosity of the party leadership. In addition, the house leaders and caucuses have staff that may number more than 150 for the majority. This staff helps with bill analysis for individual members and public relations for individual members as well as the party.

There are over 2,000 legislative aides. It is not unusual for majority legislators to have 13 or 14 staff members. Minority members may have only 4 or 5. While most aides are modestly paid, some—especially highly valued committee consultants—make over $150,000. The total personnel budget for legislative workers in 2009 was

$129.3 million. The median salary for a staff member in the Assembly was about $51,000 and in the Senate, $61,000. These aides are supplemented with members of the prestigious Assembly and Senate Fellows program and many college interns.

There are three important and well-regarded groups of staff who are nonpartisan and work for the entire legislature. The first is the Legislative Analyst's Office, which analyzes budget proposals and the fiscal impact of ballot propositions. The second is the Legislative Counsel, which helps write bills, analyze ballot propositions, and provide legal advice. The third is the State Auditor's Office, which handles management and fiscal audits of the executive branch.

The Legislative Process

There are three types of items that may pass the legislature: bills, which if successful become laws; constitutional amendments, which require a two-thirds vote of both houses and a referendum by the voters; and resolutions, which are largely symbolic expressions of opinion. For the remainder of this section we are concerned primarily with bills.

Bills are introduced only by legislators, even if the content was originally proposed by someone as politically important as the governor. Indeed, bills are often not written by the person who introduces them. Many bills may be written by, or in conjunction with, lobbyists, and the nonpartisan Legislative Counsel's office may help in drafting language. Senators are limited to introducing 65 bills in a two-year session, whereas Assembly members may introduce only 30. Bills may be introduced for a variety of reasons, such as impressing constituents or paying off a political favor, and most go nowhere. In the 2009–10 legislative session, 1,495 bills were introduced in the Senate and 2,799 in the Assembly. Of these, 1,922 reached the governor's desk and 1,385 became laws. In the 2011–12 legislative session, 1,884 bills passed the legislature and reached the governor's desk. He signed 1,636 of them, vetoing 248, some of which were strongly supported by his allies. This is far fewer than was common 20 years ago. In 1989 and 1990, 3,174 new laws were enacted. Bills must pass both houses with identical language before they are forwarded to the governor for his or her signature.

Once bills are introduced, the rules committee of the appropriate house assigns the bill to a standing committee or perhaps two committees, depending on their content. The bill is also numbered and printed. Committees cannot act on a bill until it has been in print for 30 days to allow comment from interested parties. Committees hold hearings, scrutinize the language carefully to make sure that it says what members intend, add amendments, and pass or reject bills. An absolute majority of the committee must vote favorably to report a bill out. If a bill is reported out of committee, it goes to the floor for discussion by the entire house. Amendments may be added at this time. Amendments require only a majority vote. Bill passage requires an absolute majority (41 in the Assembly, 21 in the Senate). Once a bill has passed one house, it goes to the other house for similar consideration. If a bill is successful in both houses and the wording is the same, it goes to the governor for his or her signature. If the governor vetoes a bill, then it requires a two-thirds vote in each house to override the veto.

Most likely, a bill passing both houses will have different wording. In this case one house may acquiesce to the wording of the other house or a conference committee will be established to work out the differences. A conference committee

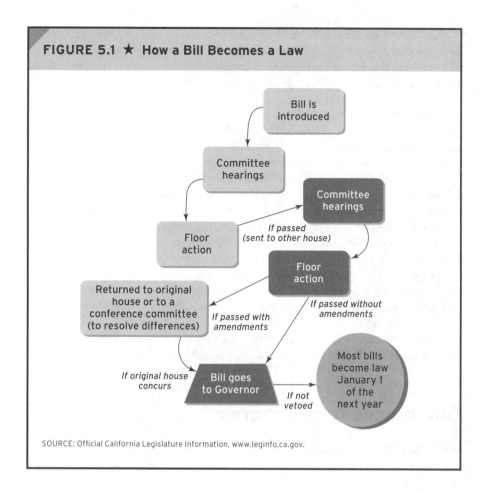

FIGURE 5.1 ★ How a Bill Becomes a Law

Bill is introduced

Committee hearings

Floor action

If passed (sent to other house)

Committee hearings

Floor action

If passed without amendments

Returned to original house or to a conference committee (to resolve differences)

If passed with amendments

If original house concurs

Bill goes to Governor

If not vetoed

Most bills become law January 1 of the next year

SOURCE: Official California Legislature Information, www.leginfo.ca.gov.

is a joint committee consisting of three members from each body. The Assembly members are appointed by the speaker, and Senate members are appointed by the Senate Rules Committee. They suggest compromise language that must pass both houses. If this attempt fails, two additional attempts may be made before the bill is put to rest.

This is the textbook approach. However, much legislation is able to shortcut some of these steps, especially near the end of a legislative session, when bills tumble over one another and deals are made in back rooms in a rush to adjourn. Many bills reappear as amendments to other bills, with even less public attention than in the normal process. At this time, the party leaders become more important because they are able to grease the skids for compromises and logrolling. (Logrolling is vote trading, the process by which members exchange votes—the classic "You vote for my bill, and I will vote for yours.")

A common end-of-session legislative tactic is to hijack a bill and then "gut and amend" it. A bill that started out to deal with state courts could suddenly reappear—with no public notice or hearings—as a bill offering in-state tuition to undocumented immigrants. Or take 2001 bill AB 1389 (insiders always refer to bills by numbers, like AB 1389 or SB 1785). This bill started out dealing with squid fishing and came back as a bill dealing with transferring public lands for development of a cruise ship terminal in San Francisco.[1]

End-of-session periods in Sacramento reflect quintessential American politics: a system that favors insiders, corporations, and big money. And while this goes on all year long, these back-room strategies work best when time is compressed and the media and other outsiders cannot follow what is going on or, if they can, they cannot do anything about it.

At the end of the session there is much pressure to get things done. As noted earlier, 988 bills passed in 2011 and many others were in play. Insiders and lobbyists know what is going on, and their attention is focused on a single bill or a small number of bills that are important to their clients. Large corporations and other interest groups hire full-time lobbyists and lawyers, sometimes a full platoon of them, to follow the important bills, develop the strategy, and take the necessary actions to ensure the desired outcome. All of which can be written off as business expenses.

These insiders work out deals behind the proverbial closed doors and provisions to bills are added and removed at the last minute. Often the junior members voting on the floor have no idea of what they are voting on.

Before the legislature was term-limited, members were extremely well-versed about their policy interests and had long memories about what tricks lobbyists and other legislators had tried to pull in previous sessions, which meant that it was more difficult to make unnoticed changes in legislation which would benefit a special interest. There is no such institutional memory now among legislators. The experience and skills rest mostly with lobbyists and agency representatives.

Differences from Congress

While the California legislature is modeled closely on the national legislature, there are important differences, and collectively, these make the California legislature a weaker body.

Term Limits

Unlike members of Congress, who can serve as long as they are reelected, California legislators are limited to three two-year terms in the Assembly and two four-year terms in the Senate. Term limits were enacted by the passage of Proposition 140 in 1990. There were numerous reasons for the success of this proposition. In part it was a reaction to the highly effective Assembly Speaker Willie Brown, a flamboyant politician who was immensely unpopular with conservative voters. In part it was a reaction against divided government (a Republican governor and a Democratic legislature) and gridlock. Partly it was a reaction against the large fund-raising efforts of incumbents. Partly it was a reflection of a national trend against entrenched incumbents. Finally, it was a belief among some Republicans that term limits would be a way to get rid of the Democratic majority. The effort has reduced the ability of the legislature to act effectively while neither reducing the Democratic majority nor eliminating gridlock.

Item Veto

In Washington, the president has to sign or reject bills passed by Congress in their entirety. He cannot approve parts that he likes and reject parts that he dislikes.

In California, as in most states, the governor has a line-item veto on appropriations, including those in the budget. This power allows the governor to reduce or eliminate a specific spending item, although he cannot increase items. This means that the legislature cannot force the governor's hand by including an item that he opposes in a larger bill, most of which he supports.

Apportionment and District Size

Both houses of the California legislature are apportioned by population, unlike Congress, in which the Constitution allots two senators to each state, regardless of size. Wyoming, with about the same number of residents as Long Beach, has the same number of senators as California, which is about 70 times larger. Because California is so populous (about 37 million people) and because its legislature is relatively small, its legislative districts are among the largest in the nation. Senate districts have over 900,000 constituents, while Assembly districts contain over 450,000 residents. New Hampshire, with 400 members in its lower house, has one representative for about every 3,000 residents. While its representatives are very accessible and elections are not expensive, most cannot wield very much influence in their very large chamber. California senators, unlike any other legislative body, represent more constituents than members of Congress and more than the U.S. senators of seven states. This means that they are considerably less accessible than their counterparts in other states and that their elections are considerably more expensive.

The fact that both houses are apportioned by population has led some informed observers to suggest that a unicameral legislature of 120 members would make more sense. This would result in smaller districts and increased accessibility among legislators.

Media Visibility

In Washington the president dominates the news. The media interpret the national government's actions by focusing on the president. Members of Congress are generally used to give more depth to a presidential story. Most often, these are party leaders, committee chairs, or the occasional legislator who has managed to make a name for himself or herself on a given issue.

The same is true in Sacramento, but the difference is that the statewide media, especially television, rarely cover news in Sacramento. Only the four party leaders receive air time, and because they hold their positions for so few years, the public has difficulty knowing who they are. Consequently, most of what happens in Sacramento occurs out of the spotlight.

Court Appointments

Some of the greatest legislative battles in Congress have been the Senate's hearings to confirm judicial appointments, especially to the Supreme Court. In California many judges are elected. Those who are appointed by the governor are approved by the Commission on Judicial Appointments. The Senate does get to approve many other gubernatorial appointments to executive positions and regulatory boards and commissions, including the governing boards of both the California State University and the University of California. For both bodies, they have rejected recent nominees over policy differences.

Filibusters

In the U.S. Senate—a body that is not apportioned on the basis of one person, one vote—41 percent of the members, potentially representing slightly more than 30 million people (fewer than the 37 million represented by California's two senators), can block the passage of most legislation through use of the filibuster. California has no such provision. Indeed, in most cases the majority rules. The principal exception is raising taxes, which requires a two-thirds vote.

Initiatives

Unlike the U.S. Constitution, the California constitution provides several means of taking issues directly to the voters. Most significant is the initiative. This is important in the legislative context because those who are thwarted in their attempts to get legislation passed can always threaten to take it or an even more extreme measure to the voters. This tactic can persuade the legislators to vote for measures that they would otherwise oppose and significantly weakens the legislature.

Seniority

In the U.S. Congress, seniority is used as an informal rule in appointing members to committees and choosing each committee's majority and minority leaders; once members are appointed to their committee positions, they are almost never removed. In the California legislature, both the appointment and removal power resides with the Assembly speaker and Senate majority leader, with seniority playing a much smaller role. Both the speaker and the Senate majority leader in 2007 and 2008 removed members of both parties from committee leadership roles for disagreeing with the leadership over various issues.

Problems, Real and Perceived

When voters pay attention to the legislature, it is most often to complain or criticize its actions. At times these objections are on target, at times not. State government currently is dysfunctional, and the legislature is an easy target. It is easy to be repulsed by the contentious process of arriving at legislative agreements. Moreover, the misbehavior of any one of the 120 legislators is amplified out of proportion and reflects badly on the whole institution. (In 2009, Orange County assemblyman Mike Duvall resigned after having been videotaped bragging about being in bed—literally—with a lobbyist.) Individual members often attack the legislature to play up their own importance, or they run for the legislature by running against it.

Among the most common valid criticisms of the legislature are the following:

Money

In the California legislature, as is the case throughout American politics, money carries a great deal of clout. Elections are expensive, and the money for elections comes from many sources, including the candidate's personal wealth, small contributions from many individual contributors, and larger contributions from business, unions, and other special interests. Large contributions are generally given to ensure support for a particular interest. Although legislators claim that their vote cannot be bought and that contributors are buying only access, that claim would be difficult to support, as the previous chapter has shown. Moreover, simply having access that the ordinary voter does not have is a significant advantage. We have the best legislature that money can buy, and short of moving to public financing of campaigns—an idea rejected by the voters in June 2010—those with money will always have an advantage over those who do not.

Money is usually distributed to those who support the position of a given interest or to those who might be swayed by the offer of monetary support. It also goes to party leaders, who then distribute it to solidify their support both within their party and against the other party. Indeed, it was the amassing of a large war chest that contributed to the distrust and dislike of Speaker Willie Brown and led to the proposing and passing of Proposition 140, setting term limits. However, term-limited legislators, having little background in fund-raising, have become more dependent than their predecessors on large donations from special interests. Jesse Unruh once said, "If you can't take their money, eat their food, drink their booze . . . and then vote against them, you don't belong here."[2] On this basis, there are probably more legislators now than before that "don't belong here."

Term Limits/Lack of Experience

It was believed that term limits would remove a remote professional class of legislators and bring in a new breed of legislators with closer ties to their districts. The ballot argument said that term limits "would remove the grip that vested interests have over the legislature" and create a "government of citizens representing their fellow citizens."[3] The expectations for this proposition were overhyped, and the results were unfortunate.

Legislative politics works best as an ongoing game among a relatively stable group of experienced players. Many of the aphorisms about politics, such as "Politics makes strange bedfellows" and "Don't burn your bridges," are based on ongoing relationships played out over a period of years. Over time legislators learn not only the game and how to play it but also whom they can trust, whom they can work with, and whom they should avoid. This knowledge facilitates cooperation across party lines. Legislators come to learn that not all good is on their side of the aisle and not all evil on the other side. In a short six years, legislators cannot all learn that; the players change too rapidly. The people who can work out effective compromises seldom emerge, and even if they were to emerge, they would not know with whom to work.

Nor can effective leadership emerge in six years. In recent years, to give leaders more time in office, the Assembly Democrats have chosen freshmen legislators as committee chairs and as speaker. But a freshman legislator, no matter how talented, cannot effectively lead a large collegial body. Contrast this with Congress, in which members may serve a decade or more before assuming a leadership position, and where Speaker Boehner and former Speaker Nancy Pelosi each served more than 20 years before assuming that position. Had they been in Sacramento, they would have been out of the Assembly for 14 years by that time.

Nor in 6 short years is there time to develop expertise in process or subject matter, the ordinary skills of a legislator. In Congress, by the time they assume leadership positions, members know the subject matter, the history, and the players. By the time 10 years have passed in Sacramento, members have been gone for 4 years. This dilemma was summed up by a lobbyist:

> I feel sorry for the first-term members who faced the energy crisis. They don't know who's smart; they don't know who knows what they're doing; they don't know the policy; they don't know the politics. And they are faced with a crisis.[4]

In Sacramento, effective power has shifted to the Senate, whose members are more experienced. Senators can spend eight years in the Senate, and many have already spent six years in the Assembly. But real power has shifted from the legislature to the permanent establishment—the bureaucracy and interest groups. Members in these institutions may spend a career in Sacramento outlasting five sets of Assembly members.

Much as they were dissatisfied with the legislature, it is doubtful that the voters wanted to shift power to either of those two groups. In June 2012 voters made a change in term limits which on balance may shift some power back to the legislature. Proposition 28 reduced the time a legislator could serve in Sacramento from 14 years (6 in the Assembly and 8 in the Senate) to 12 years, but now those years could all be served in one house. This will give each house more stability and should result in the selection of leaders with greater experience. It will probably mean that senators will generally be less experienced, but whatever is lost in that body will be gained by the much greater experience that Assembly members will be able to gain before being forced to leave. The result could be a more knowledgeable and effective legislature which is at least marginally better able to deal with lobbyists and bureaucrats.

If there has been a positive aspect to term limits, it is in the increased diversity of the legislature. The percentage of Latino legislators rose from 6 percent in 1990 to 25 percent in 2009, before declining to the current 19 percent. The percentage of women increased from 17.5 percent in 1990 to 32 percent in 2008 before dropping to the current 28 percent. The current speaker of the Assembly, John Pérez, is an openly gay Latino. The previous speaker, Karen Bass, is an African American woman. Members of ethnic groups and women regularly occupy positions in the Democratic leadership of both houses.[5]

Partisanship

Many believe that partisanship has increased in the legislature in recent years. This trend is often attributed to recent districts having been safe, where representatives were elected who couldn't lose in a general election and who were responsive to only their party's majority, which determines the primary election outcome and which is more extreme than the average voter. Safe districts resulted in increased partisanship and less willingness to compromise.

As usual, the issue is more complex than this, although the new more competitive general elections might result in the election of more moderates. The problem is not that there are strong partisans in the legislature, however. This has always been so. But in recent years, the quality of public discourse has become less civil, and the participants have come to have less regard for their opponents and have become less willing to work with them. Part of this incivility is a reflection of national politics brought on by the fact that the two national parties' leadership has become homogeneous and much more polarized. Part may also be attributed to term limits. Recognizing that they will not have to deal with them for years into the future, legislators make less effort to develop civil working relationships with their opponents.

But legislators should be partisan. We elect representatives on a partisan basis. Parties should stand for something. If we vote for Republicans rather than Democrats, then the Republicans should deliver on their partisan promises. Even those who rail against partisanship still want their interests to be forcefully proposed and protected.

Some of the greatest legislatures in the world, such as the British Parliament, are fiercely partisan and yet manage to govern. The difference is that in those bodies, the majority is permitted to rule. In our system, which permits a minority veto, bipartisan cooperation is essential; and when it is not forthcoming, the system cannot function.

Gridlock, Minority Rule, and Lack of Accountability

Although Democrats regularly control both legislative houses by majorities of more than 60 percent, our system has many checks and balances that make it difficult for a majority to rule. Our founding fathers distrusted the masses as much as they distrusted a strong executive. They were more comfortable with a system that did not work well than with a system that might do something that they did not like. While California does not have the filibuster that thwarts majority rule in Congress, it does have two major checks on effective majority governance. One is that the legislature and the governor are elected separately and may represent different parties. The second is that a two-thirds majority is required to get taxes raised, necessitating, in the absence of an overwhelming one-party majority (highly unusual, but which was achieved in the 2012 elections), that the two parties work together to produce realistic spending measures.

Perhaps no other provision of California governance has contributed more to the dysfunctional state of the state than this provision. Californians may elect a majority in the legislature and even a governor of the same party, but unless that party controls two-thirds of each house, it cannot control fiscal policy. Voters blame the majority party for gridlock, when in fact the control rests with the minority party. This provision is even more restrictive than the filibuster, which often locks up the U.S. Senate. The filibuster can only work with 40 percent of the Senate actively backing it, while California fiscal policy is held hostage to a one-third minority sitting on its collective hands, insuring gridlock. As Peter Schrag relates it:

> More than any other structural flaw, it [the two-thirds rule] diffused accountability and brought on much of the budgetary gridlock that California became notorious for in the 1980s and early 1990s.[6]

This structural flaw has been there for several decades, but one of the biggest changes in recent years and the one that contributes the most to our current state of dysfunction is that the minority party—using this "structural flaw"—refuses to compromise on the most critical issue before the state, the need for adequate and stable sources of revenue. Indeed it is this lack of compromise that has made this the critical issue.

Jerry Brown is one of the most experienced individuals to serve as governor. He is also a skilled negotiator. If he had the political culture of the 1970s, when he first served, he would be a successful governor. But skilled as he is, he is unable to find negotiating partners in the minority party leadership. According to a long-time associate of the governor, Jodie Evans, "He is aghast. He reports on some of his conversations like he couldn't believe the narrowness or lack of comprehending by public officials. . . . Some of my old tools are not going to work."[7] Brown himself says that the Republicans have a "perverse fidelity to each point in the Republican gospel."[8] These points are reinforced in the party caucuses.

The Republicans, of course, see it differently. Senator Bob Dutton says that "He's all talk and no go. He throws a few scraps out there . . . let's demonize the Republicans, and that's supposed to fix a problem?"[9] *Los Angeles Times* columnist George Skelton says, "The entire legislative system has been corrupted by Democrats' fear of angering labor unions and Republicans' subservience to a few anti-tax opportunists and entertainers."[10] But while the governor has shown a willingness to oppose the unions on pensions and organizing child care workers, the Republicans seem unwilling to agree to increasing revenues.

Initiatives

Initiatives are often used to bypass the legislative process. That this can be done reduces the need to carefully construct legislation that can pass. If an interest group believes that it can get an initiative proposition on the ballot with a populist appeal, however poorly worded—and there are many examples of such propositions—then they have little incentive to submit legislation for careful consideration of committees in each house of the legislature or to engage in legislative bargaining. Moreover, initiatives have passed that have weakened the legislature or weakened the legislature's ability to make responsible policy. Proposition 140, which instituted term limits, greatly weakened the ability of the legislature to function effectively, by ensuring that there are rarely any experienced legislators in Sacramento. Propositions 13 and 98 each limited the ability to make responsible fiscal policy, the first by limiting the use of a stable tax tool, the second by locking up a huge chunk of the available funds for a single purpose—education.

We will probably see many more propositions because it may be easier to get agreement with a majority of the voters than with two-thirds of the legislature. We appear to be in a destructive cycle. The voters feel dissatisfied with the legislature and pass a proposition that makes the legislature work less effectively. That makes voters more dissatisfied, and they vote for another proposition. And so on. An effort to put an initiative on the ballot in 2012 making the California legislature part-time failed.

California Legislature: Where Are We Now?

The legislature serves two principal functions: policy making and representation. The different requirements of these two functions create tensions. Legislators are also pressured by the needs versus the wants of the district; state versus local interests; the demands of interest groups, campaign contributors, party leaders, and the governor. California is a large state with many competing wants and needs. Legislative districts are among the largest anywhere. These factors turn the making of policy into a complex and often unseemly process. It is a process moved by imperfect humans who will always be somewhat flawed. Even the highly regarded legislature before term limits passed some bad legislation and left problems unaddressed.

Yet it could work better than it does. The state is dysfunctional, and in many ways the legislative process is key to this dysfunction. It is valid to ask if the legislature is the creator or the victim of this impaired system. In large part, this problem has been created by outside forces. Term limits and the two-thirds vote requirement for passing tax legislation are the most notable outside factors. The declining level of civility in the legislature is a reflection of the impact of term limits and of the increasing political polarization in the nation. But it is also caused in part by the safe districts created in the last legislative redistricting, a process carried out for the most part in the legislature. Legislators representing safe districts do not have to pay attention to moderate elements in their party or voters from the opposition party. Perhaps Propositions 11 and 14 will moderate this. Perhaps not. And 2012 may prove a crucial year in testing these changes. Finally, individuals are responsible for their own behavior. Regardless of outside forces, individual legislators of goodwill could make a difference.

As long as we have the current structure and policy limits placed on the legislature, often by initiatives, it is difficult to see how the system can improve. Given the diverse nature of the state and an electorate that is itself divided and tends to elect a legislature that is also divided on many important issues—which in a democracy should be a plus—positive change cannot be anticipated. Moreover, the public has little understanding of legislative functions or the legislative process, making positive change through the initiative process even more unlikely. Indeed, as mentioned, more draconian measures, such as a part-time legislature, have been suggested. As the popular cartoonist Walt Kelly's Pogo said, "We have met the enemy and he is us."

FOR FURTHER READING

Cain, Bruce E., and Roger G. Noll, eds. *Constitutional Reform in California: Making State Government More Effective and Responsive*. Berkeley, CA: Institute of Governmental Studies Press, 1995.

California Journal and State Net. *Roster and Government Guide*. Sacramento: California Journal, 2004.

de Sá, Karen. "How Our Laws in California Are Really Made." *San Jose Mercury News*, July 10, 2010. www.mercurynews.com/politics-government/ci_15452125. Accessed 6/26/12.

Institute of Governmental Affairs. "IGS Goes to Sacramento to Assess Ten Years of Term Limits." *Public Affairs Reports* 42, no. 3 (fall 2001).

Mathews, Joe, and Mark Paul. *California Crackup: How Reform Broke the Golden State and How We Can Fix It*. Berkeley: University of California Press, 2010.

Muir, William K., Jr. *Legislature: California's School for Politics*. Chicago: University of Chicago Press, 1982.

Schrag, Peter. *California: America's High-Stakes Experiment*. Berkeley: University of California Press, 2006.

———. *Paradise Lost: California's Experience, America's Future*. New York: New Press, 1998.

Wilson, E. Dotson. *California's Legislature*. Sacramento: Office of the Chief Clerk, California State Assembly, 2000.

ON THE WEB

California State Assembly Democratic Caucus: www.asmdc.org

California State Assembly Republican Caucus: www.republican.assembly.ca.gov

California Choices.org: http://californiachoices.org (accessed 6/26/12).

California State Senate: www.sen.ca.gov (accessed 6/26/12).

California State Assembly: www.assembly.ca.gov (accessed 6/26/12).

Capitol and California: www.sacbee.com/capitolandcalifornia (accessed 6/27/12).

Legislative Counsel: www.leginfo.ca.gov (accessed 6/26/12). The Legislative Counsel of California's official site, maintained by law.

Rough & Tumble: www.rtumble.com (accessed 6/27/12). Daily summary of California news.

Senate Democrats: www.democrats.sen.ca.gov

Senate Republicans: www.republicans.sen.ca.gov

University of California, Berkeley, Institute of Governmental Studies Library: http://igs.berkeley.edu/library (accessed 6/27/12).

SUMMARY

I. Legislatures are not well understood, but are critical to a democratic form of government. Indeed, a working legislature is practically a definition of a democratic government.

II. The California legislature is, for the most part, modeled on the U.S. Congress.
A. It is bicameral.
B. Members are elected from single-member, geographically based districts.
C. Unlike the U.S. Congress, both houses are based on population.

III. Legislators must both represent their constituents and make policy.
A. These two items are not always compatible.
B. In representing their districts, members must decide whether to follow the wants or the needs of their constituents and whether to follow directions from the district or use their own best judgment.
C. Poor communication from constituents makes these actions difficult.
D. Legislators have offices both in Sacramento and in their districts.

IV. The California legislature was once the most professional of all state legislatures.
A. Proposition 140, the term-limit proposition, greatly weakened the legislature by limiting members to serving six years in the Assembly and eight in the Senate.
B. As a result, legislators are always inexperienced, compared to the bureaucracy and lobbyists.

V. The California legislature is relatively small.
A. Therefore, it has some of the largest legislative districts in the world (863,000 for the Senate and 431,000 for the Assembly).
B. Districts are gerrymandered to provide safe seats for both Republicans and Democrats.

VI. The leader of the Assembly is the speaker; the leader of the Senate the president pro tempore.
A. Each is elected by all of the members in that body, but the majority party caucus usually determines the outcome.
B. The speaker controls most of the resources and is very powerful.
C. The speaker and the president pro tempore are term-limited.
D. The president pro tempore shares powers with the Senate Rules Committee.

VII. The bulk of legislative work is done in committees.
A. Bills are read and amended here.
B. Committees are made up of a group of individuals—lobbyists, staffers, members, and bureaucrats—who make and control policy in a given substantive area.

VIII. Professional staff members make the legislature possible.
A. Some of them work in districts, some in members' offices, some for committees, and some for the leadership.
B. The best-paid staff members are usually subject-matter experts working for committees.

IX. The legislative process has several steps.
A. Bills are first introduced by members and sent to committees.
B. Bills must pass the floors of both houses (with identical wording) before they are sent to the governor for his signature.
C. If the governor vetoes a bill, it takes a two-thirds vote of each house to override it.
D. Budget, appropriation, and tax bills also require a two-thirds vote, giving the minority party immense power in the legislature and making it difficult for the majority party to govern.

X. The state legislature is different from the U.S. Congress.
A. Members are term limited.
B. The governor has an item veto (he can cut or eliminate any item in a budget bill, while not rejecting the entire bill).
C. Both houses are based on population.
D. The legislature does not have a filibuster, unlike the U.S. Senate (which requires an absolute 60 percent vote to cut off debate and pass a bill).
E. The two-thirds money-bill requirement has a similar impact in thwarting the majority.
F. California also has the initiative process, which allows the legislative process to be bypassed, most often by interests with deep pockets.

XI. The effectiveness of the California legislature is limited
A. by term limits and lack of experience.
B. by the two-thirds-vote rule, which keeps the majority party from governing and makes accountability difficult.
C. by increasing partisanship.
D. by the power of big money.
E. by district size, making communication difficult.

PRACTICE QUIZ

1. An item veto allows
   a) the governor to reject any single item in an appropriations or budget bill.
   b) the speaker or the president pro tempore to pull any single item from the agenda.
   c) a single member to block a single piece of legislation by signing a written objection.
   d) a petition by a group of 10 legislators to block any single piece of legislation.

2. Proposition 140
   a) limits the time that legislators can serve in Sacramento.
   b) limits the legislature from raising property taxes.
   c) sets aside 40 percent of the budget for education purposes.
   d) requires the speaker to assign staff to the minority party.

3. The legislature is composed of
   a) 80 members in the Senate and 40 in the Assembly.
   b) 120 members in a single body.
   c) 60 members in each body.
   d) 80 members in the Assembly and 40 in the Senate.

4. A two-thirds vote is needed to pass
   a) appropriation bills.
   b) budget bills.
   c) tax bills.
   d) all of the above.

5. Partisanship in the legislature
   a) has declined because of apportionment.
   b) has declined because of the blanket primary now in effect.
   c) has led to greater ease in getting budgets improved.
   d) has increased in recent years.

6. The power of the speaker of the California Assembly includes all of the following *except*
   a) the power to assign parking spaces.
   b) the power to assign office space.

   c) the power to assign members to committees but not to remove them during the current term.
   d) the power to assign a member to a committee against both the member's wishes and the wishes and needs of his or her constituency.

7. Proposition 140 resulted in all of the following *except*
   a) an increase in office budgets.
   b) the establishment of term limits.
   c) a reduction of committee staff and personal staff.
   d) laying off some of the most knowledgeable staff experts from committees.

8. The legislative process is biased in favor of
   a) issues favored by the public.
   b) the status quo.
   c) change that interest groups favor.
   d) legislation proposed by the governor, who can introduce a limited number of bills directly to both houses, bypassing some of the steps of the legislative process.

9. California has some of the largest legislative districts in the nation. This means that
   a) elections in California tend to be expensive.
   b) citizen access to legislators is unusually good because legislators need to face the voters so often.
   c) staff levels are unusually high to handle the volume of business from constituents.
   d) California has an unusually large number of legislators.

10. Term limits have resulted in the following:
    a) an increase in expertise among legislators, who have only a few years to make a name for themselves
    b) an increase in citizen legislators, people with little or no political experience who are able to run because seats are open
    c) an increase in staff members, who are needed to help legislators with little experience
    d) a decline in the knowledge needed to pass good-quality legislation

CRITICAL-THINKING QUESTIONS

1. Should a legislator vote for what his or her constituents want or what his or her constituents need?
2. Who should apportion the legislature?
3. What criteria should be used to apportion a legislature?
4. Should a legislator take orders from constituents or use his or her own best judgment, even if it is unpopular?

5. How much access should lobbyists have to legislators?
6. When should a legislature have rules that allow a minority to block legislation?

KEY TERMS

At this point you should have a general understanding of the following concepts and terms:

apportionment (p. 109)
Assembly Rules Committee (p. 103)
Assembly Speaker (p. 103)
bicameralism (p. 98)
committees (p. 104)
gerrymander (p. 101)

gridlock (p. 113)
"gut and amend" (p. 107)
lack of accountability (p. 113)
line-item veto (p. 108)
minority rule (p. 113)
representation (p. 99)

Senate president pro tempore (p. 104)
staff (p. 104)
term limits/Proposition 140 (p. 108)
two-thirds vote (p. 106)
veto (p. 106)

6 The Governor and the Executive Branch

WHAT CALIFORNIA GOVERNMENT DOES AND WHY IT MATTERS

Consider the following activities in the executive branch of our state government:

★ After complaints from the oil industry about delays in permitting, Governor Jerry Brown fired the head of the Division of Oil, Gas, and Geothermal Resources, who had expressed concerns about "fracking."

★ Governor Brown commuted the prison sentence of a grandmother who spent a decade in prison for a crime she probably did not commit involving the death of her grandson.

★ The governor vetoed a bill requiring kids to wear helmets while skiing, stating that "Not every human problem deserves a law."

★ Upon entering office, Governor Brown reduced the size of the governor's press staff from 17 to 3, yet is widely seen as more accessible than was Governor Schwarzenegger.

★ Attorney General Kamala Harris, through hard, independent bargaining, got a better deal for the state and homeowners from banks in a home foreclosure abuse settlement than did her fellow attorneys general.

★ In 2010, when the U.S. District Court ruled that Proposition 8, which outlawed same-sex marriage, was unconstitutional, the attorney general and governor at the time—Jerry Brown and Arnold Schwarzenegger, respectively—declined to appeal the ruling.

Governor Brown commemorated the first anniversary of his third term in office with no press release trumpeting the milestone to the press. Blogger William Bradley says that no one talks much about Brown.[1] Brown likes it that way and substantially reduced the governor's press staff when he entered office. He need not have bothered because the press corps, never large, has declined drastically in recent years as newspapers retrench. TV has never paid much attention to Sacramento, and fewer viewers pay attention to TV news. Rarely is there more than a single out-of-town TV reporter in Sacramento.

California government operates largely out of the public view and it does not operate well. The term-limited legislature and the two-thirds vote requirement for passing revenue measures make it difficult for even a skilled governor to put together working coalitions on important budgetary matters—and Jerry Brown is a skilled governor. When governing fails, political leaders often turn to the initiative process, asking the public to make the final decision. But the members of the public have been kept largely uninformed up to this point and often do not understand the issues that they are asked to vote on.

Uninformed voters, inexperienced legislators, constitutional provisions that do not facilitate majority decision making, and an invisible executive. It is not a surprise that our state government does not work well.

The Invisible Governor?

While he is the most visible political figure in the state, the governor is almost invisible in comparison to the president of the United States. There are a number of reasons for this invisibility. We depend on the media for most of what we know about our government, and for the most part the media in the state are not interested in state politics or governance. From the media's perspective, there is little that is newsworthy about Sacramento: it is a long way from the major population centers of the state, and what happens there just does not capture the audience the way a good car chase does. The media work best by focusing on a well-known or riveting personality. But the governor is often perceived as boring—think of governors Davis, Wilson, and Deukmejian, and if you cannot remember them, that may have something to do with the media coverage they received. With the exception of U.S. senators, long-serving, high-visibility politicians are rare in our term-limited government.

The president's job is analytically divided into two roles: head of government and head of state. So, too, the governor, but while the head-of-government role is similar in both cases, the head-of-state role is vastly different, and it is that role that gives the president most of his visibility.

The role of the head of government is to govern—that is, to develop policy, get it passed through the legislature, and implement it via the bureaucracy. It is often divisive. Think of the prime minister of Great Britain, who not only develops policy, gets it passed, and implements it but actually appears on the floor of Parliament to answer questions, often shouted, from his own and opposition parties. In contrast, the queen is the head of state in Great Britain. Her role is highly visible, ceremonial, important for bringing people together. She cuts ribbons, attends public events, greets foreign visitors, participates in parades. In fact, this is her major role. Most of the time when you see the president between campaigns, it is in his role as head of state: welcoming the troops home, attending funerals, dedicating buildings, posing for pictures with foreign dignitaries, dipping his hands in Gulf oil, or making major or minor public announcements. Being head of state is largely a symbolically positive, noncontroversial role offering lots of photo ops for the media. In this role the president represents the entire nation, acting for all of us.

The governor does not have this range of opportunities for public visibility, or, if he or she does, the events are at so low a level that no one cares. Few dignitaries of note visit Sacramento, and the press simply does not warm to filming the governor talking to teachers or highway patrolmen, although pictures of Governor Schwarzenegger congratulating Jet Propulsion Laboratory scientists on a successful Mars landing were in all the papers in 2004. It is hard to imagine similar coverage if Governor Brown did the same thing. It is not worth the cost for profit-oriented TV stations to keep reporters and camera crews in Sacramento for these largely uninspiring moments—unless the governor has his own star power, as Schwarzenegger did. Jerry Brown is much more at home with governing and the minutiae of policy and has little interest in photo ops and the other elements of being head of state.

Nothing else so clearly demonstrates the difference between the chief executive of the United States and the chief executive of one of the most important states in the union than this difference in visibility.

There are important similarities between the two positions as well, and most notable here is that these are offices of limited powers. It is hard for the public to understand that the most powerful political leader of the most powerful nation on earth has strictly limited powers; the same is true of the governor of the most populous state in the union. Just as the president does not run the nation, the governor does not run the state. Our founding fathers feared a strong executive, having experienced such rule under a king and under capricious colonial governors. Consequently, they created a system in which the powers of the executive were secondary to the legislature and where the powers of all institutions were strictly limited.

The governor does have important powers, in some cases more than the president, but as Richard Neustadt has documented for the president, the governor's power is mostly the power to persuade.[2] His power to command and direct in any way he chooses is seriously limited.

As with the president, people have many incomplete, incorrect, and conflicting views of the governor. Tom Cronin and Michael Genovese compiled a list of what they call the paradoxes of the presidency:

- We want the president to be an effective politician while being above politics.

- We want him to be a common person and an extraordinary person at the same time.

- We want him to be powerful but not too powerful.[3]

In part, we want the president to be all things at all times, and, of course, this is not possible.

The governor is not burdened with as much symbolic baggage as is the president, and yet many misperceptions carry over to this office as well. These misperceptions are amplified by the fact that people think that they understand the office. After all, it is an executive office, a position with which all of us who work in organizations have some familiarity. But it is much more than, and much different from, being president of a corporation. It is a *political* executive office, and that is an entirely different position in an entirely different organization, an organization that does not respond well, if at all, to direct orders.

Our greatest misperception is thinking that the governor is more powerful than he or she in fact is. Our state government is modeled on the weak executive federal government that our founding fathers created. The governor does not control the legislature, and it is difficult to make policy without the cooperation, or at least acquiescence, of legislators who may have little reason to support the governor. He or she can get this cooperation only through persuasion—perhaps hardball persuasion, but persuasion nonetheless. Within the executive branch, it is possible to be more direct. But the executive branch is large and in many cases very remote from the governor. How does the governor get a highway patrolman in San Diego or a park ranger in Marin County to do what he or she wants?

Moreover, much of the executive branch is insulated from direct gubernatorial influence. The executive branch comprises many independently elected executives, known as the plural executive, often from the opposing party of the governor. And some organizations, such as the University of California, are governed by boards that can be influenced only by appointments, budgetary threats, or strongly voiced public opinion.

Besides, we often elect governors who are not especially knowledgeable about government agencies, Sacramento politics, or the many interests in our very large and diverse state. Arnold Schwarzenegger held no political office before being elected governor, and the 2010 Republican nominee for governor, Meg Whitman, did not even vote for many years. More important than formal powers are political skills, political resources, a favorable environment, and luck. Ability to bargain, friends in important positions, a good economy, and an absence of natural disasters, collectively and individually, are sometimes more important than formal powers.

Schwarzenegger was nearly unique in California politics initially, even exceeding the popularity of Ronald Reagan. By sheer dint of personality and the threat to go to the public with initiatives, he managed a series of impressive victories—in the early days. But it did not last. He overreached himself, and he antagonized the members of his own party with his moderate positions on many issues. His attempt to pass four initiatives in a special—and costly—election in November 2005 was a disaster. Near the end of his time in office, his approval ratings had reached a low of 23 percent in a Public Policy Institute of California poll.[4]

Jerry Brown is the polar opposite of Arnold Schwarzenegger. He is one of the most knowledgeable governors California has had in recent years. He loves the details of policy making, knows the intricacies of governing, and does not need the limelight. He knows how to bargain and make deals, but he is faced with a bad economy, huge revenue shortfalls, and an opposition party that will not bargain on revenue issues. It is too early to assess his success or failure in office, but in his first two years he was unable to put together the necessary support to address the long-term revenue crisis facing the state.

Formal Powers of the Governor

The formal powers of the governor, while limited, are still formidable. The governor has powers—most important, the line-item veto—that are denied to the president. Yet impressive as this list of powers is, these powers are most important as vantage points on which the governor bases his informal powers or powers to persuade. A governor who expects to use only his formal powers to govern will not accomplish much. He must use those powers as a basis to persuade other political actors to support his goals. For instance, he can use his appointment power to try

The governor has important formal and informal powers, among which are

FORMAL POWERS

organizing and managing the executive branch, including appointing many top
executives

independent executive actions

commander in chief of the National Guard

appointing people to head executive agencies, to independent boards and
commissions, and to the judiciary

drawing up the budget

making legislative recommendations

vetoing legislation

line-item vetoes of budget and appropriation items

granting of clemency, including pardons and reprieves

INFORMAL POWERS

bargaining with legislators and other independent power sources

access to the public to make his case

developing a vision or agenda for the state

raising money for political campaigns

to persuade an important legislator to support his budget by promising to appoint one of the legislator's supporters to an important state commission.

The state constitution vests supreme executive power in the governor. What those words mean is not clear, but it probably is both more and less than meets the eye. Less, because the governor's office is an office of limited powers in which nothing is supreme. More, because executives often reach beyond what was constitutionally intended. When a governor overreaches, recourse through the legislature or the judiciary takes time, and the results are often unclear.

Organizing and Managing the Executive Branch

The governor is empowered to organize and manage the executive branch. *Organize* means he can make a number of administrative appointments. *Manage* means that many of these appointees must report to the governor, at least indirectly, and he can remove them from office. Again, this power can be overstated. First, the state government does not do as much as one might think. Much of the money that it collects is passed on to local government and school districts to spend. Second, the rest of the elected executive branch, most notably the attorney general, limits his actions, and some state employees report to these elected officials—5,000 to the attorney general alone. Third, some of the appointments that the governor makes are to boards that can, and do, act independently of the governor; these appointments may be for fixed terms. The best known of these independent boards is the Regents of the University of California. This 26-member board consists of 7 ex officio members, who sit on the board because they occupy another office, including the governor himself; one student; and 18 members appointed by the governor for 12-year terms—terms that are longer than his. Control over this board, if he wishes to exert it, is possible only through new appointments, through the loyalty of previously appointed members, and through persuasion. Fourth, the governor must make appointments to agencies about which he knows little, often appointing individuals about whom he knows little. Information coming out of these agencies is limited, so the governor is often in the dark about what is happening until something goes terribly wrong and appears in the press.

Independent Executive Actions

The governor's powers are constitutionally restricted by the legislature, but he is able to act independently of the legislature in some cases. These are actions permitted by the constitution or under laws passed by the legislature. They are most significant in times of an emergency.

Few laws passed by the legislature are self-implementing. Most require positive action on the part of the administration. This process of implementation involves clarification of the law and the assembling of finances and an administrative structure to allow action to take place. All of this requires prioritization and the finding of funds, decisions that will have to be made by the governor's appointees or by the governor himself. This is a process that allows for far more influence by the governor than might be apparent on the surface.

Commander in Chief

The governor is the commander in chief of the California National Guard. This role is of little significance until times of civil disorder or natural disaster; and then the significance is in the calling out of the guard rather than actually directing its actions.

Appointments

Making appointments is one of the governor's most significant powers. The governor appoints four distinct groups of individuals: his personal staff, heads of major administrative divisions, some judges, and members of a variety of boards and commissions. Some of these appointments require confirmation by other bodies, some do not; some appointees work at his pleasure, whereas others serve for fixed terms; some are answerable directly to the governor, and others are several steps removed or protected from his intervention. Over the course of his administration, a governor can make more than 2,500 appointments. At the start of his term there will be about 500 positions to be filled.

The governor appoints his personal staff, which consists of about 100 individuals who make the governor's life possible—the individuals who structure the life of the governor, package him, and present him to the public. Governors hire, fire, and move these individuals about at will. No confirmation is required.

Next closest to the governor are the members of his cabinet. The governor determines who will serve in the cabinet and what role, if any, the cabinet plays in policy development. The heads of the superagencies of state government are in the cabinet as well as the director of finance and others whom the governor finds useful and appropriate. These positions require confirmation by the Senate, but the governor can fire them as he wishes.

The governor also appoints the heads of major departments, most of whom are in the superagencies. These individuals have the responsibility of overseeing more than 200,000 state employees.

In addition, the governor appoints members to more than 325 boards and commissions, important and unimportant, visible and invisible. Once appointed, individuals do not have to answer to the governor, although political pressure, including budget pressure, can be brought to bear in many ways.

Stating that "The state's bureaucracy is a labyrinth of disjointed boards, commissions, agencies and departments,"[5] Governor Brown in 2012 proposed a restructuring and consolidation of agencies. The previous year he eliminated 25 boards and commissions. There is no political payoff in this. Few outside of the government will notice. But it is important and illustrative of Brown's attention to policy detail.

Legislative Powers

Much of the success of the governor depends on his ability to persuade the legislature to go along with his programs. This is a difficult task because the legislature owes him little. He does not help elect them. They represent smaller and different constituencies, with legislators often looking out for local rather than statewide issues. They are on different career paths with different time constraints. Because they are term limited, they are relatively inexperienced in bargaining and do not have a long-term commitment to the Sacramento governing process. Their next jobs may be in the private sector, perhaps as lobbyists.

The governor's ability to persuade legislators depends on his political skills as well as many factors beyond his control, including the partisan makeup of the legislature and the political and economic environment. Although much of this influence depends on the governor's informal powers and the use of his other formal powers, he does have several specific powers that are directed primarily toward influencing the legislature, including preparing the budget, vetoing bills or provisions of bills, and making legislative recommendations.

Budget

Perhaps the governor's most significant power is that of preparing the budget, along with the line-item veto of budget provisions. At the federal level, the president presents Congress with a budget proposal, but it is only that, a proposal; the House of Representatives has constitutional authority over fiscal matters. The California constitution gives the power of preparing the budget to the governor. This means that all budget requests from executive branch agencies must pass through the governor. The actual work on this process is done by the Department of Finance.

The budget is prepared and sent to the legislature by January 10, with revisions following later in the spring (the May revise) as the financial picture becomes clearer. The governor then has the job of getting the budget approved by the legislature. Until 2012, a super majority of two-thirds was required to approve a budget (now only a simple majority plus one is required). Although a super-majority vote is no longer needed to pass a budget, it is still required to raise new revenues. Because current budgets do not have adequate revenues, the support of the minority party remains critical. Obtaining this support may require some expensive trade-offs with recalcitrant legislators who withhold their support until they receive an offer they cannot refuse. There are in effect five major players in the budget game—the governor and the leaders of both parties in both houses of the legislature. The need for one or two marginal votes may introduce even more major players. Because of his role at both ends of the budgetary process, and because one person needs to broker the deal, the governor usually has the key role, but even he can be held hostage by recalcitrant legislators. In recent years, Republican legislators have become adamant about not supporting tax increases, which, more than anything else, has led to the current system being unworkable. Any system that permits a minority to block action on important legislation requires compromise and bipartisan cooperation. Neither Schwarzenegger, a Republican, nor Brown, a Democrat, have been able to persuade the two parties to work together to shape revenue legislation.

Veto and Line-Item Veto

The second most significant power of the governor is the veto. Just as in Congress, all bills passed by the legislature can be vetoed by the governor. The legislature passes about 1,000 bills each year and the governor may veto up to one-third of them. The veto can be overridden only by a two-thirds majority of each house of the legislature, but that rarely happens. Equally important, and unlike the national government, the governor has a line-item veto, which permits the governor to reduce or delete any appropriation in a spending bill. That means that legislators cannot force the governor to accept funding for programs that he does not like by burying them inside a large spending bill that he must sign. The governor cannot add items, but the ability to reduce or eliminate the favorite programs of legislators is a powerful tool. It is a key item in the governor's box of bargaining tools, one that no other player has.

Legislative Recommendations

At the beginning of a legislative session, as required by the constitution, the governor presents a State of the State speech to the legislature. This speech may be short or long, general or specific. It is normally not covered in detail by the media, unlike the president's State of the Union speech. This speech may contain the governor's legislative program, but whether or not it is spelled out there, most governors have a program that addresses the problems of the state as they see them and that they hope to get passed through the legislature.

The governor cannot introduce legislation but can readily get allies to introduce his specific proposals. As the most prominent political figure in the state, he is in a position to press for action on these proposals. His success once again depends on a variety of factors, including his political skills. Because of his star power, Governor Schwarzenegger had greater access to the public through the media and could bring more outside pressure to bear on the legislature than most governors. But he squandered those resources, in part by supporting ill-advised initiatives, and in the end his governorship is widely seen as being filled with wasted opportunities. Jerry Brown prefers to work on the inside, using his not insignificant personal political skills. But he, too, needs public support for tax increases, and his public appearances may have more impact simply because they are so rare.

Judicial Powers

The governor has the power to grant pardons and commute or shorten sentences. He can also reverse parole decisions or delay a death sentence. These are significant powers, but they are used relatively rarely and with extreme caution because such decisions can have serious political consequences. Among other judicial powers of the governor is that of nominating justices to the supreme court and appellate courts and appointing other judges if positions are opened by retirement or resignation.

Public Roles of the Governor

While the governor's role as head of state does not provide as much access to the public as the president has, he still is occasionally seen cutting a ribbon, bestowing an honor upon some citizen, attending a funeral, or observing a natural disaster. These and other ceremonial and symbolic appearances may have little policy content, but they keep the governor in the public eye and give the impression that he is on top of things and that the state is in good hands. While far less visible than the president, governors do not underestimate these appearances. They remind people that the governor is on the job, that he does care about their concerns, and that, in the case of a disaster, the governor and the resources of the state will be available.

Occasionally there are some issues of such overwhelming importance—the budget crises are prime examples—that the media are willing to give the governor significant air time. On other occasions he can stage policy-related events, such as showing up at a school to emphasize his education policies (or to mask his actual opposition to certain education policies).

The governor also moves into the public spotlight during elections, and not only when he is campaigning for reelection. California governors often think they have a chance to become president—and why not, since governors of far less populous or attention-getting states have been elected. When governors sense a chance for the presidency, they try to get in the national media as much as possible. Jerry Brown did this regularly during his first two terms in office, to the detriment of his governing.

Governors also campaign for political allies—perhaps a candidate for president or a loyal endangered assemblyperson. Finally, they may take an active role in an initiative or referendum campaign, either to bolster the chances of an initiative that they support or to gain more public attention. In spite of his mixed success in this arena, Governor Schwarzenegger continued to be involved right through the elections of 2010, endorsing the successful Proposition 14 in June and leading the successful effort in November to defeat Proposition 23, which would have suspended an air pollution control law (AB 32).

The governor's extensive fund-raising appearances also may gain significant public attention. This attention is useful because it shows the opposition that the governor has a formidable war chest and shows the party faithful that the governor is out there stumping on their behalf.

Jerry Brown as Governor

Jerry Brown is the son of Pat Brown, one of California's most popular governors, who in the 1960s helped develop the education system and infrastructure that made California the envy of the nation. In 1974, seven years after his father left office, Jerry Brown was elected governor for two consecutive terms. He earned a reputation as a fiscal conservative as well as a visionary and as a bold politician who could ignore the wishes of his allies. He was also a frequent candidate for the Democratic Party nomination for president.

As a visionary, he was often parodied as Governor Moonbeam for advocating such things as establishing a space academy and purchasing a communications satellite for the state. His advocacy of fiscal restraints (which reflected his personal lifestyle) did not go over well in a state that still remembered his father, who had presided over an era of seemingly unlimited promise.

After a long time in the political wilderness, Brown reestablished his career, starting at the local level as mayor of the troubled city of Oakland and continuing on to be attorney general from 2007 to 2011. He was elected governor to a third term in 2010, after a hard-fought campaign against billionaire eBay entrepreneur Meg Whitman. Whitman had little political experience but a lot of money, and her self-financed campaign was the most expensive in California history. Brown won with far less money by emphasizing his political experience and an ability to work with the opposition Republicans.

Jerry Brown's predecessor in office, Arnold Schwarzenegger, was elected in the October 2003 recall of Governor Gray Davis. Davis was recalled due in part to the state's inadequate response to a manipulated energy crisis, to legislative budgetary stalemates, to fund-raising scandals, and to his own remoteness. Hoping for change, the voters turned to the inexperienced but flamboyant movie actor who stood out in a weak field of possible replacements.

Schwarzenegger's first and biggest challenge was to deal with the budget crisis. He proposed two financial initiatives for the March 2004 ballot, both of which the legislature endorsed and the voters approved, and that first year he balanced the state budget through a combination of cuts, borrowing, moving funds from one fiscal year to another, and the other traditional means that many governors use to balance the budget without raising taxes.

But the following year, he attacked the political establishment and called for a special election, asking voters to approve several propositions that came from the conservative part of the political spectrum. The result of the special election was a stunning defeat for the governor and his supporters. Not only did all four propositions that the governor supported fail but the governor's approval ratings fell from over 50 percent in January 2005 to between 30 and 40 percent by August and September of that year.

Most of the Schwarzenegger years were characterized by extreme state budget deficits that the governor and legislature were unable to close on a long-term basis. Year after year, the deficits were $15 billion or more of the approximately $100 billion general fund. There were yearly standoffs lasting for months between two groups: the governor and the Democrats on one hand, both willing to close a good portion of the gap with budget cuts and (in one year) revenue increases of approximately equal size, and the Republicans on the other hand, unwilling to raise taxes and revenues under any circumstances and demanding that budget cuts close at least half the gap before negotiations could begin.

In the end, the Schwarzenegger governorship failed to resolve the crises in California politics. Certainly the state was no better off when he left office than when Gray Davis was removed.

In 2010, the state voters had the opportunity to select between an experienced Democratic politician in Brown and a successful Republican Internet entrepreneur in Meg Whitman. The voters chose political experience over business acumen.

Although Brown is perhaps the most experienced nonincumbent elected to governor, his time in office has not been easy. Although he has achieved real accomplishments, the dysfunctions of the state have impeded his ability to make the degree of progress toward solving the state's problems that both he and the voters had anticipated.

From his predecessor, Brown inherited a budget deficit of $25 billion as well as an established pattern of constructing budgets largely with smoke and mirrors. Perhaps Brown's greatest accomplishments to date have been to cut the structural deficit by more than half while offering budgets that are far more honest than those of recent years. But he has had to do this with no support from Republican legislators and has had to make deep cuts in popular government programs, including cuts to higher education.

As of late 2012, Brown has signed 1884 new bills into law, vetoed 248 bills cut 5,500 positions from government, gotten Amazon.com to agree to pay state sales tax, "realigned" many services back to the local level, eliminated local redevelopment agencies, and persuaded the electorate to increase taxes to close a huge budget gap. He has also taken symbolic actions, such as eliminating a few boards and cutting back on issuing cell phones and state cars to public employees.

He remains visionary and is a strong supporter of such future-oriented programs as a high-speed rail and making California a leader in green energy and technology. But as former Senate President Pro Tempore John Burton pointed out, "'You cannot be proactive from a Democratic standpoint unless you have money.'" Burton concluded, as many political observers have, that Brown "'did as good as he could do with the cards that were dealt him.'"[6]

The cards were different from those he had when he was first governor. First, the legislature is now term limited, and as such its members are far less skilled at legislating and making deals than earlier legislators. Even more important is that the Republican legislators have become united and adamant about not raising taxes or creating any new ones. Because the California constitution requires a two-thirds vote on tax measures, the minority party generally has a veto, and without its support, creating an adequate and stable source of revenue is not possible. And that support will not be given. The Republicans do pay a price for this stance, however; their votes are not relevant on legislation that requires only a majority vote.

It is more the system than the individual politicians who are to blame for this longstanding political stalemate. Our system does not let the majority rule, and the minority in recent years has demonstrated an unwillingness to compromise on tax and revenue increases. Until the system is changed, or until the Republicans are willing to compromise on taxes, or until the Democrats are willing to disassemble most of the state functions, our state will remain in gridlock.

The highly unusual—and likely temporary—supermajority that the Democrats gained in 2012 may make at least a difference. So long as this lasts, Republican votes are not needed for tax changes. Yet, as noted in Chapter 5, several of the new Democrats are from marginal districts and may be reluctant to cast votes for unpopular tax measures that will be used against them in the next election. Further, the new changes in how districts are formed were intended to produce more moderate legislators, meaning these new Democrats may not be as adamant about tax increases as Democrats in the legislature have generally been in recent years.

Structure of the Executive Branch

The executive branch of California has several significant divisions: the governor's personal staff, the appointed cabinet and other department heads, the other elected officials of the executive branch, appointed boards and commissions, and the more than 300,000 state employees, divided into more than 85 agencies and 30 educational institutions. Not all of these agencies and employees are under the control of the governor. Figure 6.1 provides a graphic representation of the executive branch.

Personal Staff

Closest to the governor is his or her personal staff. The members of this staff include schedulers, speechwriters, and press officers. In addition there are individuals who oversee the appointments process, the general development of policy, and liaison with the legislature. They structure the governor's day, develop statements for the press and the public, arrange relations with various groups, and set up appearances throughout the state. Members of this staff are expendable, and they tend to be young and transient. Their positions totally depend on staying in the governor's good graces.

The Cabinet and Agency Heads

The governor uses his cabinet as he determines. It has no official policy function as a body but can be used to help formulate policy. The cabinet is often more a symbolic body than an integral structure of governing. The executive branch is divided into seven superagencies, and the heads of these agencies, called secretaries, are generally in the cabinet. These are State and Consumer Services; Youth and Adult Corrections; Environmental Protection; Health and Human Services; Labor and Workforce Development; Business, Transportation, and Housing; and Resources. These superagencies contain most of the agencies of the state. It is the individual agencies, not the umbrella superagencies, that actually carry out functions, and they may act independently of the superagency secretaries. The governor appoints these agency heads, although he often does not have a free choice. He needs to appoint someone with expertise in the area, and sometimes the qualifications are spelled out in law. These agencies and superagencies are called *line agencies*, the term used to describe organizations with their own statutory authority to carry out functions and provide services.

In addition, the governor has several staff advisory agencies, including the Department of Finance, the Office of Planning and Research, and the Department of Personnel Administration. Perhaps the most important of these is the Department of Finance, which prepares the governor's budget.

The Plural Elected Executive

One of the most notable features of California government is the number of state-wide elected administrative offices. It has seven of these positions, plus the Board

FIGURE 6.1 ★ Executive Branch of the California State Government

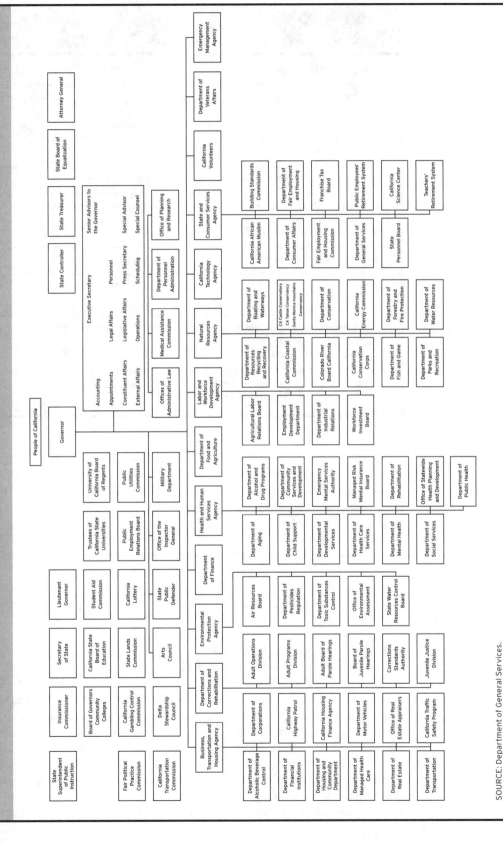

SOURCE: Department of General Services.

BOX 6.2 / The Plural Executive

In addition to the selected duties listed below, all sit ex officio on various state boards.
Governor: Organizes the executive branch, prepares the budget and legislation, signs or vetoes bills
Lieutenant Governor: Replaces the governor if he or she is out of the state or incapacitated or leaves office for any reason
Attorney General: Enforces laws, oversees and assists district attorneys
Secretary of State: Holds elections and oversees the records and archives of the state
Treasurer: Manages state money
Insurance Commissioner: Regulates insurance companies
Controller: Monitors collection of taxes, provides fiscal controls for receipts and payments
Superintendent of Public Instruction: Administers the state role in public education, sits on the state Board of Education
Board of Equalization: Oversees the assessment and administration of property taxes and the collection and distribution of sales taxes and the collection of excise taxes. The controller is a member of this body.

of Equalization, which oversees the administration of property, sales, and excise taxes. This means that there are seven independent bases of power that do not report to the governor and which do not need to adhere to his wishes. This differs from other states which have a single elected leader who appoints lesser state executives. While this distribution of power may limit the governor's freedom to make or implement policy, most of these positions do not deal with substantial policy issues. Generally, only the Attorney General is a real policy competitor (and possibly an electoral competitor as well).

It is not the plural executive, but rather the dysfunctional legislature and the restraints placed on the government by initiatives, that make governing difficult in California.

THE LIEUTENANT GOVERNOR The lieutenant governor exists to replace the governor if he or she becomes incapacitated. He also acts in the governor's absence from the state, providing occasions for great mischief. He can also preside over the Senate, breaking tie votes. He is often of a different party from the governor. Perhaps more than others, this position captures the imagination of those who would restructure government, who would either eliminate the office or link the election of the lieutenant governor to that of the governor, as is the case in other states such as Illinois. The lieutenant governor serves on several important boards, including the governing boards of both the University of California and the California State University system. The office is currently occupied by Gavin Newsom, the former mayor of San Francisco and a rising star in the Democratic Party, but the office does not provide much visibility.

THE ATTORNEY GENERAL The attorney general oversees the department of justice, which employs more than 5,000 persons and has responsibility to see that the laws are enforced. She has the freedom to set priorities for which areas get the most attention and resources. She has oversight responsibilities for local district attorneys and county sheriffs. She is legal counsel to the state and defends the state in lawsuits. She has no obligation to cooperate with the governor and is often viewed as a rival. In 2004 the governor ordered the attorney general to intercede with the state supreme court to stop gay marriages in San Francisco. The governor had no statutory basis for giving such an order, and although the attorney general ultimately did just that, he did it on his own authority. This office is very powerful, and incumbents often see themselves as leading candidates for governor—Jerry Brown used this office to launch his campaign for governor in 2010—although few have successfully made this transition. The attorney general is able to set her own

---

| BOX 6.3 | How Many State Employees Are There? |

How many people are employed by the state of California? We actually don't know. The national ratings of how well the state is managed are C at best, in the lower half of the states nationally, symbolic of the fact that one reason we don't know how many employees there are is because the state is not well managed and its computer systems are out of date. The estimates range from 176,000 to almost 500,000.

First, when most people speak of "state employees," they mean those who report to the governor. But in fact because of the plural executive branch, UC/CSU, the legislative and judicial branches, and other independent boards, only half to two-thirds of state employees report to the governor.

The state also lacks a consistent definition of an employee. Some employees are full-time and have civil service protection. Others are full-time and temporary. Others are part-time with long-term contracts. Still others are part-time and temporary—although some of them work for years. (And some are nonstate employees who are employed under state contracts, just to complicate the situation.) Many, definitely not counted as state employees, actually work for local government but with state funding.

The bottom line is that without modern management practices and a consistent definition of who is who over time, we are left with estimates. The California Budget Project estimates the total personnel-years for state employment as 350,609 in 2008–09, but part-time employees here would be included only as a proportion of full-time, so the total number of people employed by the state is even higher. The budget crisis is no doubt lowering this figure.

Compared with other states, California has relatively few employees. The U.S. Census Bureau comparison tables show that in 2005, the latest figures available, California is fourth from the bottom, with 107 state employees per 10,000 population, compared with the national average of 142 and the highest state, Hawaii, with 426. The average for the top 10 states was 271. Most of the states that are most "efficient" are larger states, suggesting that economies of scale for larger states will yield fewer employees to do similar amounts of work. For total state and local employees, California is seventh from the bottom in 2005, with 490 total employees per 10,000 population, compared with the national average of 537 and the average for the top 10 states of 699.[a]

[a]California Budget Project, *Budget Backgrounder–Professors and Prison Guards: An Overview of California's State Workforce*, April 2010, www.cbp.org/pdfs/2010/1004_bbg_Professors_and_Prison_Guards.pdf (accessed June 2010).

agenda, and it may run counter to the governor's agenda. She can use her substantial powers to counter or even embarrass the governor.

The current attorney general is Kamala Harris, another rising Democratic star, but unlike the lieutenant governor she has been able to grab the headlines on several occasions with settlements against major corporations.

THE SECRETARY OF STATE The secretary of state's office oversees the records and archives of the state. It also has the responsibility for holding elections, including publishing election pamphlets, certifying initiative petitions, keeping records, and publishing the results of elections.

THE CONTROLLER The controller is the fiscal officer for the state and oversees the state's money and the collection of taxes. The controller sits on a large number of boards, including the very important Board of Equalization and Franchise Tax Board, discussed later.

THE TREASURER The treasurer manages the money after it comes in and before it is spent. It manages the investment of this money and the sale of bonds.

THE SUPERINTENDENT OF PUBLIC INSTRUCTION The superintendent is the chief administrator of the Department of Education. Unlike the other elected statewide officers, the superintendent is elected on a nonpartisan basis. Education administration is a confusing policy area; the superintendent shares power with an appointed Board of Education. This arrangement ensures controversy and was even more confusing until Governor Brown eliminated the position of the appointed secretary of education in 2011.

THE INSURANCE COMMISSIONER The insurance commissioner's office was made elective by Proposition 103 in 1988, the only position of the plural executive created by an initiative. The commissioner regulates the insurance industry, and Proposition 103 passed because the public felt that the appointed commissioner was not doing his job. It is not clear that making this an elective post has improved matters because most of the contributions to the campaigns for this position come from the insurance industry.

In addition to these positions, voters elect by district four members to the Board of Equalization, which oversees the assessment and administration of property taxes, although much of the work is done at the county level; collection and distribution of sales taxes; and the collection of excise taxes. Income taxes are handled by a different nonelected body, the Franchise Tax Board.

Agencies and the Bureaucracy

Most of the work of California state government is carried out by more than 200,000 state employees housed in over 85 agencies. Most of these agencies are located within the seven superagencies, and most are invisible to the general public, leading to the idea that state government runs by itself. A few agencies, such as the DMV and Caltrans, are well known if not well understood. Others, such as the Office of Small Business Development or the Department of Aging, rarely make it into the news or the public consciousness. Few Californians could name anyone in the executive branch up to and including department heads; few governors could do that either. Many of these individuals are permanent experts on policy subjects who quietly go about doing their jobs.

Most California employees have civil service protection. Many are also represented by unions. A few of these unions, notably the prison guards' union, are very powerful and politically well connected to the point at which the wishes and desires of the union are more likely to become state policy than the wishes and desires of the governor, the head of the Department of Corrections, or the administration of the department.

There are more than 325 state boards and commissions. Positions on these boards are filled by the governor subject to approval of another body, most often a legislative body. These boards and commissions include important ones, such as the Air Resources Board, the Public Utilities Commission, and the Gambling Control Commission. Again, probably the most visible are the Board of Regents of the University of California and the Trustees of the California State University, which together are responsible for more than 100,000 employees. On the other hand, boards such as the Board of Chiropractic Examiners and the Apprenticeship Council are probably known only to those with a direct interest in that area. Most members serve for fixed terms, some as long as 12 years, and, once appointed, do not have to respond to the governor's wishes.

California Executive Branch: Where Are We Now?

As of 2012, several tentative steps have been taken toward tackling the biggest long-term structural problems facing the state and providing the governor with a greater capacity to lead. First, Proposition 25 removed the two-thirds vote requirement to pass a budget. An important step, it loses much of its impact when revenues cannot be similarly raised. (And it may come back to haunt the Democrats some day, should the Republicans control all parts of the state government and can cut programs at will).

Second, although some doubt it will have any real impact, Proposition 11, approved in November 2008, has taken the power to draw the state legislative districts from the legislature and given it to a citizens' commission. This committee has created new districts that have a closer partisan balance and have at times pitted incumbents of the same party against one another. The hope is a legislature willing to cooperate and compromise both with itself and with the governor. (see Chapter 5).

Along similar lines, Proposition 14, approved in June 2010, substitutes a system of preliminary and final elections for the party primary (see Chapter 4). Voters will vote in the "primary" or preliminary election for the candidate of their choice for each office from a single list of all candidates from every party, and the top two candidates will go on to the November election, which will be like a runoff. Again, the ambition is to create a less partisan legislature. The unexpected consequence of these two propositions has been to create supermajorities for the Democrats in both houses of the legislature. How that will play out cannot be predicted at this time.

However, with the exception of Proposition 28 in June of 2012, which shortened the time that legislators could stay in Sacramento but permitted them to serve that entire time in one house, no firm steps have been taken toward addressing the lowered competence of the term-limited legislature. Indeed, there was a 2012 proposal to make the legislature operate only on a part-time basis, though it failed to get on the ballot. If such a motion ever passed, it would carry its own risks. A term-limited, largely inexperienced legislature has resulted in increased difficulty in reaching agreement and in much more power being wielded by experienced professional lobbyists. A part-time legislature will only exacerbate this situation without necessarily giving the executive branch more power to realize its agenda or enact crucial policies.

Finally, nothing has been done about fixing the distortions caused by both Proposition 13, the 1978 proposition that limited property tax increases, and the series of initiatives that have locked in certain parts of the budget and made creating a stable and adequate revenue stream close to impossible. California's revenues are far more volatile than those of other states, and Californians' willingness to govern by initiative remains undaunted.

The ineffectiveness of both Governors Schwarzenegger and Brown at working with the legislative minority to address the state's needs starkly demonstrates what is wrong with our political system: although this is a democracy, ordinary majorities are not able to govern. It remains to be seen if extra-ordinary majorities will do better.

FOR FURTHER READING

Cain, Bruce E., and Roger G. Noll, eds. *Constitutional Reform in California: Making State Government More Effective and Responsive*. Berkeley, CA: Institute of Governmental Studies Press, 1995.

California Performance Review. *Prescription for Change, Report of the California Performance Review*. Vols. I–IV. Sacramento: California Performance Review, 2004. http://cpr.ca.gov/#cpr. Accessed 6/30/12.

Gerston, Larry N., and Terry Christensen. *Recall! California's Political Earthquake*. Armonk, NY: M. E. Sharpe, 2004.

Lubenow, Gerald C., ed. *Governing California: Politics, Government, and Public Policy in the Golden State*. 2nd ed. Berkeley: Institute of Governmental Studies Press, University of California, 2006.

Mathews, Joe. *The People's Machine: Arnold Schwarzenegger and the Rise of Blockbuster Democracy*. New York: Public Affairs Press, 2006.

Schrag, Peter. *California: America's High-Stakes Experiment*. Berkeley: University of California Press, 2006.

———. *Paradise Lost: California's Experience, America's Future*. New York: New Press, 1998.

ON THE WEB

California Choices.org: http://californiachoices.org (accessed 6/30/12).

California Department of Finance: www.dof.ca.gov (accessed 6/30/12).

Center for Governmental Studies, Los Angeles: www.cgs.org (accessed 6/30/12).

Governor of California: www.gov.ca.gov (accessed 6/30/12). The official site of the Office of the Governor, where you can find background information and up-to-date news, and even e-mail the governor.

Public Policy Institute of California: www.ppic.org (accessed 6/30/12).

Rough & Tumble: www.rtumble.com (accessed 6/30/12). Daily summary of California news.

University of California, Berkeley, Institute of Governmental Studies Library: http://igs.berkeley.edu/library/.

SUMMARY

I. The office of the governor is modeled on that of the U.S. president. There are significant differences between the two offices, mostly having to do with visibility.

II. Each job has two analytical roles.
   A. Head of state, which is largely ceremonial, symbolizing the unity of the state or country. In this role, the governor or president makes public appearances

in activities that bring people together. The president, in this role, is on TV almost every evening. The governor has less opportunity to play this role, and even when he does, the state TV stations seem uninterested.

    B. Head of government, which involves making policy and trying to get it passed by the legislature and implemented by the executive branch. That role is partisan and divisive. It is also an almost invisible role.

III. The formal powers of the office are greater for the governor than for the president.

    A. The governor's formal powers include making appointments and organizing the executive branch; having independent executive actions permitted by law; being commander in chief; proposing the budget; making legislative recommendations; and exercising the veto, including the line-item veto.

    B. The governor has most of the powers of the president in domestic policy but also has a line-item veto, which gives him or her more control over the political process of the budget.

    C. But California has an initiative process that a popular governor can use to bludgeon a legislature into action.

    D. California is different, too, in requiring a two-thirds vote of the legislature to pass a budget that may hamper the governor.

IV. The governor's public roles (head of state) include cutting ribbons, signing bills, observing natural disasters. Non-head-of-state public roles include campaigning and fund-raising, and advocating for initiatives.

V. Like the presidency, the office of governor is one of limited powers, which are restricted by the legislature, the judiciary, the plural elected executive, and the permanent executive branch.

VI. The structure of the state government includes the following:

    A. the governor's personal staff

    B. the governor's cabinet, which includes the heads of major departments

    C. the 385 or more agencies that make up these departments

    D. more than 300 boards and commissions, including the Public Utilities Commission and the Regents of the University of California

VII. In addition to the governor, the state is headed by a plural elected executive, which includes the lieutenant governor, the attorney general, the secretary of state, the controller, the treasurer, the superintendent of public education, the insurance commissioner, and the state board of equalization.

VIII. California employs the equivalent of more than 300,000 full-time employees to staff the government.

PRACTICE QUIZ

1. Which of the following is *not* part of the plural executive?
    a) the chancellor of the California State University
    b) the secretary of state
    c) the attorney general
    d) the controller

2. Which power does the governor have that the president does not have?
    a) legislative veto
    b) line-item veto
    c) power to declare war
    d) power to appoint judges

3. Which of the following activities of the governor would be considered part of his role as head of government?
    a) proposing a budget
    b) vetoing legislation
    c) proposing new air quality standards
    d) all of the above

4. Which of the following group of employees are under administrative control and report ultimately to the governor?
    a) legislative aides
    b) supreme court clerks
    c) highway patrol
    d) professors at California State University, Fullerton

5. How many state boards and commissions are there?
    a) fewer than 50
    b) between 50 and 150
    c) between 150 and 250
    d) between 250 and 350

6. The California governor is "invisible" under normal conditions for all of the following reasons *except*:
    a) California's governors appear in events where they are visible to the public, but for the most part, there is little interest in them.

b) for almost every recent governor, there has been little media interest in Sacramento.

c) the governor splits his or her power with other state executives, who are also trying to attract the media.

d) the governor's star power is only of interest to those who like superhero movies.

7. The governor manages the executive branch, but this power is limited by all of the following *except*:

a) the governor appoints so many people that many of them will be appointed to agencies the governor doesn't know much about.

b) some of California government is outside the power of the governor to supervise, like the University of California and the California State University.

c) the boards and commissions that the governor makes appointments to are mostly, except in extreme cases, outside of his power.

d) the attorney general must approve appointments to many boards and commissions, and that appointment power is difficult to obtain.

8. The line-item veto allows the governor to adjust any appropriations item up or down, including reducing it to zero.

a) true

b) false

9. All of the following are true of the governor's appointments to the cabinet *except*:

a) most cabinet appointments are routine, given to the governor's political supporters and campaign contributors.

b) the cabinet as a whole has no official policy function, unless the governor wants to give it a role.

c) some cabinet and subcabinet positions require an appointment of someone with qualifications that are spelled out in law.

d) the superagency heads are usually considered part of the governor's cabinet.

10. The job of the lieutenant governor, one columnist wrote not entirely in jest, consists of getting up in the morning, checking that the governor is still alive, and then making arrangements for lunch!

a) likely to be true.

b) likely to be false.

CRITICAL-THINKING QUESTIONS

1. Is the state government too large?
2. Does the plural elected executive contribute to effective or efficient government?
3. What is the value of having independent boards such as the Regents of the University of California that employ large numbers of people?
4. Which is more important for governing, the formal or informal powers of the governor? Think about this question in terms of "necessary" versus "sufficient" powers.

KEY TERMS

At this point you should have a general understanding of the following concepts and terms:

boards and commissions (p. 135)
cabinet (p. 124)
formal powers (p. 122)

head of government (p. 120)
head of state (p. 120)
informal powers (p. 122)

line-item veto (p. 126)
personal staff (p. 130)
superagencies (p. 130)

7 The California Judiciary

WHAT CALIFORNIA GOVERNMENT DOES AND WHY IT MATTERS

While the judiciary is ostensibly the least political of all of the branches of government, state courts are not insulated from a state's political culture or the actions of other state institutions. Moreover, state courts, although independent, do make judgments and rulings that become part of our larger, federal political system. This is because most law in the United States is enacted by states, and most legal challenges or cases appear in state courts first. Because of this, state courts are commonly called on to mediate important political issues that affect politics beyond their borders and become issues of national importance. This is especially true for California courts given the types of legal questions they are asked to address and the number of cases they handle each year. Two issues in particular reflect the dynamics of the relationship we find when we examine politics, courts, and federalism in California: medical marijuana (which we discuss later in this chapter) and same-sex marriage.

On May 15, 2008, the California Supreme Court ruled in the case *In re Marriage Cases* that the state of California does not have a compelling state interest to limit marriage to the traditional definition—one man and one woman—and that prohibiting same-sex couples from marrying is a violation of the equal protection clause. The repercussions from this ruling have been significant. Mobilization of interest in opposition to the ruling was swift, and as a result Proposition 8, which sought to eliminate same-sex marriage in California, appeared on the November 2008 ballot. This ballot measure was written specifically to overturn the California Supreme Court's ruling. The 2008 California "Official Voter Information Guide," which provides arguments for and against ballot propositions, quoted Proposition 8 advocates Ron Prentice of the California Family Council and Rosemarie Avila, governing board member of the Santa Ana Unified School District: "It overturns the outrageous decision of four activist Supreme Court judges who ignored the will of the people." Over 52 percent of the electorate agreed and Proposition 8 passed.

Politics are dynamic, however. The California courts, including the California Supreme Court, have ruled several times on the constitutionality of Proposition 8. In May 2009, the California Supreme Court addressed three consolidated cases involving the constitutionality of the state's ban on gay marriage (see *Strauss v. Horton*, *Tyler v. State of California*, and *City and County of San Francisco v. Horton*). In summary, the court ruled 6 to 1 that the amendment was not unconstitutional. But it also added that the amendment did not apply retroactively. This means that those 18,000 same-sex couples who married before the date that Proposition 8 went into effect are still legally married in the state of California.

But the saga didn't end there. In 2010, a federal district court judge found Proposition 8 to indeed be unconstitutional because it violated the Equal Protection and Due Process clauses of the U.S. Constitution by denying same-sex couples the right to marry (*Perry v. Brown*, formerly *Perry v. Schwarzenegger*). This decision was appealed and went to the Circuit Court of Appeals for the Ninth Circuit. A three-judge panel of the ninth circuit upheld the district court judge's ruling. Another appeal was filed with the ninth circuit for a rehearing of the case, which is referred to as an *en banc* (full court) hearing, but the court refused to review and reconsider its prior ruling, issuing an order to that effect on June 5, 2012. The U.S. Supreme Court is the only remaining legal venue for appeal for this particular case. Because the justices on the U.S. Supreme Court have what is called "discretion," they will have to vote to decide whether they wish to review *Perry v. Brown*; it will take at least four "yes" votes from the nine justices for them to review the case.

The consequences for action or inaction on the part of the highest court in the nation vary. For example, if the Supreme Court decides not to review the case, the ruling of the ninth circuit will remain in effect, which means that same-sex marriage is legal in California. If the Supreme Court chooses to review the case, they could rule in four possible ways. First, they could overturn the ninth circuit's ruling, which would have the effect of reinstating Proposition 8 and making same-sex marriage illegal again in California. Second, they could uphold the decision of the ninth circuit but limit the scope of that ruling to only California. Third, they could uphold the decision but apply it to only those states in the Ninth Circuit's jurisdiction. Fourth, and most dramatic, they could uphold the decision and apply the ruling broadly to all states, legalizing same-sex marriage nationally. Considering Proposition 8 itself was a product of California's unique reliance on direct democracy, we can see how the state's institutional design touches even the judiciary, with far-ranging consequences.

Judges and State Government

State courts are an integral and necessary component of state government. They exist and function to ensure that a state's citizenry is guaranteed due process of law and that the other branches and levels of government within the state uphold the state's statutes and code as well as the provisions in the state constitution. Therefore, judges play a much larger role than simply punishing criminals or imposing fines on a polluting company. Courts make decisions that are often political and sometimes very controversial. These decisions have the potential to affect more individuals than simply the parties to a case. Their rulings can have far-reaching consequences that not only ignite more political debate but also have an iterative effect. This is especially true in California, where the politics can be very contentious and the state witnesses a high rate of litigation. And while some cases that come before the California courts gain a significant amount of statewide and national media attention, other cases may remain under the radar yet still have an impact on our daily lives.

For example, on June 21, 2010, the California Supreme Court announced its ruling in *Kleffman v. Vonage Holdings Corp*. At issue in this case was the legality of commercial electronic advertising. Craig E. Kleffman sued Vonage on the basis that its use of multiple domain names to advertise its product and services through unsolicited e-mails (or spam) violated provisions in the California state code. The California high court ruled unanimously that "sending commercial e-mail advertisements from multiple domain names for the purpose of bypassing spam filters is not unlawful under [the state code]." This recent ruling, as well as the Proposition 8 cases discussed in the introduction, serves to illustrate the importance of the California judiciary. When individual citizens or groups of citizens believe that private entities or government have trampled on state law or on their civil liberties or civil rights, they turn to the courts. The judges serving on California's courts must decide if the state's laws or the rights of Californians have been violated.

There is also a recent trend to criminalize more behavior and increase the penalties for offenders. For example, California, like many other states, has modified its laws to allow juveniles to be tried as adults in some criminal cases. Although the intent of this law may have been to let juveniles know that California has little tolerance for certain types of crime, regardless of the defendant's age, the effect has been to shift cases from the courts of judges who deal exclusively with juveniles to the already overburdened courts handling crimes involving adults. In addition, victims' rights legislation, which has elevated some misdemeanors (nonserious crimes) to felonies (serious crimes), increases not only the severity of the penalties for the accused but also the workload for the courts. California's three-strikes law, which was enacted to punish repeat offenders, has had a similar impact. Keep in mind that these are just a few examples.

To be sure, most of the civil cases filed in California's civil courts will be resolved through negotiation between the parties and their attorneys. The courts are still involved, however, in processing the paperwork and dealing with the other administrative issues each civil case may involve.

It is also true that in reality, most of the criminal cases in the state's criminal courts will be resolved through plea bargaining, in spite of what we see in film or on television. Full court trials for the prosecution of high-profile crimes, like that of the music producer Phil Spector, who was charged with murdering Lana Clarkson in 2003 and was later convicted in 2009 after an earlier mistrial, are rare. A plea bargain is the norm. Even so, the courts are still involved in the process. Even if a criminal case never goes beyond the formal filing of charges against a defendant, judges are part of a plea bargain. As a referee, the judge's job is to determine if the plea bargain is appropriate and if the defendant entered into the plea bargain knowingly. The judge asks defendants if they understand the terms of the plea bargain and if they agreed to the terms voluntarily. If the judge decides that the terms of the plea bargain are inappropriate, it may be thrown out. The same applies to the defendant's ability to comprehend the terms of the plea and whether it was truly entered into voluntarily. If the judge concludes that any of these elements are problematic, then a new plea may have to be negotiated or the case may actually go to trial. Regardless, this single case involves many people in the criminal courts, from clerks to administrators and, of course, a judge.

To understand the role courts play in California government and politics, consider the following: from 2009 through 2010, approximately 10,075,000 cases were filed in California Superior Courts (trial courts of general jurisdiction).[1] Of these, over 85 percent were criminal in nature. And each one of these approximately 10,075,000 cases had to be handled individually by the appropriate state court in one way or another until it was resolved. To put this into context, let's consider the number of people living in this state. According to the U.S. Census Bureau, California's population was estimated at 37,691,912 as of September 2012. This number includes all persons who could be counted from newborns to the very old, people who are incarcerated and institutionalized, small children, and people with challenges that may inhibit them from participating in a range of activities.[2] Age, health, disabilities, and other factors exclude a number of Californians from committing crimes. Even if we grant that some individuals may be involved in more than 1 of 9.5 million lawsuits, almost 11 million cases filed in one state's courts in a single year is phenomenal. What is more, despite the incredible workload, California's criminal courts typically resolve cases involving felonies within 12 months. Civil cases are also resolved fairly quickly; on average, 65 percent of civil cases filed in a given year are resolved within a year.

It is easier for an individual to go to criminal court—just drive over the speed limit and get caught—than to civil court. Civil courts have rules about the types of cases they can hear. In civil disputes, parties must also have what is known as "standing to sue." To bring a case to court, an individual must suffer personal and real injury. Typically, one cannot sue on the behalf of another. As well as requiring standing, California courts, like the federal courts, will not handle collusive suits. Collusive suits are lawsuits in which both parties want a similar or the same outcome. Our legal system is an adversarial one, in which it is presumed that parties want opposite outcomes, and when one party wins, the other loses.

Both criminal and civil courts in California are limited as to the cases and controversies they handle because of jurisdiction. *Jurisdiction* refers to the kind of law the court handles. For example, there are criminal courts that deal with violations of state and local laws, and there are civil courts that hear cases involving disputes between individuals or classes of individuals. Civil courts may rule on cases involving breach of contract, tort liability, and wrongful-death suits, to name a few. *Jurisdiction* also refers to geographic boundaries. There are 58 superior court divisions in California, with at least one branch in each county. Cases are assigned to these courts depending on where the parties in civil suits reside or where alleged crimes have been committed in criminal cases.

Federalism and the California Courts: The Case of Medicinal Marijuana

In 1996 through the initiative, voters in California approved Proposition 215, the Compassionate Use Act (CUA). This act provides for the medical use of marijuana for seriously ill persons. It requires that a physician recommend that a patient's health would benefit from using marijuana to alleviate symptoms of serious illness. In addition, the act also shields patients and their caregivers from criminal prosecution for cultivating or possessing marijuana for use approved under the act.

Confusion ensued shortly after the act was implemented. First, there were many (successful) attempts at expanding the scope of the law. Second, the state law came directly in conflict with federal law that classifies marijuana as a controlled substance and makes its cultivation, possession, sale, and consumption illegal.

Seven years after the CUA was passed, Governor Gray Davis signed Senate Bill 420, the Medical Marijuana Program Act (MMPA) into law. The MMPA was designed to flesh out the parameters of the CUA. Among other things, the MMPA sought to create collective cooperatives in the state where marijuana could be cultivated and sold to qualified patients and caregivers. The cooperatives would be regulated by state and local agencies and the patients and caregivers would be issued identification cards that would help law enforcement more easily determine whether persons were covered by the CUA and, therefore, not subject to criminal prosecution under state law. The MMPA also allows for persons who fall under the classifications of cooperatives, caregivers, or patients, to raise a defense if they are charged with violating state laws involving the cultivation, possession, sale, or consumption of medical marijuana.

The MMPA had immediate implications regarding federalism. Although both the CUA and the MMPA are technically "good law" (meaning they are still current and enforceable), various attempts have been made by the national government to exercise preemption (this involves the national government claiming that it has authority over a particular policy area when it comes to legislation and thus preempts state and local regulations) over the issue of medical marijuana. For example, in 2005, the U.S. Supreme Court reviewed the case *Gonzales v. Raich*. At issue was whether Congress's power to regulate the manufacture and possession of marijuana under the Controlled Substances Act (21 U.S.C. §§ 801) allowed the national government to preempt California's laws on medicinal use of marijuana. The Supreme Court ruled in a 6 to 3 decision that the Commerce Power gives Congress the authority to regulate and to punish the manufacture and cultivation of marijuana despite California law that allows for compassionate use. It is worth noting that the dissenting Supreme Court justices argued that this was a violation of federalism and that the state law should prevail because no interstate commerce was taking place and this was purely local or *intrastate* commerce.

Since this ruling in 2005, many local governments have seized on the opportunity to create new zoning ordinances to limit the expansion of dispensaries. In fact, one tactic commonly used by local governments to close down marijuana dispensaries involves calling the U.S. attorney's office. The U.S. attorney has the authority to order these shops to discontinue their operations under the threat of having their property forfeited or seized, as well as other criminal sanctions under federal law.

Despite the U.S. Supreme Court's ruling in *Gonzales v. Raich*, California courts have continued to try medical marijuana cases according to state law. For example, a 2009 case, *People v. Colvin*, involved a co-owner (William Frank Colvin) of two nonprofit medical marijuana dispensaries, Holistic I (in Santa Monica) and Holistic 2 (in Hollywood). The dispensaries are registered with the city of Los Angeles and have been incorporated for several years. In addition, they are often reviewed by local law enforcement to ensure they meet the requirements and restrictions of the MMPA. Like other similar dispensaries, and according to the MMPA, Holistic 1 and 2 grow some of their marijuana on site but also belong to a cooperative that includes growers in Los Angeles and Humboldt. In March 2009, Colvin was less than a block from Holistic 2 en route to Holistic 1. He was stopped by police, taken into custody, and charged with violating state laws for possession of cocaine, sale or transportation of marijuana, and possession of marijuana. He did have an identification card for medicinal use and showed it to the arresting officer at the time. He also presented evidence to the trial court that he was registered to run the Holistic dispensaries. The trial court judge agreed that Colvin's dispensaries seemed to be in compliance with both the CUA and the MMPA, which are still California law despite the decision in *Raich* which gives the national government the power to preempt them with its own policy. Colvin's attorneys argued that he was only transporting the marijuana (one pound) from one dispensary to another. However, the trial court judge disagreed and ruled that the MMPA did not cover the transportation of marijuana. Colvin was found guilty of all three charges, placed on probation, and given community service. Colvin appealed this conviction, and the court of appeals determined that the transportation of marijuana from one dispensary to another fell within the scope of the MMPA. Because Colvin's possession of the pound of marijuana was for purposes of transporting it from one dispensary to another, it was also protected by the act. Therefore, the court of appeals reversed the trial court's decision with respect to two of Colvin's convictions (transportation and possession; the cocaine conviction was not appealed).

However, both parties to a case have the right to appeal, and the state appealed the decision of the court of appeals. The California Supreme Court had to determine whether it would take the case and rule on its merits or if it would choose not to hear the case and allow the court of appeals decision to stand (remain in effect). In May 2012, the California Supreme Court denied review, noting that medicinal marijuana remains an issue that has important implications for local, state, and federal law. It also cited that the *Colvin* case is only one of many that continue to be filed in the courts dealing with this policy issue. It is an interesting case study in the principle of federalism, particularly in those circumstances in which state and national law clearly conflict over a very controversial issue.[3]

How Are the California Courts Structured?

California courts have three levels: superior courts (trial courts), courts of appeals, and the California Supreme Court.

Superior courts adjudicate cases that involve violations of state and local criminal and civil law. These are the trial courts of California. When cases come before the superior courts, a jury or judge reviews the facts of the case and determines guilt or innocence in a criminal proceeding. If it is a civil case, the jury or judge determines which side presents the best case and awards damages accordingly. There are 400 courts located in the state, with approximately 1,500 judges presiding. The superior courts are also staffed with commissioners and referees. The superior courts are also the busiest courts of the state court system.

The California Courts of Appeals are intermediate appellate courts; those who lose their cases at the superior court can appeal first to the California Courts of Appeals. The purpose of this intermediate appellate court is to review the trial or the superior court records for error. California courts of appeals are divided into six districts across the state; 105 justices preside over these courts. These judges sit in 3-judge panels to review cases.

The California Supreme Court is the highest court in the state. Like the California Courts of Appeals, it is an appellate court that reviews appeals from losing parties in the lower courts. When a party to a case is unhappy with the ruling of

Member of the California State Supreme Court as of December 31, 2010. In January 2011, Tani Gorre Cantil-Sakauye (seated, center) succeeded Ronald George as Chief Justice of the Court. The Court's newest member, Justice Goodwin Liu (standing, far right), replaced retiring Justice Carlos Moreno in September 2011. (Courtesy of the Supreme Court of California. Photo by Wayne Woods.)

the California courts of appeals, the next step would be to appeal to the California Supreme Court. In California, the supreme court has what is known as discretion. Discretion allows the justices on the state supreme court to decide which cases they wish to review. Therefore, there is no guarantee that an appeal filed with the California Supreme Court will automatically get reviewed. This is the only court in California that has discretionary authority that provides the high court with a tool to moderate its workload. Justices on the supreme court cannot exercise discretion regarding death-penalty sentences or disciplinary cases involving judges or attorneys. All death-penalty sentences are automatically appealed and go directly to the California Supreme Court for review. Four out of the seven justices must agree in order for a party to win the case. The supreme court includes one chief justice and seven associate justices. (Table 7.1 provides a list of current California Supreme Court members.)

The court is diverse in regard to gender and race/ethnicity: four of the justices are women and three are nonwhite. On July 14, 2010, Chief Justice Ronald M. George publicly announced that he would not be seeking retention on the California Supreme Court in the November 2010 election. This announcement created a future vacancy, and Governor Schwarzenegger appointed Tani Gorre Cantil-Sakauye to replace Chief Justice George. Her appointment was confirmed by the Commission on Judicial Appointments on August 25, 2010, and Justice Cantil-Sakauye was retained by the voters on the November 2010 ballot. She became the 28th chief justice of California on January 3, 2011. Governor Brown appointed Goodwin Liu in 2011 to replace retired Justice Carlos Moreno.

However, the court is not as diverse ideologically. Five of the seven justices seated on the court were appointed by Republican governors. Why should this matter? Generally, Republicans are more conservative than Democrats on issues of ideological preference, such as civil rights or civil liberties. For example, a liberal

TABLE 7.1 ★ CURRENT MEMBERSHIP OF THE CALIFORNIA STATE SUPREME COURT
Tani Gorre Cantil-Sakauye, Chief Justice, appointed by Governor Arnold Schwarzenegger in 2010
Joyce L. Kennard, appointed by Governor George Deukmejian in 1990
Marvin R. Baxter, appointed by Governor Pete Wilson in 1991
Kathryn M. Werdegar, appointed by Governor Pete Wilson in 1994
Ming W. Chin, appointed by Governor Pete Wilson in 1996
Carol A. Corrigan, appointed by Governor Arnold Schwarzenegger in 2005
Goodwin Liu, appointed by Governor Edmund G. Brown in 2011

judge is more likely to uphold laws that involve regulating business than a conservative judge. This expectation, that ideology or party identification translates into differences in judicial decision making, is even more important when we consider issues such as affirmative action, voting rights, freedom of expression, and capital punishment. Because the decisions of the California Supreme Court are binding on all persons residing in the state, the composition of the state's high court and the judges' political ideology can be very important.

Governors who have the opportunity to appoint judges to the courts take advantage of this possibility and put qualified jurists on the bench whose political beliefs most closely resemble their own. From time to time, a governor may be very open about who should be serving on the state supreme court. In the 1980s, former governor George Deukmejian spoke out to the press and public about his desire to put more conservatives on the state supreme court because the liberals serving on the bench at the time were making decisions he vehemently disagreed with. In addition, governors may have other political goals for the bench. They may, for example, seek to place more women and minorities on the state supreme court so that it is more representative of the state's diverse population.

From time to time, judges who have served on the California Supreme Court have had success at being promoted to the federal bench. The most recent promotion from the state high court to the federal courts of appeals met with significant political opposition. Janice Rogers Brown's appointment to the U.S. Court of Appeals for the District of Columbia Circuit was nonetheless confirmed in June 2005. Her confirmation was a result of a political compromise after a two-year bipartisan battle between Democrats and Republicans in the Senate over several of President Bush's judicial nominees. Janice Brown, a Republican and conservative, was appointed to the California Supreme Court in 1996 by Governor Pete Wilson. President George W. Bush attempted to nominate Judge Brown to the D.C. Circuit Court of Appeals in 2003, but he was unable to get her nomination confirmed by the U.S. Senate. The reason her nomination was initially unsuccessful was political. Justice Brown's detractors argued that her voting record as an appellate judge on California's Supreme Court reflected a much too conservative bias. In addition, organized interests such as the National Organization for Women (NOW) noted that Justice Janice Brown received an "unqualified" rating from the California State

Bar Association. She is the only member of the state supreme court to receive such a rating since the state bar has been evaluating judicial nominees.

Justice Brown's confirmation struggle also illustrates the debate regarding judicial independence versus judicial accountability that we will address later in this chapter. Federal court judges are appointed by the president and confirmed by the Senate for terms of life with good behavior. This selection method was designed to protect the federal judiciary from political influences, including public opinion. Because their appointments are for life terms, many interest groups and other interested members of the Senate pay close attention to judicial appointments and the nominee's positions on important issues and voting records. Appointments to the federal bench, unlike elections to state courts, are often the topic of heated partisan debate. Once a judge is appointed to a federal court, the only way to remove him or her is through impeachment. Thus it isn't possible to hold federal judges to the same level of accountability as most state judges. Therefore, partisans and interest groups act as gatekeepers, blocking nominations of those jurists whose political preferences differ from their own.

Judicial Selection

California's court system is the largest in the nation. Serving on the bench involves two things: (1) a person must be qualified, and (2) the qualified person must be selected to serve. The qualifications for judge are the same for the three court levels. Potential jurists in California must have at least 10 years of practice of law in the state of California or service as a judge of a court of record.

Judges serving on the California Supreme Court and California Courts of Appeals are initially nominated to serve on the appellate bench by the governor. The Commission on Judicial Appointments must approve the governor's nominations. The Commission on Judicial Appointments consists of the chief justice of the supreme court, the attorney general, and a presiding judge on the California Courts of Appeals. In addition, all nominees for California's appellate courts are reviewed by the State Bar of California's Commission on Judicial Nominees Evaluation. This body evaluates the nominees by conducting thorough background checks on their qualifications as judges and as citizens. The governor may use the commission's decision as a source of information when making his or her selections but is not bound by the commission's findings. After a judge's appointment is confirmed, the judge holds office until the next retention election. To remain on the appellate courts in California, judges must face a retention election. These elections are noncompetitive; the voters are simply asked whether the judge should remain on the appellate bench.

Likewise, judges serving on California's superior courts must face nonpartisan retention elections. However, in most cases, as with the appellate bench judges initially come to the superior court bench by gubernatorial nomination. Vacancies on the superior court occur because a judge retires, leaves due to poor health, or dies. Although judges are elected to the trial courts of California, the reality is that these elections typically draw very little attention. California voters are not highly aware of the judicial candidates for these positions, nor are they as concerned about judicial offices as they are about other political offices, such as state representatives or executive officials. From time to time, however, voter awareness about a judge's performance on a particular case or rulings in a specific issue area may lead voters to remove a judge from the bench.

Removing Judges from the Bench

As we have already discussed in this chapter, voters may remove judges from the bench during an election. There are other means for removing judges if there are concerns regarding judicial misconduct or judicial competency.

- *Impeachment*—California's judges may be impeached by the assembly and convicted by a two-thirds majority of the state Senate.

- *Recall election*—Like the governor, California judges are subject to recall election if the voters petition a recall.

- *Regulatory commission investigation*—The Commission on Judicial Performance may, after investigation of complaints regarding misconduct or incapacity, punish, censure, or remove a judge from office.

Who Has Access to the Court?

The California constitution and its statutes provide rights to the people of California regarding access to the courts. Former Chief Justice Ronald M. George had become engaged in overseeing the pursuit of reforms to statewide court access. According to "California Courts, Reference—How to Use: Guide to California Courts" Californians have:

- the right to sue for money owed and for other relief;

- the right to defend oneself against a lawsuit;

- the right to be presumed innocent if charged with a crime;

- the right to defend oneself against all criminal charges;

- the right to a public and speedy trial by jury if charged with a misdemeanor or a felony;

- the right to an attorney at public expense if one is charged with a felony or misdemeanor and cannot afford an attorney.

These rights apply to citizens of the state and noncitizens alike. These rights do not mitigate against concerns about quality of legal representation for indigent persons. The lack of resources in some local court jurisdictions, especially in smaller localities, and the impact of the current budget crisis on the state's judiciary as a whole, will affect the access to the courts.

Judicial Independence versus Judicial Accountability

Unlike the federal judiciary, which consists of appointed judges who serve life terms with good behavior, many states have some form of election system for selecting their judges. The reason federal judges are appointed is to allow for an independent judiciary. Theoretically, appointed judges are less likely to be influenced by politics in their decision making because they do not have to rely on the electorate to maintain their jobs on the bench. Most of the states, however, adopted some kind of election system for selecting their judges or retaining their judges, because states wanted judicial accountability. Elections allow for accountability by giving the voters the opportunity to select members of their courts and also to remove them through the election process if the jurists make decisions that are contrary to the public's preferences.

Although the voters rarely pay much attention to competitive judicial races or judicial retention elections, there have been instances when judges have lost their seats on the bench because of voters' perceptions about judicial rulings. In the November 1986 election, six of the seven justices serving on the California Supreme Court were seeking retention. Of these six, Governor George Deukmejian targeted three and spoke out publicly against their retention on the state supreme court. Deukmejian criticized these judges for their rulings in death-penalty cases. The governor was especially critical of Rose Bird, who was the chief justice of the California Supreme Court at that time. He warned Bird and two associate justices, Cruz Reynoso and Joseph Grodin, that if they didn't change their rulings in death-penalty appeals and uphold the death-penalty sentences, he would oppose their retention elections. Numerous interest groups and political action committees joined the governor's campaign against Rose Bird and her two colleagues. Political advertisements against the retention of Bird, Grodin, and Reynoso aired on radio and television. In response, Chief Justice Rose Bird produced a television ad explaining her decision-making record to the voters. Her explanations did not satisfy the electorate, however, and on November 4, 1996, Bird, Grodin, and Reynoso lost their seats on the California Supreme Court. Shortly thereafter, Governor Deukmejian appointed three justices to replace them, including Malcolm Lucas, who was nicknamed "Maximum Malcolm" because of his rulings sentencing convicted criminals to maximum penalties, including death.

Despite the low visibility of judicial elections, these elections have many political scientists and jurists concerned, particularly over the amount of money being spent by candidates in judicial elections.

A 1995 study of contested elections in Los Angeles County Superior Court reported that campaign spending by trial court judges had risen a great deal in the years between 1976 and 1994. In 1976, the median cost of a judicial campaign for a Los Angeles County Superior Court seat was approximately $3,000. By 1994, the median skyrocketed to $70,000. Incumbents running for reelection spent, on average, $20,000 more than the median challenger, or $95,000 in 1994. Compare that to the $1,000 median campaign expenditure of an incumbent in 1976.

The Civil Justice Association of California (CJAC), a group of citizens, taxpayers, and professionals, reviewed campaign contributions to the California judiciary from 1997 to 2000 and found the following:

- from 1997 to 2000, contributions to candidates in contested superior court elections totaled over $3 million for four counties;

- in a single race in Sacramento County, over $1 million was raised;

- attorneys are the largest contributors to most judicial races;

- two supreme court justices seeking retention in 1998—remember, these are uncontested elections—received contributions of $887,000 and $710,000.

The escalation of campaign spending in judicial elections is controversial, because it usually requires judicial candidates to seek funding support from outside sources. Like candidates seeking election to state legislative or executive offices, judges are now receiving and even soliciting financial support from organized interests. This phenomenon has even spilled over into retention elections for the state supreme court, even though they are noncompetitive. Judges must solicit campaign contributions to retain their seats on the bench. Contributors often include trial lawyers' associations and other special interests. This connection has raised concern because when interest groups contribute financially to a judge's campaign the potential for influence over judicial decision making arises. Although elections allow for accountability, the notion is that accountability is to the citizens or voters, not to the more narrow preferences of an organized interest group. This concern has mobilized a national movement for reform. One of the most active advocates is former Associate Justice of the U.S. Supreme Court Sandra Day O'Connor. Retired Justice O'Connor has been a vocal critic of state judicial elections because of the amounts that judicial candidates are soliciting and spending, and because of the public perception that money buys influence.

Most people consider the judiciary the least political of all of the branches of government, yet the increased spending in competitive and noncompetitive elections for judgeships compromises this assumption. Even judges are expressing concern. In 2001, an opinion survey, "Justice at Stake Campaign," revealed that 53 percent of California judges are dissatisfied with the current climate of judicial campaigning in the state. Over 80 percent of the judges surveyed believed that voters knew little about candidates for the bench and were electing judges based on criteria other than qualifications for office. The majority of judges polled agreed that reform of campaign financing of judicial elections is necessary and that public financing of these elections would be an appropriate alternative.

In response to stories in the media, including a series of articles published in the *Los Angeles Times*, and the concerns of the public, judges, public officials, and others, a task force was created to examine judicial campaigns in California. The Judicial Campaign Task Force for Impartial Courts was established in 2007. It consists of 14 members appointed by former California Supreme Court Chief Justice Ronald M. George, and it is investigating several issues, including the structure of California judicial elections as well as the filing, reporting, and accessibility of judicial campaign contributions and spending. The findings to date of this commission were reported in a 408-page volume in December 2009.[4] Many problems were noted with respect to judicial campaigns and elections, most notably the amount of money spent by candidates for judicial elections and, ironically, the poor quality or low level of information disseminated by judicial candidates to the public. The commission is not finished with its work, and additional reports are expected. It is also worthwhile to note that reforms and current state policies include the following:

- Judicial candidates are prohibited from making statements that commit or appear to commit them with respect to cases, controversies, or issues that could come before the courts.

- Judicial candidates may not knowingly misrepresent the identity, qualifications, present position, or other facts concerning themselves or an opponent.

- Judicial candidates are not prohibited from soliciting campaign contributions.

- Like all other state political candidates, judicial candidates are required to report all campaign contributions and expenditures.

- Any contributions to or expenditures of judicial candidates of $100 or more must be itemized. Judicial candidates for superior court may file a candidate statement to be included in the voter's pamphlet. These statements are very expensive, however, and the cost is prohibitive for most candidates.

There is one further caveat that should be mentioned. Whenever limits or rules are placed on campaign spending, the rights of freedom of expression and freedom of association guaranteed by both the California and U.S. constitutions may be abridged. Campaigning for political office is guaranteed by the right to speak freely, and in today's political contests, it is becoming increasingly expensive. Therefore, it is almost impossible to impose limits on campaign spending. So judges running for retention on the California Supreme Court or running to serve on the state's trial courts must exercise their own restraint—not an easy thing to do if your opponent or opposing forces are spending a lot of money to keep you off the bench.

The Politicization of the Judiciary

Every term, judges serving on the California bench across all court levels (trial, intermediate appellate, and supreme) are confronted with cases that require them to make political decisions or decisions that have political effects. One example of this is political redistricting. The redrawing of electoral districts is always a political process. Political parties seek either to maintain or to increase their odds of getting candidates reelected through the redrawing of district lines. It is very common for redistricting plans to end up contested in the courts by political parties, elected officials, candidates seeking political office, and/or organized special interests. Since the 1980s, the California courts have been involved in many cases and controversies regarding redistricting. Perhaps the most controversial was in 2005, when Governor Schwarzenegger and others proposed an initiative, Proposition 77, that would reform redistricting procedures in the state. Rather than having legislators redraw district lines after each census, the responsibility would be given to a panel of three retired judges (selected by legislative officials). This ballot measure was contested in the California Courts of Appeals before it even appeared on the ballot. Those opposed to the measure argued that judges should not be put in the role of redrawing or creating new political districts. Although there was some success with procedural challenges to the initiative at the courts of appeals, attempts to block the initiative from the ballot finally failed, and the voters had the opportunity to decide in November 2005 whether retired judges should be redrawing the state's electoral district lines. The voters vetoed the measure by a margin of approximately 19 percent.

As we can see, there are certainly political dimensions of the judiciary. While it is most common for us to consider the "political branches" such as the legislature and the executive first when we think about politics, it is important to remember that courts play a significant role in political processes and that this is especially true in California. The presence of the initiative, referendum, and recall facilitate this role further. The increased spending on judicial campaigns at the trial and appellate levels adds another dimension that may call some of these other political actions into question.

Judicial Review and the Statewide Initiative

Another issue of concern regarding the judiciary in California is the relationship between direct democracy and judicial review. It is vitally important to keep in mind that, regardless of the method of selection of judges, judicial decisions or rulings may have far-reaching consequences for all of us. California is one of 26 states in the United States that allows for citizens to propose and enact their own legislation through the initiative. Moreover, the California state constitution permits citizens to use the initiative to enact statutes and constitutional amendments.

The popular initiative was implemented in this state during the early twentieth century by Progressives such as the Lincoln-Roosevelt League, along with other like-minded groups seeking political reform in California government. As an alternative policy-making tool, the initiative allows citizens to circumvent the legislature and write and enact policies reflecting their own political preferences. Theoretically, the initiative performs as another check against unresponsive government. Therefore, when citizens believe the legislature is not responding to their demands—that is, when the legislature is not enacting the laws that they would like them to—the people may propose their own laws and, if they are successful at getting them on the ballot, persuade the voters to enact them.

The initiative, however, is also subject to judicial interpretation and judicial review, just like a piece of legislation coming out of the state legislature. Since the success of Proposition 13, the property tax reform initiative, in 1978, the use of the initiative in California has increased greatly. Organized interests and citizen-based movements have attempted to use the initiative to enact policies in California in nearly every conceivable issue area. Victim's rights and penalty enhancements for criminals, such as the three-strikes law, have been enacted through the initiative. The decriminalization of marijuana for medicinal purposes was adopted via the initiative. Term limits for many of California's elected officials were also ballot initiatives. Voters in California have also enacted policies for insurance reform, registration of sex offenders, harsher penalties for human trafficking in the sex trade industry, anti-affirmative action laws, and most recently, a temporary tax to fund education and modifications to the state's "three strikes and you're out" law over the past 30 years. While it is erroneous to argue that all initiatives in California reflect controversial issues such as those listed, it is clear that the initiative has been used increasingly in the past to enact a wide array of policies that reflect citizen dissatisfaction with elected state government.

When the initiative is used to enact controversial policies, it is usually debated in the press, and if that controversial initiative is successful at getting voter approval, there is a very strong likelihood it will be contested in the courts. In fact, the constitutional validity of each of the initiatives described in the preceding paragraph has been challenged in at least one court of law. The outcomes of these court cases have varied. But what is important is this: just like judges on federal courts, state court judges have the power of judicial review. When state judges have the power to overturn laws enacted by the people as well as laws composed by state legislators, the tension between lawmaking and law reviewing is heightened.

Is this tension all that important? Many scholars and many voters would argue that it is. In fact, the common opinion among the electorate in California is that the initiative as an alternative policy-making tool has become an exercise in futility, precisely because of legal intervention. The consensus among California voters is that once an initiative passes at the ballot box, it ends up in a court of law. In truth, courts are reactive bodies. Judges must wait until a case comes to their courtrooms to make a legal decision. So why do so many initiatives end up in the California courts? The answer is simply politics. California is a very diverse state, and our diversity can be measured in a number of ways. We are diverse in race and ethnicity, we are diverse in culture, we are diverse economically, we are even diverse in terrain and climate. Given so many dimensions of diversity, there is no dearth of conflict in our state regarding which political problems are important and which solutions to these problems should be adopted. Hence California courts also function as another arena for the continuation of political debate. The response to the State Supreme Court's 4–to–3 ruling in *In re Marriage Cases* and the subsequent proposal, adoption, and reversal of Proposition 8 illustrate this well.[5]

California Courts: Where Are We Now?

A number of issues currently confront California's courts. As discussed earlier, the caseload continues to increase for all court levels. And while the superior courts and appellate courts have been managing this load fairly efficiently, there are legitimate concerns about the system's ability to continue to do so, given the state's continued fiscal crisis.

Courts are also subject to similar constraints that affect state agencies. It is fairly easy to argue that the greatest of these constraints, setting jurisdiction (decision-making power and authority) aside, is the state's economy and budget. Most recently, the court system in California has found itself constrained by the extraordinary challenges of the state's budget. Chapter 8 discusses the budgetary process and more of the political implications in greater detail, but here we can examine the impact of this budgetary crisis on the courts.

On the face of it, a discussion about budgets and courts may not appear all that interesting. However, when Governor Brown signed the budget on June 27, 2012, it included $6 billion of automatic cuts—hundreds of millions to the court system—severely affecting both its day-to-day operations and its future construction plans. It is important to note that these cuts come on top of other actions that have been taken to reduce the size of court administration throughout the state. Because most courts are obviously located at the local level, counties and municipalities have taken the brunt of these budget cuts. Responses to the ramifications of these cuts have included threatened strikes by state court administrative personnel and the elimination of some innovative, albeit controversial, programs at the local level. One such program involves nonviolent misdemeanor crimes by juvenile offenders in the Los Angeles area. This program is part of a relatively recent, legal movement known as "problem-solving justice," or the good courts movement. It served as an alternative to more punitive, traditional forms of dealing with juvenile low-level crime. The nontraditional court served more than 100,000 children each year, but has been shut down by the county because of budget cuts.[6]

In addition, the new chief justice, Tani Gorre Cantil-Sakauye, has had to respond to some criticisms by organized interests and other parties about wasteful spending on projects and the growth of the state's Administrative Office of the Courts (AOC). A relatively new (2009) interest organization, The Alliance of California Judges, has been pressuring the chief justice and the judicial council to respond to past and present budget cuts more proactively. The alliance has been arguing that both should pay closer attention to wasteful spending, predicting (accurately) that like his predecessors, Governor Brown would include more cuts to the state courts' budgets in the new fiscal year. More specifically, this organization targeted the now defunct electronic Court Case Management System. According to the *Courthouse News Service*, "even as trial courts were closing, the [Judicial] Council voted repeatedly, with only one or two dissenting votes, to continue pouring hundreds of millions into that now failed IT project. That money came primarily from trial court funds." The *Courthouse News Service* article goes on to claim that "over half a billion" dollars was spent before the Court Management Case System was terminated.[7]

On top of this, C. J. Cantil-Sakauye released a report "prepared by a committee of state judges" in late May 2012 criticizing the AOC for understating the number of its employees and for paying "hundreds" of its personnel six-figure salaries. The report noted that this growth in both size and salaries paid was taking place during a hiring freeze. The investigation concluded, among other things, that the AOC had circumvented the hiring freeze and had violated some of its own personnel rules. It also recommended that there be significant cuts in the staff and that the organization be consolidated to allow for more oversight and, presumably, more efficiency.[8]

Finally, reforming judicial campaigns in the state is also a critical agenda item. Some attempts at reform, such as campaign finance reporting, have been implemented and have not been found unconstitutional. However, when voters amended the state constitution in 1986 to prohibit political parties from endorsing judges, who run in nonpartisan elections, the California Supreme Court found the initiative unconstitutional because it violated our rights to freedom of expression and freedom of association. Obviously, judges have a lot of say when it comes to these reforms, and it is up to the individual judge to decide how much is too much when it comes to campaign spending.

FOR FURTHER READING

American Judicature Society (AJS). "Judicial Selection in the States." www.judicialselection.us. Accessed 8/16/12.

Bonneau, Christopher W., and Melinda Gann Hall. *In Defense of Judicial Elections*. New York: Routledge Press. 2009. This book is a critique of previous empirical studies of judicial elections. Bonneau and Hall argue that elections as a selection method for judges is actually beneficial to democratic society.

California Courts, Guide to California Courts. www.courtinfo.ca.gov/courts. Accessed 9/27/12.

Civil Justice Association of California. "Campaign Contributions to the California Judiciary 1997–2000." Accessed 8/16/12.

The National Organization for Women. "NOW Opposes Extremist Judicial Nominees—Regardless of Gender." www.now.org/press/11-03/11-13.html.

Streb, Matthew J., ed. *Running for Judge: The Rising Political, Financial and Legal Stakes of Judicial Elections*. New York: New York University Press. 2007. This edited book is a collection of contemporary research conducted by professors who study state courts and judicial elections. Each chapter examines current issues and controversies that are confronted by state courts and state court judges.

ON THE WEB

The American Judicature Society (AJS): www.ajs.org. Accessed 8/16/12. The AJS is a nonpartisan organization made up of legal professionals and citizens. It seeks to provide a better understanding of the judiciary and the justice system.

The California Supreme Court Historical Society (CSCHS): http://cschs.org. Accessed 8/16/12. CSCHS catalogs and archives information about the California Supreme Court's history.

The National Center for State Courts (NCSC): http://ncsconline.org. Accessed 8/16/12. NCSC is an organization that provides services for court administrators, practitioners, and others interested in state courts. The website includes information, datasets, and articles about state courts and court-related topics.

SUMMARY

I. Introduction: judges and state government.
   A. Judges play an integral role in California politics.
   1. Court rulings can impact all Californians, such as the recent rulings on Proposition 8 (the ban on gay marriage).
   2. Controversial rulings can lead to political mobilization against the justices serving on California's courts. In some instances, justices have lost their retention election bids to keep their seats on the California Supreme Court.
   B. California courts have a very high caseload.
   1. Increase in criminalization and penalties increase the caseload.
   2. Despite the high workload, California courts remain fairly efficient and are able to dispose of a significant percentage of their criminal and civil caseload at all court levels.

II. Federalism and California Courts
   A. Legal challenges to Proposition 215, the Compassionate Use Act (CUA), illustrate the tension between state and federal government. California permits the use of medical marijuana under certain conditions, but the federal government does not. There are many continuous attempts by federal law enforcement to close marijuana dispensaries that would otherwise be operating legally under the CUA.
   B. Local governments are also adopting ordinances to regulate or even prohibit dispensaries from operating in their communities. At times, local governments will even use federal law enforcement to assist them with closing dispensaries.
   C. The California courts currently have a number of cases across all levels examining this policy.

III. Structure of the California courts.
   A. Superior courts are the trial courts of the California court system. They are courts of "first instance" and triers of fact. The California Courts of Appeals are intermediate appellate courts. They are divided into six districts across the state. All cases except for death-penalty cases are first appealed to the California Courts of Appeals. The supreme court is the highest court in the state. It is composed of seven justices and, like the courts of appeals, is an appellate court—that is, it reviews cases that were first heard in lower state courts such as the courts of appeals or a superior court.
   B. The California courts are diverse in terms of both gender and race. In July 2010, Chief Justice Ronald M. George announced that he would not seek to be retained on the California Supreme Court. This announcement created a vacancy, and Governor Schwarzenegger nominated Tani Gorre Cantil-Sakauye to fill this vacancy. She is the first female chief justice on the supreme court. Her appointment also creates a female majority, with four female justices and three males.
   C. Justices serving on the California Supreme Court have been promoted to the federal bench from time to time. Some of these appointments have been met with little opposition, and some have been unsuccessful, such as President George W. Bush's nomination of Janice Brown to the U.S. Courts of Appeals in 2003.

IV. Judicial selection.
   A. Methods of selection for the California courts include nonpartisan elections for superior court and merit selection for appellate courts.
   B. Methods of removal from the bench include recall elections and impeachment. In addition, because all judges in California face some sort of election (direct or retention), voters may choose to vote for another judicial candidate or they may choose to vote against retaining an appellate court judge.
   C. Access to California courts is widely available. However, there is concern about the cost of litigation and legal representation.

V. Judicial independence versus judicial accountability.
   A. There are two competing theories regarding judicial selection—appointment and election. Those who favor judicial independence argue that appointment is a better method for selecting judges because it insulates them from politics. Conversely, those who favor accountability argue that election as a method of selection is essential in a democracy and that judicial elections allow citizens to hold judges accountable for their decision making similar to the way other elected officials are held accountable for their actions in office.
   B. Recent controversies about judicial campaigning and campaign finance have led to some high-profile jurists (for example., retired U.S. Supreme Court Associate Justice Sandra Day O'Connor) and others to call for reforms. The most radical reforms proposed would eliminate judicial elections entirely. The increasing cost of judicial campaigns, which are low-saliency and low-turnout elections, have many members of the bar and legal community concerned.
   C. The politicization of the California courts is another issue of concern. Judges on California courts are increasingly asked to decide on cases involving very controversial issues such as the death penalty and gay marriage.

PRACTICE QUIZ

1. All death-penalty sentences are automatically appealed directly to the California Supreme Court for review.
   a) true
   b) false
2. The California Supreme Court is similar to the U.S. Supreme Court in that it has nine justices.
   a) true
   b) false
3. Most criminal cases in California are resolved through plea bargaining.
   a) true
   b) false
4. Voters in California are highly informed about the candidates running in judicial elections.
   a) true
   b) false
5. Initiatives passed in California are not subject to judicial interpretation and judicial review.
   a) true
   b) false
6. In recent years, campaign spending in judicial elections
   a) has increased.
   b) has decreased.
   c) has remained the same.
   d) cannot be determined.
7. Chief Justice Rose Bird and Associate Justices Cruz Reynoso and Joseph Grodin were voted out by voters who were angry about the judges' decisions concerning
   a) same-sex marriage.
   b) the death penalty.
   c) Proposition 13.
   d) term limits.
8. Judges selected by the governor to serve on the supreme court and the courts of appeals in California must be approved by
   a) the state legislature.
   b) the attorney general.
   c) the Commission on Judicial Appointments.
   d) none of the above.
9. Superior courts in California adjudicate the following types of actions:
   a) civil and criminal cases.
   b) only civil cases.
   c) only criminal cases.
   d) appeals only.
10. One method of removing judges in the state of California is
    a) removal by the governor.
    b) censure by the state legislature.
    c) agreement between the speaker of the Assembly and the attorney general.
    d) a recall election.

CRITICAL-THINKING QUESTIONS

1. Given the concern over the role of money in judicial elections, what kinds of reforms might be implemented that would still allow for accountability? Is it possible to keep money or special interests out of judicial elections?
2. What factors do you believe are responsible for the tremendous criminal caseload in the California superior courts?
3. Is judicial independence important for state court judges?
4. What kinds of checks are there on the California judiciary? How do the other branches and other political actors hold the state courts accountable?

KEY TERMS

At this point you should have a general understanding of the following concepts and terms:

appellate jurisdiction (p. 144)
civil courts (p. 141)
judicial accountability (p. 148)

judicial discretion (p. 145)
judicial independence (p. 148)

retention election (p. 147)
superior courts (p. 144)

8 The State Budget and Budgetary Limitations

WHAT CALIFORNIA GOVERNMENT DOES AND WHY IT MATTERS

Why Does Student Tuition Keep Rising?

The answer to rising student tuition is actually simple. Higher education is a major category, the third or fourth largest in most years, of the state budget, and charts that float around Sacramento make it look as if students, until very recently, paid relatively low tuitions/fees by national standards. The charts came from the California Postsecondary Education Commission, a research agency created by the legislature to be independent of the three systems of higher education, or from the Legislative Analyst's Office. Figure 8.1 presents an example from the 2006–07 school year. Everyone involved in higher education policy sees this chart: the governor's department of finance, the legislative committees and their staff, the bureaucracy, and one of this book's authors, who was on the California State University (CSU) statewide academic senate for several years. Once you have seen the chart, there is very little you can argue to legislators on the hunt for an extra several hundred million dollars to cut from the budget that can prevent them from saying, "Well, the students are paying relatively little by U.S. standards; just increase the university's fees to cover the difference."

And that was the process that occurred, year after year, for over a decade. By 2012, CSU's fees were no longer at the bottom of the list, but rather the middle. The University of California (UC) started higher on the list, but the same process has operated. All told, the legislature has cut hundreds of millions of dollars from the UC, CSU, and community college budgets. Table 8.2 on page 169 shows the expenditures for 2012–13 at $10.1 billion and 7 percent of total state expenditures. Over the four years from 2008 to 2012, higher education lost $2.8 billion in funding, about 22 percent of its total. Some of this has been replaced by student fee and tuition increases, but the budget cuts are

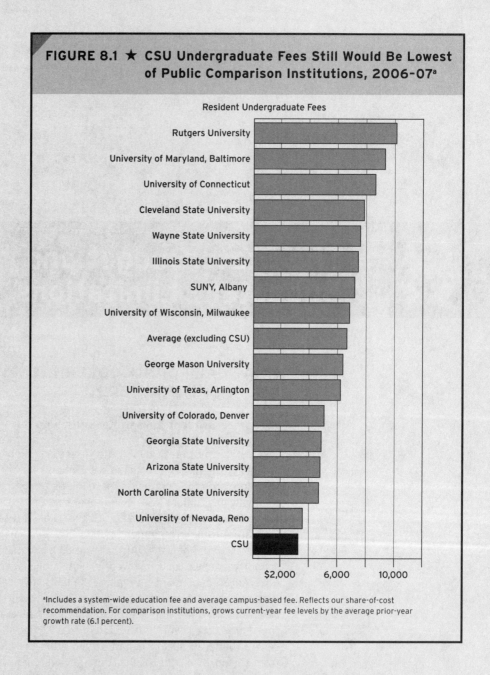

FIGURE 8.1 ★ CSU Undergraduate Fees Still Would Be Lowest of Public Comparison Institutions, 2006-07[a]

Resident Undergraduate Fees

- Rutgers University
- University of Maryland, Baltimore
- University of Connecticut
- Cleveland State University
- Wayne State University
- Illinois State University
- SUNY, Albany
- University of Wisconsin, Milwaukee
- Average (excluding CSU)
- George Mason University
- University of Texas, Arlington
- University of Colorado, Denver
- Georgia State University
- Arizona State University
- North Carolina State University
- University of Nevada, Reno
- CSU

$2,000   6,000   10,000

[a]Includes a system-wide education fee and average campus-based fee. Reflects our share-of-cost recommendation. For comparison institutions, grows current-year fee levels by the average prior-year growth rate (6.1 percent).

the reasons classes are difficult to obtain and there seems to be less money available for other projects.

Students aren't the only citizens heavily impacted by California's budget woes. With a budget of over $130 billion, California represents one of the largest economies in the world. Its projected *deficit in* recent years has been larger than the entire budgets of all but the 5 to 10 largest states. Over 2.5 million workers in California—1 out of 6—work for the federal, state, or local governments, and some of the rest are indirectly funded by the public sector.[1]

For something this important to so many people, it is amazing that the process to approve the budget and some of the items in it is so controversial. The public itself is split—most Californians are opposed to spending cuts in public programs as well as increases in taxes or fees. They are also distrustful of state government and disapprove of the job their politicians are doing. One political party won't increase taxes under any circumstances; indeed, one group of legislators considers the entire budget so illegitimate that it won't vote for the budget under any realistic set of circumstances (in fact, at least one of them didn't vote for a budget for over a decade). The legislature came within one vote of increasing the sales tax in 2002, but that one vote couldn't be found. The amount—and intensity—of political controversy over this budget, a document that embodies the values and decisions of the citizens, its legislature, and its leaders, is truly remarkable.

Passing the budget is at the center, both in difficulty and in scope, of what state government does each year. Since the passage of Proposition 13, state government has received less revenue, which has become more volatile, rising and falling with the economy. The state constitution states that the legislature is to pass the budget by June 15. Since 1990, the legislature has met the deadline only six times. Two of those were budget surplus years, when it is easier to pass a budget. The other two were 2011 and 2012, when Proposition 25 required only a majority vote to pass the budget.

How Is the Budget Formed?

The process of forming a budget has four steps. Most governments today follow a similar process—proposal by the executive branch, enactment by the legislature, approval by the governor, and implementation by the executive branch. Box 8.1 shows the process. Note that the preparation, enactment, and implementation of a single fiscal year's budget takes almost three calendar years.

Executive Proposal

Each fall, state agencies send their budget proposals to the governor through the State Department of Finance. The governor formulates his budget proposal and sends it to the legislature in January. In late spring, he revises the proposal in what is called "the May revise."

Actually, before 1922, agencies proposed their budgets directly to the legislature; there was no unified state budget proposed by the governor or anyone else. "Budgeting was the domain of interest groups, department heads, and ranking committee members."[2] Progressive Governor Hiram Johnson in 1911 asked for justification for the amounts contained in the appropriations bills sent to him. Finding little or no justification, he created the Board of Control to advise him on the fiscal justification for each appropriation.

In 1922, California adopted its own version of new federal legislation (1921) *unifying* the budget process. The legislation called for a consolidated administration proposal in the form of a governor's budget that must be balanced, contain justifications for the amounts proposed, and be accompanied by bills in each house that legislative leaders are required to introduce, thus providing a starting point for the

BOX 8.1 California's Budget Process

CALENDAR YEAR 1

JULY–SEPTEMBER

- Agencies prepare requests, proposals.

- Requests sent to Department of Finance.

OCTOBER–DECEMBER

- Department of Finance reviews requests, consults governor.

CALENDAR YEAR 2

JANUARY–MARCH

- California constitution requires governor to send a balanced budget to the legislature by January 10.

- Governor's budget proposal is introduced in both houses as identical budget bills.

- Legislative Analyst's Office prepares extensive analysis.

- Extensive budget hearings held in both houses.

APRIL–JUNE

- May—Governor sends revised and updated projections of revenues and expenditures to legislature (the May revise).

- June 15—California constitution requires legislature to pass (by a majority vote) a balanced budget by this date. As of November 2010, all members of the legislature permanently forfeit salary and expenses every day until the budget is passed.

- Governor signs budget, uses item veto, if desired, to lower any appropriation items. Legislature can override by a two-thirds vote.

JULY–SEPTEMBER

- July 1—California's fiscal year begins. This is the first quarter. (The federal fiscal year, in contrast, begins October 1.)

OCTOBER–DECEMBER

- Second quarter of California's fiscal year.

CALENDAR YEAR 3

JANUARY–MARCH

- Third quarter of California's fiscal year.

APRIL–JUNE

- Fourth quarter of California's fiscal year.

---

negotiations and decisions each year. The existence of a governor's budget was an improvement over the situation before 1900, when "government structures . . . hid more than they revealed to the public."[3]

Legislative Adoption

The legislature adopts a balanced budget based on the governor's proposal. As of 2011, both the Assembly and the state senate must adopt the budget by a majority of the entire membership of the body. The Assembly and senate budget committees and their subcommittees hold hearings on the budget bills, receiving testimony and input from individuals and groups, including the affected departments and agencies, the Department of Finance, the Legislative Analyst's Office, committee staff, and interest groups.

The Legislative Analyst's Office provides nonpartisan and independent review of the entire budget, including alternative ways to accomplish the same goals and objectives. The former legislative analyst Elizabeth Hill was called "the Budget Nun . . . because her fiscal reports are incorruptible. They're the bible. The one source of truth. . . . She's the most influential non-elected official in the Capitol."[4] The current legislative analyst, Mac Taylor, was appointed in 2008 and has 30 years of experience in the office.

Before 2011, when the Assembly and senate budget bills differed, a Budget Conference Committee was appointed to work out the differences. However, with the passage of Proposition 25 in 2010, only a majority vote is required to pass the budget, so the endless compromising with the Republican Party that used to occupy Sacramento through the summer in the 1990s and 2000s is over. In 2011 and 2012, the budget passed by June 15, the official deadline in Proposition 25 to prevent legislators from losing their salaries on every day that the budget is late. Raising a tax, however, still requires a two-thirds vote of both the Assembly and the state Senate. In 2012, the Democrats achieved majorities of over two-thirds in both the Assembly and Senate, allowing them for the time being to raise taxes without any Republican support.

The "Big 5" group, consisting of the governor, Assembly speaker, senate president pro tempore, and the Assembly and senate minority leaders, that used to be so important in soliciting a few Republican votes to pass the budget under the old two-thirds requirement, is now irrelevant, or at least it was in the first two years under the new system.

Gubernatorial Action

The governor may use the line-item veto to lower any line-item appropriation in the budget, including lowering it to zero. The legislature may override the governor's veto by a two-thirds majority in each of the two houses and replace the lowered number with its own amount, although doing so is rare.

Implementation

Agencies implement the budget as passed, with the fiscal year beginning July 1. The Department of Finance states explicitly that agencies and departments are expected to operate within their budgets and comply with any provisions enacted

1. Within the first 10 days of the calendar year, the governor must submit to the legislature a unified budget that is balanced, contains an explanation for each proposed expenditure, and is accompanied by a budget bill itemizing the recommended expenditures.

2. The budget bills must be introduced immediately in each house by the respective appropriations chairs.

3. The legislature must pass the budget by June 15 of each year. As of 2004, the budget must be balanced.

4. Appropriations from the general fund must be passed in each house by a majority vote of the membership. Note that the requirement is "of the membership," not just those present and voting.

5. When the governor signs the budget bill(s), he or she is allowed to reduce or eliminate an appropriated dollar amount. This is the line-item veto, a powerful tool.

by the legislature. "The general expectation is that state agencies comply with the legislative intent."[5] There is some flexibility in implementation, but, compared to other states, the governor's flexibility is limited, as we shall see.

Other Groups Involved in the Budget Process

In addition to the governor and legislature, who are at the center of the process, the agencies mentioned earlier—the Department of Finance on the executive side and the Legislative Analyst's Office on the legislative side—are closely involved in the process, as are two other groups:

- The courts have sometimes ruled on the constitutionality of particular budget actions, particularly on proposed administrative actions taken in the absence of a budget when the legislature has been late. They have also had to decide the constitutionality of various budget provisions, like the Proposition 13 limits.

- Moody's, Fitch Ratings, and Standard & Poor's rate the ability of the states to repay their bond issues. The rating is one of several factors that influence the cost of selling a bond issue. The lower the credit rating, the higher the interest rate that must be paid to induce investors to purchase the bonds. In 2003, Moody's rating of California's bonds was the lowest rating given for any state. Nothing symbolizes the state's continuing inability to reconcile its desire for high services with its desire to pay low taxes than the fact that its bond rating continues to be in the bottom two or three among all states, one or two steps above "junk-bond status." The budget crises of 2009 and 2010, in which the state had to issue IOUs to its creditors in 2009, brought the rating back down to the lowest level of any state in 2010, although the bonds were still considered to be "investment-grade." In 2012, the state still had one of the lowest state credit ratings.

What Is in the Budget?

Every state budget contains the following information:

- economic assumptions—how the economy should respond during the forthcoming fiscal year, and what that response means for revenues and expenditures
- revenues expected in the various categories
- expenditures appropriated by department and program

Revenues

Looking at all sources of revenue, both general funds and special funds, we see the revenue sources are as follows, according to the governor's budget proposal in January and May 2012 (see Table 8.1 and Figure 8.2):

PERSONAL INCOME TAX California's personal income tax ranges from 0 to 9.3 percent of income, with a substantial credit per child or dependent. The income tax is considered highly progressive, with the top 5 percent of taxpayers

TABLE 8.1 ★ Revenue Sources, 2012–13 Budget, May 2012 Governor's Revise

REVENUE SOURCES	DOLLARS (IN BILLIONS)	PERCENT OF TOTAL REVENUE
Personal income tax	61.6	46
Sales tax	31.0	23
Corporation tax	8.5	6
Highway users' taxes	5.7	4
Motor vehicle fees	5.7	4
Insurance tax	2.5	2
All others	17.7	13
Total	132.7	

SOURCE: California Department of Finance, "2012–13 Enacted Budget," www.ebudget.ca.gov (accessed 9/9/12).

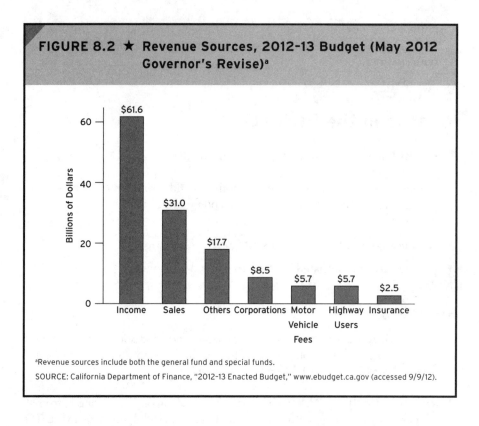

FIGURE 8.2 ★ Revenue Sources, 2012-13 Budget (May 2012 Governor's Revise)[a]

[a]Revenue sources include both the general fund and special funds.

SOURCE: California Department of Finance, "2012-13 Enacted Budget," www.ebudget.ca.gov (accessed 9/9/12).

paying about two-thirds of the income tax, while the bottom 40 percent pay less than 1 percent.[6] This is one of the most progressive personal income taxes in the nation. Regular income (salaries and wages) does not vary that much from year to year, but capital gains income (income from selling stock that has appreciated in value, for example) varies considerably from one year to the next, making revenues from the income tax fluctuate considerably.

Governor Jerry Brown's initiative proposal on the November 2012 ballot established three new brackets for taxpayers who make more than $250,000 per year: at 10.3, 11.3, and 12.3 percent of income. The new brackets are temporary, lasting for seven years, from 2012 to 2018. They make the California state income tax even more progressive than it is at present, reflecting the income level of the state (higher than the nation's; see Chapter 1).

SALES TAX The state sales tax is 7.5 percent. Counties or taxing districts are allowed to add between 0.13 and 0.5 percent per local district for local services. In some areas there is more than one district tax in effect. The average sales tax in California is 7.75 percent. The minimum in any area is 7.5 percent. The maximum is in two cities in Los Angeles County, Pico Rivera and South Gate, at about 10 percent. Economists consider the sales tax regressive—that is, as individual or household income increases, the proportion of income paid through the tax decreases, because lower-income households spend a higher proportion of their incomes on consumption goods that are taxed compared with higher income households. In California, the state refunds 1.25 percent of its share to the local city and county;

this feature has led many cities to search for businesses that are both clean industries and have a high sales volume, such as big-box shopping centers and automobile dealerships.

A state sales tax has existed in California since 1933, with the rate being raised on the average every five years. Governor Jerry Brown's proposal on the November 2012 ballot raised the state sales tax one-quarter of 1 percent temporarily, from 2013 to 2015.

The sales tax is based on an older conception of the economy in which most of the economy consists of goods that are bought and sold. The modern economy is over half services, but these are not taxed at all in California, as the sales tax was developed over 50 years ago and has not been updated. In many states, at least some services are taxed. Having a broader base on the sales tax would enable the rate to be lowered from its current high level, but finding a two-thirds majority in the legislature to pass a tax reform act is close to impossible.

PROPERTY TAX All owners of property pay California's property tax, limited under Proposition 13 to 1 percent of the assessed value in 1975 or the value of a more recent sale. Once acquired, annual tax increases are limited to 2 percent or the amount of inflation, whichever is less. Proposition 13 passed overwhelmingly in 1978 and contains provisions requiring special votes greater than 50 percent for legislators and voters to raise taxes. Proposition 13 rolled back property taxes in California by more than half, and the state has endeavored to make up the difference ever since. Local property tax revenue available for cities, counties, and school districts has been substantially reduced. As a result, all local government entities are more reliant on the state for revenue, and decision-making power has substantially shifted, in the eyes of virtually all observers, from the local level to the state level. School districts are an excellent example of the effects. Whereas California once had some of the best-quality and best-funded schools in the nation, its expenditures per pupil have fallen in comparison to the rest of the nation, its staff per student ratio is now 70 percent of the average for other states, its student achievement levels lag behind the rest of the nation, and a substantially greater proportion of high-income families send their children to private schools compared to the pre-1978 period. At the same time, teacher salaries are relatively high because of the cost of living, in particular housing prices, and the desire to attract good-quality recruits to the profession. The infrastructure discussion in Chapter 10 has more examples.

CORPORATION TAX The corporation tax taxes corporate profits and provides about 6 percent of state revenues, according to Table 8.1 and Figure 8.2. The corporation tax structure is cited favorably by *Governing* magazine in its appraisal of the state's tax system as "tough on the creation of tax-dodge subsidiaries, and the law covers a firm's property and assets, not just its sales."[7] Almost 500,000 corporations filed tax returns in 1999, but "the 1.9 percent with taxable incomes in excess of $1 million paid 80.1 percent of the tax. The ten largest corporations pay 20 percent of the tax in any given year."[8]

The overall tax structure, compared to other states, depends more on taxes that are volatile—that is, they go up and down with the economy (income tax, sales tax)—and less on taxes that don't vary with the economy (the property tax) because of the Proposition 13 limits. The average state obtains 29 percent of its total state and local tax funds from the property tax, but because of Proposition 13's limits, California obtains only 22 percent.

INDIAN GAMBLING Governor Schwarzenegger attempted to increase the amount of revenue received for the General Fund from Indian gambling operations in California. In 2005–06, the state received only $27 million for the General Fund of the $301 million the state got as a result of the tribal–state gambling compacts negotiated by the governor and ratified by the legislature. In 2008–09, the governor's budget projected $430 million in revenues, but much less was actually received. In the current budget, the subject isn't even mentioned.

How Well Does the Taxing System Function?

The taxing system seems to be functioning poorly. *Governing* magazine's February 2003 analysis, "The Way We Tax," gave California one star out of four in the category "Adequacy of Revenue," two out of four in "Fairness to Taxpayers," and two out of four in "Management of System."[9] Only Tennessee received a lower overall rating, and four other states were tied with California. Some of the problem areas:

- The "highly progressive—and volatile" income tax depends too much on capital gains being taxed at the same level as regular income. Thus, when the stock market soared in 2000, tax revenues soared also, but the state received only half this amount the very next year. In 2008, for example, the forecast for the income tax dropped 13 percent in just six months due to the downturn in the economy.

- Although the state income tax is highly progressive, the sales tax is highly regressive and the entire tax system is regressive as a whole, meaning that those at the bottom of the income distribution pay a higher proportion of their incomes as taxes to the state than those at the top. Figure 8.3 shows the percentage that each quintile, or fifth, paid to the state in all taxes in 2009: sales tax, business taxes, property tax, and personal and corporate income taxes.

- In 2009, Governor Schwarzenegger and the legislative leadership agreed to establish the Commission on the 21st Century Economy to suggest ways to modernize California's out-of-date revenue structure. A majority of the bipartisan commission recommended reducing the personal income tax substantially and eliminating the state sales tax and corporate tax, substituting in their place a "business net receipts tax," not to exceed 4 percent, that would be applied to the net receipts of all businesses. Small businesses with less than $500,000 in annual receipts would be exempt. Perceived as a conservative report, it was thoroughly rejected by liberals in the legislature. As a result, nothing came of the recommendations.

- "The state tax structure is highly elastic and, increasingly, . . . spending is inelastic," according to John Ellwood, a professor at the University of California, Berkeley. An elastic tax structure is one that would vary considerably as the economy expands and contracts, whereas an inelastic structure would not vary in those circumstances. So taxes received go up and down as the economy changes over time, but expenditures for the most part do not change, or change very slowly.

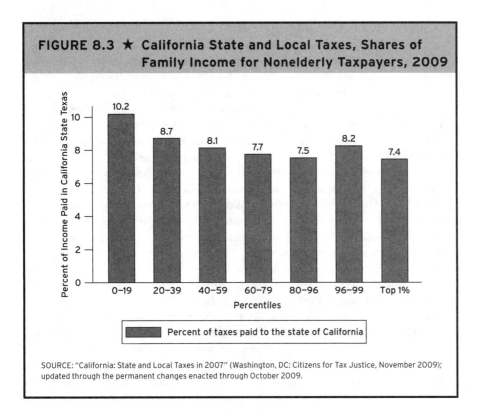

FIGURE 8.3 ★ California State and Local Taxes, Shares of Family Income for Nonelderly Taxpayers, 2009

SOURCE: "California: State and Local Taxes in 2007" (Washington, DC: Citizens for Tax Justice, November 2009); updated through the permanent changes enacted through October 2009.

- The sales tax focuses on goods that are sold, reflecting the manufacturing economy in place when the tax was developed. But the modern economy has shifted toward services, which are not taxed—for example, a doctor's office visit or the labor charge when your automobile is fixed. Broadening the base of the sales tax would enable the high rate (compared to other states) to be lowered.

- "Ballot measures have imposed rigid spending demands" (discussed in the section "Budgetary Limitations," later in the chapter).

- Tax subsidies have proliferated as the legislature has added them in recent years as inducements to obtain the two-thirds majority necessary to pass the budget.

- Tax administration is split among the Franchise Tax Board, the Board of Equalization, and the Employment Development Department, considered an inefficient arrangement.

Is California Overtaxed?

Conservatives certainly think California is overtaxed. The California Taxpayers Association makes the case that "the extraordinary level of taxation in California can provide more than enough in tax revenue to fund police and fire services, education for our children, and public works projects and health and welfare services for California's poor."[10] Taxes are so high, in their view, that the state is becoming economically uncompetitive with other states.

California is a relatively rich state. Its household and median family incomes are some $5,000 (or more) higher than the U.S. averages. The income and sales tax rates are among the higher tax rates of all American states. However, there are numerous exemptions that bring the total tax rate lower—sufficiently low that the total state and local tax burden for 2009, according to the U.S. Bureau of Economic Analysis and the Census Bureau, is 20th among all states at 15.99 percent of personal income, compared to the national average of 15.43 percent.[11]

The most important thing about California's tax structure is not that it is high or higher but that it is outmoded. It reflects the economy of the 1950s and Proposition 13 decisions made in the 1970s. The property tax collects less money than other wealthy states because of Proposition 13. The sales tax is based on the purchase of goods (with food exempted), not on the modern economy, which is based on services. Lower- and middle-class families with children are largely exempted from the personal income tax. The bottom line is that, like so many areas of the state's governmental structure, California's tax structure needs to be reformed. Without tax reform, California will continue to be a battleground for both liberals and conservatives, with conservatives seeking to lower the highest rates, and liberals seeking exemptions for the poor and middle class.

Most conservative groups rate California's business climate as one of the worst of any state due to the high levels of taxes; the taxation of capital gains at regular tax rates; and the number of regulations and permits that must be taken account of to establish, run, and expand a business. Nevertheless, many large corporations are located in California, particularly in Silicon Valley (the area between San Francisco and San Jose) because of the wealth of skilled talent in the area's labor market.

Moreover, business has many benefits in the tax system. Although the bank and corporation tax is almost 9 percent, there are so many exemptions that the tax rate on the $1 trillion California economy is about two-thirds of 1 percent. Proposition 13 gives businesses relatively low property tax rates, especially because the turnover rate for business and commercial property is much lower than the rate for private homes. All told, however, most do not find that the benefits for business outweigh the poor business climate. Whether California can simplify the vast array of permitting and regulatory agencies characteristic of large, diverse states is another question. So far, little progress has been made.

One question is whether California's level of taxes reduces the growth the state would otherwise experience. An analysis of the growth rates of nine states with a high rate of personal income taxation compared to the nine states that lack any personal income tax shows that there is no conclusive relationship. In fact, the states that grow the most seem to be those that have high rates of population growth, and several of the nonincome tax states have economic resources (oil in particular, which is why they don't have a state income tax) not available to other states.[12]

Expenditures

Again looking at all expenditures, the following are the major categories of the budget for 2012–13:

Table 8.2 indicates that the largest category is "health and human services," at $44.9 billion for 2012–13 and about 32 percent of the entire budget. This category includes Medi-Cal, California's Medicaid program, which provides health cover-

TABLE 8.2 ★ State Expenditures by Category, 2012-13 Budget[a]

EXPENDITURES	DOLLARS (IN BILLIONS)	PERCENT OF TOTAL EXPENDITURES
Health and human services	44.9	32
Education (K–12)	39.6	28
Business, transportation, housing	15.8	11
Higher education	10.1	7
Corrections and rehabilitation	9.0	7
Legislative, judicial, executive	6.1	5
Resources	6.0	5
Environmental protection	1.9	2
General government	2.6	2
Others	1.8	1
Total	122.6	

[a]Includes the General Fund, special funds, and bond funds.
SOURCE: California Department of Finance, "2012–13," www.ebudget.ca.gov (accessed 9/9/12).

age for the poor as well as for senior citizens in nursing homes; the public health system; Healthy Families, California's state children's health insurance program; welfare; Temporary Assistance for Needy Families; and the state contribution to food stamps and the Women, Infants, and Children (WIC) supplemental food program, among many others.

"Education (K–12)" is the second largest portion of the state budget at $39.6 billion and 28 percent of total expenditures. There is a long, gradual upward trend in the proportion of the budget devoted to education, although there is a slight decline in the last several fiscal years because of declining state revenues. With the passage of Proposition 13, a gradually increasing proportion of the state general fund has been spent on K–12 education. The money in this category supplements property tax revenues for education, collected by each county.

The third largest category is "business, transportation, and housing," at $15.8 billion or 11 percent of the state budget. This area includes Caltrans, which maintains the state's roads; the Department of Motor Vehicles (DMV); and the departments that regulate corporations, alcoholic beverages, real estate, managed health care, and high-speed rail, among others. (The high-speed rail area includes only $15 million for state positions to manage the high-speed rail authority; if the high-speed railroad is actually implemented, construction funds will come from the federal government and bond issues.) Most programs in the business, transportation, and housing area are largely funded by special funds and taxes, not through the general fund.

"Higher education" is the fourth largest category at $10.1 billion and 7 percent of total expenditures. Higher education includes funding for the community college system (112 campuses), the CSU system (23 campuses), and the UC system (10 campuses). Since 1980–81 there has been a trend downward in the proportion of the budget devoted to higher education. In recent years, state funding for higher education has been cut severely, as indicated in the opening vignette to this chapter. Tuition increases have partially replaced the lost state funding.

The "corrections and rehabilitation" category provides funding for the state prisons and youth authorities. This category increased steadily from 1980–81 through the mid-1990s as the public demanded three-strikes laws and similar measures, but has since leveled off.

The "others" category provides funding for everything else in the state budget, from the coastal commissions to the state bureaucracy.

Figure 8.4 depicts the 2012–13 budget.

Why Do Revenues Vary So Much?

California's budget goes up and down each year, soaring when the economy is healthy and plunging in even the mildest recessions. Here is why:

- The economy. Revenues from the sales tax and the personal income tax depend on how the state economy performs each year.

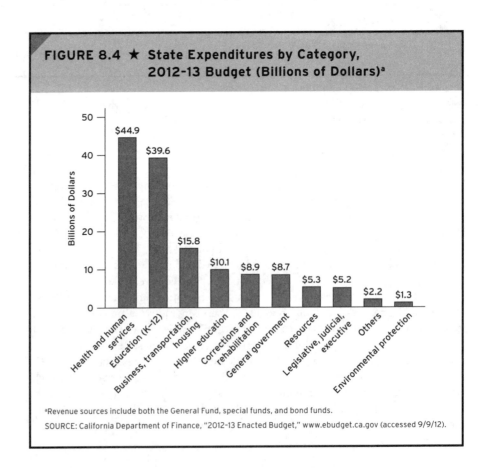

FIGURE 8.4 ★ State Expenditures by Category, 2012-13 Budget (Billions of Dollars)[a]

[a]Revenue sources include both the General Fund, special funds, and bond funds.

SOURCE: California Department of Finance, "2012-13 Enacted Budget," www.ebudget.ca.gov (accessed 9/9/12).

- Compared to other states, the budget relies more on the personal income tax, the capital gains portion of which soars when stock options are cashed out, than on the property tax, limited in 1978 by Proposition 13.

Budgetary Limitations

In addition to passing bond issues, through initiatives California voters have limited what the state government can do in some very significant areas. Here are the most significant:[13]

- **Proposition 13 (1978)** cut property taxes to 1 percent of the assessed valuation of the property in 1975 and allows reassessment only when the property is sold. If justified by inflation, the tax can rise a maximum of 2 percent in between assessments.

- **Proposition 62 (1986)** requires a vote of the electorate on all taxes that might be used to replace revenues lost under Proposition 13.

- **Proposition 98 (1988)** requires that at least 40 percent of the general fund be devoted to K–14 education, including community colleges; annual increases are to be at least equal to the increase in school enrollment and the cost of living.

- **Proposition 99 (1988)** mandated a 25¢ tax on cigarettes, with the proceeds to be spent on antismoking campaigns and medical research.

- **Proposition 111 (1990)** increased the gas tax and trucking fees, with the proceeds required to be spent on transportation projects.

- **Proposition 5 (1998)** mandated the state to negotiate a compact to allow tribal casinos in California.

- **Proposition 42 (2002)** requires that the sales tax on gasoline be devoted to transportation-related projects.

- **Proposition 49 (2002)**, supported by actor and (at that point) potential Republican candidate for governor Arnold Schwarzenegger, requires that several hundred million dollars be spent on after-school programs.

- **Proposition 71 (2004)** authorizes the sale of $3 billion in bonds to fund stem-cell research in the state.

- **Propositions 1A, 1B, 1C, 1D, 1E, 84 (2006)** authorizes over $40 billion in bonds to be spent on infrastructure improvements in the state. The interest on these bonds is paid from the budget each year.

- **Proposition 1A (2008)**, the "Safe, Reliable High-Speed Passenger Train Bond Act for the 21st Century," authorizes the sale of $9.9 billion in bonds to build a high-speed train connecting San Diego, Los Angeles, Bakersfield, San Francisco, and Sacramento. The interest from the bonds, when sold, will be $600 million per year out of the General Fund.

Of these, the two that have had the most effect are Propositions 13 and 98. Proposition 13 has made the state budget more reliant on taxes that vary with the economy and less reliant on sources of income that don't vary with the economy, particularly the property tax. Proposition 98 dictated that a certain proportion of the budget, almost half when higher education is included, must be devoted to one policy area.

Because the initiative requires only a majority vote, it is relatively easy to authorize expenditures through the initiative compared with going through the legislature. California has become a state in which it is easy to lower taxes/budget items and to authorize expenditures through the initiative but increasingly difficult to raise the funds to pay for all these items that the voters find so popular.

Recent California Budgets and the Budget Process

In each of the recent years, California lawmakers and the governor have closed the budget gap with the standard techniques used in other states—incremental tax increases; cuts in education, health, and social services, the largest portions of the budget; and borrowing through bond issues that are repaid over a 5- to 10-year period to cover a portion of the yearly deficit. California Forward, a new bipartisan group aimed at fixing some of California's perennial budget process problems, stated in 2008 that

> the current budget process is largely a relic of the mid-20th Century, with the focus on how much to increase spending (or how much to cut), rather than the value that public services bring to Californians over time. These annual budget decisions often either push California's fiscal systems toward long-term solvency or away from it. The ongoing and chronic imbalance between revenues and expenditures is one indicator of system failure. Changing how budget process decisions are made could enable public leaders to deal with the more intractable and complex problems involving the revenue system and the state-local relationship.

They identify, as we have, the key problems of budgeting:

> The costs of operating state programs are growing faster than the revenue base that supports them. The revenue system is highly sensitive to changes in the economy, producing significant volatility. The single-year budgeting horizon encourages short-term fixes, rather than long-term solutions. The budget does not take a strategic approach to ensure a return on public investments and there is a lack of public and legislative review of how money is spent.[14]

Many commentators noted the cumulative effect of the fees and caps that have been proposed more and more frequently in recent years.[15] Traditionally, California tried to supply sufficient services for all, on the principle that "if you're eligible, we'll serve you." The community colleges guarantee, for example, that any high school graduate can go to college. That principle has been shifting, though. The Schwarzenegger budget for 2004–05 in particular had caps on the number of individuals who can be served in various programs; immigrants in Medi-Cal and the program that supplies drugs for those with AIDS are both capped at the level of January 1, 2004. California's fees for students attending CSU and community colleges used to be among the lowest in the nation; they have increased substantially in recent years. Measures are often proposed as emergency measures, but few emergency measures have been repealed in the past. In short, there is a lowered expectation for services that has become particularly apparent in the Schwarzenegger and Jerry Brown eras but has been in the background for the last decade or more.

BOX 8.3   What Exactly Is Proposition 13?

Proposition 13, passed overwhelmingly by the voters in June 1978, had the following provisions:

- All property taxes are rolled back to a maximum of 1 percent of the value of the property in 1975-76.

- The value of the property, and thus the tax paid, was allowed to increase by the rate of inflation, but the inflation rate was capped at 2 percent per year.

- When ownership changed, property would be revalued at the current market value.

- No new property taxes could be imposed, either by the state or by local governments.

- Any "special taxes" could be imposed only by a two-thirds margin of the voters in the particular area (the state legislature was already under a two-thirds approval rule for raising taxes, a rule in force since 1933).

- All property taxes collected were to be distributed "according to law," and because no law existed, the legislature had to create one, which it did in 1978 and 1979.

The most immediate change was to local governments. Before 1978, they had each established their own property tax rate, designed to produce sufficient revenues to accomplish the particular function of the agency. Now, instead, each agency's property tax rate was irrelevant; the state would decide "according to law" which agency got which amount of money. The total property tax collected fell by over half. The state, however, had a $5 billion surplus, which helped bridge the gap for several years.

The single biggest change is that the state assumed considerable authority over what used to be local government issues.[a] Local governments used to set the local tax rate to produce sufficient funds for the level of public services that each locality desired. Instead, those decisions are now made by the state, and "clearly, the property tax is now really a state tax."[b]

Another consequence flows from the provision that requires a two-thirds vote of the local area to impose or raise a tax. Many localities have had votes of 60 to 66 percent, just short of the required two-thirds, and have not been able to do such things as acquire land for parks. School bond issues, however, require only a 55 percent vote as a result of Proposition 39 in 2000, which authorized bonds for the repair and construction of school facilities if approved by 55 percent of the local voters, rather than two-thirds.

One of the most important consequences is called "the fiscalization of land use"– that is, the tendency of local governments not only to evaluate land use changes in terms of how much money will be brought to the local government but to make decisions on that basis. Because localities receive a share of the state sales tax, land use changes that produce a lot of sales tax revenues are preferred. Big-box shopping centers and auto malls have been favored by many cities in preference to housing developments. Along with favoring certain kinds of developments, development fees and other ways to obtain revenue that is not available through the property tax have increased substantially.

Finally, we have seen the development of many "arcane" financing techniques, those intricate enough to be understood only by a few. These are also designed to help obtain revenues to replace property taxes.

a. The best description of Proposition 13 and its implications is Jeffrey I. Chapman, "Proposition 13: Some Unintended Consequences," Public Policy Institute of California, September 1998, www.ppic.org (accessed 7/27/12).
b. Chapman, "Proposition 13," p. 22.

The California Budgetary Process: Where Are We Now?

As of 2012, the budgetary process needed substantial reform. Dan Walters, a respected California journalist, states that the inability of the legislature to deal with the budget crisis and fiscal matters in general seems to be a reflection of three structural factors:

1. The extremely short term limits on the legislature, meaning that few politicians present in the twenty-first century were also present in the early 1990s during the last budget crisis. The leadership is inexperienced compared to other states, and "current members [are relieved] of responsibility for past decisions."[16]

2. The bipartisan gerrymander of legislative districts after the 2000 Census, which produced an overwhelming number of safe districts and seems to have reduced the willingness of legislators to work for bipartisan solutions and compromise. In 2008, voters approved Proposition 11, which formed a citizens' commission to draw the state's Assembly and Senate districts after the 2010 Census. The 2012 election results showed that more of California's legislative districts were competitive than in earlier elections.

3. The two-thirds majority requirement for passing budgets and imposing tax increases. This, as we know, was modified by Proposition 25 in November 2010 to require only a majority to pass the budget each year. The two-thirds requirement still holds for tax increases and for the badly needed tax reform that would broaden the tax base and lower tax rates.

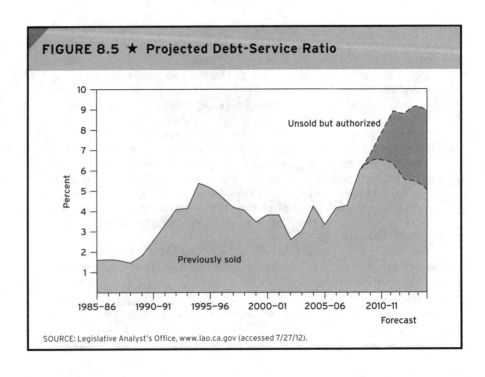

FIGURE 8.5 ★ Projected Debt-Service Ratio

SOURCE: Legislative Analyst's Office, www.lao.ca.gov (accessed 7/27/12).

In addition, there is a fourth factor—the citizens of California, who are willing to authorize all manner of financial allocations from the General Fund through the initiative process. These allocations vary from the self-serving to those with which no one would argue. But none has a dedicated new revenue source—each is an additional allocation from the General Fund, reducing the funds available for existing programs. Higher education, in particular, has been hurt by these actions. The willingness of the voters to authorize bond issues is leading to substantial additional debt payments from the General Fund, as pictured in Figure 8.5 from the Legislative Analyst's Office.

Data from the Census and Moody's show that California's net tax supported debt per capita and its debt as a proportion of 2010 personal income are number two in the nation, after New York.[17] The national median tax supported debt per capita is $1,066; California's is $2,542. The national median for net tax supported debt per capita as a proportion of 2010 personal income is 2.8 percent; California's is 6.8 percent. California's debt is high by any standard. While Californians may no longer feel that they can have every service imaginable without paying any higher taxes, they clearly haven't decided to pay for their past debts.

FOR FURTHER READING

Barrett, Katherine, Richard Greene, Michele Mariani, and Anya Sostek. "The Way We Tax." *Governing* (February 2003): 20.

Baldassare, Mark, and Christopher Hoene. *Local Budgets and Tax Policies in California and U.S. Cities: Surveys of City Officials*. San Francisco: Public Policy Institute of California, December 2004.

Baldassare, Mark, and Matthew Newman. *The State Budget and Local Health Services in California: Surveys of Local Health Officials*. San Francisco: Public Policy Institute of California, September 2005.

———. "Budget Backgrounder, A Mini-Primer on Bonds." Sacramento: California Budget Project, February 2006.

———. *A Budget for All Californians: Improving the Transparency and Accountability of the State Budget*. Sacramento: California Budget Project, May 2006.

———. "Governor Releases Proposed 2008–09 Budget." Sacramento: California Budget Project, January 2008.

California Budget Project. "Who Pays Taxes in California?" Sacramento: California Budget Project, April 2008. www.cbp.org. Accessed 7/30/12.

California Taxpayers Association. "Cal-Tax: Taxes Are Heavy Burden in California." www.caltax.org/California.htm. Accessed 7/30/12.

Howard, John. "The Schwarzenegger Budget." *California Journal* (February 2004): 44–47.

Legislative Analyst's Office. "California's Tax System: A Primer," April 2007. www.lao.ca.gov/2007/tax_primer/tax_primer _040907.aspx. Accessed 7/30/12.

Public Policy Institute of California. "Just the Facts: California's State Budget." San Francisco: Public Policy Institute of California, April 2010. www.ppic.org. Accessed 7/30/12.

———. "Just the Facts: Proposition 13, 30 Years Later." San Francisco: Public Policy Institute of California, June 2008. www.ppic.org. Accessed 7/30/12.

ON THE WEB

California Budget Project: www.cbp.org (accessed 7/30/12).

California Forward: www.cafwd.org (accessed 11/5/12). California Forward promotes better financial policy and quality public services.

Howard Jarvis Taxpayers Association: www.hjta.org (accessed 11/5/12).

Legislative Analyst's Office: www.lao.ca.gov (accessed 7/30/12).

State of California, Department of Finance–budget update site: www.ebudget.ca.gov (accessed 7/30/12).

State of California, Department of Finance: www.dof.ca.gov/ Research/Research.php (accessed 7/30/12). California statistics and demographic information site

SUMMARY

I. What is the California budget?
  A. The governor's and legislature's views of the future.
    1. The future of the state's economy (economic assumptions).
    2. The future income of the state (revenues).
    3. Future spending of the state (expenditures).
  B. The budget is at the center of what the state does each year.

II. How is the budget formulated?
  A. Agencies send their requests to the governor each fall.
  B. The governor sends a balanced budget request to the legislature each January for the fiscal year starting the next July 1.
  C. The legislature adopts a balanced budget by June 15 each year, for the fiscal year to start July 1.
    1. The budget is almost always late. Only four budgets have been on time in the last two decades, and those were budget-surplus years.
    2. In recent years, the volatility of the state's revenues has caused the budget to be substantially readjusted during the fiscal year.
  D. The governor has a line-item veto, allowing him or her to reduce any line-item dollar amount downward, even to zero. However, the governor may not raise any line item.
  E. The legislature is assisted by its own neutral budget office—the Legislative Analyst's Office.
  F. If the Assembly and state senate versions of the budget differ, a "budget conference committee" will attempt to iron out the differences.
    1. If this fails, the Big 5 (the governor and the majority and minority leaders of both the Assembly and senate) will meet.
    2. Until 2011, this process was not successful, with budgets approved in late summer or early fall at best.
    3. In 2011 and 2012, because only a simple majority was needed to approve the budget, budgets were approved close to the deadline of June 15.
  G. Agencies then implement the approved budget, including studies to be carried out and presented to the legislature.

III. Revenues.
  A. Personal income tax—the largest source of income for the general fund and highly progressive.
  B. Sales tax—the next largest source of income, increased by 1 percent for 2009–10 and 2010–11. Local governments can add a small amount to the state sales tax. A portion of the tax is refunded to them. Many localities have added to their communities sales-tax-producing businesses such as big-box shopping centers and automobile dealerships specifically because of the revenues they would receive from the state.
  C. Corporate tax—the third largest source of revenues. A new method of calculating what is owed may reduce the state's revenues from this tax substantially starting in 2011–12.
  D. The California tax system is very volatile, compared to other states. It depends on the ups and downs of the economy and produces greater surges in revenue and precipitous falls when the economy booms or a recession takes place.

IV. Expenditures.
  A. Education (K–12)—the largest single expenditure. Proposition 98 requires K–12 expenditures to be over 40 percent of the state General Fund. K–12 education and higher education expenditures together equal or are greater than 50 percent of the state General Fund.
  B. Health and human services is the next highest category.
  C. Business, transportation, and housing is the third-highest category.

V. Limitations on the budget.
  A. The most substantial limitations have come from initiatives passed by the voters.
  B. Proposition 13, which limits the property tax to 1 percent of the value of one's house, and Proposition 98, which guarantees a certain amount to K–12 education, are the most important of these limitations.
  C. Cumulatively, the limitations have guaranteed well over half the General Fund and at least half of all expenditures, giving the governor and legislature less flexibility than they would have in other states. That was the intent of the initiatives—to limit what the governor and legislature can do. The level of distrust the voters have for the governor and legislature is very high in California.

VI. Recent state budgets have been characterized by huge and fluctuating gaps between revenues and expenditures.
  A. These have made it difficult to find the middle ground necessary to obtain a two-thirds vote in the legislature for a budget. Starting in 2011, only a majority will be required.
  B. Legislators and the governor have rolled over part of the debt in some recent years by borrowing against the future, through a bond issue. In general, this is a poor practice because the interest payments on the bonds become another amount that is "locked in" next year's budget and those of subsequent years as well.

VII. Why is budgeting such a problem in California?
  A. California's term limits are too short. Legislators do not get enough time to learn the intricacies of their jobs.
  B. Gerrymandered legislative districts have produced safe seats, so that legislators generally do not have to worry about losing in the next election. The process has produced even more partisan legislators than we would see otherwise. Proposition 8, approved in 2008, authorized the formation of a citizens' commission to redistrict the Assembly and state senate in 2011, after receiving the results of the 2010 Census. The first election held under the new seats was in 2012.
  C. The two-thirds majority for passing a budget and raising taxes has made the process difficult for both parties.
    1. Because one party generally supports high levels of services and taxes, and another takes the opposite approach, compromise has been difficult.
    2. Few states require a two-thirds majority to pass the budget. More do so to raise taxes.
  D. The initiative process makes it relatively easy for interest groups to sponsor initiatives to allocate proportions of the General Fund for themselves. The state's voters are too willing to approve such initiatives.

PRACTICE QUIZ

1. Both the governor and the legislature are obliged by the California state constitution to pass a balanced budget.
   a) true
   b) false
2. The state of California cannot pass its budget each year starting in 2011 unless the Assembly and state Senate pass the budget by
   a) 50 percent plus 1 vote.
   b) 55 percent.
   c) 66.7 percent.
   d) 75 percent.
3. The state of California cannot raise state taxes unless the Assembly and state Senate pass the relevant law by
   a) 50 percent plus 1 vote.
   b) 55 percent.
   c) 66.7 percent.
   d) 75 percent.
4. Proposition 13 requires
   a) property taxes to be lowered to the level when the property was last sold. Property tax values can rise 2 percent per year.
   b) property taxes to be set at 1975 levels; property is reassessed when it is sold. Property tax values can rise 2 percent per year.
   c) property taxes to be lowered to 1945 levels; property is reassessed when it is sold. The level of the tax can rise 3 percent per year.
   d) Property taxes to be raised to the appropriate level when the property on both sides of a house or business has been sold—all the property is then reassessed at current values. The level of the tax can rise 2 percent per year if the property is not sold.
5. Proposition 98 requires education spending to be at least
   a) 50 percent of the entire state budget.
   b) 50 percent of the general fund.

   c) 33.3 percent of the general fund.
   d) 40 percent of the general fund.
6. How do term limits affect the budget process?
   a) More minority and female legislators are elected, and they are more willing to compromise to enact the budget.
   b) Former senior legislators, while not able to hold their current seats, return to the legislature each year to offer their ideas about how to solve the budget crisis.
   c) Term limits have produced majority and minority leaders in both the Assembly and Senate who are willing to compromise and get the job done.
   d) Term limits have produced a less experienced leadership who have found it difficult to compromise and enact the budget.
7. The governor's line-item veto allows
   a) the governor to lower any appropriation item.
   b) the governor, in conjunction with an agency, to veto any bill in its entirety.
   c) the governor to "pencil out" any line or sentence in any bill.
   d) the governor to raise or lower any appropriation item, including lowering the item to zero.
8. The governor's line-item veto may be overridden by a 50 percent plus one vote in both houses of the legislature.
   a) true
   b) false
9. The credit rating assigned to the state of California by Moody's, Fitch Ratings, or Standard & Poor's is important because
   a) the credit rating influences the size of the deficit or surplus California may have in any given fiscal year.
   b) when the credit rating goes down, the interest rate that the state pays to float its bonds goes up.

c) when the credit rating goes up, the amount of interest the state pays goes down.
d) all of the above
e) none of the above
f) a and b above, but not c

10. Indian gambling revenues have become an extremely significant source of income for the state of California.
a) true
b) false

CRITICAL-THINKING QUESTIONS

1. How might California's tax system be made more predictable and less dependent on the economy than it is now? How might *Governing* magazine rate your proposed changes?
2. How should the budget process in California be reformed, assuming it should be reformed? What goals are important in reforming the process, and what changes in the process might achieve those goals?
3. Should the governor have more authority in the budget process? One of the key differences between California and Georgia was the difference in the power of the governor. Leaving aside the opinion you might have of the current incumbent, what reforms might help with the long-term budget process in California?
4. The other major player in the budget process is the legislature. How might the legislature's consideration of the budget be changed to make California's budget more predictable and timely?

KEY TERMS

At this point you should have a general understanding of the following concepts and terms:

big-box shopping centers/automobile dealerships (p. 165)
Budget Conference Committee (p. 161)
Department of Finance (p. 159)
governor's budget (p. 159)

Legislative Analyst's Office (p. 161)
line-item veto (p. 161)
May revise (p. 159)
Moody's, Fitch Ratings, Standard & Poor's ratings (p. 162)

personal income tax (p. 163)
progressive (p. 163)
regressive (p. 164)
sales tax (p. 164)
unified budget (p. 159)

9 Local Government

WHAT CALIFORNIA'S LOCAL GOVERNMENTS DO AND WHY THEY MATTER

Governing California would be hard to imagine without the more than 5,000 local governments that help run the state. Local officials and workers in cities, counties, school districts, special districts, and regional bodies all play an essential role. By late spring 2012, however, many local governments were in trouble, especially in the cities, and some of them were struggling to survive.

The complexity of the state's local government system makes it hard to generalize about what local governments do. But a short list would include the following:

★ General-purpose local governments, like cities and counties, do everything from putting out fires to cleaning the streets and seeing that the buses run on time. They protect the health, safety, welfare, and overall quality of life of all who live within their jurisdictions.

★ Limited-purpose governments, such as school districts and other special districts, deliver specific public services such as public education, pest abatement, and irrigation to meet particular needs within defined territorial boundaries.

★ Regional governments address problems such as air pollution and population growth that affect broad areas across many jurisdictions and that require comprehensive study and planning to solve.

★ Many local governments do the actual work involved in implementing state and federal laws, from control of water quality and production of affordable housing to homeland security.

★ Most local governments provide citizens with opportunities to learn about public problems, express their opinions, practice hands-on democracy, and collectively exercise some degree of popular control on issues they really care about close to home.

★ Some local governments experiment and innovate to pioneer new ways of serving citizens better or improving the democratic process. Often these local initiatives spread and can have major impacts in reforming how government works at the state and national levels.

Times have been hard for Californians the last few years. A prolonged and severe economic recession had taken its toll. But by spring 2012 things seemed to be getting better. For local government officials, however, hard times had become even harder as they coped with slashed budgets, reduced staffing, cutbacks in services, and projected revenue shortfalls as far as the eye could see. Many local officials, especially in the state's larger cities, also discovered, sometimes too late, that they faced unsustainable financial obligations to their current and retired employees. In some cases the projected costs of promised pensions and health benefits had already escalated out of control. One city, Vallejo, faced with such problems, had already declared bankruptcy in 2008. Another, Stockton, filed for bankruptcy in June 2012, followed by San Bernardino, in August 2012. Making things worse, an important source of revenues for many cities was suddenly extinguished in 2011. The state government, backed by the California Supreme Court, terminated the existence of nearly 400 community redevelopment agencies in one fell swoop and seized their money to help solve its own budget crisis. The state government was in trouble, too, and local governments would have to fend for themselves. If local government leaders could expect little support from the state, they could expect even less from the federal government, which continued to be paralyzed by legislative gridlock and polarized partisan politics.

On top of these multiple hardships, the youth-led Occupy Wall Street Movement that erupted in September 2011 in New York City had inspired scores of Occupy demonstrations and encampments in cities across the nation. This spontaneous grassroots movement gave voice to the anger and resentment of the 99 percent toward the rich and powerful 1 percent. It shifted the focus of national political discourse from important concerns about deficits and austerity to the even deeper issues of expanding income inequality, social injustice, and the plutocracy our democracy had seemingly become. But in many California cities, even the more liberal ones like San Francisco and Oakland, local governments bore the brunt of protest demands, the occasional outbreaks of violence, and the financial impact of all this disruption on local budgets and commerce. On December 12, 2011, for example, an estimated 3,000 marchers from Occupy Oakland, for the second time, shut down the Port of Oakland for a day. A few months later, on May 1, 2012, a band of self-described anarchists infiltrated an Occupy San Francisco protest in the city's Mission district and damaged over 30 businesses. (Occupy San Francisco leaders condemned the violence and raised funds to partially reimburse business owners for the costs of repairs.) Occupy demonstrations also flared up on some state college campuses. In November 2011, for example, student activists at UC Berkeley and UC Davis put up tents on their campuses and helped organize student protests of recent education budget cuts and skyrocketing tuitions. Later attempts by police to remove these encampments resulted in violent confrontations, including a notorious pepper-spraying incident at UC Davis.

Despite these challenges, if there is hope for economic recovery and democratic renewal in California, much of it lies with the state's local governments, especially in the cities, where most people live and work, where democracy still thrives, and where protests often give rise to needed political reforms. Local governments do a lot under extremely harsh conditions, and all of it matters.

The Legal Framework: Dillon's Rule, Home Rule, and Local Powers of Governance

The U.S. Constitution assigns power and authority to the national and state governments, but it says nothing about local governments. Counties, cities, special districts, and other forms of local government have no inherent rights or powers. What rights and powers they do have are conferred on them by the state constitution or state legislature.

The constitutional doctrine that gives states ultimate authority over local governments is known as Dillon's Rule. In 1868, Iowa judge John F. Dillon ruled that "municipal corporations" such as counties and cities are mere "creatures of the state" and may exercise only those powers delegated to them by the state.[1] Upheld by the U.S. Supreme Court in 1903 and again in 1923, Dillon's Rule is firmly established, at least in theory, as the basic legal framework for relations between state and local governments. In practice, however, only a few states, like Alabama, Idaho, and Nebraska, demand strict obedience to Dillon's Rule and require local governments to seek their permission in order to act. California, like most states, has passed government codes and home-rule laws that allow significant local discretion and autonomy. Within broad limits, county and city residents can select their own form of government, manage their own elections, raise their own revenues, and choose what kinds of functions to perform and at what levels of service.[2]

In California, under the provisions of Article XI, Section 5, of the state constitution and various court rulings,[3] most of the more populous cities and counties have adopted home-rule charters, which allow the maximum discretion and autonomy to local governments. The others are designated as general law cities and counties that fall more directly under state authority and control. To get an idea of just how far home-rule powers can be taken in asserting local autonomy, see Box 9.1 on home rule and local autonomy in San Francisco.

A more practical restraint on state meddling in local government is based on the maxim that all politics is local. State legislators, after all, are elected by local constituencies to protect their local interests, and they won't last long if they forget who brought them to the dance. These political realities have shielded local governments from the full blast of arbitrary state authority.[4] Finally, as part of the so-called devolution revolution that began in the 1970s, federal and state authorities have been only too eager to delegate responsibility to local governments to fend for themselves and solve their own problems, using their own money.

In sum, Dillon's Rule is very liberally construed in California. The state's constitutional and legal framework confers broad formal powers of local governance, especially in charter cities and counties. Home rule on paper, however, does not necessarily translate into home rule in reality. In recent years, as we shall see, the state's chronic budget crises and other financial disasters have been strangling the life out of some local governments and crippling the powers of others to govern. Formal authority minus needed resources equals impotent local government. That equation threatens to reduce the ideal of home rule and local autonomy to a myth.

BOX 9.1 — San Francisco: Pushing the Envelope of Home-Rule Powers

As a consolidated city and county, San Francisco has pushed the limits of home-rule powers about as far as they can go. Some examples:

CITY OF REFUGE LAWS

In the early 1980s, San Francisco declared itself a "sanctuary city." It has since passed a number of "city of refuge" laws to protect immigrants from illegal search and seizure by state and federal authorities.

LIMITS ON GROWTH AND NEW LABOR STANDARDS

Since the 1980s, San Francisco has imposed increasingly severe restrictions on high-rise construction, waterfront development, and land use generally. The city also began charging developer fees to raise new local revenues for affordable housing and public-transit improvements. In 2003, the city required all city employers to pay a high minimum wage and in 2006 to provide paid sick leave to all employees. In 2007, the city began offering affordable health care to all uninsured city residents.

GOVERNMENT REORGANIZATION AND ELECTORAL REFORMS

In 1995, San Francisco voters approved a charter amendment that consolidated the city's divided bureaucracy under mayoral authority. The following year, voters changed how they elected their Board of Supervisors, rejecting the at-large system in favor of district elections. In 2002, the city adopted ranked choice voting for district elections and citywide offices, the first major city in the nation to do so.

SOCIAL AND CULTURAL POLICY

In 1996, San Francisco passed its landmark Equal Benefits law, which requires all businesses and nonprofits that have contracts with the city to provide equal benefits to married employees and those with same-sex domestic partners. In February 2004, Mayor Gavin Newsom directed that official marriage licenses be granted to same-sex couples. A month later, more than 4,000 gay and lesbian couples had been married under the new local policy. The California Supreme Court ordered the city to halt the practice, pending judicial review. In May 2008, the court ruled that the state's ban on same-sex marriage was unconstitutional and that such marriages would be legal effective June 2008 for residents and nonresidents. On November 4, 2008, however, the state's voters approved an initiative constitutional amendment, Proposition 8, eliminating the right of same-sex couples to marry. The California Supreme Court ruled in 2009 that Proposition 8 was constitutional. On appeal, a federal district judge ruled in August 2010 that Proposition 8 violated the U.S. Constitution. Ban supporters, in turn, appealed to the U.S. Ninth Circuit Court of Appeals, which affirmed the District Court ruling in 2012. It is highly likely this case will reach the U.S. Supreme Court for final resolution.

As these examples illustrate, San Francisco often acts as if it were a state unto itself and not merely the creature of one. The decision to certify gay marriages, in particular, created a storm of legal challenge and political controversy across the nation. San Franciscans, however, seem to enjoy sparking conflict by pushing the envelope of their home-rule powers. Where they succeed, others may follow.

SOURCES: Richard Edward DeLeon, *Left Coast City: Progressive Politics in San Francisco, 1975–1991* (Lawrence: University Press of Kansas, 1992).
"San Francisco and Domestic Partners: New Fields of Battle in the Culture War," in *Culture Wars and Local Politics*, ed. Elaine B. Sharp (Lawrence: University Press of Kansas, 1999), pp. 117–36.
Rich DeLeon, "Only In San Francisco?: The City's Political Culture in Comparative Perspective," *SPUR Newsletter*, Report 411, November 12, 2002, www.spur.org/documents/pdf/021101_article_01.pdf (accessed 8/2/12).
"San Francisco: The Politics of Race, Land Use, and Ideology," in *Racial Politics in American Cities*, ed. Rufus P. Browning, Dale Rogers Marshall, and David H. Tabb, 3d ed. (New York: Longman, 2003), pp. 167–98.
Dean E. Murphy, "San Francisco Mayor Exults in Move on Gay Marriage," *New York Times*, February 19, 2004.

County Governments

At the first meeting of the California legislature in 1850, lawmakers divided the state into 27 counties for the purpose of administering state laws. Since then many new counties have been created, mostly by subdivision. The state's current 58 counties have been with us since 1907, when the last addition, Imperial County, was carved out of the old San Diego County (see Figure 9.1). Political movements have arisen from time to time that attempted to split an existing county to make a new one. An 1894 amendment to the state constitution, however, made it virtually impossible to do so by requiring a favorable majority vote in both the entire county affected and in the territory of the proposed new county.[5]

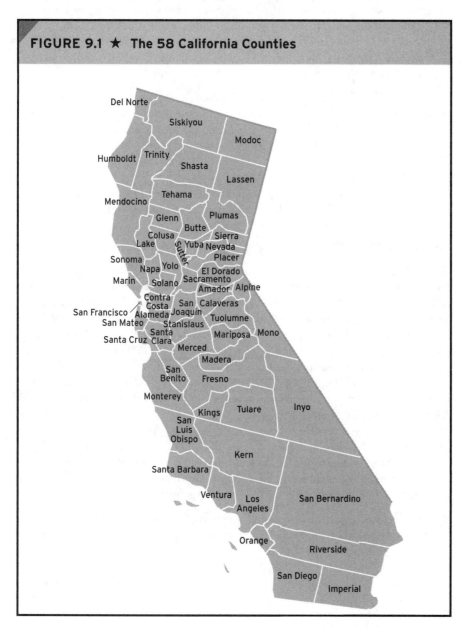

FIGURE 9.1 ★ The 58 California Counties

California's 58 counties vary greatly in their territory, population, and demographic characteristics.

- *Territory*—Just in terms of size, the differences are vast. For example, you could fit 427 areas the size of San Francisco County (47 square miles) within the borders of San Bernardino County (20,053 square miles). The differences in physical geography are equally extreme, ranging from deserts to rain forests, from flat farmlands to tall mountains. Some counties are densely urban and covered with cities, whereas others are so rural that coyotes outnumber people.

- *Population*—Alpine County's grand total of 1,061 residents could all live comfortably in one San Francisco precinct. Los Angeles County, at the other extreme, is bursting with nearly 10 million people, representing more than 28 percent of the state's entire population. The lowest-ranking 29 counties combined contain only 5 percent of the state's total population; the 5 most populous counties (Los Angeles, Orange, San Diego, San Bernardino, and Santa Clara) hold about 55 percent of the state's total.

- *Demography*—If you tour the state's 58 counties, you'll discover vastly different social and economic worlds. The populations of some counties are relatively poor, others relatively rich. Some are mostly white, others mainly nonwhite. Some are dominated by homeowners, others—for example, San Francisco—by renters.

Table 9.1 reports the lowest- and highest-ranking counties on these and other selected indicators to illustrate the extremes observed among California's counties.

Legal Framework

The state constitution provides a general legal framework for the governing of most counties, which are known as *general-law counties*. It prescribes the number and functions of elected county officials, how they are selected, and what they may or may not do in raising revenue, spending money, delivering services, and so on. Fourteen counties, however, have adopted a *home-rule charter*, which gives voters greater control over the selection of governing bodies and officers, more flexibility in raising taxes and revenues, and broader discretion in organizing to deliver services. All of the state's most populous counties and one small county, Tehama, with its 57,000 residents, are now *charter counties*. Voters can adopt a charter for their county government by a majority vote.

- Long content to live without a charter, the voters of Orange County finally adopted one in March 2002. They did so mainly to prevent the governor from appointing his own choice to fill a vacancy on the county board of supervisors, which he had the authority to do under the general-law provisions.

- San Francisco is an unusual case. It is governed under a single charter as a consolidated county and city, an arrangement that is unique in the state and rare in the country.

County charters vary widely in content and in the range of powers claimed for local control. When a charter does not mention a subject, that subject is governed by the general law.

TABLE 9.1 ★ Comparing the Counties of California

	LOWEST	HIGHEST
Total population (2011)	1,102 (Alpine)	9,889,056 (Los Angeles)
Land area (square miles)	47 (San Francisco)	20,053 (San Bernardino)
Population density (2011)	1.6 (Alpine)	17,179 (San Francisco)
White non-Hispanic (2011)	16.3% (Imperial)	87% (Sierra)
Hispanic (2011)	7.4% (Trinity)	80.6% (Imperial)
Asian/Pacific Islands (2011)	0.5% (Sierra)	34.4% (San Francisco)
Black (2008)	0.1% (Alpine)	15.2% (Solano)
Homeowners (2008)	39.5% (San Francisco)	73.1% (Placer)
Aged 25+ years with BA degree (2008)	10.1% (Kings)	56.9% (Marin)
Median family income (2008)	$37,936 (Imperial)	$91,982 (Marin)
Below poverty (2008)	6.1% (Marin)	22.9% (Imperial)
Unemployment (2012)	6.6% (Marin)	28.2% (Imperial)

SOURCES: 2008 data: U.S. Census Bureau, American Factfinder, 2008 American Community Survey 1-Year Estimates. http://factfinder.census.gov; 2011 data: U.S. Census Bureau, http://quickfacts.census.gov/qfd/states/06/06025 .html; 2012 data: California Economic Development Department, www.labormarketinfo.edd.ca.gov/Content .asp?pageid=170 (all accessed 8/2/12).

Government Organization

In all counties except San Francisco, an elected five-member board of supervisors exercises both legislative and executive authority. Given the extremes in the size of county populations, it shouldn't surprise you that small five-member boards yield huge disparities in political representation. For example, each board member in tiny Alpine County represents, on average, only 212 residents. In mammoth Los Angeles County, on the other hand, each board member represents nearly 2 million people, a number greater than the entire population of New Mexico.

County boards of supervisors, whose members are elected by districts for staggered four-year terms, not only pass laws, called *ordinances* at the local level, but also control and supervise the departments charged with administering them. This combination of legislative and executive authority gives county supervisors great power. From time to time, someone suggests a formal separation of powers and greater executive accountability. But nothing has changed in this regard and probably never will.

FIGURE 9.2 ★ Los Angeles County Organizational Chart

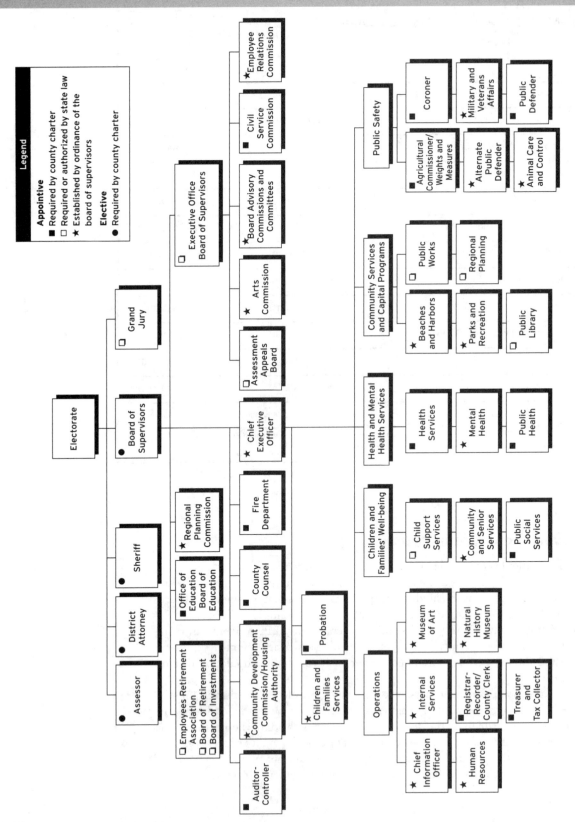

SOURCE: *County of Los Angeles Annual Report 2009–2010*, p. 5. Several departments report directly to the Board of Supervisors or are headed by elected officials, but work with the chief executive office through the clusters. These are assessor, auditor-controller, executive office of the Board of Supervisors, county counsel (Operations), community development commission (Community and Municipal Services); sheriff, district attorney, and fire (Public Safety).

As always, there is an exception: In the consolidated city and county government of San Francisco, an elected 11-member board of supervisors has legislative authority. An independently elected mayor has executive authority and some control, shared with many boards and commissions, over the bureaucracy.

In addition to the board of supervisors, other elected county officers required by general law include a sheriff, who enforces the law in areas outside the cities; a district attorney; and an assessor. A 1998 constitutional amendment consolidated municipal and superior trial courts into a single layer of superior court judges elected by county voters. Elections for all offices are nonpartisan. In terms of appointed positions, charter counties have considerable latitude in creating departments and agencies to serve their needs, either by charter provision or by ordinance. Other offices are required or authorized by state law. Some charter counties, like Los Angeles County, have appointed a chief administrative officer to manage their sprawling bureaucracies under board supervision.

Figure 9.2 shows Los Angeles County's organization chart. It illustrates the complexity of local government authority and responsibility that can be found in counties with large and diverse populations. By way of contrast, Figure 9.3 shows Placer County's organizational chart, which is much simpler and more typical of counties with small populations.

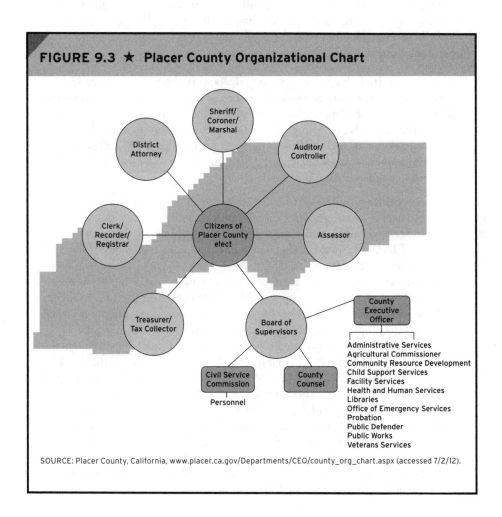

FIGURE 9.3 ★ Placer County Organizational Chart

SOURCE: Placer County, California, www.placer.ca.gov/Departments/CEO/county_org_chart.aspx (accessed 7/2/12).

County Government Functions and Responsibilities

County governments have major functions and responsibilities, most of them man-dated by state or federal law, especially outside the jurisdictions of cities. County responsibilities include bridges and highways, public safety, public health, employ-ment, parks and recreation, welfare and public assistance, public records, tax collection, general government, court administration, and land use. In the larger counties, the public workforce required to manage all this can be truly massive. Los Angeles County, for example, now has over 101,296 employees. The revenues needed to pay for their efforts can be equally huge. In 2011–12, for example, Los Angeles County raised and spent over $23.3 billion. Most of this money was received from intergovernmental transfers ($10.2 billion) and property taxes ($4.6 billion). Most of it was spent on public assistance ($5.9 billion), public safety ($6.2 billion), and health services ($6.7 billion).[6]

Decisions on land-use policy are perhaps the most important and controversial ones a county board of supervisors can make. If you're ever in the mood to watch a good political fight, attend a typical county board of supervisors meeting in places like Napa County or San Diego County. Areas like these still have plenty of open land outside the cities and fast-growing populations that fuel a demand for new housing construction, schools, and public infrastructure (sewers, highways, etc.). Landowners and developers typically badger the county board of supervisors to allow them to build, often with the result that conservationists, environmentalists, and other groups mobilize in opposition to push them back.

- In January 2010, Napa County supervisors were the target of several developer and environmentalist lawsuits related to land use. The economic downturn in the Napa Valley wine industry had created pressure to convert agricultural lands into homes. The developers sued the county to block overregulation of such lands and to protect private property rights. The environmentalists sued the county, charging that officials were failing to protect such lands from development.[7]

- More recently, on July 31, 2012, the Riverside County Board of Supervisors met to decide whether to "fast track" approval of Granite Construction's application to build a surface mine known as Liberty Quarry near the small town of Temecula. Fast-tracking would allow skipping the county planning commission's standard review and thus expedite the board's final decision on the project. The public debate at the crowded meeting was impassioned on both sides. Orange-shirted opponents faced off against green-shirted supporters. Representatives of the chamber of commerce, labor unions, and other groups backed the proposal, arguing that the quarry would stimulate the local economy and create badly need jobs. Temecula city officials, environmentalists, and leaders of the Pechanga Band of Luiseño Indians contended that the quarry would pollute the air, wreck the economy, and destroy a nearby sacred tribal site. One supervisor called Liberty Quarry "the most divisive project in county history." The board voted 3–2 to fast-track approval, prompting cheers from the green shirts and cries of outrage from the orange shirts. This story then ended abruptly and happily for all concerned. On November 15, 2012, just days before the board was scheduled to give its final approval, leaders of the Pechanga Band announced that they had reached an agreement with Granite Construction to purchase the Liberty Quarry site for $3 million and pay the firm an additional $17.35 million to cover its project costs. Granite was permitted to build its mine elsewhere miles from Temecula and the sacred tribal lands. The Pechanga Band promised to preserve the original site as it was. And Temecula officials would drop their lawsuit to stop the board from voting on a controversial decision it no longer had to make.[8]

As California's population continues to grow and to spread from the cities into the state's remaining farmlands and rural areas, you can expect to see more land-use battles erupting in the political arenas of county governments.

Local Agency Formation Commissions

All 58 California counties have a local agency formation commission (LAFCo), whose members are appointed by the county board of supervisors. These commissions play a critical role in resolving conflicts among the many local governments that often compete with one another for power and resources within their county jurisdictions. A county's LAFCo is responsible for

- reviewing and approving the incorporations of new cities, the formation of new special districts, and any proposed changes of jurisdictional boundaries, including annexations and detachments of territory, secessions, consolidations, mergers, and dissolutions.

- reviewing and approving contractual service agreements between local governments and between local governments and the private sector.

- defining the official spheres of influence for each city and special district.

- initiating proposals for consolidation, dissolution, mergers, and reorganizations if such changes seem necessary or desirable.

These powerful commissions are especially busy in counties that are rocked by large-scale land-use battles, such as San Diego County, Napa County, and Contra Costa County, or that teem with masses of people, multitudes of governments, and major secession movements, such as Los Angeles County.

City Governments

Legal Framework

Like counties, California's cities derive their powers as municipal corporations from the state constitution and state legislature. Within that legal framework, as of June 2010, the state's 481 incorporated cities fell into three categories: general-law cities (371), charter cities (109), and the unique case of San Francisco's consolidated city and county. The state Government Code, enacted by the legislature, specifies the general powers and structure of general-law cities. Broader home-rule powers are granted to charter cities, giving citizens more direct control over local affairs. Under these different arrangements, all cities have the power to legislate, as long as their local policies don't conflict with state or federal law. They have the power to raise revenues, levy taxes, charge license and service fees, and borrow. They may also hire personnel as needed; exercise police powers to enforce local, state, and federal laws; and condemn property for public use.

Incorporation: How Cities Are Born

The state grants powers to cities, and in that sense cities are indeed creatures of the state. But cities themselves are created only by the request, and with the consent, of the residents in a given area. In California, this process of *municipal incorporation* is typically initiated by a citizen petition or by a resolution of the county board of supervisors. Landowner petitions are also possible but rare. Some of the more important reasons that motivate residents to seek incorporation are

- to limit population growth, or perhaps to accelerate it.
- to provide more or better-quality services than those provided by the county.
- to prevent annexation by a nearby city.
- to create a unit of government more responsive to local needs and concerns.

A petition for municipal incorporation must be submitted to the county's LAFCo. The LAFCo panel reviews the proposed plans for the new city, its boundaries, service provisions, governing capacity, and financial viability. The LAFCo also studies the likely financial and other impacts of the proposed incorporation on neighboring local governments, including the county itself. If the petition for incorporation survives this initial review and a later public hearing and possible protests, it moves to an election. If a majority of voters living within the boundaries of the proposed new city approve, a new city is legally born.

New cities are created by incorporation quite frequently. Between 1962 and 2011, the number of cities in the state grew from 373 to 482.[9] Most recently, for example, on March 8, 2011, the residents of Jurupa Valley, an unincorporated community of about 95,000 in Riverside County, voted for cityhood effective July 1 that year. Residents in other unincorporated places, however, have rejected the opportunity to incorporate as a city and run their own show. The prospect of rapid growth and development, for example, scared many of the 57,000 residents of Castro Valley. In November 2002, they voted three to one against incorporation. They were happy to remain Northern California's largest unincorporated community and to continue being governed locally by the Alameda County Board of Supervisors.

City Government Functions and Responsibilities

City governments provide a wide range of services and facilities that directly affect the lives of their residents: fire and police protection; street construction and maintenance; sewage and waste disposal; health, social, and recreational programs; and planning and zoning to determine land use consistent with a community's needs and values. Most city governments provide water, and some run public transit systems. A few, like Los Angeles and Sacramento, own and manage municipal electricity or natural gas utilities.

Residents in most cities are content if the basic services, such as police, fire, and waste management, are provided reliably and efficiently, either directly by the municipality itself or, as in many smaller cities, by contracting services from other local governments and the private sector.[10] In some places, however, residents demand more from their city government than just the basics. In some cities, for example, business leaders and entrepreneurs often pressure city hall to promote rapid economic growth and development. In other cities, such as Berkeley and San Francisco, community activists often pressure city hall to limit growth and development and to pursue ambitious social agendas on the world stage.

City Government Revenues and Expenditures

As shown in Table 9.2, the typical city budget in California relies most heavily on current service charges and taxes for most of its revenues. Most of what it spends goes for public safety, community development and health, public utilities, and transportation. We will have more to say about city finances later in this chapter in the context of the state's continuing budget crisis.

Forms of City Government and the Legacy of Progressive Structural Reforms

The overall vision and structural reforms advanced by the Progressives nearly a century ago have had an enduring impact on the form of municipal government in California. Progressive reformers sought to replace government by corrupt bosses running partisan, ward-based, big-city political machines with government by reputable civic leaders and nonpartisan experts managing local affairs in the public interest. The structural reforms implementing that vision called for

- strong managers and weak mayors.
- nonpartisan elections.

TABLE 9.2 ★ Typical Sources and Uses of Municipal Funding (Excluding City and County of San Francisco)

REVENUES		EXPENSES	
Taxes	31.8%	Public safety	26.7%
Current service charges	37.9%	Community development and health	17.4%
Intergovernmental agencies	9.5%	Public utilities	19.8%
Revenues from use of money and property	2.7%	Transportation	18.0%
Special benefit assessments, licenses and permits, fines and forfeitures	3.5%	Culture and leisure	8.0%
		General government	9.5%
Other revenues and other financing sources	14.6%	Other	0.6%
	_____		_____
	100%		101%*

*Total expenses add up to over 100 percent due to rounding.
SOURCE: California Controller's Office, *Cities Annual Report FY 2009–2010*, www.sco.ca.gov/Files-ARD-Local/LocRep/0910cities.pdf, pp. v, xx (accessed 8/2/12).

- at-large council elections.

- nonconcurrent elections.

- the tools of direct democracy (the initiative, referendum, and recall).

Other Progressive reforms included civil service (merit-based) systems of municipal employment and, especially in the larger cities, professionally run city planning commissions and departments.[11] Reformers were particularly successful in the southwestern states, where populations were growing fast and new cities were popping up everywhere, isolated from the influence of eastern-style partisanship and urban machine politics.[12] Municipalities that have all or most of these institutional features are known as *reform governments*. Most medium-size American cities and nearly all of California's cities qualify for that label.

COUNCIL-MANAGER PLAN VERSUS MAYOR-COUNCIL SYSTEM Under the *council-manager* form of government, the voters elect a city council, which in turn appoints a professionally trained city manager to run the administration. The city manager directly controls the bureaucracy and supervises the performance of department heads. The council restricts itself to legislative policy making, while retaining the ultimate authority to fire or replace the appointed manager. Fully 96 percent of the 456 California cities surveyed in 2002 are governed by the council-manager plan,[13] including some big ones like San Diego and San Jose. Mayors are directly elected in about a third of these cities, but with few exceptions (e.g., San Jose) they perform mainly ceremonial duties and have no independent executive powers, such as the veto or budgetary control.

The rest of California's cities are governed by *mayor-council systems*. Most are very small cities that can't afford a professional city manager. In the larger cities that have mayor-council systems, like San Francisco and Los Angeles, the voters elect a mayor and a city council in separate elections. The mayor serves as the city's overall chief executive and exercises independent veto and budgetary powers. The council (or, in the case of San Francisco, the board of supervisors) is responsible for legislative policy making. Typically, as in Los Angeles and San Francisco, various appointive boards and commissions set overall policy and supervise administration of important city departments, such as police and fire, thus limiting the mayor's direct control of the bureaucracy.

In practice, formal and informal power arrangements vary markedly across both systems. In recent years, many council-manager cities have strengthened mayoral authority to become more responsive to their political environments.[14] Some mayor-council cities, on the other hand, have hired professional managers to achieve greater administrative control and efficiency. Personal ambition, political skill, and leadership style are key factors that determine just how powerful a given mayor or manager really is in running things and shaping public policy.[15]

NONPARTISAN ELECTIONS California law requires that all local elections be officially nonpartisan. In nonpartisan elections, no information about a candidate's political party membership is shown on the ballot. Unofficially, of course, many local contests are fiercely partisan, especially because the courts some years ago permitted political party organizations to endorse candidates in local races. For example, in San Francisco's 1999 mayoral runoff election between Willie Brown and Tom Ammiano, the local Republican Party reluctantly endorsed the state GOP's archenemy, Democrat and former Assembly Speaker Willie Brown.

Shocked and humiliated by this action, some outraged GOP leaders sought to expel the local chapter from the state party organization.[16]

AT-LARGE VERSUS DISTRICT COUNCIL ELECTIONS A recent survey found that nearly all California cities (93 percent) conduct at-large council elections, in which voters elect council members citywide rather than by districts or wards.[17] Under the *at-large system*, for example, if a number of candidates compete for one of the three vacant seats on the council, all of the city's voters have the opportunity to vote for any three of them, and the top three vote-getters are declared the winners. About 5 percent of cities use the *district election method*, which divides the city into districts and requires the voters in each district to elect one of the candidates running in that district to represent them on the council. The remaining cities—Oakland is an example—use some hybrid combination of at-large and district elections to elect their councils.

Some cities, most prominently San Francisco in 2000, have changed from at-large to district elections. San Francisco's switch to the district system was a response to voter demand for greater representation of neighborhoods and minority groups, reduced influence of big money on elections, and a wider field of candidates who otherwise could not afford to run citywide campaigns.[18] Of course, the district system by itself doesn't guarantee a more neighborhood-oriented council, less costly campaigns, or political life on a smaller scale. The 15 members of the Los Angeles City Council, for example, are elected by districts. But each council member represents nearly a quarter of a million residents on average and must run expensive campaigns over vast territories to get elected.

NONCONCURRENT ELECTIONS Progressive reformers sought to insulate local government from the corrupting influence of national partisan politics. One way they accomplished this goal was to require many cities to conduct nonconcurrent elections for council seats. That is, they scheduled local elections in nonpresidential election years or at odd times, deliberately out of sync with the national election calendar. A recent survey found that only about 19 percent of California cities hold council elections concurrently with the presidential general election or presidential primaries.[19] As discussed later, nonconcurrent elections have been blamed as the number one structural cause of the dismally low voter turnout rates in California cities.

DIRECT DEMOCRACY At the local level of government, just as at the state level, ordinary citizens have access to the tools of direct democracy (the initiative, referendum, and recall) bequeathed to them by Progressive Era reformers. Specifically, if citizens gather the required number of valid signatures on formal petitions, they can

- initiate direct legislation, including proposed ordinances and charter amendments, by placing such measures on the ballot for voter approval.

- suspend implementation of council legislation until the voters approve it at a referendum election.

- subject incumbent elected officials to a recall vote and possible dismissal before the next scheduled regular election.

Local referenda are quite rare. Local recall elections are even rarer, except in places like the contentious little town of Pacifica, where voters have successfully petitioned for five recall elections over the last 30 years. The use of local ballot initiatives,

The Ralph M. Brown Act of 1953 required that "all meetings of the legislative body of a local agency shall be open and public, and all persons shall be permitted to attend any meeting of the legislative body of a local agency, except as otherwise provided in this chapter." The intent of the Brown Act, also known as the "open meetings law," was to support transparency and prevent secret meetings and backroom dealings of local government officials in the conduct of public business. (The Bagley-Keene Act of 1967 later extended the same open-meetings requirement to state government agencies.) The Brown Act did allow closed meetings for personnel decisions and the like to protect community and individual rights. Critics like Peter Scheer, however, argue that the original narrow exemptions were stretched too far in the 1990s to include meetings negotiating local collective-bargaining agreements, which the public may see only after they are signed—often too late to raise hard questions and objections about the financial implications. Despite its limitations, the Brown Act is consistent with the state's Progressive reform tradition. It gives citizens timely access to vital information about what local government officials say and do in their name.

SOURCES: League of California Cities, *Open & Public IV: A Guide to the Ralph M. Brown Act* (2007). Peter Scheer, "Public Employee Unions: Losing the Image Battle," *San Francisco Chronicle*, June 13, 2010, p. N5.

however, is much more frequent and widespread, although not nearly to the extent observed at the state level. Direct legislation by citizen initiative has become almost routine in some cities, such as San Francisco, especially around land-use issues. A recent study, however, found that only 43 of 387 cities surveyed (11 percent) had even one citizen initiative on their most recent ballot.[20] Also see Box 9.2 on the Brown Act, the "open meetings law," which gives citizens yet another tool of direct democracy for becoming more informed about the decision-making process and for holding their local government officials accountable.

LOCAL VOTER TURNOUT AND POLITICAL REPRESENTATION Voter participation is low and still falling at all levels of government in California. At the local level, a recent survey revealed that only 48 percent of a city's registered voters, on average, cast ballots in the most recent council elections. That same survey found that "California residents who are highly educated, wealthy, old, and white are much more likely to participate than residents who are poor, young, less educated, and nonwhite."[21] The political exclusion of the state's large and growing noncitizen immigrant population only adds to the problem of achieving democracy for all (see Box 9.3). Clearly, at least at the local level, California's active electorate is not very large and is demographically not representative of the state's population.

Certain institutional reforms could boost voter turnout and eventually produce more representative and responsive local government. One electoral reform in particular would likely have a major impact: the rescheduling of local nonconcurrent elections to coincide with high-turnout presidential elections. Doing so in a given city "could well mean a doubling of voter turnout."[22] A number of California cities have recently moved to concurrent elections, partly as a cost-saving measure.

Without such electoral reform or some kind of new political mobilization of the inactive electorate, the unrepresentative active electorate will continue to choose who governs at the local level.

Special Districts

Special districts are limited-purpose local governments. They fill the need or desire for services that general-purpose governments such as counties and cities cannot or will not provide. If residents or landowners desire new or better services, they can take steps to establish a special district to pay for them. As a popular guide to special districts notes: "Special districts *localize* the costs and benefits of public services. Special districts allow local citizens to obtain the services they want at a price they are willing to pay."[23] Examples of special districts include fire protection districts, cemetery districts, water districts, recreation and park districts, storm water drainage and conservation districts, irrigation districts, and mosquito abatement districts.

School and Community College Districts

California's school and community college districts are a unique type of special district. As of 2010–11, there were 1,037 K–12 school districts in the state, a number whittled down, mostly by consolidation, from the 1,630 districts that operated in 1962.[24] School districts derive their authority from the state Education Code and are governed by locally elected school boards. Each board sets general policies and appoints a superintendent as chief executive officer, who serves at the pleasure of the board. The superintendent has overall responsibility for managing the system and its various schools and programs. In 2012, the state's community college system of two-year public institutions had 112 colleges organized into 72 districts. Serving more than 2.6 million students, nearly 25 percent of the nation's community college student population, it is the largest system of higher education in the world. In 1988, the legislature enacted Assembly Bill 1725, giving community colleges status as institutions of higher education. AB 1725 also strengthened the advisory role of local academic senates and of the Student Senate for California Community Colleges in working with state government officials in making higher-education policy. Each community college district is governed by a locally elected board of trustees that sets general policies and appoints a chancellor as chief executive officer. As discussed elsewhere in this book, the state of the state's K–14 public education system and especially the financial crises that surround it continue to be a major focus of policy debate and political battle.

Nonschool Special Districts

Excluding the school districts, the state had 4,792 special districts in 2009–10, according to the most recent California State Controller's report on special districts.[25] These special districts can be classified in three different ways: single-purpose versus multiple-purpose special districts, enterprise versus nonenterprise special districts, and independent versus dependent special districts.

- About 85 percent of the state's special districts perform a single function, such as fire protection or mosquito abatement. The others are multifunctional, such as the state's nearly 900 County Service Areas (CSAs), which provide two or more services, such as enhanced recreation services and extended police protection.

- About one in four special districts are enterprise districts, which are run like businesses and charge user fees for services. Nearly all water, waste, and hospital districts are enterprise districts of this sort. The state's many nonenterprise districts provide public services such as fire protection and pest control that benefit the entire community, not just individual residents. Typically, property taxes rather than user fees pay the costs.

- About two-thirds of the state's special districts are independent districts. An independent district is governed by its own separate board of directors elected by the district's voters. Dependent districts are governed by existing legislative bodies. All CSAs, for example, are governed by a county board of supervisors.

These three ways of classifying special districts are not mutually exclusive, and examples of all possible combinations exist.

Legal Framework

Like all local governments in the state, special districts must conform to the state constitution and the legislature's Government Code. Statutory authority for special districts derives either from a principal act or a special act of the state legislature. A *principal act* is a general law that applies to all special districts of a given type. For example, the Fire Protection District Law of 1987 in the state Health and Safety Code governs all 386 fire districts. About 60 of these principal law statutes are on the books and can be used to create a special district anywhere in the state. Another 120 or so *special acts* have been passed by the legislature to adapt a special district's structure, financing, and authority to unique local circumstances. The Alameda County Flood Control and Water District, for example, was formed under such a special act.

How Special Districts Are Created

To form a special district, the voters in the proposed district must apply to their county's LAFCo. After the LAFCo reviews and approves the proposal, it moves to an election in which only the voters residing inside the proposed district boundaries may vote. A simple majority is required for approval in most cases. A two-thirds majority is required if new special taxes are involved. The total number of special districts has increased only slightly in recent years, from 4,750 in 2005–06 to 4,792 in 2009–10, according to the latest available reports. However, the modest net change in total numbers can conceal a considerable churning of old districts dying and new ones being born. During the 2009–10 fiscal year, for example, 50 new districts were created and 27 were dissolved.[26]

The Advantages and Disadvantages of Special Districts

The advantages claimed for special districts include

- the flexibility that such districts allow in tailoring the level and quality of service to citizen demands.
- the linking of costs to benefits, so that those who don't benefit from a district's services don't have to pay for them.
- the greater responsiveness of special districts to their constituents, who often reside in smaller geographic areas of larger city and county jurisdictions.

The disadvantages of special districts include

- the overlapping of jurisdictions and the resulting duplication of services already provided by cities and counties or by other special districts.
- the reduced incentives for needed regional planning, especially in providing water, sewer, and fire protection services, which are typically offered by a host of special districts governed by independent boards without any central coordination.
- the decreased accountability that results from the sheer multiplicity of limited special districts, which overwhelms the average citizen's ability to find out who is in charge of delivering specific services.

These critics would abolish most special districts and centralize their functions in established general-purpose city and county governments. One contends that special districts "make a mockery of the natural connections that people have with a specific place. Special districts lie beyond the commonsense experience of most citizens; their very purpose is to divorce a narrow element of policy from the consideration of those charged with the maintenance of the common interest."[27]

Regional Governments

A number of regional governments have formed in California to cope with problems such as air pollution, waste management, growth control, affordable housing production, and transportation gridlock—problems that affect large geographical areas and millions of people living in many different city and county jurisdictions. Some of these regional bodies have strong regulatory powers. Others are mainly advisory in function.

Regulatory Regional Governments

Examples of state regional governments that have strong regulatory powers include the California Coastal Commission, the South Coast Air Quality Management District, and the San Francisco Bay Conservation and Development Commission.

CALIFORNIA COASTAL COMMISSION (CCC) Appointed by the governor and the state legislature, the 12-member CCC has state-empowered regulatory authority to control all development within the 1,000-yard-wide shoreline zone along the entire California coast. Exercising its powers to grant or withhold permits for development, the CCC has succeeded over the years in opening public access to beaches, protecting scenic views, and restoring wetlands.

SOUTH COAST AIR QUALITY MANAGEMENT DISTRICT (SCAQMD) The 12-member SCAQMD board has state-granted regulatory authority to control emissions from stationary sources of air pollution (e.g., power plants, refineries, gas stations) in the state's south coast air basin. This region encompasses all of Los Angeles and Orange Counties and parts of Riverside and San Bernardino Counties, an area of 12,000 square miles and home to more than 12 million people, nearly half the state's total population. This area also has the worst smog problem in the nation. Over the years, the board, which is appointed by city governments in the basin area, has conducted many studies, monitored air pollution levels, developed regional pollution abatement plans, and vigorously enforced federal and state air pollution laws. In large part thanks to its efforts, the maximum level of ozone in the basin has been cut to less than half of what it was in the 1950s, despite the tripling of population and quadrupling of vehicles in the region over that same period.

SAN FRANCISCO BAY CONSERVATION AND DEVELOPMENT COMMISSION (BCDC) The 27-member BCDC was created by the state legislature in 1965 in response to growing public concern about the future of San Francisco Bay, which was rapidly being dredged and polluted at an alarming rate by landfill projects. The commission includes members appointed by the governor, legislature, and various state and federal agencies, as well as four city representatives appointed by the Association of Bay Area Governments and nine county supervisors— one from each of the nine bay area counties. The commission is charged with regulating all filling and dredging in the bay; protecting the Suisun Marsh, the largest wetlands in California; regulating proposed new development within the first 100 feet inland from the bay to ensure maximum public access; enforcing the federal Coastal Zone Management Act; and other regulatory functions. By exercising its permit powers, BCDC not only stopped development that eventually could have reduced the bay to a pond but also actually added hundreds of acres of new open water.

Advisory Regional Governments

In addition to regional regulatory bodies, the state also has a number of regional planning, research, and advisory institutions. The most important are various regional councils of government (COGs). COGs are assemblies of delegates representing a region's counties and cities who join voluntarily and meet regularly to discuss common problems and regional issues. The state's two most prominent COGs are the Southern California Association of Governments (SCAG), the nation's largest COG, and the Association of Bay Area Governments (ABAG).

SCAG's regional jurisdiction encompasses 15 million people living in an area of more than 38,000 square miles, while ABAG's boundaries include 6 million people living in an area of 7,000 square miles. Both SCAG and ABAG have general assemblies that represent the broad membership of counties and cities located in each region. In both COGs, the serious work is done by smaller executive committees, a 75-member regional council in the case of SCAG and a 38-member executive board in the case of ABAG. Like most COGs, both SCAG and ABAG have professional staffs that conduct extensive research and planning studies of regional problems. Both regularly host regional conferences and forums on a range of substantive issues. And both have been designated by the federal government as metropolitan planning organizations for their regions, with the mandate to draw up plans for regional transportation, air quality, growth management, hazardous waste management, and production of affordable housing.

Both SCAG and ABAG have raised public awareness of regional problems and issues. They have also encouraged more regional planning and collaborative decision making. Neither COG, however, has the effective power or authority to enforce its policy recommendations on other local governments in their regions. Many Bay Area local officials, for example, pay lip service to ABAG's recommended fair-share quotas for production of affordable housing but then routinely ignore them when making decisions.

Occasionally, a serious organized effort is made to create a truly comprehensive regional government with broad regulatory authority and strong enforcement powers. In the early 1990s, for example, an attempt was made to establish a powerful Bay Area regional government under the banner of BayVision 2020.[28] That proposal failed, like all the others, because most of the region's local governments were unwilling to surrender local autonomy and delegate some of their powers to a new, higher authority.

On a more hopeful note, Governor Schwarzenegger signed Senate Bill 375 into law in September 2008, moving the state at least a few steps in the direction of creating stronger regional governments, particularly in the areas of transportation, housing, and environmental protection. This landmark legislation requires the state's Air Resources Board to collaborate with metropolitan planning organizations and local government officials in developing "sustainable community strategies" and setting regional targets for the reduction of greenhouse gas emissions.

Progress in implementing SB 375 over the next few years will depend on economic conditions and mostly voluntary cooperation from city and county officials. But SB 375 also comes armed with an array of penalties and incentives that might actually work in time to nudge local officials into some form of regional governance that can make a difference.[29]

Indeed, by early summer 2012, the Air Resources Board had set precise regional targets for reducing greenhouse gas emissions by 2020 and 2035. Even more encouraging, the board had already approved the sustainable community strategies proposed by the Sacramento and Southern California metropolitan planning organizations (MPOs), and the state's other MPOs were lining up to get the board's green light.

California's Community Redevelopment Agencies, R.I.P.

In late December 2011, nearly 400 redevelopment agencies operated throughout the state in sponsoring cities and counties. By May 2012, only a few months later, they were all gone. What happened to them is the subject of a mini-case study starting on page 202. Here we'll offer only a short obituary explaining how they were born, what they did, and why their death was greeted with both cheers and jeers, along with some tears.

California's redevelopment agencies were born on paper in 1945 when the state legislature passed the Community Redevelopment Act, which authorized the formation of such agencies "to prepare and carry out plans for the improvement, rehabilitation, and redevelopment of blighted areas."[30] These new agencies were to be placed under the control of sponsoring local governments, mainly cities and counties, and were authorized to acquire property by the power of eminent domain, dispose of it by lease or sale without public bidding, clear the land, construct infrastructure needed for building on project sites, and make other improvements. To ensure that these powerful agencies served a public interest priority, they were required to spend at least 20 percent of their funds on affordable housing. As to their funding, redevelopment agencies did not have the power to tax, but they could issue revenue bonds. The first redevelopment agencies received most of their funding from federal grants. Later they would be allowed to earn revenues through property tax-increment financing. If a project site generated higher property tax revenues than it otherwise might have produced without redevelopment, the increment in revenues over the baseline would be returned to the agency to pay for the project site investments. In time, many of these agencies became flush with cash. Following passage of Proposition 13 in 1978, fiscally starved cities and counties began using their redevelopment agencies to raise additional property tax revenues, which were otherwise forbidden under the limits imposed by that landmark constitutional amendment.

In the typical case, redevelopment agencies would buy and assemble parcels of land, enhance the infrastructure, and then transfer the land to private parties "on favorable terms for residential and/or commercial development."[31] Over the years, the state's redevelopment agencies produced a lot of affordable housing, rescued a lot of land from blight and decay, and often became engines of local economic development. Their collective track record was blemished, however, by instances of abuse of agency power and misuse of funds for projects that served only private interests and profits. These projects destroyed more affordable housing than they created and bulldozed entire communities out of their neighborhoods. In some cases, as happened recently in Oakland, financially desperate city officials dipped into their redevelopment funds to pay basic salaries for police officers and to cover other expenses unrelated to the purpose of fighting blight and urban decay.[32] Moreover, some studies showed that redevelopment projects really didn't stimulate new economic development but merely relocated it from one poor area to another within a region with no net gain in jobs or tax revenues. Madeline Janis, a former commissioner on the Los Angeles Community Redevelopment Agency, offers the example of "a garment factory that was given CRA/LA-owned land and a $2-million subsidy in 2009 to move from South Gate to South Los Angeles, creating very few new jobs—and taking jobs away from another needy community."[33]

By 2010, redevelopment agencies had become chronically controversial, loved by some and hated by others. The precise mix of love and hate was determined by an agency's location and its history there. When the state government dipped down that year to take its own big bite out of redevelopment funds, redevelopment officials and their allies chose to fight rather than compromise. It was a political battle they couldn't win.

Two Case Studies in Local Government Revolt

The following two mini-case studies dramatically illustrate how California's local governments have coped with recent crises that have threatened to tear cities apart and undermine home rule. The first looks at what happened when the citizens of San Fernando Valley attempted to secede from the city of Los Angeles in 2002. The second examines the revolt of local officials against the state government in 2010 when Sacramento legislators tried, once again, to balance the state budget by grabbing property tax money from the cities, counties, and redevelopment agencies. The revolt turned out well for the cities and counties, but not so well, to say the least, for the redevelopment agencies.

Breaking Up Is Hard to Do: The San Fernando Valley Secession Movement

Nearly all of California's local governments have developed stress fractures of one kind or another from trying to cope with growing populations, increased demands for service, shrinking financial resources, and a state government that seems determined to make things worse rather than better. On top of all that, the state's largest city, Los Angeles, has been beset by internal conflicts that threaten to tear it apart. On November 5, 2002, that city's voters rejected a citizen referendum that would have allowed the San Fernando Valley and its 1.35 million residents to secede from Los Angeles and become a separate city. If the measure had passed, the new city would immediately have ranked as America's sixth-largest city, while what remained of Los Angeles south of the Santa Monica mountains would have fallen from second- to third-largest in terms of population.

This secessionist revolt did not come out of the blue. It was only the latest in a long string of failed secession attempts that began 30 years earlier with the predominantly white valley's opposition to Los Angeles's school integration and busing policies. Since then, however, the valley's population has grown in size and diversity. Its political and business leaders have become more organized and sophisticated. And its list of grievances against Los Angeles city hall, codified in a latter-day "Declaration of Independence," have expanded to include complaints and demands that can no longer be easily dismissed by Los Angeles power elites as narrow, selfish, or racist.

Encouraged by a 1997 state law that prevented city councils from simply vetoing secession attempts, Valley Voters Organized toward Empowerment (Valley VOTE) and other secession groups gathered over 100,000 signatures to place the referendum on the ballot. They secured LAFCo approval based on studies showing that both cities, old and new, would be economically viable following the split. They argued their case that valley residents paid more in taxes than they received in services from the distant, unresponsive politicians and bureaucrats who ruled Los Angeles city hall. And key leaders, including many developers and business owners, most of them white, appealed to Los Angeles voters to "Free the Valley!" by giving valley residents control of their own city government—presumably more friendly to small businesses, more inclined to cut taxes and improve services, and more responsive to the valley's needs and aspirations.

Los Angeles mayor James Hahn and other city officials were slow to take this latest secession attempt seriously and respond to it. Alarmed, downtown business leaders, city hall lobbyists, and public service employee union chiefs organized "LA United Together" to fight the valley secession referendum and another one by Hollywood on the same ballot. They raised over $7 million for the antisecession campaign, outspending the valley and Hollywood cityhood advocates by more than two to one. They unleashed a blitz of TV ads declaring that secession would not solve any problems and would only make things worse. In the middle of a statewide economic downturn and budget crunch, Mayor Hahn warned, valley secession would cause a citywide financial disaster of "biblical proportions." Among other complications of the proposed "divorce," valley kids would still belong to the Los Angeles Unified School District, Los Angeles city departments and agencies would have to provide a wide range of contractual services to valley residents until the new city established its own bureaucracy, and the new city would also be required to pay Los Angeles an "alimony" totaling $2 billion over 20 years under LAFCo-arranged compensation for lost revenue. Leading up to the referendum vote, these arguments gave pause to many valley residents, especially Latinos who depended on jobs and services dispensed by Los Angeles city hall.

Under the 1997 state law, formal secession required majority approval both from the entire Los Angeles city voter population and from the breakaway subpopulation of Valley voters themselves. The referendum passed narrowly in San Fernando Valley, achieving at least a moral victory. The measure failed by a wide margin in the citywide vote, however, thus squelching this latest secession attempt. Nonetheless, the stresses and strains that had given rise to the movement in 2002 were still active in 2012 and could erupt once again in the years ahead.[34]

The Great Redevelopment Agency Massacre of 2011

The second case study illustrates just how complicated and combative the process of governing California can be when budgets are involved and when local governments fight the state government over money. This case features just about every major governing institution and political actor covered in the textbook, including the governor, the state legislature, the court system, many local governments of different types, and the workings of direct democracy, public opinion, interest groups, elections, and the state constitution itself. All were brought together in a collision in 2011 caused by only the latest in a seemingly never-ending cascade of budget crises. The study also shows how a local government revolt against the state can succeed—and then go awry. At the end of the story, the budget crisis will have been only partly solved, nearly 400 local government agencies will have been erased, and the future of state and local government relations will have been plunged even deeper into turbulence and uncertainty. It is a revealing case, sad in its way, and full of irony.

BRIEF HISTORICAL BACKGROUND In February 2004, the state's budget deficit had grown massive and out of control. Herb Wesson Jr., speaker of the state Assembly at the time, wrote that the staggering $35 billion deficit was "a hole so deep and so vast that even if we fired every single person on the state payroll, we would still be billions short."[35] The story of how that hole was dug starts in 1978, when the state's voters passed Proposition 13. Most of the state's fiscal misery, short term and long term, branches out from there (see Chapter 8). Surveying the damage that Proposition 13 had caused over the last 25 years, Peter Schrag recited the familiar list: reduced public services at all levels of government, the declining quality of public education, the neglected and rotting infrastructure, and so on. But as bad as that was, Schrag wrote, the biggest impact "was the seismic shift in California's governmental structure, accountability and power: from local to state government; from representative democracy to direct democracy through the initiative process; from a communitarian ethic in how we paid for public services to a fee ethic."[36]

The next major chapter in this story was written in 1988, when the state's voters passed Proposition 98, which required the state's annual budget to allocate approximately 40 percent of the general fund to the schools. When the state later faced serious revenue shortfalls, the legislators found a way to balance the state budget while also complying with Proposition 98. They deposited a major portion of the collected local property tax revenues into educational revenue augmentation funds (ERAFs) and directed that those funds be spent on schools to meet the obligations imposed by Proposition 98. But what about the financial needs of other local governments, whose property tax revenues (thanks to Proposition 13) were now placed under state government control and being handed out to the schools? In what can only be described as a shell game, the state tried to solve that problem by giving some money back to local governments from other funds. That solution might have worked, except that most of those other funds had strings attached, including paying for state-mandated programs that had little or nothing to do with local priorities. To make matters worse, the state and federal politicians continued to crank out new mandated programs for local governments to administer without providing any additional funding—so-called unfunded mandates.

According to one study, California's cities and counties had become "net donors to the state general fund" and were "at the mercy of the state as long as the Legislature is in session." Put bluntly, from the local government point of view, the state budget process had been lowered to the level of a "fiscal street mugging."[37] To some critics these trends spelled doom for effective home rule.[38] To adapt and survive, many local governments were forced to slash public services, lay off employees, defer infrastructure maintenance, and charge new user fees wherever they could. Many also pursued the "fiscalization of land use."[39] That is, they changed

Like all cities with storm drains that flow to rivers and oceans, the small City of Bellflower (population 73,000) must comply with the federal Clean Water Act. That law prohibits municipal storm water discharges without a National Pollutant Discharge Elimination System (NPDES) permit. In California, the NPDES permit program is administered by the State Water Resources Control Board and nine regional water quality control boards. To obtain the needed permit, a city must at minimum develop and implement storm water pollution prevention plans that include management and monitoring programs, controls on industrial runoff, and public education. In recent years, the state regional boards have imposed even more stringent and costly requirements on municipal storm drain operators. The Los Angeles regional board, for example, required Bellflower and other cities seeking NPDES permits to eliminate all litter from their storm drains. "If a single Styrofoam cup should reach the ocean," wrote Charles Summerell, "these agencies would be in violation of federal law." While imposing this new mandate with the best of intentions, the federal and state governments refused to fund it. Local governments had to pay for it out of their own hides. For many cities, reported Summerell, the effects of this unfunded mandate have been "financially devastating." In October 2002, for example, the City of Bellflower was forced to cut $358,000 from its limited budget to comply with the new regulations. To prevent that plastic foam cup from reaching the ocean, Bellflower residents paid the price in terms of one fewer gang specialist deputy probation officer ($24,013); one fewer recreation staff position ($54,500); reduced law enforcement overtime ($15,000); reduced sidewalk, curb, and gutter improvements ($40,791); postponed purchase of an emergency generator ($55,000); and slashed funding for other important local services.

SOURCE: Charles Summerell, *The Fiscal Condition of California Cities: 2003 Report* (Sacramento: The Institute for Local Self Government, 2003), p. 34.

their economic development and land use policies to discourage new residential housing (whose property taxes now go to the state, not to the local governments) in favor of attracting new businesses, such as shopping malls and automobile dealerships, that would capture sales tax revenues for starved local treasuries.

By early 2004, local government officials had grown tired of the governor and state legislators using local government property tax revenues to balance out-of-control state budgets. Leaders of the League of California Cities, the California State Association of Counties, and other local government organizations formed a political coalition that forced Governor Arnold Schwarzenegger and the state legislature to place a proposed constitutional amendment, Proposition 1A, on the November 2004 ballot. In return for local government acceptance of two more years of reduced funding to help balance the state budget, Proposition 1A would prohibit the state from reducing local sales tax rates or altering the method of allocation, from shifting property taxes from local governments to schools or community colleges, from decreasing local-earmarked vehicle license fee revenues without providing replacement funding, and from enforcing unfunded state government mandates. Redevelopment agencies, it is important to note, were not explicitly covered by these protections. Proposition 1A would further require a declared fiscal emergency, a two-thirds vote of both houses of the legislature, and the governor's approval to shift local government property tax revenues to the schools. In such an emergency, those diverted revenues would have to be repaid, with interest, within three years.[40] In the November election, Proposition 1A passed overwhelmingly with 84 percent of the vote. Many of California's local government officials celebrated Proposition 1A as the new Magna Carta of state–local fiscal relations. It was a landmark constitutional amendment that would "restore predictability and stability to local government budgets."[41]

YET MORE BUDGET CRISES, PROPOSITION 22, AND THE DEATH OF REDEVELOPMENT AGENCIES
We now fast forward to December 2008. Governor Schwarzenegger, confronted with yet another budget crisis, declared a fiscal emergency. The state legislature quickly invoked Proposition 1A to borrow $2 billion in property taxes from local governments to help close a $20 billion gap in the state's 2009–10 budget. Under the terms of Proposition 1A, that money presumably would be repaid with interest (set at 2 percent) within three years. The governor and legislature also tapped another $2 billion from the state's many local redevelopment agencies, which were not covered under Proposition 1A and thus not entitled to any reimbursement, much less with interest.

Advocates of redevelopment agencies fought these mandated givebacks, mainly through the courts. They called such givebacks a form of theft and pointed out that these agencies were funnels for a lot of federal economic stimulus money. The capacity to leverage tens of billions of dollars in new jobs and investments, they argued, would be lost if redevelopment projects were defunded.[42] The most furious reaction to the state legislature's perceived money grab, however, came once again from the cities and counties. Leaders of county and city governments, redevelopment agencies, labor and business groups, and urban professional associations formed the Californians to Protect Local Taxpayers and Vital Services Coalition to mobilize for political war with state government officials. Coalition leaders expressed their total lack of trust in the good intentions of state government officials: "The borrowing [under Proposition 1A] was meant to provide an outlet in short-term budget emergencies," the Coalition's website declared, "but it's instead being used to paper over structural budget problems. For example, the State has no clear way to pay back the $2 billion plus interest in local property taxes that the state is borrowing as part of this year's 2009–2010 State budget, yet lawmakers borrowed these funds anyway."[43] The League of California Cities derided the state's all-too-familiar budget fix as an illegal and reckless Ponzi scheme.[44] The coalition gathered 1.1 million qualifying signatures to place a new initiative constitutional amendment, Proposition 22, on the November 2010 election ballot. The official voter guide summarized the proposition's intent: "Prohibits the State, even during a period of severe fiscal hardship, from delaying the distribution of tax revenues for transportation, redevelopment, or local government projects and services."[45] If approved by the voters, the proposed constitutional amendment would close the loopholes in Proposition 1A that had allowed the state to continue borrowing money from local treasuries with no intention of paying it back. Proposition 22 would block such borrowing even under conditions of "severe fiscal hardship." Further, unlike Proposition 1A, Proposition 22 explicitly protected the state's redevelopment agencies. Their funds would also be placed in the lockbox of property tax revenues to be reserved for local government use only, safe from the sticky fingers of desperate state legislators.

Representatives of the state's teachers, nurses, and firefighters wrote the argument against Proposition 22 in the official voter guide. They warned that the proposed amendment would significantly reduce funding for public schools, affordable health care, and public safety. The prohibition on state borrowing of local funds particularly worried them because in a "real fiscal crisis" such inflexibility would leave "schools, children's health care, seniors, the blind and disabled with even less hope." Their most vehement objection to Proposition 22, however, was that it "locks protections for redevelopment agencies into the State Constitution forever. These agencies have the power to take your property away with eminent domain. They skim off billions in local property taxes, with much of that money ending up in the hands of local developers." "Your tax dollars," they concluded, "should go first to schools, public safety, and health care. They should go LAST to the developers and the redevelopment agencies that support this proposal."[46]

On November 2, 2010, Proposition 22 passed easily with 61 percent of the vote. Feckless state legislators could never again balance their state budgets on the backs of the cities, counties, and redevelopment agencies. Or so it might have seemed to the victors. Perhaps forgotten, however, was a very important point made at the beginning of this chapter. Dillon's Rule established that local governments are creatures of the state. And the state's power to create local political entities is also the power to destroy them.

When Jerry Brown became governor (for the second time) in January 2011, he faced yet another huge budget deficit of $25 billion. As part of his response, he announced a plan to terminate the state's nearly 400 redevelopment agencies and redirect their property tax revenues to pay for schools, health services, and other programs placed in jeopardy by the budget crisis. Those property tax revenues totaled $5.7 billion (about 12 percent of all property tax revenues collected by the state). Governor Brown's goal the first year, however, was to transfer only $1.7 billion to the state, leaving the remaining funds to the agencies to complete redevelopment projects underway and to close up shop.

To execute Governor Brown's plan, two bills were introduced in the state Assembly. The first, AB 26, would dissolve all the redevelopment agencies. The second, AB 27, was a compromise measure pushed mainly by legislators who worried that killing the redevelopment agencies would eliminate a major source of funding for new affordable housing. This bill would allow cities and counties to reconstitute their redevelopment agencies on a smaller scale but only on the condition that they make substantial payments twice a year to a state fund set up to benefit schools and other programs. Redevelopment officials might have worked with legislators at this stage to make a better deal, but they were in no mood to compromise. As AB 26 and AB 27 made their way through the legislative process, local redevelopment officials across the state, seeing the writing on the wall, rushed to lock in funds before the curtain came down and their money taken. In San Diego, for example, these preemptive lock-in moves were made not only to guarantee funding for current projects but also for those set to start in the distant future, as far away as 2048.[47]

After AB 26 and AB 27 became law in June 2011, the California Redevelopment Association, League of California Cities, and other petitioners promptly sued the state and took their case to the California Supreme Court. Based in large part on their claim that these two laws violated the provisions of Proposition 22, they challenged the constitutionality of both laws and requested a stay of action. The state supreme court justices granted the stay, heard oral arguments in November, and announced their ruling on December 29, 2011.[48] First, the court ruled that AB 26 was constitutional. As creatures of the state, redevelopment agencies could be dissolved by the state. Nothing in Proposition 22 or the rest of the state constitution explicitly protected these agencies from such dissolution. The state's redevelopment agencies as they stood then were toast. Second, the court ruled that AB 27 was unconstitutional because it required newly reconstituted redevelopment agencies to make payments to the state as a condition for survival. Such mandatory "pay to play" payments violated Proposition 22, which prohibited the state from making such "raids" on redevelopment funds. The court's decision was the worst possible outcome for redevelopment agency supporters. The state could kill redevelopment agencies with AB 26, but it could not resurrect them with AB 27 because of Proposition 22. Redevelopment agency officials, the most aggressive advocates of Proposition 22, were thus hoisted by their own petard.[49]

By May 2012, redevelopment agencies no longer existed in California. The 1,500 or so employees who had worked for them were laid off or reassigned to other positions. Some agency funds were distributed to cities and counties to complete existing projects, and the rest were transferred to the state. City and county officials immediately began pleading with state legislators to pass a new and improved version of the old redevelopment program that might survive legal scrutiny. As summer approached, however, there was no response, at least no response that might win Governor Brown's approval. Meanwhile, some cities and counties began launching new redevelopment projects under their own more limited authority and using their own resources.[50] And the budget crisis? As of late May 2012, the governor and the state legislators still had to find another $16 billion to close the gap. The money squeezed from the now-extinct redevelopment agencies turns out to have been only a drop in the bucket.

Local Government: Where Are We Now?

California's local governments, especially the cities, face three major problems, all related. First is the continuing economic distress caused by the collapse of the housing market bubble and the meltdown of national financial institutions. Second is the long-term destructive impact of unsustainable local government pension and benefit programs. And third, by far the most important problem but also the least solvable, is the lack of support from the state and federal governments as cities and other local governments try to fend for themselves while bearing the brunt of economic hard times and national political upheaval. Despite these formidable challenges, however, some local government leaders are seizing the opportunity found in crisis to adapt and innovate and inspire new movements of political and social reform.

The Great Recession and Its Impact on Local Governments

The Great Recession, which officially began in December 2007, hit California especially hard. This fact should not be surprising because California was a "pivotal site" and one of the "wellsprings" of the Great Recession itself.[51] Across the state, 95 percent of voters reported in January 2010 that California's economy was in "bad times" (up from 52 percent in 2007), 79 percent that unemployment was a "very serious" problem (up from 39 percent in 2007), and 59 percent that their personal financial well-being was "worse off" than the year before (up from

33 percent in 2007).[52] The Associated Press reported that between October 2007 and April 2010 the state's unemployment rate increased from 5.4 to 12.3 percent, residential and commercial property foreclosure rates from 1.5 to 3.2 percent, and bankruptcy fillings from 0.5 to 1.7 percent.[53] All the state's 58 counties suffered economic hardship during this period, but some much more than others. The Associated Press Economic Stress Index, which combines statistics on unemployment, foreclosures, and bankruptcies, rose from 7.2 points to 16.6 points for the state as a whole between October 2007 and April 2010. This index of hard times increased by "only" about 6 points in the relatively well-off counties of Santa Barbara and San Francisco. The index jumped more than 14 points (from 12.0 to 24.2) in Merced County, however, and even higher in less populated counties like San Benito (15 points) and Colusa (16 points). And in Imperial County, a shift from 21.8 to 32.0 points on the index reflected very bad times there becoming even worse.

At the national level, the widespread fear and anger triggered by deepening recession helped fuel the political mobilization that gave Barack Obama his stunning victory in the November 2008 presidential election. At the level of California's 27 most populous counties, the link between the severity of economic stress and the demand for political reform was particularly clear. As Figure 9.4 shows, the counties hit hardest by the recession tended to be those whose voters shifted most toward supporting the Democratic Party's candidate in the 2008 election. This spike in voter support for Democrats proved to be quite durable. The Democratic candidate gained an average of 7 percentage points in these counties from 2004 to 2008. And despite a recovering state economy and lower unemployment, voter support for President Obama fell back by only an average of 2 points from 2008 to 2012, when he was reelected. Politically, therefore, these county electorates had become 5 points more "blue," on net, since just before the Great Recession.

At the level of cities, the recession caused many business failures, massive job losses, widespread home foreclosures, a rising demand for local government services, and a plunge in the tax revenues needed to pay for them. The recession's negative impacts were so severe in some cities that local governments were pushed to the brink of bankruptcy. The city of Vallejo, for example, buckled under the burden of unrestrained spending, reduced tax revenues, and out-of-control pension and benefit costs. In 2008, this city of 117,000 finally surrendered to the inevitable and declared bankruptcy. Three years later, after a federal judge released the city from bankruptcy, Vallejo's fiscal condition had improved but was still bleak. City leaders grappled with austerity budgets, reduced staff, unhappy citizens, and lingering anger from the public employee labor union leaders who had sued to stop the bankruptcy in the first place. The bankruptcy had cost Vallejo $8 million in legal fees alone, money that could have been spent on urgently needed services. City leaders now had to search for new revenue sources while coping with the stigma of management failure that has repelled investors and would-be new residents alike.[54]

Stockton, a city of 290,000, suffered an even worse fate than Vallejo's. By late May 2012, the city was in dire financial straits because of its depressed local economy, 20 percent unemployment rate, projected large budget deficits with no reserves, and unsustainable pension and benefit liabilities. Most daunting were the mounting debt-service costs to be paid on gross overinvestment in poorly conceived and wildly optimistic redevelopment projects like a new baseball park, marina, sports arena, and city hall.[55] On top of those financial miseries, the state government's recent dismantling of Stockton's redevelopment agency had reduced the city's property tax revenues from that source by 60 percent. Finding no other

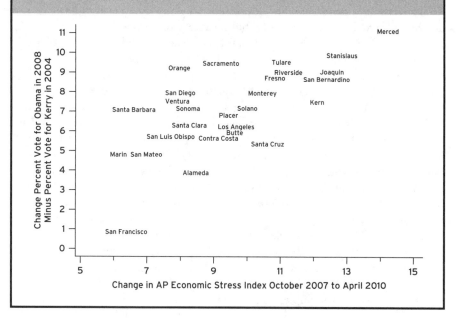

FIGURE 9.4 ★ Economic Stress Triggers Voter Support for Political Change in California Counties

This scatter plot shows the shift in voter support for the Democratic Party's presidential candidate from 2004 to 2008 (*left scale*) versus the shift in the AP Economic Stress Index from October 2007 to April 2010 (*bottom scale*). (Technical note: The data point labels are slightly jittered for readability. The correlation is *R* = .66, and the linear regression model fit is *y* = 0.80 + 0.66*x*, indicating that a 1 percent increase in the AP Economic Stress Index was associated with a 0.66 percent increase in voter support for the Democratic Party's candidate.)

way to escape financial disaster, city officials prepared to declare bankruptcy. They negotiated with the city's creditors in a process mandated by a new state law (AB 506) that forces municipalities to take more time and explore more alternatives before seeking bankruptcy protection. After those negotiations failed to produce a better solution, the city council voted on June 26, 2012, to declare bankruptcy. That decision, according to *The Economist*, made Stockton "the biggest municipal insolvency in American history."[56] Only a month later, San Bernardino, a city of 210,000 coping with its own financial emergency, also filed for bankruptcy protection.[57] By late fall 2012, no additional cities had filed for bankruptcy. A widely quoted analysis by Moody's Investor Service, however, showed that Modesto, Riverside, and other cities in the severely stressed Inland Empire were following exactly the same path Stockton took into bankruptcy. Moody's outlook for the future of this region was grim: "In the current environment, as more municipalities approach the economic or political limit to raising taxes or adjusting spending, we expect an increase in defaults and bankruptcies over the next few years." It is possible that further economic recovery combined with the recent passage of Proposition 30 in the 2012 election will sufficiently improve the "current environment" to allow cities like Modesto and Riverside to escape Stockton's fate. But much will depend on how quickly and how well city leaders can bring their employee compensation packages and pension obligations under stricter control.[58]

"Where Politicians Fear to Tread": GASB and Pension Reform

Financial horror stories like those of Vallejo and Stockton worry local government leaders around the state, particularly in areas where economic recovery from the prolonged recession has been slow.[59] Even in the more economically robust cities like Los Angeles and San Francisco, however, the projected long-term costs of local government pension and health benefit programs could lead to financial ruin and bring them down unless painful but necessary reforms are made.

Until fairly recently, most local politicians were blissfully unaware of (or in denial about) the long-term implications of their pension plans and health benefits for current and retired employees. In 2006, however, the national Governmental Accounting Standards Board (GASB) issued new accounting and reporting rules that required all U.S. local governments (starting first with the big cities) to estimate and report the full long-term costs of health benefits and other nonpension-related contracts over 30 years. Local officials, once they were informed about those projected costs, were expected to begin immediately storing away funds each year to pay for them. The old "pay–go" system—that is, thinking and budgeting only one year ahead—was out the window.[60] In his article, "Where Politicians Fear to Tread," John Diaz of the *San Francisco Chronicle* called attention to the new GASB rules and wrote: "If you want to see a California politician run for cover, ask him or her about the acronym 'GASB.'"[61] Most elected politicians operate with very short time horizons. What they were forced to see when GASB took their blinders off was shocking.

Former mayor Richard Riordan, for example, warned in 2010 that his city of Los Angeles would face the prospect of bankruptcy in four years if the city didn't stand tough against the public employee unions and convert their pension funds from defined benefits to 401(k)s.[62] Local politicians on the left, who typically rely heavily on public employee labor unions for votes, may have a tougher time confronting and coping with such harsh fiscal realities. In liberal San Francisco, for example, a civil grand jury report in 2010 warned about the coming "Pension Tsunami." The study projected that the city's pension and health care costs would increase from $413 million in 2010 to nearly $1 billion in five years, devouring fully a third of the city's current general fund.[63] Simply telling the truth about such matters can be politically risky, especially in what one reporter accurately described as a "political culture that routinely rewards public employee unions with little thought about the future."[64] After the city's progressive public defender, Jeff Adachi, appealed to fellow progressives to support pension reform, he was branded as a traitor by the city's public employee labor union leaders and shunned by the *San Francisco Bay Guardian* and other media voices on the left.[65] The city's voters, however, demanded action. In the November 2011 election they overwhelmingly supported a modest pension reform package placed on the ballot by interim mayor Edwin Lee. At the same time, the voters also chose Lee, a political moderate, to become the city's new permanent mayor. During his campaign, Lee had announced that negotiations with the public employee unions on pension reform "must save at least $300 million to $400 million per year to save the city from near-certain bankruptcy."[66] Hard times, both economically and politically, lay ahead for San Francisco. And if wealthy San Francisco is in trouble, so are, to an even greater extent, many other California local governments confronting the same kinds of problems with weaker economies, fewer resources, and little or no political support.

On the Brighter Side

Despite hard times, California's local government officials and community activists have taken positive steps to solve their own problems, while also trying to clean up the various messes made by the state and federal governments. For example, by mid-June 2010, the mayors of 136 California cities had signed the U.S. Conference of Mayors Climate Protection Agreement. This initiative was launched by Seattle Mayor Greg Nickels on February 16, 2005, the day that the Kyoto Protocol became law for the 141 countries that had, by that date, ratified it. President George W. Bush had rejected the protocol and dismissed the science of global warming that had prompted it. But these California mayors, along with 906 others from across the country, pledged to meet or beat the Kyoto Protocol targets in their own cities and to urge their state governments and the federal government to do the same.[67]

San Francisco, in particular, has arguably become the nation's vanguard city of progressive reform and social change. In 2002, for example, San Francisco became the first major U.S. city to adopt ranked choice voting for local elections. In 2003, the voters required all city employers to pay their employees a high minimum wage, and in 2006 also to provide them with paid sick leave. In 2004, then-mayor Gavin Newsom boldly authorized same-sex marriages in San Francisco, an action that met with strong opposition at the time and that continues to have legal and political repercussions at the state and national levels. In 2007, Supervisor Tom Ammiano and Newsom initiated a pioneering universal health care program serving the city's estimated 73,000 uninsured residents. "Cities shouldn't have to do this," Newsom said, "but I'm very proud that our city is doing it."[68]

But Local Governments Cannot Do It Alone:
The State, the Feds, and the Occupy Movement

Gavin Newsom's comment that "cities shouldn't have to do this" prompts one last point on the topic of where we are now in California local government. The point is simply that California's local governments can't function very well or for very much longer without major support from the state and federal governments. Yet the state government remains in perpetual crisis mode, coping with one massive budget deficit after another and repeatedly calling on local governments to bail it out of financial disaster rather than the other way around. And the federal government has neglected urban problems for decades, slashed most of its urban assistance programs, and provided little in the way of direct stimulus funding to state and local governments to help them help their local economies pull out of recession. The continuing political paralysis, polarization, and gridlock at both the state and federal levels of government is eroding the foundations of American federalism by allowing, through neglect, one city after another, like Vallejo and Stockton, to sink beneath the waves.

The Occupy Movement and all of its diverse branches in American cities may prove to be the political catalyst needed to restore a sense of democratic renewal,

Occupy San Francisco encampment near Justin Herman Plaza, November 2011.
(Photo by Richard DeLeon.)

national community, and shared responsibility for collectively mobilizing to do something about the root causes of income inequality and social injustice in this country. In California, however, the relative success of the various urban-based Occupy movements has varied greatly with the local political culture, economic circumstances, and leadership skills found in each city.

In San Francisco, for example, most of the city's elected officials supported the first Occupy San Francisco demonstrations and encampments near the federal reserve building and Justin Herman Plaza. Interim Mayor Edwin Lee and his police chief waited a long time and negotiated patiently with the occupiers before dismantling the encampments in December 2011 with relatively few arrests. The Occupy San Francisco movement since then has diversified and specialized in targeting specific neighborhoods (e.g., Occupy Bernal), financial institutions (e.g., Occupy Wells Fargo), and types of actions, such as preventing bank foreclosures on homes. There have been sporadic flare-ups of violence in some city neighborhoods, particularly the Mission, but the self-described anarchists who instigated them have been condemned by the local Occupy leaders.

In Oakland, on the other hand, just across the bay, the Occupy Oakland movement took root in a more economically distressed city and with many more working-class and unemployed participants than in San Francisco. Occupy Oakland also operated on a much larger scale, with more outbreaks of violence and greater economic disruption, including a general strike involving thousands of protesters who closed down the city's port for a day, and with a more repressive response from city officials, especially the police. Reflecting the distrust many protesters felt toward the city's police, they renamed Frank H. Ogawa Plaza, the site of their main encampment in front of city hall, the Oscar Grant Plaza after a young man killed on the BART system by a police officer in 2009. The dismantling of that encampment and others was accompanied by violent resistance and many arrests. Mayor Jean Quan, a progressive elected in 2011, has had difficulty controlling events and mediating between angry protesters, angry business owners, the police, and others. In late May 2012, a signature-gathering campaign to recall Mayor Quan was under way, even as Occupy Oakland leaders continued to refuse to make a pledge of nonviolence or to screen their participants for weapons.[69]

As this brief comparison of two Occupy protests in California cities suggests, the Occupy Movement itself is too volatile and uncoordinated and leaderless to have much of a direct impact in transforming America's political system and governing institutions. Indeed, by late 2012, nearly all of the Occupy encampments in California cities had disappeared. Many of the original protestors had moved on to agitate for social change in more conventional ways, including active engagement in the November election campaigns. The visible face of the movement had largely faded from view. In retrospect, the Occupy Movement may come to be seen mainly as a short-lived but vital catalyst of urban-based democratic renewal and progressive reform. It forced the issues of income inequality and social justice into the spotlight of the 2012 presidential election, and it moved government leaders at all levels, including the local, to pay more attention to the forgotten 99 percent.

FOR FURTHER READING

Baldassare, Mark. *A California State of Mind: The Conflicted Voter in a Changing World*. Berkeley: University of California Press, 2002.

Bridges, Amy. *Morning Glories: Municipal Reform in the Southwest*. Princeton, NJ: Princeton University Press, 1997.

DeLeon, Richard Edward. *Left Coast City: Progressive Politics in San Francisco, 1975–1991*. Lawrence: University Press of Kansas, 1992.

Hajnal, Zoltan L., Paul G. Lewis, and Hugh Louch. *Municipal Elections in California: Turnout, Timing, and Competition*. San Francisco: Public Policy Institute of California, 2002.

Rodriguez, Daniel B. "State Supremacy, Local Sovereignty: Reconstructing State/Local Relations under the California Constitution." In *Constitutional Reform in California: Making State Government More Effective and Responsive*. Ed. Bruce E. Cain and Roger G. Noll. Berkeley: Institute of Governmental Studies Press, University of California, 1995, pp. 401–29.

Sonenshein, Raphael J. *Politics in Black and White: Race and Power in Los Angeles*. Princeton, NJ: Princeton University Press, 1993.

ON THE WEB

California Department of Finance/Research: www.dof.ca.gov/Research/Research.php (accessed 7/6/12). The Department of Finance produces detailed and up-to-date statistical reports and studies on local government finances, the state budget process and its impacts on localities, and a wide range of demographic and economic information on cities and counties.

California Employment Development Department: www.edd.ca.gov (accessed 7/7/12). Valuable source of up-to-date statewide and county-level information on employment and labor market conditions.

California Secretary of State: www.sos.ca.gov/elections (accessed 7/7/12). Excellent source of information on county-level election results for statewide candidate races and ballot propositions.

California Special Districts Association: www.csda.net (accessed 7/7/12).

California State Association of Counties: www.csac.counties.org (accessed 7/7/12). Useful source of wide-ranging news and information on California's counties, with a main focus on policy and administration.

Institute for Local Government: www.ca-ilg.org (accessed 8/4/12). The research arm and affiliate of the League of California Cities and the California State Association of Counties. Very good source of in-depth studies of key policy issues facing the state's local governments.

League of California Cities: www.cacities.org/index.jsp (accessed 7/7/12). An excellent source of news, information, and data on all aspects of governing California's cities.

U.S. Conference of Mayors: www.usmayors.org (accessed 7/7/12).

SUMMARY

I. Overview of California local governments.
   A. California has more than 5,000 local governments of various types, including general-purpose governments like counties and cities, specific-purpose governments like school districts and special districts, and regional governments.
   B. Local governments provide essential services, ranging from law enforcement and fire protection to waste management and street maintenance to air- and water-quality control.

II. Legal framework for local government: the state has ultimate authority over local governments.
   A. Under Dillon's Rule, local governments are "creatures of the state" and have no inherent rights or powers except those given to them by the state constitution or legislature.
   B. California, like most states, gives counties and cities significant powers to govern themselves, make policies, enforce laws, raise revenues, borrow, and generally control local affairs as long as their decisions don't conflict with state or federal laws.
   C. The more populous cities and counties have adopted home-rule charters, which allow maximum local autonomy in self-governance.
   D. The other cities and counties operate as general-law counties and cities, which have to abide more strictly to the state legislature's local government code.

III. County governments.
   A. California's 58 counties are extremely diverse in terms of territorial extent, population size, demographic characteristics, and political culture.
   B. Except for the unique case of San Francisco's consolidated county/city government, all counties are governed by five-member boards of supervisors that exercise both legislative and executive powers.
   C. Counties perform important functions, many of them required by state government laws and mandates.
   D. Counties also provide essential services, especially in unincorporated areas outside the cities and other jurisdictions, and they are major arenas for making large-scale land-use and development policies.
   E. Each county also has a local agency formation commission (LAFCo), which plays a critical role in creating, merging, or dissolving new local governments, like cities and special districts, and resolving disputes among competing jurisdictions.

IV. City governments.
   A. The state has 481 cities, most of them general-law cities, the rest charter cities that have significant home-rule powers and local autonomy.
   B. Cities are legally created through a process of municipal incorporation that requires LAFCo review and approval, and a final majority vote of the community seeking formal city status.
   C. Nearly all cities have a form of government modeled on the vision of Progressive Era reformers. Called reform cities, most have strong city managers, weak mayors, nonpartisan elections, at-large council elections, nonconcurrent elections, and direct democracy (the initiative, referendum, and recall). Important exceptions to such reform cities are cities like Los Angeles and San Francisco, which have strong mayors and, in the case of San Francisco, district elections.

V. Citizen participation in local government.
   A. The Brown Act of 1953, known as the "open meetings law," requires that all meetings of local legislative bodies be open and public unless specifically exempted, and that all citizens be permitted to attend such meetings.
   B. Voter turnout in city elections has been steadily declining in recent years.
      1. Those who do vote in city elections tend to be whiter, older, richer, and more educated than those who don't.
      2. In particular, the state's growing population of noncitizens have little political voice or formal representation in local government.
      3. Certain electoral reforms, such as a shift from nonconcurrent to concurrent elections, could markedly increase voter turnout levels.

VI. Special districts.
   A. Special districts are limited-purpose local governments.
   B. Excluding the state's 1,042 K–12 school districts and 72 community-college districts, California has nearly 5,000 special districts.
   C. Special districts provide a range of services—for example, irrigation, pest abatement, parks and recreation, water, fire protection—which are not provided at all (or in sufficient amounts) by general-purpose governments like counties and cities.
   D. Special districts are created by a LAFCo-approved citizen petition and a majority vote.
   E. Most special districts are independent agencies that provide one type of service received and paid for by residents in smaller territories of larger jurisdictions, like counties.
   F. Some special districts are enterprise districts that charge individual user fees for service.
   G. Most special districts are funded by taxes or special assessments from service recipients.
   H. The advantages of special districts include greater flexibility and responsiveness in tailoring service and the levels of cost and benefit to citizen demands.

I. The disadvantages of special districts include duplication of services, lack of coordination, and unclear structures of authority and accountability.

VII. Regional governments.
   A. The state's regional governments address problems like air pollution and population growth that affect large areas and multiple local government jurisdictions.
   B. Some regional governments, like the San Francisco Bay Conservation and Development Commission and the California Coastal Commission, have strong regulatory authority and enforcement powers.
   C. Other regional governments, like the Southern California Association of Governments, the Association of Bay Area Governments, and other councils of government (COGs), mainly perform research, planning, and advisory functions and have little or no power or authority to impose their decisions on local jurisdictions.

VIII. Community redevelopment agencies.
   A. Nearly 400 redevelopment agencies were active throughout the state in 2011.
   B. They no longer exist. How and why they disappeared are discussed in the text.

IX. Five major problems facing local governments.
   A. The challenge posed by internal conflicts and secessionist movements exists in some local jurisdictions, as illustrated by the last San Fernando Valley secession attempt in Los Angeles.
   B. A second problem is figuring out how to cope with the continuing impact of the Great Recession on local economies, housing markets, employment, and local government revenues and services.
   C. Lawmakers routinely try to fix the state government's chronic budget crisis by raiding local government treasuries, thus depriving cities and counties of needed resources and undermining effective home rule.
   D. If the long-term costs of local government pension and health benefit plans are not controlled soon, the result could be financial ruin and even bankruptcy.
   E. Local governments cannot function effectively without state and federal government support, which is unlikely to come in today's political climate. The Occupy Movement might change things—or not.

PRACTICE QUIZ

1. Cities and counties that have home-rule charters have the authority to make their own laws even if they violate state and federal laws.
   a) true
   b) false
2. The U.S. Constitution gives local governments inherent rights and powers which cannot be taken away by state governments.
   a) true
   b) false
3. County boards of supervisors have both legislative and executive authority.
   a) true
   b) false
4. Most cities are governed by manager-council systems.
   a) true
   b) false
5. At the local government level, citizens cannot petition for a referendum or recall election.
   a) true
   b) false
6. Which of the following is *not* a characteristic of reform government at the local level?
   a) at-large council elections
   b) nonpartisanship
   c) city manager plan
   d) concurrent elections

7. Which of the following counties operates under a single charter as a consolidated city and county?
   a) Los Angeles
   b) Sacramento
   c) San Francisco
   d) Orange
8. Which of the following is *not* a tool of direct democracy?
   a) referendum
   b) incorporation
   c) initiative
   d) recall
9. Which of the following elected officials will be found only in county governments?
   a) sheriff
   b) mayor
   c) council member
   d) manager
10. The fiscalization of land use is one way some local governments have found to
   a) encourage the construction of new affordable housing.
   b) prevent the building of new shopping malls.
   c) promote new businesses that will return a local share of state-collected sales taxes.
   d) raise property taxes to pay for new schools and sewage systems.

CRITICAL-THINKING QUESTIONS

1. Do you think the Progressive Era reform vision for local governments is still a good one today and that the state's local governments should continue to be run by professional managers and insulated as much as possible from state and national party politics? Why or why not?

2. Should local governments, such as cities, be given more home-rule powers and greater local autonomy free of state interference? Test case: Would it be okay with you if all California cities asserted their home-rule powers and local autonomy to the extent that San Francisco has? Why or why not?

3. Do you agree with some critics that most special districts should be abolished and their functions centralized under the control of county and city governments? Why or why not?

4. Do you agree with some observers that California needs more and stronger regional governments? Why or why not? If you agree, what are some of the problems facing those who seek to form such governments, and what steps would you take to create them? How would you balance your recommendations with the principles of home rule and local autonomy?

5. Do you think communities such as those in San Fernando Valley should be allowed to secede from established jurisdictions and form their own cities? If so, do you think it should be easier or harder for them to do so than it is now?

6. Do you support or oppose the rebellion of local governments against the state as a response to the state's attempt to use local government property tax revenues to solve its budget deficit problem? Why or why not?

KEY TERMS

At this point you should have a general understanding of the following concepts and terms:

advisory regional governments (p. 199)
at-large elections (p. 193)
charter cities and counties (p. 181)
cities (p. 189)
council-manager plan (p. 192)
councils of government (COGs) (p. 199)
counties (p. 183)
Dillon's Rule (p. 181)
direct democracy (p. 193)
district elections (p. 193)
educational revenue augmentation funds (ERAFs) (p. 203)

enterprise districts (p. 196)
fiscalization of land use (p. 203)
general-law cities (p. 189)
general-law counties (p. 184)
Governmental Accounting Standards Board (GASB) (p. 210)
home rule (p. 181)
independent districts (p. 196)
local agency formation commission (LAFCo) (p. 189)
mayor-council plan (p. 192)
municipal incorporation (p. 190)
nonconcurrent elections (p. 193)

nonpartisanship (p. 192)
Occupy Movement (p. 211)
ordinances (p. 185)
redevelopment agencies (p. 200)
reform governments (p. 192)
regional governments (p. 198)
regulatory regional governments (p. 198)
school districts (p. 195)
secession (p. 201)
special districts (p. 195)
tax-increment financing (p. 200)
unfunded mandates (p. 203)
user fees (p. 196)

10 Public Policy in California

WHAT GOVERNMENT DOES AND WHY IT MATTERS

Duroville

Riverside County, east of Los Angeles, has some 300+ trailer parks, many inhabited by migrant agricultural workers who pick the vegetables and fruit that grow so abundantly in the county's irrigated valleys. In 1999, the county cracked down on several trailer parks that cater to migrant workers, finding that they had substandard and dangerous conditions. Harvey Duro Sr., a member of the Torres Martinez Desert Cahuilla Indian Reservation, spread the word of a new trailer park on reservation land where the displaced workers could move. Many farm workers moved in; they pay about $500 a month per trailer to live there.[1]

The conditions aren't good. The trailer park, officially called Desert Mobile Home Park but unofficially known as Duroville, is next to a dump that burns from time to time. There have been heaps of tires and construction debris piled in the area, the streets are dusty (and muddy when it rains), and the area's sewage goes into a pond next door. In 2002, the teachers in the local schools noticed many students from the park with asthma and rashes; the likely culprit was determined to be the dump. The Bureau of Indian Affairs, which had jurisdiction because the trailer park was on the reservation, moved to close the park because of the unsanitary conditions. In 2009 the local U.S. attorney said in court that the park had "leaking sewage, 800 feral dogs, piles of debris and fire hazards," along with 5,000 tenants. The cost of bringing it into compliance would be more than $4 million, which the owner could not afford.

After several years of litigation, a federal judge in 2009 decreed that there was no other place for the residents to go, and the park could stay open. It holds anywhere from 2,000 to 6,000 people, depending on the time of year and economic conditions. Many of them are undocumented. Many earn less than $10,000 per year. And many of them are Purépechas, an indigenous people from Michoacán, Mexico. Many, in fact, are from a single town in Michoacán.

By 2010, most of those selling drugs in the park were gone, the feral dog problem was substantially reduced, and the rotting garbage had been cleared. But there was still no place for the residents to move, and the quality of the trailers was no better.

Riverside County has a public housing project under construction intended for Duroville residents, but public housing projects require residents to be in the United States legally, and many residents of Duroville are not. In addition, the project requires more money to be finished; $12 million in redevelopment agency money has been targeted as the source, but as we saw in Chapter 9, the governor and the state department of finance convinced the legislature to end redevelopment agencies in California in 2012, and there is no money to finish the project. The $12 million, according to the *Desert Sun* newspaper, was intended to purchase new double-wide trailer homes for 181 families from Duroville.[2]

Duroville still exists, and whether it will close remains undecided. It has up to 6,000 residents, its own Wikipedia entry, and new resident councils and representatives to help ensure that residents adhere to the rules. Articles about the community occasionally appear in the *New York Times* and *Los Angeles Times* as well as in the local newspapers. The residents have been encouraged to leave, but they are not compelled to do so. The issue of housing, and many other policy areas in California politics, reveals the challenges posed throughout this book, challenges related to California's enormous diversity and unique institutions.

You may have concluded by now that California is a land of contrasts. The same state that has Beverly Hills and the communities of Silicon Valley also has its Durovilles. Public policy in California includes areas that are like Duroville—that is, areas that are not doing so well—and other areas that are in better shape. It is difficult to generalize as to what the average state of affairs is.

We know from earlier chapters in this book that California has been close to being ungovernable during the last two decades. We have a public that demands a high level of services but refuses consistently to pay for them. Many members of the public still feel that the free tuition and low fees in higher education during the Pat Brown era are still possible in an era when the state's people and politics have changed profoundly. The public is often willing to approve initiatives to undertake new projects that lack funding and is even more willing to curtail the use of taxes except for special functions, many of which happen to benefit the interests sponsoring the relevant initiative. The latter fact doesn't seem to bother the voters.

We have institutions that function, but in some cases barely so. The legislature still makes decisions but is paralyzed on restructuring the state's tax structure, which is now over 50 years old. Some new institutional changes—most the top-two primary system and the new nonpartisan legislative redistricting system notably—will benefit the functioning of the legislature, but we will have to see over the next few years how they perform. The 50 percent majority necessary to pass a budget has already ended the needless budget haggling that used to paralyze Sacramento all summer and for part of the fall, but the cost is cuts that have devastated the state's public schools.

We also know that major steps have been taken to improve the quality of the political process in California. The top-two primary, the 50 percent rule for passing the state's budget in the legislature, and the commission to handle redistricting every 10 years in a neutral and nonpartisan fashion may be just the beginning of a wave of reform that could take most of the next decade to straighten out the state.

Meanwhile, our question in this chapter is the current state of public policy in California. *Public policy* means what government actually does or "produces" in various policy areas, such as health, welfare, education, higher education, water, and the like. These areas are different in each state. For the California of the 1950s and 1960s, education and water policy were proud, if politically difficult, achievements, and the state was one of the nation's leaders in solving its problems and supporting its schools and colleges. For the California of the 2000s, these are areas of profound disappointment.

For example, even with Proposition 98 of 1988 "guaranteeing" the public schools some 40 percent of the general fund, California's finances have been so tight that K-12 spending is among the lowest of the 50 states. Spending per student in 2010-11 was 46th out of the states, at $8,908 per student, compared with a national average of $11,761. The number of K-12 students per teacher was 50th, and California has the largest class sizes in the entire country at 20.5 students per teacher, compared with the national average of only 13.8. The number of students per guidance counselor was 810; the national average is 433.[3]

Likewise, the University of California, the California State University, and the state's extensive community college system have all seen cutbacks in pay and course offerings as well as substantially higher tuition and fee payments. How much higher these can go is a major and unanswered question, but there are few alternatives in the current economic climate.

One could write several books about California public policy, so in this chapter we have picked four areas that are interesting. They are typical in the sense that they show some of the best and worst areas in which the state is involved. The first of these is health insurance. The second is immigration, a problem that affects several areas of public policy. The third is the state's infrastructure, widely assumed to be experiencing similar spending issues as K-12 education. And the fourth is gambling, sanctioned by the state on Indian reservations.

Health Insurance in California

One of the problems that the legislature and governor have had to face the last several decades is that many people in California, over 20 percent of the population, do not have health insurance. The reasons vary, but two stand out. One is that many people in California, more than the national average, work in small firms, and small firms tend not to offer health insurance nearly as often as large firms. The second is that California's population has a large proportion of immigrants, and immigrants tend to have a much lower probability of having health insurance than are native-born Americans. Figure 10.1 shows the last 10 years of health insurance in California, with figures from 2000 and 2010. The graph includes only people under 65 because those 65 years and over have a 0.99-plus probability of having Medicare.

California has the highest proportion of noncitizens in the nation, at 15 percent, and almost half of them don't have health insurance (47 percent), but four other states have a higher proportion of their noncitizens uninsured, led by Texas at almost 62 percent. The categories are discussed in the following sections.

Employer-Sponsored Insurance

About 53 percent of Californians under age 65 have employer-sponsored insurance (ESI)—that is, they get their insurance through their employer, who will typically subsidize some of the cost. ESI has been declining nationally, and the recession of 2008–09 accelerated the process, which means that there could be

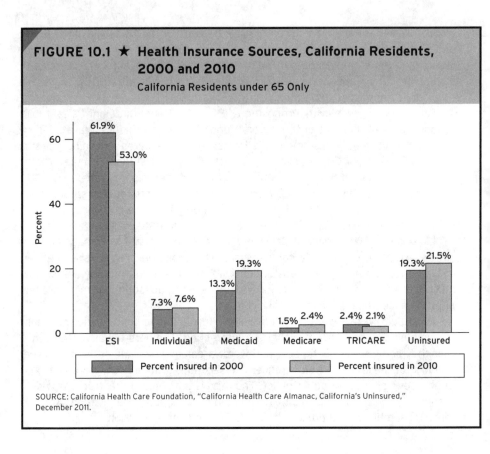

FIGURE 10.1 ★ Health Insurance Sources, California Residents, 2000 and 2010

California Residents under 65 Only

Percent insured in 2000 — ESI 61.9%, Individual 7.3%, Medicaid 13.3%, Medicare 1.5%, TRICARE 2.4%, Uninsured 19.3%

Percent insured in 2010 — ESI 53.0%, Individual 7.6%, Medicaid 19.3%, Medicare 2.4%, TRICARE 2.1%, Uninsured 21.5%

SOURCE: California Health Care Foundation, "California Health Care Almanac, California's Uninsured," December 2011.

some improvement over the next few years. Only seven states have a higher proportion of their population uninsured than California: Texas (which leads the nation at more than 27 percent), New Mexico, Florida, Nevada, Mississippi, Arizona, and Arkansas. In 2009, individuals paid $428 per month for health insurance, with employers paying all but $47 of that cost. Families paid $1,127, with employers paying all but $283 of the cost.

Individual Health Insurance Marketplace

In the individual health insurance marketplace, people purchase a health insurance policy directly from the insurance company. Two and a half million Californians, 8 percent of the population, participate in this market, which in California has been characterized by extremely large price increases from year to year (one large insurer asked for a 39 percent price increase from 2010 to 2011) and by insurers that have dropped policyholders who have become sick and filed large claims, on the grounds that their applications were not truthful. So many of these situations were highlighted in the newspapers that the new federal health insurance law, the Patient Protection and Affordable Care Act of 2010, specifically outlawed dropping policyholders when they get sick—called a *rescission*—effective September 23, 2010.

Medi-Cal

Medi-Cal is California's version of the federal Medicaid plan for the poor. The federal government sponsors two large federal health insurance programs, Medicare and Medicaid. Medicare, aimed primarily at senior citizens, is paid for with federal funds and beneficiary premiums, deductibles, and co-pays. Medicaid, in contrast, is aimed at low-income people, and the financing is split between the federal government and the states, with the federal government providing an average of 57 percent of the funding and some national standards, and the states providing the other 43 percent of the funding plus basic program administration and decision making. The proportion of the funding that each state provides is determined by a formula based on state per capita income, and because California is a relatively rich state, it receives 50 percent federal funding, the minimum. (Mississippi received the maximum federal funding rate at 74.2 percent in 2012.)

California's policy makers face a higher proportion of uninsured residents compared with other states, and the legislature and governor have attempted, successfully, to fill in the gap by expanding Medi-Cal. Medi-Cal now covers almost 30 percent of the population, compared with the national average of 22 percent.[4]

However, the downside to this expansion is that California's average cost per Medi-Cal recipient is the lowest of any state, mostly because provider payments— the payment to each hospital and doctor for providing a Medi-Cal-covered service—is the lowest in the country. Consequently, access to doctors, particularly specialists, is limited for Medi-Cal beneficiaries in many parts of the state because many medical practices either will not take Medi-Cal beneficiaries at all or limit the numbers they are able to see for financial reasons.[5]

Medicare

Figure 10.1 shows that about 2 percent of Californians are on Medicare. Remember that the chart shows only those under 65 years of age; for those 65 and over, Medicare is universal, and over 4 million Californians 65 and over are on it. For those under 65, anyone with ALS (Lou Gehrig's disease) or end-stage renal disease is immediately eligible for Medicare, and those who are on Social Security disability are eligible for Medicare after a two-year wait. Those under 65 who are on Medicare thus have a disability of some kind, although not all those with disabilities are eligible for Medicare.

TRICARE

In Figure 10.1, the TRICARE bar includes TRICARE and other military-related programs. These are the health care programs for military retirees and their dependents, including some members of the military reserves, with some civilian health benefits for military personnel as well. The category also includes those who receive their health care from the U.S. Department of Veterans Affairs (VA).

Uninsured

The last bars in Figure 10.1 are for those who lack health insurance—almost 22 percent of the under-65 population of California. This proportion is significantly higher than that of the United States as a whole, where 17 to 18 percent of the population is uninsured. The following are some facts about the uninsured:

- Some 23 percent of workers lack insurance in California, compared with 19 percent in the nation.

- Most heads of household without insurance have a job. The proportion who work full time for the whole year in California, some 62 percent, is about the same as the national figure of 61 percent.

- Only 14 percent of heads of household without insurance did not work, compared with the national figure of 17 percent.

- It is estimated that most *children* without insurance are eligible for Medi-Cal or Healthy Families, California's State Children's Health Insurance Program (SCHIP, which is a federal program aimed at those whose incomes are just above the Medicaid/Medi-Cal eligibility levels). Between 58 percent and 69 percent of children without insurance are eligible for either program; between 4 percent and 11 percent of adults are eligible.

- The 25- to 34-year-olds are the largest age group represented among the uninsured (26 percent), but every age group under 65 is represented. So-called preretirees, 55- to 64-year-olds, are 9 percent of the total.

- Of those without health insurance, 41 percent have incomes under $25,000 per year. Most of them will be covered by Medicaid/Medi-Cal under the new federal health insurance law when it comes into full effect by 2014.

- Ethnically, most people without health insurance in California are Latino (about 58 percent). Whites represent the next most frequent group, at 24 percent. Asians compose 11 percent of the total, and African Americans 5 percent.

- Of those without health insurance, 63 percent are American citizens; 37 percent are not.

The new federal health insurance law contains a requirement that all Americans have health insurance as of 2014. Those who are poor will be covered by an expanded Medicaid (Medi-Cal in California), mostly at federal expense. Those who lack the funds to purchase health insurance will receive a federal subsidy. Employers are encouraged to continue their coverage of those who have ESI as of this point. Whether the new law will eliminate those without health insurance in California is an open question. It seems likely that a good number of those who lack health insurance now will have it in 2015. We shall have to wait and see.

Immigrants in California

When a large proportion of a state's population is born in other countries and a substantial proportion of that population is not in the United States legally, there are many public-policy implications. In Chapter 1 we noted that

- 27 percent, or 10.2 million people, of the state's population in 2010 was born outside the United States. Of those, almost half are from Mexico.

- of the 38 million people in California, 2.6 million, almost one-quarter of the foreign-born population, are undocumented.

What issues arise from immigration?

Work Issues

Because one-quarter of all Californians are immigrants and because the immigrant population is concentrated among those of working age—25- to 64-years-old—

many jobs at all levels are held by immigrants, and policy issues arise as to how employers check that the applicant has the proper legal documentation to work and so forth. Immigrants are such an important part of the California labor force that the legalization of some undocumented workers, the so-called path to citizenship, has been noticeably more popular in California than in other states. One of the largest demonstrations in the nation took place recently in Los Angeles, where over a million people demonstrated for immigrants' rights. But legalization is *not* a cure-all. A Public Policy Institute of California study of the effects of legalizing some unauthorized immigrants concluded, based on a survey of immigrants who became legal permanent residents in 2003, that "legalization is not likely to increase the occupational mobility or wages of most unauthorized immigrants, at least in the short run."[6]

Campaign Issues

Immigration itself is an issue in many state campaigns. Governor Pete Wilson ran for reelection in 1994 in part on a stance opposing illegal immigration, as did 2010 Republican gubernatorial candidate Meg Whitman. Recent governors have actually sent bills to the federal government for extra payments that they allege arise from the level of immigration, which is a federal government responsibility.

School Issues

Immigrants tend to have more children than those who have lived in this country for several generations, and consequently areas that have more immigrants need more schools. Schools entail both construction costs and ongoing expenses for teachers and supplies. In six of California's largest cities, immigrants make up a majority: Glendale, Santa Ana, Daly City, El Monte, Union City, and Alhambra. Santa Clara (36 percent), San Francisco (36 percent), and Los Angeles (35 percent) are the counties with the highest percentages.

Costs of State Welfare and Health Programs

Because immigrants tend to be poorer than those born in the United States, the state's costs for welfare, Medi-Cal, and public health programs are substantially higher than they would be otherwise. The immigrant population's poverty rate is 18 percent, compared with 12 percent for those born in the United States.[7] These costs are the basis for the state's asking the federal government for assistance because of the disproportionate impact of immigration, a federal government responsibility.

We should note that *undocumented* immigrants are not eligible for welfare or Medi-Cal, although their U.S.-born children are eligible and may receive services. Hospitals must take care of those who arrive sick at the emergency room. Schools, by law, educate children without regard to citizenship status. And, of course, if you commit a crime and are caught, undocumented immigrants as well as others are sent to jail or the state's prisons. Overall, there is no reliable study of the fiscal effect of illegal immigration.[8]

Driver Licenses

Should noncitizens, particularly those who are not legally in this country, receive driver licenses? A decision by the legislature and the Davis administration to grant driver licenses to undocumented immigrants in 2003 was a major issue in the vote to recall Governor Davis in October of that year. The law required applicants to have other forms of identification, such as a federal individual taxpayer identification number, and the DMV was given discretion to specify the type of identification required. After the recall in 2003, Governor Schwarzenegger asked the legislature to repeal the law, and it did.

Voting

A policy issue that could arise in the future is the question of whether noncitizens should be allowed to vote in any elections at the state or local level. The options include allowing noncitizens to vote in all state and local elections, city elections only, neighborhood councils within cities only, or something similarly restricted. While *federal law* and the U.S. Constitution do not allow noncitizens to vote in federal elections for president, U.S. senator, or congressional representative, the *state* could change its constitution and laws to allow noncitizens to vote in state and local elections, using the differences between the total population and the voting population as justification. Maryland allows noncitizens to vote in state and local elections, and the question was debated in 2004 in New York, another large state with a substantial immigrant population. UCLA's Chicano Studies Research Center issued a policy paper in 2003 stating that immigrants were more than 25 percent of the population in over 85 California cities and calling for efforts to increase their political participation.[9]

It is not immigration per se that has led to these public-policy problems. What makes immigration such a difficult issue is the concentration of immigrants, both legal and illegal, in certain border states, producing costs that are higher than those of the average state. These costs are a result of federal immigration policies, over which the states have little control. Although the federal government formulates and implements immigration policy, it does not reimburse states for costs that are above the average level of other states as a result of those policies.

California's Infrastructure

Infrastructure is the part of government that citizens come into contact with the most—highways, schools, universities, commuter buses, and rail. California's infrastructure deteriorated significantly into the mid-2000s, but the five bond issues approved by the voters in November 2006, totaling over $40 billion, for infrastructure improvements to transportation systems, housing, public education, higher education, and disaster/flood control should make a significant difference in these systems over time as the bonds are issued and construction takes place. One factor that makes the maintenance of the state's infrastructure difficult is what Bruce Cain of University of California, Berkeley's Institute of Governmental Studies calls California's "infrastructure ambivalence." On the one hand, Californians want modern facilities and infrastructure, but "we don't want what often comes with those things. There are, for instance, unavoidable environmental costs. Water projects can endanger fisheries in the Delta. New roads and housing can separate and destroy ecosystems."[10] Consider the following examples.

Highways

California's public road system is worth approximately $300 billion. The American Association of State Highway and Transportation Officials, using Federal Highway Administration data, issued a report in 2009 indicating California's pavement conditions, including interstates, freeways, and major urban routes, as 35 percent poor, 31 percent mediocre, 16 percent fair, and 18 percent good. The "good" percentage is tied for the lowest in the nation with Rhode Island. The national average of the "poor" percentage is 13 percent; California's 35 percent is exceeded only by New Jersey's at 46 percent. A 2008 survey of the nation's bridges found 25 percent of them structurally deficient or functionally obsolete, with some 6,977, or 29 percent, of California's bridges falling into the deficient/obsolete category. Some progress is being made using funding from the 2006 infrastructure bond issues.

Fire Prevention

In early March 2004, voters in San Diego County considered seven attempts to raise more money for fire prevention and to "beef up fire departments that were overwhelmed in the deadly wildfires of last fall."[11] The city of San Diego is a good example. The proposal was to increase the hotel room tax, what is often called the tourist tax, from 10.5 percent to 13 percent of the price of a hotel room, a rate similar to what is charged in other large tourist-oriented cities in California. It attracted a 61 percent positive vote, a landslide in most elections, but the state constitution and laws, as amended by Proposition 13 and its follow-up legislation and constitutional amendments, require any new tax or increase in any existing local tax to be approved by two-thirds of the voters (see Chapter 8). The increase would have provided an extra $8 million for the fire department, $3 million for the police, and $7 million for tourism promotion projects.

Meanwhile, in the unincorporated areas of the county, many now served by volunteer fire departments that were overwhelmed by the fires of fall 2003, three tax increases failed. In one of them, the ballot statement opposing the $50 a year per parcel increase read: "Taxes won't stop. Next year, another tax. Taxing will continue until they break you financially." After the fires in fall 2003, the consensus was that the poor communications, volunteer fire departments, lack of coordination among agencies, and poor training had been major contributors to the quick spread of the fires and to the hundreds of homes lost. In spite of that, supporters could not muster a two-thirds vote.

In 2010, San Diego County remained the only county in the state *without* a unified countywide fire department, and in 2008 the county needed more than 20 additional fire stations and 800 additional firefighters to meet national fire-service accreditation standards. A *Los Angeles Times* series in mid-2008 pointed out that not only were fire departments across the state short of firefighters and equipment but a major factor in the increased losses from forest fires was the tendency of new developments to be located adjacent to wildlands. The state Department of Forestry and Fire Protection now estimates that "about 40% of the more than 12 million homes in the state are on land with a high or extreme threat of wildfire."[12] In wealthier areas, the recent tendency is to pay a private firefighting service a premium of "at least $10,000 per year . . . [to protect] homes with a value of at least $1 million."[13]

Levees

In 1986, a levee broke along the Yuba River and inundated the small town of Linda in the Central Valley, causing several hundred million dollars' worth of damage. In 2004, 18 years later, the state supreme court ratified a court of appeal decision that found the state of California liable because it had not repaired the stretch of levee that broke. While the state resisted liability for the break and its consequences, the courts have found that the state will have to pay for the consequences of its neglect.[14]

The *Sacramento Bee* published a series of articles that detailed the several governmental agencies that were responsible for flood control and maintenance of the levees along the Sacramento River. Although the agencies have not been able to find the funds to repair over 150 sites where the levees could fail during a major flood, builders and developers have continued to construct large developments in the Central Valley near Sacramento in areas where levees hold back rivers that are capable of flood damage to thousands of homes and businesses.[15]

In mid-2004, just after the publication of the *Sacramento Bee* series, a dirt levee broke suddenly in the Delta region, instantly changing 12,000 acres of farmland into a 12,000-acre lake. Officials found that a second levee was in danger of breaking, and a third needed to be shored up to prevent a road from being flooded, cutting the only connection to two islands housing 178 residents.[16] Total damage: $35 million to buildings and crops, plus another $36.5 million to fix the levees.

The Future of California's Infrastructure

The neglect of the state's infrastructure in these instances is obvious. The reasons why infrastructure repair and upkeep are not a higher priority are less obvious. One is that infrastructure is a long-term problem, and our political system, based on two- and four-year terms of office, thinks short term. This factor is magnified by the term limits imposed on the legislature, traditionally a body in which legislators spent several decades of their careers and could think in longer terms than the governor and the executive-branch officials, who are elected for only one or two four-year terms. Now with term limits, the members of the legislature are subject to the same short-term time constraints.

A second factor is the impact over time of the public employee unions that represent potential votes for politicians and whose emphasis, as one would imagine, is on maintaining or increasing personnel in the public sector, not on fixing infrastructure.

All of this changed with the destruction wreaked by Hurricane Katrina on the Gulf Coast and the subsequent failure of government in many places to fulfill its emergency responsibilities. The public-works package of bond issues approved by the voters in November 2006 included Proposition 1E, the Disaster Preparedness and Flood Prevention Act of 2006, which authorized $4.1 billion in bonds to rebuild flood-control structures, including the delta levees. The money authorized is providing a solid start toward rebuilding the eroding facilities.

Every governor in recent years has appealed to the federal government for extra help. Except for the Clinton administration's response to the Northridge earthquake in 1994, the federal government has not responded with anything out of the ordinary. California remains a relatively wealthy state that pays more to the federal government in taxes than it receives in federal benefits.

Many current construction projects in California were funded by the 2006 initiatives and the Obama administration's stimulus act of 2009. These have made some progress in upgrading the state's infrastructure, although much more remains to be done.

Indian Gaming in California

In 1931 the first casino opened in Nevada. Only Nevada had gambling casinos until 1976, when New Jersey voters legalized gambling in Atlantic City. Nine more states legalized gambling between 1989 and 1998, and there are now over 400 *nontribal* casinos in 11 states. In the early 1980s, Indian tribes in Florida and California began to operate bingo games with larger prizes than state regulators allowed. The cases in both states went to court; the result was a Supreme Court decision in 1987 and in 1988 the passage by Congress of the Indian Gambling Regulatory Act. The act requires tribes to have a compact with the state specifying the type of gambling permitted on their lands. Today, at least 233 of the 562 federally recognized Indian tribes run about 500 gambling casinos and other facilities, "generating about $26.5 billion per year in revenue, or one-seventh of all gambling proceeds."[17]

In California, former Governor Pete Wilson negotiated in 2009 the first compact in 1998. It placed such severe restrictions on slot machines that the tribes qualified an initiative, Proposition 5, for the November 1998 ballot, taking the issue to the voters. The campaign was the most expensive in California at that time, with $90 million spent by both sides, and Proposition 5 was approved by a substantial majority. It required the governor to approve any tribal casino proposal. It placed no limits on the number of casinos statewide or the number of gambling machines or tables each casino could operate. It lowered the gambling age to 18 and allowed the tribes to continue using the video slot machines that the state and federal governments had deemed illegal. Tribal casinos would be self-regulated, governed by a tribal-appointed gaming board. There would be no direct state or local involvement in casino operations. The California Supreme Court struck down Proposition 5 in 1999. The court said the proposition violated an existing initiative law that banned casino gambling in California.

The tribes, however, found Wilson's successor, Gray Davis, more willing to negotiate compacts. He negotiated with 60 tribes, "allowing them to expand current gambling operations, allowing Nevada-style gambling . . . , legalizing video slot machines, [and] allowing casino employees to unionize." The compacts depended on the approval of Proposition 1A on the March 2000 ballot; it passed with a 65 percent majority. At this point, it is estimated that the tribes are generating revenues of approximately $7 billion per year, and they have become major contributors to California election campaigns. "Gaming has become so lucrative that hundreds of Native Americans are petitioning the Bureau of Indian Affairs for recognition of new California tribes to buy land and build casinos."[18] In 2012, the state's 109 tribes operated 67 casinos. Many more casinos are planned.

The major policy issue is the percentage of gaming revenues that should be returned to the state of California. At present, the tribes pay approximately $200 million per year, about 2.5 percent of their revenues, to the state to help other tribes that do not have gaming operations. They also make voluntary contributions to the local governments in the area of their casinos to offset increased expenses that may result from the casino. Connecticut receives 25 percent of the revenues from the Foxwoods Casino in that state; other states receive less. A recent court decision involving the Rincon tribe of San Diego County held that California could not extract taxes from Indian casinos in return for permission to expand.

Another casino-related issue is the lack of knowledge of the odds of winning at the various kinds of gambling available in California. In other states, non-Indian gambling operations must reveal their odds, but among the states with Indian gaming, only Connecticut requires the tribes to reveal the odds of winning.[19]

Tribal casinos are not required to address environmental problems, such as "damage to local roads, animal and plant life, and over demands . . . casinos placed on water supplies and public services." On his last day in office, after being recalled, Governor Davis wrote a letter releasing the tribes from any obligation to negotiate over these issues.[20]

Another contentious issue is the exclusion of hundreds of persons who thought they were members of Indian tribes and thus entitled to receive the substantial annual payments generated from casino profits that go to lawful members. Several tribes in recent years voted former members out of membership on the grounds that they were not lineal descendants of the original members of the tribe. The governor has been urged to investigate the disenrollments, which in some cases are contravened by DNA evidence, and the disenrolled members have threatened to sue in state, federal, or Bureau of Indian Affairs courts, although none of these courts normally takes on membership issues.

One interesting feature of Indian casinos in California is that because of federal law and a U.S. Supreme Court decision, the tribes have "sovereign" immunity from lawsuits filed by those who work in the casino or by patrons of the casino. Injured employees and customers have sued the casinos, but the suits have been routinely dismissed because of the sovereign immunity law. Congress has been unable or unwilling to update the law, meaning that the tribes are not required to obey laws relating to environmental quality, workers' compensation, and so forth. They are required to obey alcohol control laws, however.

Contrasting the casinos in California and Nevada, we note the following:

- Indian casinos in California do not pay property tax, sales tax, personal property tax, corporate tax, or state income tax. Persons living on Indian reservations pay federal income tax only. In contrast, Nevada casinos pay the same taxes as other businesses, and anyone who benefits from a Nevada casino has to pay the same tax as other citizens.

- Nevada casinos are regulated and policed by the state. Indian casinos in California have almost no regulation by the state and are policed by their own force, which follows its own tribal rules and is not subject to review by courts outside the reservation.

- Nevada casinos have known rates of return, regulated by the state, for slot machines and other games. Indian casinos in California operate under their own rules. The odds for slot machines in particular are not known and can be changed by the management at will.

In general, both patrons and employees have many more "rights" in Nevada because of the state's willingness to regulate the "gaming" industry and the inapplicability of the federal laws governing Indian reservations to gambling in Nevada.

The major issue facing the state and federal government in 2012 is that some of the tribes want to expand their casinos closer to urban areas. The Obama administration has loosened the rules on adding land to existing reservations. The U.S. Supreme Court in 2009 issued a ruling that the Interior Department, which houses the Bureau of Indian Affairs, could not create reservations for tribes that were not recognized in 1914, but legislation could overturn that ruling. Senator Dianne Feinstein has expressed concern over the expansion of the existing number of casinos, saying that "Enough is enough. Sixty casinos, it seems to me, is enough, more than enough."[21]

Indian gaming, then, raises a host of issues about whether private entities that profit from public infrastructure and legal rights granted by state government have any obligation to support the state in return. These are difficult issues, particularly given the history of the treatment of Native Americans in California, and they promise to be in the news for years to come.

Conclusion

We can learn something from these areas of public policy. First, there are major areas of public policy that operate reasonably well given the constraints on budgets that operate in California. Both the health care area and higher education fit this category. In health care, the state, confronted with a huge number of people without health insurance, expanded its Medicaid program, Medi-Cal, to accommodate some of these people. Because the federal government subsidizes half of all Medi-Cal costs, this is a very rational solution.

In infrastructure, the state is beginning to make progress, thanks to the bond issues approved in 2006 under Governor Schwarzenegger. We shall see if this continues in the future.

K–12 education, however, is another story. The side effect of Proposition 13 is that every policy area is more dependent on state-level policies and budgets than it was before 1978, and with that dependence the funds spent on K–12 education, in spite of the Proposition 98 guarantee, have fallen relative to what other states spend. Combined with the higher salaries paid in the public sector generally in California to compensate for the high cost of housing, the effect has been to make California's K–12 class sizes significantly higher than the norms nationally. The long-term effects of not having a well-educated workforce can be negative, as the students who are educated today are the people who will contribute to the Social Security and pension payments of the older generations.

Duroville is an example of an area where the state is hamstrung by inadequate revenues and an inability to control what happens on federal lands, in this case Indian reservations. Indian reservations are also relevant to the Indian casinos, where an interest did not like what the state had as its public policy, so it funded an initiative to change things, which passed. The initiative was written to benefit the interest, as we saw with the lack of information about betting odds and other areas that are public and regulated in Nevada, but secret and not regulated in California.

"We have met the enemy and he is us," said Pogo in a comic strip set in the Okefenokee swamp. Pogo made that statement on the first Earth Day, when he was confronted with an ocean of trash. But the same is true of contemporary California. Every few years, the voters seem to rise up against state government and approve initiatives that express their anger but tie up the government in knots that no one can undo. Consider the following:

- Proposition 13, limiting property taxes to 1 percent of the value of the property (1978)
- The failure to reconfirm three supreme court justices (1986)
- Proposition 98, requiring minimal K–12 education funding (1988)
- Proposition 140, legislative term limits (1990)
- Proposition 187, restricting services to undocumented immigrants (1994)
- Recall of Gray Davis as governor (2003)

Indeed, the goal of many initiatives is to keep the legislature from doing anything at all. As long as California is a state where it is easy to fund initiatives and difficult to enact policy through the legislature, the initiative will remain the public policy tool of choice for special interests.

We began this book with the idea that California was essentially ungovernable, that the voters had tied up state government in such a way that reasonable officials could not enact middle-of-the-road policies that would benefit the public as a whole. We have made some progress with the enactment of the top-two primary, the 50 percent legislative requirement to enact the budget, and the commission to reapportion the state's legislative districts after the census every 10 years. But we still have a way to go.

What else can be done? It is still too difficult to raise taxes, at a two-thirds majority of the legislature. The two-thirds should be lowered to somewhere in the 50 to 60 percent range, by which you would still need a supermajority to take such a serious action, but a minority of just a third could no longer hamstring the legislature. The governor still does not control the other members of the executive branch. We should be electing a governor and lieutenant governor on the same ticket and then having the governor appoint the other officials to head up the various elements of the executive. And the legislative term limits, even at 12 years in one house, are too short for legislators to invest sufficiently in learning—indeed, mastering—legislation. The legislature, compared with other states, is very small because the districts are the biggest in the nation; at a minimum, we should have a unicameral legislature with 120 seats, each a third smaller than a present Assembly seat.

The initiative process should be reformed, in the words of *The Economist*, so that "the initiative process and the legislature work together, rather than against each other."[22] The initiative should be taken at least partially out of the hands of the professional fund-raising and political consultant firms that dominate it. They do so because five months is too short a time for amateurs to collect signatures. You need paid professionals to do the job in that time. The number of signatures required is too few. And the legislature cannot amend the proposed initiative typically even decades after it is enacted. In other states legislatures can place competing and presumably better-written initiatives on the ballot themselves; this might well be an experiment worth taking given the number of poorly written initiatives that have been approved in the last two decades.

We end with our theme from Chapter 1. We have begun the long road to reform, and there is hope for a state more governable in the future. But more steps have to be taken, and we need both visionary leadership and voters who pay attention and are interested in change. We hope the readers of this book will be those voters.

FOR FURTHER READING

"Arnold's Big Chance: A Survey of California." *The Economist*, May 1, 2004, pp. 1–16.

Barrera, E. A. "A Firestorm of Controversy—Still No County Fire Department Five Years after Cedar Blaze." *East County Magazine*, August 2008, www.eastcountymagazine.org (accessed 8/17/12).

Hill, Laura E., Magnus Lofstrom, and Joseph M. Hayes. "Immigrant Legalization: Assessing the Labor Market Effects." San Francisco: Public Policy Institute of California, 2010, www.ppic.org/content/pubs/report/R_410LHR.pdf. Accessed 8/17/12.

Hans Johnson and Laura Hill. "At Issue, Illegal Immigration." San Francisco: Public Policy Institute of California, July 2011. www.ppic.org/content/pubs/atissue/AI_711HJAI.pdf. Accessed 8/17/12.

Kaiser Commission on Medicaid and the Uninsured. "Citizenship Documentation Changes." Co-published with the Georgetown University Health Policy Institute, May 2009, www.kff.org/medicaid/7896.cfm. Accessed 8/17/12.

———. "Five Basic Facts on Immigrants and Their Health Care." March 2008, www.kff.org/medicaid/upload/7761.pdf. Accessed 8/17/12.

Light, Steven Andrew, and Kathryn R. L. Rand. *Indian Gaming and Tribal Sovereignty: The Casino Compromise*. Lawrence: University Press of Kansas, 2005.

Pear, Robert. "Lacking Papers, Citizens Are Cut from Medicaid." *New York Times*, March 12, 2007.

Schrag, Peter. *California: America's High-Stakes Experiment*. Berkeley: University of California Press, 2006.

Simmons, Charlene Wear. *Gambling in the Golden State, 1998 Forward*. Sacramento: California Research Bureau, California State Library, May 2006.

"Special Report: Democracy in California, The People's Will," *The Economist*, April 23, 2011.

State of California, Legislative Analyst's Office. *A Primer: The State's Infrastructure and the Use of Bonds*. Sacramento: Legislative Analyst's Office, January 2006.

ON THE WEB

American Association of State Highway and Transportation Officials: www.transportation.org. Accessed 8/17/12.

California Progress Report: www.californiaprogressreport.com. Accessed 11/6/12. A daily briefing on politics and policy.

Center on Policy Initiatives, San Diego: www.onlinecpi.org/index.php. Accessed 8/17/12.

Public Policy Institute of California: www.ppic.org. Accessed 8/17/12.

UCLA Chicano Studies Research Center: www.chicano.ucla.edu/center.htm. Accessed 8/17/12.

SUMMARY

I. Duroville is a trailer park located on an Indian reservation in Riverside County. Many of its residents are agricultural workers, and the park has had particularly squalid conditions in its 12 years of existence.
   A. The federal government has filed suit to close it, but the lack of an alternative location that the several thousand residents could afford has stymied federal and state efforts to do so.
   B. The state and county have constructed a new trailer park using redevelopment funds, but the $12 million that the county would need to finish the park has been eliminated in the state budget crisis, and many of the present Duroville residents would not be able to move because they are undocumented.

II. California has a higher-than-average proportion of people without health insurance.
   A. Employer-sponsored insurance is lower in California in part because California has more small firms and in part because the state has so many noncitizens.
   B. Proportionally, more people buy their own health insurance in California than in other states. The health insurance market has been characterized by a large percentage of price increases from year to year and by "rescissions," the cancellation of policies because of inaccurate applications (the insurance company view) or because high claims have been filed (the state view).
   C. Medi-Cal covers 30 percent of Californians, a larger proportion than in other states, but the average cost per beneficiary is among the lowest among the states because provider payments are so low.
   D. In California, Medicare covers some 600,000 persons under 65 with disabilities. A similar number is covered

by TRICARE or the Department of Veterans Affairs (VA).

E. Almost 22 percent of the state's population lack health insurance, significantly more than in other states. Most people without health insurance work full time all year, are Latino, and are American citizens. Most children without health insurance are eligible for Medi-Cal or Healthy Families.

F. The new federal health insurance law is likely to ensure that many more people in California have health insurance by 2015.

III. California has the highest number and proportion of immigrants of any state. Twenty-seven percent, or 9.9 million people, of California's 37 million were born outside the United States. Almost half of those are from Mexico.

A. A quarter of those born abroad—2.6 million—are estimated to be undocumented.

B. Many issues arise from the high proportion of immigrants in California, including who pays the extra costs for them (the federal government or the state government), whether they should be allowed to have driver's licenses, who pays to build schools for them, whether they should be allowed to vote in local elections in towns or cities where noncitizens make up a majority, and so forth.

IV. California's infrastructure has noticeably deteriorated in the last 50 years.

A. The issue affects vital state services, such as fire prevention. San Diego County is particularly affected because its citizens are reluctant to pay for adequate fire protection.

B. The state's highways are in poor condition but are being gradually upgraded through bond issues passed in 2006 at Governor Schwarzenegger's urging and through federal Recovery Act funds.

C. The levees in the Delta and the Central Valley of California are being attended to by state funds provided in bond issues passed in 2006.

V. Indian casinos are widespread in California and have provided a few of the state's Indians with relatively high incomes.

A. There are presently 67 Indian casinos, with over 60,000 slot machines.

1. Some 2 to 3 percent of the proceeds from the casinos are paid to the state, mostly to a fund that compensates tribes that do not have casinos. The state General Fund receives about $25 million per year, in spite of then-Governor Schwarzenegger's efforts to increase the amount. The $25 million is less than one-tenth of 1 percent of the General Fund total.

2. The odds of winning in Indian casinos in California are not known, in contrast to Nevada's casinos, which are strongly regulated. California Indian casinos are weakly regulated.

B. *Sovereign immunity* means that those who work at or who patronize Indian casinos do not have the right to sue them for injuries or other problems.

C. The tribes determine who is and is not a member, and some tribes have excluded previous members after the casino has opened, thus increasing the money received by the other members.

VI. The book concludes with a look at the fundamental problems confronting California government, symbolized by Pogo's statement that "we have met the enemy and he is us." The voters have been willing to approve any number of initiatives that have tied the state government in knots, expressing their anger every few years with property tax limitations, the strictest term limits in the nation, recalling the governor, and approving patently unconstitutional restrictions on the services received by immigrants. However, three steps represent some hope in making California governable again: the top-two primary, the commission that has redistricted the state after the 2010 census, and the 50 percent approval rule for the budget in the legislature. More steps remain.

PRACTICE QUIZ

1. Medicaid is
   a) a national program, administered by the federal government, with little state input.
   b) a state program, administered with little federal government guidance or funds.
   c) a federal/state program, with over half the money coming from the federal government.
   d) a federal/state program, with over half the money coming from the states.

2. Duroville is a particularly difficult public policy problem because
   a) the trailer park is located on an Indian reservation, taking it out of state jurisdiction.
   b) many of the residents are undocumented, meaning they will have a difficult time qualifying for public housing.
   c) the many other trailer parks in Riverside County indicate that the problems symbolized by Duroville may be widespread.
   d) all of the above

3. In California, ESI
   a) has historically been higher proportionately than in other states because of the size and structure of California's employers and the number of noncitizens in the state.
   b) has historically been about the same as in other states.
   c) has historically been lower than in other states because of the size and structure of California's employers and the number of noncitizens in the state.
   d) has historically been higher than in other states because of the generosity of the state's medical programs.
4. The individual health insurance market in California is a model that other states might emulate.
   a) true
   b) false
5. More immigrants in California are from Mexico than any other country of origin.
   a) true
   b) false
6. Just as immigrants are spread throughout California, they are also spread throughout the United States on a roughly equivalent basis.
   a) true
   b) false
7. California's infrastructure has been neglected for all of the following reasons *except*
   a) most recent budgets have had to cut expenses, and infrastructure is among the easier items to cut.
   b) the state legislature does not put a high priority on infrastructure issues because infrastructure does not vote.
   c) most politicians in California have long time horizons.
   d) public employee unions have emphasized their members, who are voters, rather than infrastructure issues.
8. Indian gaming in California operates under the same general set of rules as the casinos in Nevada do.
   a) true
   b) false
9. Indian gaming issues in California have involved the following *except*
   a) tribal-sponsored initiatives
   b) federal court decisions over the legality of Indian casinos in California
   c) compacts negotiated by the governor and ratified by the state senate
   d) substantial gaming revenues received by local governments in California
10. According to the book, California voters are unwilling to support sufficient fire protective services in some counties because
    a) more than 33 percent of voters are opposed to paying increased taxes for this purpose.
    b) private fire protective services have largely replaced those in the public sector in these counties.
    c) only about 10 percent of existing housing in California is located in areas classified as "high" or "extreme" fire danger.
    d) it is rare for California counties to have unified countywide fire departments.

CRITICAL-THINKING QUESTIONS

1. Discuss the condition of California's highways, both in your experience and as presented in the book. What does the condition of our highway system have in common with the other infrastructure problems mentioned, such as fire prevention, city swimming pools, school buildings, and levees?
2. The involvement of many different groups makes Indian gaming a significant public-policy problem. Indicate the different groups that are involved; their goals, which may be different or conflicting; and something about their success thus far.
3. Discuss the ways in which undocumented immigration is a problem for localities (counties, cities, towns, unincorporated areas) in California. What in general can be done to solve these problems?
4. What are the two most important reforms of California government to consider in the future?

KEY TERMS

At this point you should have a general understanding of the following concepts and terms:

employer-sponsored insurance (ESI) (p. 219)

Indian Gambling Regulatory Act (p. 227)

individual insurance market (p. 220)

infrastructure (p. 224)

legal permanent resident (p. 223)

Medicaid (p. 220)

Medi-Cal (p. 220)

Medicare (p. 221)

nonpartisan legislative redistricting (p. 218)

nontribal casinos (p. 227)

Proposition 5 (p. 227)

public policy (p. 218)

redistricting (p. 218)

rescissions (p. 220)

sovereign immunity (p. 228)

tribal casinos (p. 227)

undocumented immigrant (p. 222)

unicameral legislature (p. 230)

Answer Key

Chapter 1

1. c
2. b
3. c
4. d
5. b
6. b
7. d
8. c
9. a

Chapter 2

1. b
2. c
3. a
4. c
5. c
6. c
7. a
8. c
9. d
10. b

Chapter 3

1. c
2. b
3. a
4. c
5. b
6. c
7. a
8. d
9. a
10. b

Chapter 4

1. a
2. b
3. d
4. a
5. a
6. d
7. a
8. b
9. a
10. b

Chapter 5

1. a
2. a
3. d
4. c
5. d
6. c
7. a
8. c
9. a
10. d

Chapter 6

1. a
2. b
3. d
4. c
5. d
6. d
7. d
8. b
9. a
10. b

Chapter 7

1. a
2. b
3. a
4. b
5. b
6. a
7. b
8. c
9. a
10. d

Chapter 8

1. a
2. a
3. c
4. b
5. d
6. d
7. a
8. a
9. d
10. b

Chapter 9

1. b
2. b
3. a
4. a
5. b
6. d
7. c
8. b
9. a
10. c

Chapter 10

1. c
2. d
3. c
4. b
5. a
6. b
7. c
8. b
9. d
10. a

Notes

Chapter 1

1. Dan Walters, "Ex-Governors Miss Chance to Discuss Complexities," *Santa Barbara News-Press*, February 21, 2004, p. A11.
2. James Q. Wilson, "A Guide to Schwarzenegger Country," *Commentary* (December 2003), pp. 45–49. Field Institute, *Legislation by Initiative vs. through Elected Representatives* (San Francisco: Field Institute, November 1999), www.field.com/fieldpollonline/subscribers/COI-99-Nov-Legislation.pdf (accessed 7/17/12).
3. Initiative and Referendum Institute, "Initiative Use" (Los Angeles: University of Southern California Gould School of Law, September 2010), www.iandrinstitute.org (accessed 7/17/12).
4. "Just the Facts: Immigrants in California," PPIC (Public Policy Institute of California), July 2002.
5. Jeffrey S. Passel, Randy Capps, and Michael Fix, *Undocumented Immigrants: Facts and Figures* (Washington, DC: Urban Institute Immigration Studies Program, January 12, 2004), www.urban.org/UploadedPDF/1000587_undoc_immigrants_facts.pdf (accessed 7/17/12).

Chapter 2

1. Follow the Money, "National Institute on Money in State Politics," www.followthemoney.org (accessed 6/20/12).
2. Amanda Meeker, "An Overview of the Constitutional Provisions Dealing with Local Government, Report of the California Constitutional Review Commission," (1996), pp. 87–92, www.californiacityfinance.com/CCRChistory.pdf (accessed 12/3/12).
3. Carl Brent Swisher, *Motivation and Political Technique in the California Constitutional Convention 1878–79* (New York: Da Capo Press, 1969).
4. Spencer C. Olin Jr., *California's Prodigal Sons: Hiram Johnson and the Progressives, 1911–1917* (Berkeley: University of California Press, 1968), p. 70.
5. John M. Allswang, *The Initiative and Referendum in California, 1898–1998* (Stanford CA: Stanford University Press, 2000), p. 15.
6. Richard Hofstadter, *The Age of Reform* (New York: Washington Square Press, 1988), p. 23.
7. George Mowry, *The California Progressives* (Chicago: Quadrangle Paperbacks, 1963), pp. 9, 12–13.
8. Kevin Starr, *Inventing the Dream: California through the Progressive Era* (New York: Oxford University Press, 1985), pp. 242–43.
9. Dean R. Cresap, *Party Politics in the Golden State* (Los Angeles: The Haynes Foundation, 1954), p. 12.
10. Mowry, *The California Progressives*, p. 12.
11. Mowry, *The California Progressives*, p. 15.
12. Quoted in Mowry, *The California Progressives*, p. 65.
13. Starr, *Inventing the Dream*, p. 254.
14. Many recalls take place at the local level, where volunteer groups organize recalls of city council or school board members because they simply feel strongly about a particular issue. Statewide recalls, however, are rare.
15. Debra Bowen, California Secretary of State News Release, "99 Years of California Initiatives, One Day Left to Qualify for June 8 Ballot," www.sos.ca.gov/admin/press-releases/2010/db10-015.pdf (accessed 6/20/12).
16. Allswang, *The Initiative and Referendum in California*, p. 33.
17. Allswang, *The Initiative and Referendum in California*, p. 75.

18. California Secretary of State Debra Bowen, "Referendum," www.sos.ca.gov/elections/ballot-measures/referenda.htm (accessed 6/20/12).

19. Jim Puzzanghera, "History of Recall Adds Fuel to Both Sides," *The San Jose Mercury News*, June 18, 2003, http://digital.library.ucla.edu/websites/2003_999_022/latest.news/94/index.htm (accessed 8/3/12)

20. Field Research Corporation, "Statewide Ballot Proposition Elections," October 2011, http://field.com/fieldpollonline/subscribers/COI-11-Oct-California-Ballot-Propositions.pdf (accessed 6/20/12).

Chapter 3

1. Jay Michael, Dan Walters, and Dan Weintraub, *The Third House: Lobbyists, Power, and Money in Sacramento* (Berkeley, CA: Berkeley Public Policy Press, 2002), p. 13.

2. Cary McWilliams, *California: The Great Exception* (Berkeley: University of California Press, 1999), p. 198.

3. Arthur H. Samish and Bob Thomas, *The Secret Boss of California* (New York: Crown Publishers, 1971), p. 13.

4. Debra Bowen, California Secretary of State, "History of the Political Reform Division," 2004, www.ss.ca.gov/prd/about_the_division/history.htm (accessed 6/22/12).

5. Sam Dotson, "Some Call Spending Money to Get Money Respectable but Necessary for Inland Cities and Schools," *Riverside Press Enterprise*, July 6, 1997, p. A2.

6. Debra Bowen, California Secretary of State, "Lobbying Activity: Employers of Lobbyists," http://cal-access.ss.ca.gov/Lobbying/Employers (accessed 6/22/12).

7. Chase Davis, "State Lobby Spending on Pace to Set Records," *California Watch*, November 3, 2011, http://californiawatch.org/dailyreport/state-lobby-spending-pace-set-records-13402 (accessed 6/22/12).

8. "California Lobbyist Control Gets a C," *Silicon Valley/San Jose Business Journal*, May 19, 2003.

9. McWilliams, *California*, p. 213.

10. Mark Sappenfield, "Why Clout of Lobbyists Is Growing," *Christian Science Monitor*, July 23, 2003, news.corporate.findlaw.com/csmonitor/s/20030723/23jul2003084412.html; www.csmonitor.com/2003/0722/p01s02-uspo.html (accessed 6/22/12).

11. Debra Bowen, California Secretary of State, "Lobbying Activity: Lobbying Firms," 2007–08, http://cal-access.ss.ca.gov/Lobbying/Employers (accessed 6/22/12).

12. Stephen Ansolabehere, James Snyder Jr., and Mickey Tripathi, "Are PAC Contributions and Lobbying Linked? New Evidence from the 1995 Lobby Disclosure Act," http://www.tandfonline.com/doi/abs/10.1080/1369525022000015586#preview (accessed 8/4/12).

13. National Institute on Money in State Politics, "State Overview: California 2009–10," www.followthemoney.org.

14. California Fair Political Practices Commission, "Big Money Talks," March 2010, p. 41, www.fppc.ca.gov/reports/Report31110.pdf (accessed 6/22/12).

15. Maria Lagos, "Result of Furloughs—$1 Billion Liability," *San Francisco Chronicle*, April 23, 2011, www.sfgate.com/cgi-bin/article.cgi?f=/c/a/2011/03/07/MNSQ1I2ASB.DTL&ao=all (accessed 6/22/12).

16. Steven Malanga, "The Beholden State," *City Journal* 20 (Spring 2010), www.city-journal.org/2010/20_2_california-unions.html (accessed 6/22/12).

17. Patrick McGreevy and Nancy Vogel, "Senate Travel Perks for Sales," *Los Angeles Times*, March 16, 2008.

18. Field Research Corporation, "Statewide Ballot Proposition Elections," October 2011, http://field.com/fieldpollonline/subscribers/COI-11-Oct-California-Ballot-Propositions.pdf (accessed 6/22/12).

19. Elisabeth R. Gerber, "Interest Group Influence in the California Initiative Process," Public Policy Institute of California, 1998, www.ppic.org/main/publication.asp?i=49 (accessed 8/4/12).

20. Susan F. Rasky, "Covering California: The Press Wrestles with Diversity, Complexity, and Change," in *Governing California: Politics, Government, and Public Policy in the Golden State*, ed. Gerald C. Lubenow and Bruce E. Cain (Berkeley: Institute of Governmental Studies Press, University of California, 1997), pp. 157–88.

21. Rasky, "Covering California," p. 182.

22. Jim Rutenberg, "Working to Spin Distrust of Media into Votes," *New York Times*, October 12, 2003.

Chapter 4

1. Spencer C. Olin, *California's Prodigal Sons: Hiram Johnson and the Progressives, 1911–1917* (Berkeley: University of California Press, 1968).

2. Schaffner, Brian F., Streb, Matthew, and Wright, Gerald, "Teams without Uniforms: The Nonpartisan Ballot in State and Local Elections," *Political Research Quarterly* 54, no. 1 (2001), pp. 7–30.

3. Michael Finnegan, "The Race for the White House," *Los Angeles Times*, September 8, 2004, p. A1.

4. Roper Center for Public Opinion Research, *Social Capital Community Benchmark Survey: Methodology and Documentation*, February 17, 2001, www.ropercenter.uconn.edu/scc_bench.html (accessed 8/13/12).

5. Mark Baldassare, *A California State of Mind: The Conflicted Voter in a Changing World* (Berkeley: University of California Press, 2002), p. 47.

6. Richard Edward DeLeon, *Left Coast City: Progressive Politics in San Francisco, 1975–1991* (Lawrence: University Press of Kansas, 1992).

7. "The Mormon Money behind Proposition 8," October 23, 2008, www.theatlantic.com/daily-dish/archive/2008/10/the-mormon-money-behind-proposition-8/209748/ (accessed 8/13/12).

8. S. Rasky, "Introduction to 'An Antipolitician, Antiestablishment Groundswell Elected the Candidate of Change,'" in *California Votes: The 2002 Governor's Race and the*

Recall That Made History, ed. G. Lubenow (Berkeley: Berkeley Public Policy Press, 2003).

9. Rasky, "Introduction."
10. Decker, C., "State's Shifting Political Landscape," Los Angeles Times, November 6, 2008, p. A1.
11. Decker, C., "Money Simply Is Not Enough," Los Angeles Times, November 7, 2010, p. A41.
12. Kevin Yamamura, and Torey Van Dot "California Lawmakers Secure Pay with Unfinished Budget," , Sacramento Bee, June 16, 2012, p. 1A, www.sacbee.com/2012/06/16/4566229/california-lawmakers-secure-continued.html (accessed 7/20/12).
13. "No on Prop. 29," Los Angeles Times, April 27, 2012, articles.latimes.com/2012/apr/27/opinion/la-ed-prop29-20120427 (accessed 12/3/12).
14. Adam Nagourney, "Vote on $1 Cigarette Tax Starts $47 Million California Brawl," New York Times, June 4, 2012.
15. "Young Voters Help Secure Obama Victory, Passage of Progressive Ballot Measures," Huffington Post, November 7, 2012.
16. Phil Willon, "GOP Loses Grip on Inland Empire," Los Angeles Times, November 11, 2012, p. A37.
17. Jean Merl, "California No Longer on Sidelines in Congressional Races," Los Angeles Times, November 5, 2012, p. AA3.
18. George Skelton, "Time for Initiative Reforms," Los Angeles Times, November 15, 2012, p. A2.
19. D. P. Osorio, "The Cost of Winning a Senate Race," DPOsorio.com, May 9, 2012, http://dposorio.com/blog/822/the-cost-of-winning-a-senate-race (accessed 7/20/12).
20. Rasky, "Introduction."
21. William Booth, "In Calif. Governor's Race, It's Ads Infinitum," Washington Post, May 29, 1998, p. A1.
22. Carol A. Cassel, "Hispanic Turnout: Estimates from Validated Voting Data," Political Research Quarterly 55, no. 2 (June 2002), pp. 391–408. Michael A. Jones-Correa and David L. Leal, "Political Participation: Does Religion Matter?" Political Research Quarterly 54, no. 4 (2001), pp. 751–70.

Chapter 5

1. Emily Bazar, "A Mad Dash into Confusion: As Lawmakers Race to Wrap Up for the Year the Public Often Gets Left in the Dark," Sacramento Bee, September 16, 2001.
2. Lou Cannon, Governor Reagan: His Rise to Power (New York: Public Affairs, 2003), p. 166.
3. Peter Schrag, Paradise Lost: California's Experience, America's Future (New York: New Press, 1998), p. 244.
4. Institute of Governmental Studies, "IGS Goes to Sacramento to Assess Ten Years of Term Limits," Public Affairs Report 42, no. 3 (fall 2001).
5. National Conference of State Legislators, www.ncsl.org/default.aspx?tabid=18248 (accessed 6/28/12).
6. Schrag, Paradise Lost, p. 143.
7. Adam Nagourney, "Political Shift in California Trips Brown," New York Times, September 20, 2011, www.nytimes.com/2011/09/21/us/politics/brown-says-california-gop-is-harder-to-work-with-decades-later.html?pagewanted=all (accessed 6/24/12).
8. Anthony York, "Brown and Obama Find Bipartisanship a Difficult Goal to Reach," Los Angeles Times, February 24, 2012, http://articles.latimes.com/2012/feb/24/local/la-me-jerry-brown-20120224 (accessed 6/24/12).
9. Nagourney, "Political Shift in California Trips Brown."
10. George Skelton, "California's Capitol—the Long View: A Columnist Looks Back on 50 Years Covering the Ups and Downs of Sacramento," Los Angeles Times, December 1, 2011, p. A2.

Chapter 6

1. William Bradley, "Jerry Brown 2.0 at 1," Huffington Post, January 7, 2012, www.huffingtonpost.com/william-bradley/jerry-brown-2012_b_1190844.html (accessed 6/29/12).
2. Richard E. Neustadt, Presidential Power and the Modern Presidents: The Politics of Leadership from Roosevelt to Reagan (New York: Macmillan, 1990).
3. Thomas E. Cronin and Michael A. Genovese, The Paradoxes of the American Presidency (New York: Oxford University Press, 1998).
4. Public Policy Institute of California, "Job Approval Ratings for Governor Schwarzenegger" www.ppic.org/content/pubs/other/APR_Schwarzenegger0510.pdf (accessed 8/30/12).
5. "Press Release: Governor Brown Delivers Plan to Streamline and Simplify State Government to Little Hoover Commission," March, 30, 2012, http://gov.ca.gov/news.php?id=17476 (accessed 8/30/12).
6. Nicolas Riccardi, "Brown's 2011: Tall Hopes but Taller Hurdles," Los Angeles Times, December 27, 2011, p. A1.

Chapter 7

1. 2011 Court Statistics Report, http://www.courts.ca.gov/documents/2011CourtStatisticsReport.pdf.
2. U.S. Census Bureau, American Fact Finder, http://factfinder2.census.gov/faces/nav/jsf/pages/index.xhtml
3. People v. Colvin, 203 Cal.App.4th 1029 (2012).
4. Judicial Council of California, http://www.courts.ca.gov/policyadmin-jc.htm?genpubtab.
5. 2008 Court Statistics Report.
6. "California Courts Wrestle with Budget Cuts Old and New." Retrieved from http://latimesblogs.latimes.com/california-politics/2012/06/california-court.html
7. "IT Project Sinks in Sea of Criticism." Retrieved from http://www.courthousenews.com/2012/03/27/45079.htm.
8. See "Judges Criticize Court Bureaucracy in Blistering Report." Retrieved from http://www.law.com/jsp/ca/PubArticleCA.jsp?id=1202556419264&Judges_Criticize_Court_Bureaucracy_in_Blistering_Report.

Chapter 8

1. Marla Dickerson, "State Fiscal Woes Threaten Cities' Budgets and a Leading Job Engine," *Los Angeles Times*, January 17, 2003, pp. C1, C4.
2. California Department of Finance, "History of Budgeting," February 24, 1998, www.dof.ca.gov (accessed 7/27/12).
3. California Department of Finance, "History of Budgeting."
4. George Skelton, "The 'Budget Nun' Earns Her Pay and Bipartisan Respect," *Los Angeles Times*, May 26, 2003, p. B5.
5. California Department of Finance, "California's Budget Process," October 10, 2000, www.dof.ca.gov/fisa/bag/process.htm (accessed 7/27/12).
6. Public Policy Institute of California, "California's Tax Burden," 2003, www.ppic.org (accessed 7/30/12).
7. Katherine Barrett, Richard Greene, Michele Mariani, and Anya Sostek, "The Way We Tax," *Governing* (February 2003), p. 20.
8. *Silicon Valley/San Jose Business Journal*, "Analysis details who pays taxes in California," www.bizjournals.com/sanjose/stories/2002/04/08/daily60.html (accessed 9/11/12).
9. Barrett et al., "The Way We Tax," p. 20.
10. California Taxpayers Association, "Cal-Tax: Taxes Are Heavy Burden in California," www.caltax.org/California.htm (accessed 7/30/12).
11. California Budget Project, "Who Pays Taxes in California?" (Sacramento: California Budget Project, updated April 2012).
12. Institute for Taxation and Economic Policy, "'High Rate' Income Tax States Are Outperforming No-Tax States," February 2012, www.itepnet.org (accessed 7/27/12).
13. James D. Savage, "California's Structural Deficit Crisis," *Public Budgeting and Finance* 12, no. 2 (summer 1992), pp. 82–97.
14. California Forward, "Curing Deficits and Creating Value: Principles for Improving State Fiscal Decisions," s3.amazonaws.com/zanran_storage/www.caforward.org/ContentPages/1903423.pdf (accessed 12/3/12).
15. Peter Nicholas and Virginia Ellis, "Budget Signals Narrowed Ambitions," *Los Angeles Times*, February 18, 2004, p. A1.
16. Dan Walters, "California's Crisis of Governance Undermines Democratic Theory," *Sacramento Bee*, July 4, 2004, p. A16.
17. Texas Bond Review Board, "Debt Affordability Study," February 2012, Appendix F, www.brb.state.tx.us/pub/bfo/DAS2012.pdf (accessed 7/27/12).

Chapter 9

1. Bernard H. Ross and Myron A. Levine, *Urban Politics: Power in Metropolitan America*, 6th ed. (Itasca, IL: F. E. Peacock, 2001), p. 90.
2. Dale Krane, Platon N. Rigos, and Melvin B. Hill Jr., *Home Rule in America: A Fifty-State Handbook* (Washington, DC: CQ Press, 2001).
3. Daniel B. Rodriguez, "State Supremacy, Local Sovereignty: Reconstructing State/Local Relations under the California Constitution," in *Constitutional Reform in California: Making State Government More Effective and Responsive*, ed. Bruce E. Cain and Roger G. Noll (Berkeley: Institute of Governmental Studies Press, University of California, 1995), pp. 401–29. Krane, Rigos, and Hill, *Home Rule in America*. Melvin B. Hill, *State Laws Governing Local Government Structure and Administration* (Washington, DC: U.S. Advisory Commission on Intergovernmental Relations [ACIR], 1993).
4. Ross and Levine, *Urban Politics*, p. 91.
5. John Taylor, "What Happened to Branciforte County?" (Sacramento: California State Association of Counties, 2000), www.counties.org/defaultasp?id=52 (8/4/12).
6. *County of Los Angeles Annual Report 2011–2012*, http://lacounty.gov/wps/portal/lac/employees/ (accessed 8/2/12). See also for budget figures http://ceo.lacounty.gov/pdf/11-12/2011-12%20Adopted%20Budget%20Charts.pdf (accessed 8/2/12).
7. Jillian Jones, "County's Legal Troubles Tied to the Value of the Land," *Napa Valley Register*, January 30, 2010, http://napavalleyregister.com/news/local/article_31d6dfe0-0d71-11df-a0e3-001cc4c03286.html (accessed 8/4/12).
8. Aaron Claverie and David Downey, "Pechanga to Buy Quarry Site," *The Californian*, November 15, 2012, www.nctimes.com/news/local/swcounty/region-pechanga-to-buy-quarry-site/article_a17a4dde-0a5a-597d-a8f9-057ba5c3eddf.html (accessed 11/16/12).
9. U.S. Census Bureau, *2007 Census of Governments* (Washington, DC: Government Printing Office, 2007). California Association of Local Agency Formation Commissions, "California Cities by Incorporation Date," www.calafco.org/resources.htm#incorp (accessed 8/4/12).
10. Zoltan L. Hajnal, Paul G. Lewis, and Hugh Louch, *Municipal Elections in California: Turnout, Timing, and Competition* (San Francisco: Public Policy Institute of California, 2002), pp. 23–24.
11. Ross and Levine, *Urban Politics*, pp. 165–78.
12. Amy Bridges, *Morning Glories: Municipal Reform in the Southwest* (Princeton, NJ: Princeton University Press, 1997).
13. International City/County Management Association (ICMA), "Officials in U.S. Muncipalities 2,500 and Over in Population," in *The Municipal Year Book 2003* (Washington, DC: ICMA, 2003), pp. 195–200.
14. H. George Frederickson and Gary Alan Johnson, "The Adapted American City: A Study of Institutional Dynamics," *Urban Affairs Review* 36, no. 6 (2001): 872–884. Susan A. McManus and Charles S. Bullock III, "The Form, Structure, and Composition of America's Municipalities in the New

Millennium," in *The Municipal Yearbook 2003*, ed. ICMA, pp. 3–18.

15. Bruce E. Cain, Megan Mullin, and Gillian Peele, "City Caesars? An Examination of Mayoral Power in California," presented at the 2001 annual meeting of the American Political Science Association, August 29–September 2, San Francisco.

16. Richard Edward DeLeon, *Left Coast City: Progressive Politics in San Francisco, 1975–1991* (Lawrence: University Press of Kansas, 1992).

17. Hajnal et al., *Municipal Elections in California*, p. 25.

18. DeLeon, *Left Coast City*. A recent study of over 7,000 U.S. cities found that district systems were better than at-large systems in achieving diversity on city councils only where underrepresented groups are highly concentrated geographically and constitute a sizable share of the population. See Jessica Trounstine and Melody Ellis Valdini, "The Context Matters: The Effects of Single-Member Versus At-Large Districts on City Council Diversity," *American Journal of Political Science* 52, no. 3 (July 2008): 554–69.

19. Hajnal et al., *Municipal Elections in California*, p. 19.

20. Hajnal et al., *Municipal Elections in California*, p. 26.

21. Hajnal et al., *Municipal Elections in California*, p. 3.

22. Hajnal et al., *Municipal Elections in California*, p. 64.

23. Senate Local Government Committee, *What's So Special about Special Districts? A Citizen's Guide to Special Districts in California*. 3rd ed. (Sacramento: California State Senate, 2002), p. 3.

24. California Department of Education, http://www.cde.ca.gov/ds/sd/cb/ceffingertipfacts.asp (accessed 8/2/12).

25. California State Controller's Office, *Special Districts Annual Report 2009–2010*, http://www.sco.ca.gov/Files-ARD-Local/LocRep/districts_reports_0910_specialdistricts.pdf, p. vi (accessed 8/2/12).

26. California State Controller's Office, *Special Districts Annual Report 2009–2010*.

27. Brian P. Janiskee, "The Problem of Local Government in California," *Nexus, a Journal of Opinion* (Spring 2001), pp. 219–33.

28. Gabriel Metcalf, "An Interview with Joe Bodovitz," *SPUR* report no. 378 (September 1999).

29. The text of the SB 375 law is available at www.leginfo.ca.gov/pub/07-08/bill/sen/sb_0351-0400/sb_375_bill_20080930_chaptered.pdf (accessed 8/2/12). The Institute for Local Government provides a useful resource center with detailed background on SB 375. See http://www.ca-ilg.org/sb-375-resource-center (accessed 8/2/12). To track progress in implementing SB 375, see http://www.arb.ca.gov/cc/sb375/sb375.htm (accessed 8/2/12).

30. California Supreme Court, quoting from the Community Redevelopment Act, in *Cal. Redevelopment Assn. v. Matosantos*, S194861, December 29, 2011, http://www.courtinfo.ca.gov/opinions/archive/S194861.PDF, p. 9 (accessed 5/23/12).

31. *Cal. Redevelopment Assn. v. Matosantos*, S194861 (December 29, 2011), www.courtinfo.ca.gov/opinions/archive/S194861.PDF, p. 9 (accessed 5/13/12).

32. Marisa Lagos, "Calif. Wins OK to Abolish Redevelopment Agencies," *San Francisco Chronicle*, December 30, 2011, p. A-1.

33. Madeline Janis, "Rethinking Redevelopment in California," *Los Angeles Times*, February 8, 2012, http://articles.latimes.com/print/2012/feb/08/opinion/la-oe-janis-redevelopment-20120208 (accessed 5/13/12).

34. For more information on the secession movement and its outcome, see Tom Hogen-Esch, "Urban Secession and the Politics of Growth: The Case of Los Angeles," *Urban Affairs Review* 36, no. 6 (2001): 783–809. Martin Kasindorf, "L.A. Secession Drives Faltering as City Hall Warns about Risks," *USA Today*, October 30, 2002, p. 3A. William Booth, "L.A. Secession Campaign Tests Hahn's Mettle," *Washington Post*, September 22, 2002, p. A4. David Devoss, "Secession Is Dead, but Self-Rule Dream Lives," *Los Angeles Times*, November 9, 2002, p. 3.

35. Herb J. Wesson Jr., "Cutting to the Bone," *Western City* (February 2003).

36. Peter Schrag, "25 Years Later," *San Diego Union-Tribune*, June 22, 2003, p. G1.

37. Michael Coleman and Bob Leland, "State Intrusion Creates Fickle Fiscal Future for Cities," *Western City* (April 2003).

38. Michael Coleman and Michael G. Golantuono, "Local Fiscal Authority and Stability: Control and Risk in California City Revenues," *Western City* (August 2003).

39. Dean J. Misczynski, "The Fiscalization of Land Use," in *California Policy Choices*, ed. John J. Kirlin and Donald R. Winkler, vol. 3 (Los Angeles: University of Southern California, 1986). Paul Lewis and Elisa Barbour, *California Cities and the Local Sales Tax* (San Francisco: Public Policy Institute of California, 1999), www.ppic.org/content/pubs/report/R_799PLR.pdf (accessed 8/4/12).

40. For a detailed analysis of Proposition 1A, see League of Women Voters of California Education Fund, "Proposition 1A," November 2004, http://ca.lwv.org/lwvc/edfund/elections/2004nov/pc/prop1A.html (accessed 7/6/12).

41. Michael Coleman, "A Primer on California City Finance," *Western City*, March 2005.

42. Keeley Webster, "Controversial CRA Givebacks Hinder Development," *California Lawyer Magazine* (April 2010). For a contrary perspective, see Steven Greenhut, "Court Wise to Take Redevelopment Cash," CalWatchdog.com, May 23, 2010.

43. Californians to Protect Local Taxpayers and Vital Services Coalition, "Questions & Answers," www.savelocalservices.com/node/27 (accessed 6/14/10).

44. League of California Cities, "League of California Cities Condemns Proposed State Budget As Reckless Ponzi Scheme," press release, July 21, 2009.

45. Attorney General, "Proposition 22: Official Title and Summary," http://voterguide.sos.ca.gov/past/2010/general/propositions/22/title-summary.htm (accessed 5/22/12).

46. Attorney General, "Proposition 22: Arguments and Rebuttals," http://voterguide.sos.ca.gov/past/2010/general/propositions/22/arguments-rebuttals.htm (accessed 5/22/12).

47. Liam Dillon, "San Diego to Brown: How You Like Them $4 Billion?" *Voice of San Diego*, February 17, 2011, www.voiceofsandiego.org/government/thehall/article_95760260-3b01-11e0-bbac-001cc4c03286.html (accessed 5/19/12).

48. *Cal. Redevelopment Assn. v. Matosantos*, S194861 (December 29, 2011), www.courtinfo.ca.gov/opinions/archive/S194861.PDF (accessed 5/23/12).

49. See Marisa Lagos, "Calif. Wins OK to Abolish Redevelopment Agencies," *San Francisco Chronicle*, December 30, 2011, p. A-1.

50. For a thoughtful essay on the uncertain future of redevelopment in Los Angeles and other cities, see Madeline Janis, "Rethinking Redevelopment in California," *Los Angeles Times*, February 8, 2012, http://articles.latimes.com/print/2012/feb/08/opinion/la-oe-janis-redevelopment-20120208 (accessed 5/13/12).

51. Ashok Bardhan and Richard A. Walker, "California, Pivot of the Great Recession," Working Paper Series (Berkeley: Institute for Research on Labor and Employment, University of California, March 2010).

52. Field Research Corporation, *The Field Poll, Release #2320*, January 19, 2010.

53. Associated Press, *AP Economic Stress Index: Measuring Financial Strain across the U.S.*, http://hosted.ap.org/specials/interactives/_national/stress_index/ (accessed 6/14/10).

54. Maria LaGanga, "Lessons of Hard Times in Vallejo," *Los Angeles Times*, May 26, 2010. Carolyn Jones, "Vallejo's Bankruptcy Ends after 3 Tough Years," *San Francisco Chronicle*, November 2, 2011, p. C-5.

55. Alison Vekshin, "The Building Boom That's Sinking Stockton," *BusinessWeek.com*, April 12, 2012, www.businessweek.com/articles/2012-04-12/the-building-boom-thats-sinking-stockton.html (accessed 5/24/12).

56. "Stockton's Bankruptcy: California's Greece," *The Economist*, June 30, 2012, www.economist.com/node/21557768 (accessed 8/3/12).

57. "San Bernardino Officially Files for Bankruptcy Protection," *Los Angeles Times*, August 1, 2012, http://latimesblogs.latimes.com/lanow/2012/08/san-bernardino-officially-files-for-bankruptcy-protection.html (accessed 8/2/12).

58. Moody's Investor Service, "Why Some Cities Are Choosing Bankruptcy," August 17, 2012, www.cacities.org/UploadedFiles/LeagueInternet/d4/d49b287c-0939-48ae-b8bc-834aaf6a0eeb.pdf (accessed 11/16/12). Also see Dan Walters, "Bankruptcy Filings by California Cities May Spread," *Modesto Bee*, October 22, 2012, www.modbee.com/2012/10/22/2423407/dan-walters-bankruptcy-filings.html (accessed 11/16/12).

59. Jim Christie, "Bankruptcy Talk Spreads Among Calif. Muni Officials," Reuters, May 27, 2010.

60. Robert Locke, "How GASB 45 Will Affect Your City or Agency: What You Need to Know," *Western City Magazine*, November 2006.

61. John Diaz, "Where Politicians Fear to Tread," *San Francisco Chronicle*, December 9, 2007, p. C-4.

62. Maria L. LaGanga, "Lessons of Hard Times in Vallejo," *Los Angeles Times*, May 26, 2010. Jim Christie, "Bankruptcy Talk Spreads among Calif. Muni Officials," Reuters, May 27, 2010. Richard Riordan and Alexander Rubalcava, "Los Angeles on the Brink of Bankruptcy," *Wall Street Journal*, May 5, 2010.

63. Civil Grand Jury (2009–10), "Pension Tsunami: The Billion Dollar Bubble." City and County of San Francisco, June 2010, p. 4.

64. Joshua Sabatini, "San Francisco's Public Pension System Is Drowning in Red Ink," *San Francisco Examiner*. August 14, 2011, www.sfexaminer.com/local/2011/08/san-franciscos-public-pension-system-drowning-red-ink (accessed 5/12/12).

65. Jeff Adachi, "Why Progressives Should Support Pension Reform," *Fog City Journal*, March 14, 2011, www.fogcityjournal.com/wordpress/2700/why-progressives-should-support-pension-reform (accessed 4/11/12).

66. Quoted in Corey Marshall, "Will the City's Pension Proposal Really Solve the Pension Crisis?" SPUR Blog, June 14, 2011, http://spur.org/blog/2011-06-14/will-citys-pension-proposal-really-solve-pension-crisis (accessed 7/15/11).

67. U. S. Conference of Mayors, "U. S. Conference of Mayors Climate Protection Agreement," www.usmayors.org/climateprotection/agreement.htm (accessed 6/14/10).

68. Wyatt Buchanan, "734 Businesses Sign Up for S.F. Health Program," *San Francisco Chronicle*, May 2, 2008.

69. Matthai Kuruvila, "Unruly Meeting on Occupy, Violence," *San Francisco Chronicle*, May 26, 2012, p. C-1. Wikipedia offers useful histories and valuable guides to the Occupy movement in general and the Oakland and San Francisco Occupy movements in particular, http://en.wikipedia.org/wiki/Occupy_movement, http://en.wikipedia.org/wiki/Occupy_Oakland, and http://en.wikipedia.org/wiki/Occupy_San_Francisco (all accessed 5/26/12).

Chapter 10

1. Dan Barry, "Beside a Smoldering Dump, a Refuge of Sorts," *New York Times*, October 21, 2007, www.nytimes.com/2007/10/21/us/21land.html?_r=1 (accessed 7/10/12).

2. Marcel Honoré, "Duroville Relocation Effort Suffers Blow," *Desert Sun*, May 1, 2012.

3. California Budget Project, "School Finance Facts, a Decade of Disinvestment: California Education Spending Nears the Bottom," Sacramento: California Budget

Project, October 2011, www.cbp.org/pdfs/2011/111012
_Decade_of_Disinvestment_SFF.pdf (accessed 8/10/12).

4. See Medicaid.gov for information on state enrollments in
Medicaid, www.medicaid.gov/Medicaid-CHIP-Program
-Information/By-State/By-State.html (accessed 9/11/12).

5. For more information about Medi-Cal, see the many pub-
lications of the California HealthCare Foundation at their
website, www.chcf.org (accessed 8/17/12), or the Kaiser
Family Foundation, www.kff.org (accessed 8/17/12).

6. Laura E. Hill et al., "Immigrant Legalization: Assessing the
Labor Market Effects," summary (San Francisco: Public
Policy Institute of California, April 2010).

7. Public Policy Institute of California, "Just the Facts, Immigrants in California," July 2002, www.ppic.org (accessed
8/17/12).

8. Hans Johnson and Laura Hill, "At Issue: Illegal Immigration," Public Policy Institute of California, July 2011, www
.ppic.org/main/publication.asp?i=676. (accessed 7/2012).

9. Joaquin Avila, "Political Apartheid in California: Conse-
quences of Excluding a Growing Noncitizen Population,"
Latino Policy and Issues Brief No. 9 (Los Angeles: UCLA
Chicano Studies Research Center, December 2003).

10. Bruce E. Cain, "Searching for the Next Pat Brown: California Infrastructure in the Balance," in *California's Future
in the Balance*, California Policy Issues Annual, special ed.
(Los Angeles: Edmund G. "Pat" Brown Institute of Public
Affairs, November 2001).

11. "Penny-Wise, Fire-Foolish" [editorial], *Los Angeles Times*,
March 8, 2004, p. B10.

12. Bettina Boxall, "A Santa Barbara Area Canyon's Residents
Are among Many Californians Living in Harm's Way in
Fire Prone Areas," *Los Angeles Times*, July 31, 2008, p. A1.

13. Kimi Yoshino, "Buying a Quick Response," *Los Angeles
Times*, October 26, 2007, pp. A1, A21.

14. Stuart Leavenworth, "Logjam May Break on Mending
Levees," *Sacramento Bee*, April 2, 2004.

15. Stuart Leavenworth, "Defenses Decayed: Neglected Levees
Pushed Past Limits," *Sacramento Bee*, March 28, 2004.

16. Sara Lin and William Wan, "Crews Shore Up Levees as
Concerns Rise over Upkeep," *Los Angeles Times*, June 10,
2004, pp. B1, B8.

17. Craig Lambert, "Trafficking in Chance," *Harvard Magazine* (July–August 2002), p. 40, http://500nations.com
(accessed 8/17/12).

18. "Proposition 97," Institute of Governmental Studies, University of California, Berkeley, igs.berkeley.edu/library/
elections/proposition-97 (accessed 12/17/12).

19. Paul Pringle, "Players at Indian Slots Have No Clue on
Payout," *Los Angeles Times*, February 10, 2003, p. B1.

20. Pringle, "Players."

21. Dan Morain, "Obama's Policies Help Indians, but Payback
Is Iffy," *Sacramento Bee*, July 15, 2012.

22. "Special Report: Democracy in California, The People's
Will," *The Economist*, April 23, 2011, p. 15.